The Woman Question
in Mrs. Gaskell's Life and Works

By

AINA RUBENIUS

NEW YORK / RUSSELL & RUSSELL

The English Institute in the University of Upsala

NUMBER 5 IN

ESSAYS AND STUDIES
ON ENGLISH LANGUAGE AND LITERATURE

Edited by

S. B. LILJEGREN

FIRST PUBLISHED IN 1950
REISSUED, 1973, BY RUSSELL & RUSSELL
A DIVISION OF ATHENEUM PUBLISHERS, INC.
BY ARRANGEMENT WITH AINA RUBENIUS
L. C. CATALOG CARD NO: 72-90568
ISBN: 0-8462-1717-1
PRINTED IN THE UNITED STATES OF AMERICA

CONTENTS

PREFACE

Most of the books and articles written about Mrs. Gaskell have either been of a chiefly biographical nature or have treated her works from a purely literary point of view or concentrated on her treatment of the social conditions of the poor in a large manufacturing town. With the exception of the question treated in *Ruth*, Mrs. Gaskell's attitude towards problems of special importance to women seems to have escaped the attention of commentators. Yet she lived in a period which saw the beginnings of the Women's Rights Movement, and it is evident from her books that she was well aware of many of the special problems of the early Victorian woman, both such as were new, resulting from the changed conditions of home life which the Industrial Revolution brought with it, and such as had merely assumed a new immediacy on account of the attention drawn to them by the pioneers of women's rights and the consequent debate in newspapers, magazines, and Parliament. It has therefore been of interest to examine the special female problems which faced Mrs. Gaskell in her own life, as well as her treatment of these and other women's problems in her works against the background of the actual conditions of the time and other factors which influenced Mrs. Gaskell's attitude and in some cases made her change her views or emphasize more strongly new aspects of a question which she had already treated in early stories.

Many of Mrs. Gaskell's letters quoted in this study are also printed in Haldane, *Mrs. Gaskell and her Friends*. As, however, Miss Haldane's version of the letters often differ considerably from the originals, references to Miss Haldane's work have not always been made. Owing to the present impossibility of buying Mrs. Gaskell's works in a uniform edition, page references have had to be made to different editions, specified in the Bibliography.

*   *   *

I am greatly indebted for valuable assistance in many ways, in the first place to Professor S. B. Liljegren, University of Upsala, whose suggestions, advice and criticism at various stages of the writing of this study have been of the greatest importance. I also feel sincere gratitude for the valuable criticism of Dr. Imogene Walker and Mrs. Carol King. I am grateful to the staffs of several libraries, especially for access to the Shorter Collection in the Brotherton Library, Leeds, the manuscript material concerning Mrs. Gaskell in the John Rylands Library, Manchester, the British Museum and the Victoria and Albert Museum, London, and the extensive Gaskell Collection in the Manchester Central Library, as well as for the kind permission of the librarians of the John Rylands and Brotherton libraries and the Victoria and Albert Museum to quote from manuscript material. My thanks are also due to the Bodleian Library, Oxford, the University Library, Uppsala, and the Nobel Library, Stockholm. My very special thanks are due to Mr. G. Lögdberg, headmaster of *högre allmänna läroverket* in Örnsköldsvik, for his unfailing readiness to arrange such working conditions as made possible the completion of this study. Finally, I wish to thank my friend Fil. mag. Gun Andersson for much patient listening.

Örnsköldsvik, October, 1950.

Aina Rubenius.

The Woman Question
in Mrs. Gaskell's Life and Works

CHAPTER I

THE POSITION OF WOMEN IN ENGLAND IN THE FIRST HALF OF THE NINETEENH CENTURY

(In law, in public opinion and in actual fact. Opposition. Strong women—weak men in Mrs. Gaskell's works.)

THE FIRST half of the nineteenth century was a period of vast changes in English life and thought. The Industrial Revolution radically altered the living conditions of a large percentage of the population of England and changed the forms of home life. Fundamental philosophical, political, and religious beliefs were being reconsidered. Education for the masses was becoming an admitted necessity. The new humanitarian attitude toward the oppressed in society, such as slaves and child-labourers, was gaining ground. Some women were beginning to voice their opinion that woman was considered as a mere appendage of man without any intrinsic value of her own, and public opinion was slowly awakening to the fact that English law treated women, or at least married women, as irresponsible children. The force and extent of some of the new ideas is indicated by the Roman Catholic Relief Act of 1829, the Reform Act of 1832, and the agitation for the abolition of slavery.

It is true that the Reform Act of 1832 and the Municipal Corporation Act of 1835, which extended franchise to men, were the first expressly to deprive women of this right, but, as E. A. Hecker points out[1], the very fact that "male persons" needed now to be so specifically designated in the bill, whereas hitherto the words "persons" and "freeholders" had been deemed sufficient, attests the recognition of a new factor.

---

[1] Eugene A. Hecker, *A Short History of Women's Rights* (New York and London, 1910), p. 145.

In respects other than political, a woman enjoyed the same rights as a man — but only as long as she remained single, and in a century when no professional careers were open to women, the unmarried woman was regarded as a failure; "woman's mission" was to be a wife and mother, her sphere was the home. And as a wife her existence as an independent individual was simply not recognized in English law. She "owed complete obedience to her husband . . . Her property, with a few partial exceptions, became his property, and over the children of their marriage his rights were absolute. A woman, in law, belonged to the man she married; . . . he could restrain her personal liberty".[1] As G. M. Trevelyan points out, "the law was in curious contrast to the words of the marriage service, when the man was made to say 'with all my worldly goods I thee endow'. It was really the other way round".[2] Even if her husband deserted her or she left him because of his cruelty—the only reason valid in the eyes of the law—her property remained in his possession, and his rights over their children were in no way changed.

Moreover, woman was considered by the law as essentially different from and inferior to man. "The comment in the case which decided that woman might take the office of sexton was as follows 'This is a servile ministerial office which requires neither skill nor understanding'."[3]

Public opinion endorsed this view of woman's capacity, and several works for the edification of women were written on the subject. The wife of a clergyman, Mrs. John Sandford, was the author of a typical book of this kind. Her *Woman in her Social and Domestic Character* was published in 1831 and ran through four editions in three years. It sets out to nip in the bud any aspiration on the part of women towards equality with men: "Nature has assigned her a subordinate place, as well as subordinate powers; and it is far better that she should feel this, and should not arrogate

---

[1] Erna Reiss, *Rights and Duties of Englishwomen. A Study in Law and Public opinion* (Manchester, 1934), pp. 6–7.

[2] G. M. Trevelyan, *English Social History. A Survey of Six Centuries. Chaucer to Queen Victoria* (London, New York, Toronto. Second edn. 1946), p. 488, note.

[3] Reiss, *op. cit.*, p. 41.

the superiority of the other sex, whilst she claims the privilege [indulgence] of her own."[1]

Nor could a woman, according to Mrs. Sandford, be trusted to make a decision for herself, for "Want of judgment is, indeed, one of the most common defects in female character, and it is in discernment, rather than in capacity, that the inferiority of woman consists. She chose wrong at first, and liability to error seems entailed upon her".[2]

The best thing she could do was to make a virtue of her complete helplessness: "Nothing is so likely to conciliate the affections of the other sex as a feeling that a woman looks to them for support and guidance . . . There is, indeed, something unfeminine in independence. . . . It is contrary to nature, and therefore it offends . . . A really sensible woman . . . is conscious of inferiority, . . . her weakness is an attraction, not a blemish."[3]

With this view of woman's capacity it is not surprising that Mrs. Sandford does not encourage her readers to seek new fields of activity.[4] Indeed, she can see but one reason for a wish to do so: "And what but vanity leads to the frequent intrusion of women at the present day into new and untried offices?"[5] Even a literary career is a little suspect: "though the Blue Stocking Club exists no longer, women are not proof against the vanity of letters".[6]

If her domestic life is unsatisfactory, "Resignation . . . should be as familiar to woman as her daily cross".[7]

Religion is regarded chiefly as an incitement to domesticity: "Religion is just what woman needs . . .[8] And it is the domesticating tendency of religion that especially prepossesses men in its favour, and makes them, even if indifferent to it themselves, desire it, at least, in their nearest female connections."[9]

[1] Mrs. John Sandford, *Woman in her Social and Domestic Character* (London 1831), p. 63.

[2] *Ibid.*, p. 84.

[3] *Ibid.*, p. 13.

[4] The book, according to the advertisement, was written "exclusively for her own sex".

[5] Sandford, *op. cit.*, p. 74.

[6] *Ibid.*, p. 67.

[7] *Ibid.*, p. 36.

[8] *Ibid.*, p. 43.   [9] *Ibid.*, p. 45.

Encouraged by "the favourable reception of a former work"[1] Mrs. Sandford soon wrote another book on the same subject. *Female Improvement*, which appeared five years after the publication of *Woman in her Social and Domestic Character*, shows a more liberal attitude towards woman's problems. After rather vague chapters on the importance of religion, the author goes on to plead for better education for women and for more sensible employment than "the vapid conversation of triflers . . . idle amusements, and . . . public display".[2] She also protests against the general contempt in which unmarried women were held. She does not, however, encourage them to seek work outside the home of a relative, where "The kind Sister, or Aunt, will be always welcomed".[3] She points out, though, that the kind sister or aunt could never hope to be considered as the equal of a married woman, who "occupies a higher position".

These books, as well as all the others of the time written in the spirit of Milton's "He for God only, she for God in him", were, of course, but the direct descendants of Rousseau's *Emile*. That book, in spite of its epoch-making ideas about the education of boys, shows but a poor opinion of woman. It is easy to see why passages like the following excited the fury of such women as Mary Wollstonecraft[4]:

"woman is framed particularly for the delight and pleasure of man; . . . she must render herself agreeable to man, instead of provoking his wrath . . .

"Thus the education of the fair-sex should be entirely relative to ours. To oblige us, to do us service, to gain our love and esteem, to rear us when young, to attend us when grown up, to advise, to console us, to soothe our pains, and to soften life with every kind of blandishment; these are the duties of the sex at all times, and what they ought to learn in their infancy . . . From this habitual constraint arises a docility which women stand

---

[1] Mrs. John Sandford, *Female Improvement* (London, 1836), Advertisement.

[2] *Ibid.*, I: 153.

[3] *Ibid.*, II: 172.

[4] After quoting Rousseau's "woman is expressly formed to please the man" etc, she adds the following sentence: "I shall make no other comment on this ingenious passage than just to observe, that it is the philosophy of lasciviousness." Mary Wollstonecraft, *A Vindication of the Rights of Woman*. With an Introduction by Elisabeth Robins (London. Walter Scott, no date), pp. 57–8. (The book was first published in 1792.)

in need of all their lives, since they never cease to be subject either to the persons, or opinions of men, . . ."[1]

Even Ruskin, who is sometimes represented as a pioneer for woman's education, recognizes her only in her relation to man. As late as 1864 he stated with disapproval that "there was never a time when wilder words were spoken, or more vain imagination permitted, respecting this question" [education for women]. Then he assured his audience that a woman must be "wise, not for self-development, but for self-renunciation". Woman must never, he said, venture into those fields of learning where even men have failed: "There *is* one dangerous science for women—one which let them indeed beware how they profanely touch—that of theology . . . that science in which the greatest men have trembled, and the wisest erred." Her husband's pleasure must be woman's load-star:

"A woman, in any rank of life, ought to know whatever her husband is likely to know, but to know it in a different way. His command of it should be foundational and progressive, hers, general and accomplished for daily and helpful use . . . a woman ought to know the same language, or science, only so far as may enable her to sympathise in her husband's pleasures, . . ."[2]

A great number of contemporary autobiographies show that these were actually the rules generally applied to family life. Mary Howitt, for instance, writes about her own youth in the early nineteenth century[3]: "Opposition to my father was never thought of by his family, which consisted entirely of submissive women, with the exception of his young son, who . . . had his will in all things."[4]

An extreme case, though not essentially different from the accepted ideal of the time, is quoted by Hecker.[5] A "Lady of Distinction" writes the following to a relative in 1821:

---

[1] John James Rousseau, Citizen of Geneva, *Emilius or An Essay on Education*. Translated from the French (London 1763), II: 177, 189, 197.

[2] John Ruskin, "Of Queens' Gardens". Public lecture, delivered in Manchester in 1864.

[3] She was born in 1799.

[4] Mary Howitt, *An Autobiography*. Edited by her daughter, Margaret Howitt. (2 vols., London 1889), I: 111–12.

[5] *Op. cit.*, p. 135.

"The most perfect and implicit faith in the superiority of a husband's judgment, and the most absolute obedience to his desires . . . will give the most entire satisfaction. It will take from you a thousand cares, . . . by often looking at your husband's face, by smiling on the occasions on which he does, by frowning on those things which make him frown, and by viewing all things in the light in which you perceive he does, you will acquire that likeness in countenance which it is an honour to possess, . . . When your temper and your thoughts are formed upon those of your husband, according to the plan which I have laid down, you will perceive that you have no will, no pleasure, but what is also his . . . when trifles are the subject, talk as much as any of them; but distinguish when the discourse turns upon things of importance."

The above advice was given early in the century, but as late as 1852, in the case of Mrs. Sandilands, who had left her husband, Counsel expressed his opinion that "she cannot be considered to have a will apart from that of her husband any more than a child of tender years can have a will apart from its parents". Times had moved, however, and Lord Campbell, judging the case, decided that "a husband has no such right at common law to the custody of his wife".[1]

Many women suffering under what Harriet Martineau termed "intolerable oppression" were trying to find a remedy. She learned much about their trials and wrote about one period of her life[2]:

"The stories that I could tell, from letters which exist among my papers, or from those I thought it right to burn at once, would move the coldest, and rouse the laziest. Those which touched me most related to the oppressions which women in England suffer from the law and custom of the country. Some offered evidence of intolerable oppression, if I could point out how it might be used. Others offered money, effort, courage in enduring obloquy, every thing, if I could show them how to obtain, and lead them in obtaining, arrangements by which they could be free in spirit, and in outward liberty to make what they could of life."[3]

Even before the beginning of the nineteenth century there had been isolated voices raised in protest against these conditions. Mary Wollstonecraft's *Thoughts on the Education of Daughters* was published in 1787, and her best-known work, *A Vindication of the*

---

[1] Reiss, *op. cit.*, p. 46.

[2] 1837.

[3] Harriet Martineau, *Autobiography*. With memorials by Maria Weston Chapman (3 vols., second edn, London, 1877), II: 104.

Rights of Woman, appeared in 1792. Through its very redicalness, however, it missed its mark in an age which was not prepared to consider either co-education, professional careers for women, or equality between the sexes. Mrs. Sandford simply expressed the opinion of a vast majority of ther contemporaries in her shocked disapproval: "it must be allowed that literary ladies have not always been very prepossessing. The disciple of Wollstoncraft [*sic*] threw off her hat, and called for a boot-jack; and imagined that by affecting the manners of the other sex, she should best assert her equality with them . . ."[1]

Naturally, the marriage laws had been discussed in fiction too. The heroine in Thomas Holcroft's *Anna St. Ives*, which appeared in the same year as Mary Wollstonecraft's *Vindication*, refuses to marry a suitor, because he does not approve of her principle that "husband, wife, or lover, should all be under the command of reason; other commands are tyranny".[2] To mention but one more example from the early part of the same century, Roxana, in Defoe's book of that title, refuses to marry, because "the very nature of the marriage contract was, in short, nothing but giving up liberty, estate, authority, and everything to the man, and the woman was indeed a mere woman ever after, that is to say, a slave".[3]

About the middle of the nineteenth century, however, the legal position of women was beginning to be more and more discussed. Caroline Norton's persistent struggle for the right to her children, and the scandals in high life which her case caused the public to suspect, directed attention to her problem.[4] In 1837 she published a pamphlet *The Natural Claims of a Mother to the Custody of her Children as affected by the Common-Law Rights of the Father*, and it was largely owing to her efforts that the amendment of the law

---

[1] Sandford, *Woman in her Social and Domestic Character*, pp. 21–22.

[2] Vol. IV, letter 79.

[3] Defoe, *Roxana, or, The Fortunate Mistress* (The Living Library, Cleveland and New York, 1946), p. 144. (First published in 1724).

[4] Caroline Elizabeth Sarah Norton (née Sheridan, afterwards Lady Stirling-Maxwell) was born in 1808 and married for the first time in 1827. After some years of a stormy marriage she had to leave her husband, who refused her access to their home and children. His object in claiming Mrs. Norton's contracts with her publishers was partly to make known to the world his wife's affairs concerning the income left her by Lord Melbourne. She died in 1877.

regarding the Custody of Infants was passed into law in 1839. After that date the judges of the Courts of Chancery had the power to grant a woman custody of her children if they were under seven years of age.

Mrs. Norton also suffered under the unfavourable economic conditions imposed on her by the law. Her husband took advantage of his legal right to claim the proceeds of her literary work. When he subpoenaed his wife's publishers to produce her contracts with them, she wrote her pamphlet *English Laws for Women in the Nineteenth Century*, as well as her *Open Letter to the Queen* of 1855.

Her efforts were, however, chiefly confined to the question of a mother's right to her children, and she expressed strong disapproval of some of the other aims of the woman's movement: "The wild and stupid theories advanced by a few women of 'equal rights and equal intelligence' are not the opinion of their sex. I, for one (I, with millions more) believe in the natural superiority of man as I do in the existence of God . . . I never pretended to the wild and ridiculous doctrine of equality."[1]

Once attention had been drawn to the "woman's question", a lively discussion began, which resulted in a large number of articles and books on the subject. Extremely moderate in its demands though it seems today, Mrs. Hugo Reid's *A Plea for Woman: Being a vindication of the importance and extent of her national sphere of action* shows an essentially different attitude to woman's problems from Mrs. Sandford's. It was published in 1843, in the hope that her book "may be the humble means of bringing forward more able pens on the same subject", as she wrote in the preface. The disadvantages under which women suffered were summed up as: "I. Want of equal civic rights.

---

[1] "A Letter to the Queen on Lord Chancellor Cranworth's Marriage and Divorce Bill", p. 98, quoted by Reiss, *op. cit.*, p. 128. Anybody desiring to enlist Queen Victoria's sympathies in a reform of the laws regarding the position of women would have to make such a reservation, as the Queen had strong feelings on the subject of Woman's Rights. In 1870 she called the movement "a mad, wicked folly" and proceeded to mention "all its attendant horrors, on which her poor feeble sex is bent, forgetting every sense of womanly feeling and propriety". She added: "It is a subject which makes the Queen so furious that she cannot contain herself." (Martin, *Queen Victoria*, quoted by Lytton Strachey in *Queen Victoria*, Phoenix Library. London, 1937, p. 260.)

II. Enforcement of unjust laws.

III. Want of means for obtaining a good substantial education."[1]

Mrs. Gaskell's friend Mme Mohl, who used every opportunity to make her English women friends realize the subjection under which she thought they lived, naturally approved highly of the author of *A Plea for Woman.* "Mrs. Reid is an excellent person; she will push on womankind when womankind is unpushable", she wrote in a letter.[2]

America was the first country to start an organized Women's Rights Movement, and the year 1848, when the meeting which resulted in The Women's Rights Association was held at Seneca Falls has been regarded as the first important date in the movement. But the soil was prepared in England, too. The first women's suffrage pamphlet there appeared as early as 1847; and in 1851 a petition of women, which had been agreed to at a public meeting at Sheffield, and which claimed the elective franchise, was presented to the House of Lords by the Earl of Carlisle.

Meanwhile the discussion went on. The vexed question of married women's property was already a much discussed subject in 1849, as appears from an ironical article in the April number of *Fraser's Magazine.* It is entitled "Letter of Advice from an Experienced Matron to a Young Married Lady". The Matron impresses on the addressee her duty of obeying to the letter the words in the marriage service, according to which the husband delegates to his wife all his authority in money matters: "with all my worldly goods I thee endow". The letter goes on: "every shilling your husband spends without your leave is downright *robbery,* . . . it is rebellion against *himself,* you being . . . invested with all his authority".

Herbert Spencer devoted the whole of Chapter VI in *Social Statics* (1850) to a discussion of the rights of women, and an article in the *Westminster Review* (Jan., 1850) about Woman's Mission denounced the "double moral" in sexual matters and pleaded for

---

[1] Mrs. Hugo Reid, *A Plea for Woman: Being a vindication of the importance and extent of her natural sphere of action* (Edinburgh, London and Dublin, 1843), p. 48.

[2] Undated letter to Miss Bonham Carter. M. C. M. Simpson, *Letters and Recollections of Julius and Mary Mohl* (London, 1887), p. 162.

a wider field for women's activities and more respect for unmarried women. After an account of the unjustness of the marriage laws the author asks in despair: "But does one married woman in a thousand know anything about this, much less desire to erase it from the statute-book?"[1] Harriet Taylor, afterwards the wife of J. S. Mill, published an article on the enfranchisement of women in the *Westminster Review* in 1851 (April–July)—"that notable one" as Charlotte Brontë called it in a letter to Mrs. Gaskell.[2]

When J. S. Mill married Mrs. Taylor in 1851, he wrote his statement of the relationship between husband and wife, admitting full equality and regretting that he had "no means of legally divesting myself of these odious powers"[3] as a husband. His *On the Subjection of Women* did not, however, appear until 1869.

One of the pioneers of the Women's Rights Movement in England, Barbara Leigh Smith (afterwards Mrs. Bodichon), published her pamphlet *A Brief Summary in Plain Language of the Most Important Laws Concerning Women* in 1854. She also founded a committee to collect signatures for the first petition for a Married Women's Property Act (1856). The time was not yet ripe, however, for any mitigation of the power of a man over his wife and family, and the bill was rejected. As one of its opponents expressed it, legislation must not break down "the distinguishing character of Englishmen, the love of home, the purity of husband and wife, and the union of one family".[4] Many were surprised that the petition was treated seriously at all. "Sir Erskine Perry says that, contrary to his expectation, the petition was received very respectfully in the House of Commons, without a sneer or a smile", wrote Anna Mary Howitt to her sister.[5]

---

[1] p. 368.

[2] September 20th, 1851. See Elizabeth Cleghorn Gaskell, *The Life of Charlotte Brontë* (Everyman's Library, London, 1946), p. 344.

[3] Quoted by Reiss, *op. cit.*, p. 46.

[4] Parliamentary Debates, May 14th, 1857. Vol. 145, quoted by Reiss, *op. cit.*, p. 126.

[5] March 17, 1856. (Mary Howitt, *An Autobiography*, II: 116–17.) The *Westminster Review* of October, 1856, quoted the case of a milliner in Manchester to show to what preposterous results the existing laws concerning married women's property might lead: "A lady whose husband had been unsuccessful in business established herself as a milliner in Manchester. After some years of toil she

Though the bill was rejected, the petition was not a complete failure, for in 1857 it resulted in the first divorce law. Paragraph 25 of this Divorce and Matrimonial Causes Act of 1857 contains the following regulation: "In every case of a judicial separation the wife shall, from the date of the sentence and whilst the separation shall continue, be considered as a *feme sole*[1] with respect to property of every description which she may acquire or which may come to devolve upon her; ..."[2]

In the following year, 1858, there came the Divorce and Matrimonial Causes Amendment Act, according to paragraph 6 of which "Every wife deserted by her husband ... may ... apply to the said judge ordinary for an order to protect any money or property in England she may have acquired or may acquire by her own lawful industry ..."[3]

In spite of the undoubted progress that the "woman's question" was making, the results seemed to many to be very slow in forthcoming. George Eliot mentioned Wharton's *Summary of the Laws relating to Women* in a letter of 1853[4], and added: "'Enfranchisement of women' only makes creeping progress; and that is best, for woman does not yet deserve a much better lot than man gives her." Mrs. Taylor, in her article in the *Westminster Review* about the enfranchisement of women, described the difficulties in the path of the pioneers of the movement:

"To be accused of rebelling against anything which admits of being called an ordinance of society, they are taught to regard as an imputation of a serious offence, to say the least, against the proprieties of their sex. It requires unusual moral courage as well as disinterestedness in a woman, to express opinions favourable to women's enfranchisement, ... The li-

---

realised sufficient for the family to live upon comfortably, the husband having done nothing meanwhile. They lived for a time in easy circumstances after she gave up business and then the husband died, bequeathing all his wife's earnings to his own illegitimate children. At the age of 62 she was compelled, in order to gain her bread, to return to business." Quoted by Hecker, *op. cit.*, p. 132.

[1] Single woman.

[2] *The Divorce and Matrimonial Causes Acts of 1857 and 1858, with all the decisions, new rules, orders, and table of fees,* &c. by Thomas Hugh Markham, Esq., M. A., Barrister-at-Law, of the Inner Temple. London, 1858.

[3] *Ibid.*

[4] Letter to Mrs. Peter Taylor, 1st Feb., 1853 (J. W. Cross, *George Eliot's Life.* 3 vols., Edinburgh and London, I: 247.)

terary class of women, especially in England, are ostentatious in disclaiming the desire for equality or citizenship, and proclaiming their complete satisfaction with the place which society consigns to them";

Even if Mrs. Taylor was right about the majority of "the literary class of women in England", there were exceptions. In *Jane Eyre* (1847) Charlotte Brontë had created a heroine who did not passively conform to the accepted rules for a "feminine" woman's behaviour in a love affair, and Shirley in the book of that name (1849) showed little willingness to accept a man's ideas and decisions as naturally superior to any woman's. Elizabeth Barrett Browning's *Aurora Leigh* from which Mrs. Gaskell aptly chose the motto for her *Life of Charlotte Brontë*[1], did not appear until 1857, but ten years earlier, the woman's cause had already been treated in poetry by a man. Tennyson's "The Princess" was first published in 1847. Its heroine, who is the successful founder of a university for women, attempts to save women, who have been "cramp'd under worse than South-sea-isle taboo", from being "for ever slaves at home and fools abroad" so that "you may with those self-styled our lords ally / your fortunes, justlier balanced, scale with scale".[2]

Harriet Martineau exerted an influence on public opinion in her day by means of a large number of newspaper leaders[3] and other articles, as well as various "Illustrations".[4] In her novel *Deerbrook* (1839), she found "an opportunity of expressing an opinion on most subjects under the sun"[5], among them the opportunities for congenial work for educated women. Her religious background, like Mrs. Gaskell's, was Unitarian. As A. V. Holt says, "probably no reli-

---

[1] "Oh! my God,
Thou hast knowledge, only Thou,
How dreary 'tis for women to sit still
On winter nights by solitary fires,
And hear the nations praising them far off."
(Fifth Book. The original has "My Father" for "Oh, my God".)
[2] III, l. 261; IV, l. 500; II, ll. 51–2.
[3] During a period of fourteen years she wrote three or four articles a week for the *Daily News*.
[4] *Illustrations of Political Economy* (1832–4), *Poor Laws and Paupers Illustrated* (1833–7), *Illustrations of Taxation* (1834), *Forest and Game Law Tales* (1845–6).
[5] *The Cambridge History of English Literature* (Cambridge, 1922), XIII: 343, note 1.

gious body except the Quakers has given such whole-hearted support as the Unitarians to the cause of women's freedom in all its forms".[1] Other Unitarian names associated with the new conception of women's capacity and sphere are Mrs. Somerville, Mary Carpenter, Frances Power Cobbe, Eliza Fox, Florence Nightingale, among the women, and such men as M. D. Hill, W. J. Fox[2], Sir James Stansfeld, William Shaen, P. A. Taylor[3], though it is true that some of them disclaimed any sympathy with the Women's Rights Movement in its extreme forms.

Harriet Martineau feared that the extremists might endanger the whole cause: "Lady Morgan and Lady Davy and Mrs. Austin and Mrs. Jameson may make women blush and men smile and be insolent; and their gross and palpable vanities may help to lower the position and discredit the pursuits of other women . . ."[4] On the other hand, she admired the work done by more moderate champions of better conditions for women:

"I have solaced and strengthened myself with the image of Joanna Baillie, and with remembering the invulnerable justification which she set up for intellectual superiority in women, while we may hope that the injury done to that cause by blue-stockings and coquettes will be scarcely more enduring than their .own trumpery notoriety."[5]

She was convinced that much remained to be done:

"Nobody can be further than I from being satisfied with the condition of my own sex, under the law and custom of my own country; . . . The best friends of that cause are women who are morally as well as intellectually competent to the more serious business of life, . . . The best advocates . . . women who are obtaining access to real social business—. . . the hospital administrators, the nurses, the educators and substantially successful authors of our own country."[6]

---

[1] Raymond V. Holt, *The Unitarian Contribution to Social Progress in England* (London, 1938), p. 147.

[2] He "made a fine leading article of the report of the Women's Convention". (Oct., 1839) (H. Martineau, *op. cit.*, III: 196.)

[3] Several of these, e.g. Mr. and Miss Fox, Mrs. Jameson, Mr. Shaen, and Mr. Taylor, were personal friends or acquaintances of Mrs. Gaskell.

[4] Harriet Martineau, *op. cit.*, I: 352.

[5] *Ibid.* I: 359–60.

[6] *Ibid.*, I: 400–1.

In those words she defined her own importance in this respect, as well as that of Florence Nightingale. Though the latter once professed herself to be "brutally indifferent to the wrongs or the rights of my sex[1]", her "Suggestions for Thought to the Searchers after Truth among the Artizans of England" (1860) pleads for reforms as regards the position of women, and in a letter to John Stuart Mill she wrote: "Till a married woman can be in possession of her own property, there can be no love or justice."[2]

The changed conditions of life were making new demands on a woman's time and work, and a new concept of her as an independent and responsible being was taking shape. But old ideals often clashed with new, and many women struggled with the problem of conflicting loyalties. The question of woman's position in all its aspects was indeed a burning subject.

If, now, we put a preliminary question as regards Mrs. Gaskell's attitude towards the discussion of woman's status, we note that she was the wife of a Unitarian minister with all the duties which this position involved, and the devoted mother of four daughters. But she was also a writer of fiction and tried by this means to reform many of the social evils of her time. She was well aware of new problems, both in her own life and in those of her friends and other women, and they left their mark on her writings in many ways.

"As to women's powers in relation to man", Mrs. Gaskell "had no doubts", according to Miss Haldane[3], who quotes a letter written in October 1856, where Mrs. Gaskell writes: "I would not trust a mouse to a woman if a man's judgment was to be had. Women have no judgment. They've tact, and sensitiveness, genius and hundreds of fine living qualities, but are at best angelic geese as to matters requiring serious and long scientific consideration. I'm not a friend of Female Medical Education." This letter refers, however, to the special question of woman's ability in science and medicine. In her books Mrs. Gaskell never discusses per se her own views about the relative superiority of man or woman, but even

---

[1] Letter to Harriet Martineau, Nov. 30 (1858?), quoted by Cook in *The Life of Florence Nightingale* (London, 1914), I: 385.

[2] Aug. 11, 1867. (Cook, *op. cit.*, II: 216.)

[3] Elizabeth Haldane, *Mrs. Gaskell and Her Friends* (London, 1931), p. 284.

the most cursory reading reveals the fact that most of her heroines
are strong, equal to a crisis, whereas her men are often weak, liable
to break up under heavy mental strain. While allowed to keep up
appearances as masters, they are often shown up in almost childish
helplessness in problematical situations.[1]

Lord David Cecil's assertion that she "looked up to man as her
sex's rightful and benevolent master"[2] holds good if one considers
the attitude of wives towards their husbands in her earliest stories
exclusively. But even in the early *Lizzie Leigh* Susan Palmer's
father is entirely dependent on his daughter, and in the later tales
there are too many examples of strong women and weak men for
the reader to agree with the above definition of Mrs. Gaskell's attitude towards man. Faith Benson in *Ruth* is stronger than her
brother: "It was a great relief to Mr. Benson to think that his sister
would so soon be with him. He had been accustomed from childhood to rely on her prompt judgment and excellent sense."[3] One
might also mention Margaret and her husband in *Right at Last*, Mr.
and Mrs. Hickson in *Lois the Witch*, and Thekla and Fanny in *Six
Weeks at Heppenheim*. Even Ellinor in *A Dark Night's Work* proves
to have more moral strength of character than her father.

One of the most striking examples of the same relation is Margaret and her father in *North and South*.[4] She insists on being told

---

[1] The first example of a man treated rather like a fractious child occurs in
Mary Barton, when Mrs. Jones speaks to her husband "in a soothing tone, such
as you use to irritated children". (P. 300.) Although Mrs. Robson in *Sylvia's
Lovers* "really believed her husband to have the serious and important occupation for his mind that she had been taught to consider befitting the superior intellect of the masculine gender" (p. 108), she admits that "it's dree work havin'
a man i' th' house" (p. 39) on the occasion when he pretends to understand domestic work better than the women. The minister in *Cousin Phillis* is represented
as a strong, upright character, but when his daughter is taken suddenly ill, "the
momentary terror had robbed the strong man of his strength, and he sank back
in his chair with sobbing breath", whereas his wife "seemed to know so much
better what to do than the minister, in the midst of the sick affright which blanched
her countenance". (Pp. 249–50.)

[2] *Early Victorian Novelists*. (London, 1934.)   [3] Pp. 76–7.

[4] *North and South* appeared in *Household Words* from September 2, 1854,
till January 17, 1855. The fact that the characters of Margaret and Mr.
Hale are partly copied from the models in *Pomfret* (see Appendix II) is not ir-
reconcileable with the theory that they also represent Mrs. Gaskell's idea of an
average man and woman, especially as these types of character recur in many

the truth about her mother's illnes, and this is what Dr. Donaldson thinks of her after she has been told: "That girl's game to the backbone. Another, who had gone that deadly colour, could never have come round without either fainting or hysterics. But she wouldn't do either—not she! And the very force of her will brought her round."[1]

Her father, meanwhile, has no strength to give: "Poor Margaret! All that afternoon she had to act the part of a Roman daughter, and give strength out of her own scanty stock to her father."[2]

Like Charlotte Brontë's Shirley, to whom her character owes much[3], it is Margaret who provides the money for her lover to repair his finances; like Caroline Helstone, also in *Shirley*, she wants to protect her lover from the rage of the workmen, and in Mrs. Gaskell's book she actually does so to the extent of being hit by the stone aimed at Mr. Thornton.[4] Later, she defends her behaviour in words that sum up her ideas of what constitutes "a woman's work": "I would do it again, let who will say what they like of me. If I saved one blow, one cruel, angry action that might otherwise have been committed, I did a woman's work."[5]

Like his counterpart in *Pomfret*[6], Mr. Hale leaves to his daughter the painful duty of telling his wife about his decision to leave the Church, and when he returns home after this news has been imparted to Mrs. Hale "he had a timid fearful look in his eyes; something almost pitiful to see in a man's face".[7]

When he first hears of Margaret's anxiety about her mother's health he refuses to listen:

"Mr. Hale was in exactly that state of apprehension which, in men of his stamp, takes the shape of wilful blindness. He was more irritated than

---

of her stories. She borrowed much from other writers, but only in cases where the "models" were consistent with her own ideas. Her borrowings were occasioned rather by a lack of creative power than by an absence of convictions.

[1] P. 136.

[2] P. 256.

[3] See Appendix II.

[4] Mrs. Gaskell had already used this episode in one of her short stories, *The Heart of John Middleton*, published in 1850.

[5] P. 202.

[6] See Appendix II.

[7] P. 52.

Margaret had ever known him at his daughter's expressed anxiety . . .
He walked uneasily up and down the room . . . '. . . She never would
conceal anything seriously affecting her health from me: would she, eh,
Margaret? I am quite sure she would not. So don't let me hear of these
foolish morbid ideas, . . .' "[1]

It is interesting to notice that Mrs. Gaskell apparently took this
reluctance of Mr. Hale's to face anxiety and to let others talk to
him about their worries from her husband's character. There are
numerous passages in her letters referring to his unwillingness to
let his wife talk to him about her worries[2], and in the letter to her
sister-in-law of January 10, 1865[3], she wrote: "*I* think your account of Sam[4] sounds anxious; but I don't think Wm does. But
then he does rather hate *facing* anxiety; he is so *very* anxious when
he *is* anxious that I think he always dislikes being made to acknowledge there is cause . . ."[5]

---

[1] Pp. 111-112. [2] Cf. p. 27.

[3] Quoted on p. 23.

[4] Mr. Gaskell's brother.

[5] Apparently other characters in Mrs. Gaskell's works also borrowed traits
from Mr. Gaskell. She had come to consider it a moral flaw to give way to her
great grief over the death of her only son. On April 26, 1850, she wrote to Miss
Fox: "I must not waste my strength or my time about the never-ending sorrow
. . . that is one evil of the bustling life that one has never time calmly and bravely
to face a great grief, and to view it on every side as to bring the harmony out of
it." (Copy of letter in the Brotherton Library.) According to A. W. Ward it
was Mr. Gaskell who made his wife begin to write a long story so as to take her
mind off the sorrow under which she was sinking; (See p. 34.) in *The Well of
Pen-Morfa*, Nest "bound her sorrow tight up in her breast to corrode and fester
there", (p. 364) and the Methodist preacher uses words which might well have
been spoken by Mr. Gaskell to his wife: "I do not pity you. You do not require
pity. You are powerful enough to trample down your own sorrows into a blessing for others; and to others you will be a blessing. I see it before you." (P.
369.) This kind of advice is repeated directly or by implication in later stories.
The old servant Betty, for instance, in *Cousin Phillis* tells Phillis that "we ha'
done a' we can for you, and th' doctors has done a' they can for you, and
I think the Lord has done a' He can for you, and more than you deserve,
too, if you don't do something for yourself. If I were you, I'd rise up and
snuff the moon, sooner than break your father's and your mother's hearts wi'
watching and waiting till it pleases you to fight your own way back to cheer-
fulness". (P. 256.) Mrs. Gaskell had no patience with the "womanly", simpering creatures with a habit of fainting in all exciting or difficult situations,
who usually figured as heroines in the novels of sentimentality. Mrs. Gaskell's

18

Many women who took up the question of the position of women about the middle of the nineteenth century did so for personal reasons. Mrs. Norton, for instance, was driven to fight for a mother's right to her children by her unfortunate experience of marriage.[1]

The overwhelming majority of those who have written about Mrs. Gaskell and her works have unquestioningly accepted the tradition about her happy marriage as true. Miss Dullemen and Miss Haldane, who both express their doubts concerning this tradition[2], hardly give any evidence to support their statements. It is therefore necessary to examine more closely than has previously been done the question whether Mrs. Gaskell had any such personal experiences as might have influenced her manner of treating women's problems in her works. Such an examination seems doubly necessary in view of the fact that her treatment of the position and duties of a wife undergoes a marked gradual change in the course of her career as a writer.

---

heroines hardly ever faint in order to escape a difficulty. If they faint at all they generally do so after they have grappled with a situation and weathered the crisis. And they do not sink down in a graceful swoon to evoke the protective chivalry of the hero. The heroine of *Sylvia's Lovers*, we are told, "fainted at his feet, coming down with a heavy bang on the round paving stones of the yard", (p. 270.) and, like most of Mrs. Gaskell's heroines, she has to act on the advice, in this case given by her mother: "Lass bear up! . . . thou mun cry thy cry at after!" (P. 270.)

[1] See p. 7.

[2] Miss Dullemen expresses her "impression that Mr. Gaskell as a husband and father was not always the most sympathetic and devoted of men". (J. J. Van Dullemen, *Mrs. Gaskell: Novelist and Biographer*. Amsterdam, 1924, p. 90.) Miss Haldane, too, "always has the feeling that the two, Mr. and Mrs. Gaskell, never quite understood one another". (Elizabeth Haldane, C. H., *Mrs. Gaskell and her Friends*, London, 1931, p. 301.)

CHAPTER II

MRS. GASKELL'S MARRIAGE

(Early life before marriage. Mrs. Gaskell's attitude towards her husband's pastoral work [lack of understanding]. Mrs. Gaskell's affection for her husband. Mr. Gaskell's original affection for his wife, his growing indifference and Mrs. Gaskell's reaction to it. Mrs. Gaskell's increasing independence in economic matters. Mr. Gaskell's influence on his wife's literary works.)

THOUGH in some respects Mrs. Gaskell accepted the prevalent ideas about the relative positions of man and woman, she grew up under conditions that were more favourable for a broad-minded attitude than was common. In her childhood she experienced none of the unquestioned authority of a father over his family. When little more than a year old, the motherless girl was taken to Knutsford to live with and be educated by her aunt, Mrs. Lumb (née Holland), who was separated from her husband. Apart from short visits to her father, Elizabeth Cleghorn Stevenson was with her aunt until she went to school for five years at Stratford-on-Avon.[1] Not until she left school at about seventeen years of age did she go to stay with her father in Chelsea, where she remained until his death on March 22, 1829. Before that time she had grown up chiefly under feminine supervision, although her uncle, Peter Holland, the Knutsford doctor, is said to have taken an interest in her education. Moreover, her religious background on both sides of the family was Unitarian[2], and she was re-

---

[1] A. S. Whitfield, in *Mrs. Gaskell, Her Life and Work* (London, 1929), gives the period correctly as five years. Most other biographers, for instance Sanders in his chronology (Gerald DeWitt Sanders, *Elizabeth Gaskell*. With a bibliography by Clark S. Northup. New Haven and London, 1929), give it as two years. Jane Coolidge, in the unfinished manuscript in the Brotherton Library, refers to a letter (now in the Victoria and Albert Museum, London) from Mrs. Gaskell to W. S. Landor, dated from Plymouth Grove May 22, 1854. The figure there is unmistakable: "as you quote Warwickshire (where I was 5 years at school)".

[2] Cf. pp. 12, 13.

lated to such well-known Unitarian families as the Wedgwoods, the Darwins, and the Turners.

After her father's death, Elizabeth returned to Knutsford for a visit to her aunt, and then went on to Newcastle-on-Tyne to the home of William Turner, a Unitarian minister to whom she was distantly related. In 1831 she spent several months in Edinburgh together with one of Mr. Turner's daughters. She returned to Knutsford in 1832, and on August 30, 1832, when she was not quite twenty-two years old, she married William Gaskell, junior minister of Cross Street Unitarian Chapel, Manchester, who was five years older than his wife.

There is not much evidence concerning their married life, but what little there is hardly confirms the tradition of an ideally happy marriage expressed in most biographical books and articles, especially the innumerable centenary articles of 1910. Most of these articles take it for granted that the marriage between Mr. Gaskell, with his humanitarian ideals and literary tastes, and Elizabeth Cleghorn Gaskell, the writer and social reformer, was perfect.[1] The source from which this tradition seems to derive is A. W. Ward's[2] biographical introduction to the Knutsford edition of Mrs. Gaskell's works[3], in which he writes: "Mrs. Gaskell's married life was one of unbroken happiness, and, especially in the

---

[1] Lord David Cecil accepts this view of the Gaskell marriage in *Early Victorian Novelists* (1934), and Sir Arthur Quiller-Couch writes that "her married life was one of unbroken happiness". (*Charles Dickens and other Victorians*, Cambridge, 1925, p. 204.) Mrs. Chadwick says that "Mr. and Mrs. Gaskell's tastes, aims, and aspirations were identical", (Mrs. Alice Chadwick, *Mrs. Gaskell, Haunts, Homes, and Stories*. New and revised edn. London, 1913, p. 131) and Whitfield writes about them: "Together they united both fortune and affection, and were just the happy couple they ought to have been." (*Op. cit.*, p. 15.)

[2] He is also the author of the pages devoted to Mrs. Gaskell in *The Cambridge History of English Literature* (in Vol. XIII, Chap. XI, "The Political and Social Novel").

[3] The article contains several mistakes. It states, for instance, that the authoress remained for only two years at the Miss Byerleys' school at Stratford-on-Avon (cf. p. 19), that she was present at Charlotte Brontë's wedding, and that she first met Mme. Mohl in 1854 (cf. pp. 41–2). The following rash eulogism must also be counted among the mistakes: "she was too absolutely free from literary affectation of any kind to be guilty even of the venial sin of unconscious plagiarism". (See Appendix II.)

earliest years of it, she was able to identify her interests completely with those of her husband."[1] In his introduction to *North and South* he mentions their "perfect union of tastes as well as affections". There is, however, evidence which shows that this union of interests was far from complete.

Mr. and Mrs. Gaskell spent their honeymoon of about a month in Wales, after which they returned to Manchester, where Mr. Gaskell resumed his pastoral duties. It is true that Susanna Winkworth[2], panegyrical whenever she mentions Mrs. Gaskell, adds, after enumerating all her perfections: "nor did she ever forget the special duties of a minister's wife".[3] A. C. Smith, however, who also had known Mrs. Gaskell in his youth, gives a very different picture of her:

"she no sooner settled in Manchester than she steadily and consistently objected to her time being considered as belonging in any way to her husband's congregation for the purpose of congregational visiting, and to being looked to for that leadership in congregational work which is too often expected of the 'minister's wife'. What she did was of her own

---

[1] He assures his readers that "the facts [which he gives about Mrs. Gaskell's life] ... may be taken as authentic" and that "the honoured name that she left was safe in the care of her dearly loved daughters". (Marianne was born in 1834, "Meta" in 1837, Florence in 1842, and Julia in 1846.) Meta and Julia shared the Manchester home after their father's death in 1884. They afforded A. W. Ward "invaluable assistance" (Editor's preface to Vol. I of the Knutsford edn), but at the same time Meta jealously guarded her mother's private life. She was careful never to give information which might lead anybody to suspect a lack of complete harmony in the Gaskell household. (Her own letter, quoted on p. 28, however, shows that at times no such harmony existed.) She took her mother's wish that no biography should be written of her much more to heart than her elder sister. In the Shorter collection in the Brotherton Library there are some forty letters from Mrs. Gaskell to Marianne, a few to Julia and "my dearest girls". There are none to Florence. Meta took good care that no letters from Mrs. Gaskell to herself should fall into the hands of any prospective biographer. Mrs. Gaskell was aware of this difference in her daughters, and in a letter to Marianne (undated, in the Brotherton Library) she implored her: "*Pray* burn my letters. I am always afraid of writing much to you, you are so careless about letters ... *Burn this.*"

[2] See pp. 53–4.

[3] Margaret J. Shaen ed., *Memorials of two Sisters. Susanna and Catherine Winkworth* (London, 1908), pp. 24–25.

choice and desire. The one place she did unite in willing service was the Sunday school . . .".[1]

It must not, however, be concluded that she took no interest in conditions in Manchester. She worked for the relief of the poor in "the hungry forties", the period treated in *Mary Barton*. About a similar period in 1862 she wrote to C. E. Norton: "Last autumn and winter was *such* hard work—we were often off at nine,—not to come home till 7 or $\frac{1}{2}$ past, too worn out to eat or do anything but go to bed. The one thought ran thro' all our talk almost like a disease."[2] It is remarkable, though, that the funeral sermon, which praises her literary work, makes no mention of any contribution to the welfare work in the parish.[3]

She did not always appreciate her husband's ministerial work. In most of her references to it in letters, there is a slightly complaining tone. With his literary work, such as his lectures on The Poets and Poetry of Humble Life, she showed more sympathy. She had feared that "his usual fault of procrastination" would "prevent him doing justice to it"[4], and was delighted when her apprehensions proved to be unfounded. She even assisted her husband in preparing some more lectures on the same subject[5],

---

[1] A. Cobden Smith, "Mrs. Gaskell and Lower Mosley Street. A Centenary Address." (Delivered Oct. 2, 1910. Printed in the *Sunday School Quarterly*, January, 1911.)

[2] July 13, 1863. (Jane Whitehill, *Letters of Mrs. Gaskell and Charles Eliot Norton, 1855–1865*. London, 1932).

[3] James Drummond, "The Holiness of Sorrow, a sermon preached in Cross Street Chapel, Manchester, on Sunday, Nov. 19th, 1865, on occasion of the sudden death of Mrs. Gaskell. Printed by desire of the congregation".

[4] Letter (in the Brotherton Library) to her sister-in-law Eliza Gaskell. Postmark Jy 18, 1838.

[5] On August 18, 1838, she wrote to Mary Howitt: "My husband has lately been giving four lectures to the very poorest of the weavers in the very poorest district of Manchester, Miles Platting, on 'The Poets and Poetry of Humble Life'. You cannot think how well they have been attended, and how interested people have seemed. And the day before yesterday (August 16, 1838) two deputations of respectable-looking men waited on him to ask him to repeat those lectures in two different parts of the town. He is going on with four more in the winter, and meanwhile we are *picking up* all the 'Poets of Humble Life' we can think of". (Margaret Howitt, "Stray Notes from Mrs. Gaskell". *Good Words*, September, 1895.)

and together, they wrote a poem, "Sketches among the Poor, No. 1.", which appeared in *Blackwood's Magazine* in January, 1837. This kind of collaboration over poems and lectures belonged, however, only to the earlier part of their marriage, and nothing came of the plan to write more Sketches among the Poor.

A letter written by Mrs. Gaskell in the last year of her life does not express much sympathy with her husband's work. It also shows that he had grown reluctant to talk about it in his home: "I never know what makes him so busy; as if we any of us ask him he always says 'it's so much extra fatigue going over all I have got to do'. I *fancy* a great many people refer to him on business or family difficulties: and besides the necessary thinking this requires, he writes letters *very* slowly . . ."[1] After enumerating various other items among her husband's professional duties, she goes on: "Then there's the plaguing Unitarian Herald; which takes up six or seven hours a week (at the office) & a great deal of odd time at home; . . . I think he really *likes* all these things . . . and when he *is* at home, we only see him at mealtimes . . ."

As appears from the Smith article, Mrs. Gaskell was never, even in the earliest period of her married life, "able to identify her interests completely" with those of her husband. She does not seem ever to have shown any real understanding of his chief work, and towards the end of her life Mr. Gaskell did not even want her to take an interest in it.

But even if Mrs. Gaskell neither understood nor appreciated her husband's absorption in his work, she seems to have retained a sincere affection for him all her life. Her letters to friends and relatives—none to her husband seem to have been preserved—are full of anxious thought about his health. She wrote to her daughters: ". . . beg you to write back to me, as soon as ever you recieve this, and tell me exactly how Papa is"; and the next week: "the great relief of your letter saying Papa was better . . . Do you think Papa wants me? If so, I should like to come home straight".[2] In May, 1854,

[1] Letter from Mrs. Gaskell to her sister-in-law Mrs. Nancy Robson, January 10, 1865. (In the Brotherton Library.)

[2] Undated letters from Paris (in the Brotherton Library). Mrs. Gaskell visited Paris for the first time in 1854. In a letter to Mr. Gaskell, dated from Tavistock House, 5 Feb., 1854, (in the John Rylands Library, Manchester), Dickens

she also wrote about Mr. Gaskell's health: "All last week I was *stupid* with anxiety."[1] She often tried to plan holidays for him when she thought that he looked tired or ill. Thus she wrote to C. E. Norton on June 3, 1857: "I wish Mr. Gaskell *looked* stronger, . . . I wish you could persuade him to go to America with you . . . —and I cd. soon earn the passage and travelling money. He wants change, and yet hates leaving home."[2] On other occasions she praised his affection for his children. There is no hint of any differences of opinion in the Diary which Mrs. Gaskell kept during the first few years of her daughter Marianne's life. To judge from this Diary, Mr. and Mrs. Gaskell's ideas concerning the education of their children were identical. There is one picture of happy family life in a letter from Mrs. Gaskell to Miss Fox, of 1849, describing her home-coming from London after being lionized there as the author of *Mary Barton*: "Mr. Gaskell meeting me; . . . we all six husband wife and children four, talked at once, upon different subjects, incessantly till bedtime for the younger ones."[3]

Mr. Gaskell undoubtedly began his married life with a sincere love for his wife. A short time before the marriage he wrote to his sister Eliza: "Mrs. L's[4] illness . . . served to present Elizabeth to me in a still more lovely and endearing light than I had before beheld her, and did more perhaps to knit our souls together than months could have done, without it. You can't imagine how lonely I feel without her . . . I am now writing with her rings on my fingers, . . ."[5] But later on he ceased to feel lonely without her and developed a habit of retiring from family life, which, together with his reluctance to express sympathy and affection, constituted his wife's chief source for disappointment in her marriage.

---

wrote: "You do not say that Mrs. Gaskell was delighted with the external aspect of Paris, but I suppose I may take that for granted. I am sorry, however, that her first impressions were not formed on a fine morning in the early summer . . ."

[1] Copy of letter to Forster in the Brotherton Library.

[2] Whitehill, *op. cit.* Solicitude for Mr. Gaskell's health is obviously the only reason for this plan, not a wish to get him out of the way in time for the arrival of Harriet Beecher Stowe and other guests, as Yvonne ffrench suggests in her *Mrs. Gaskell* (London, 1949), p. 68.

[3] Extract of letter in the Brotherton Library.

[4] Mrs. Lumb, Mrs. Gaskell's aunt.

[5] Letter in the Brotherton Library.

There are frequent complaints in Mrs. Gaskell's letters that her husband was too busy to have time for his family or their guests.[1] In a letter to her sister-in-law Mrs. Robson she wrote: "Wm and I have rather taken to chess. At least when he has time for oh! he is so busy."[2] To her eldest daughter she confided her apprehensions about Mr. Gaskell's probable behaviour to guests in his home: "Papa in very good spirits; but ever since he has been too busy to be talked to—and today is *quite* unapproachable . . . Think how many people are coming (possibly) in April! . . . and if Papa gets over busy; & not talkable as today!"[3] It is clear that Mrs. Gaskell and her daughters delighted in outward activity and social life in spite of the expressions of longing for rest and quiet which recur in Mrs. Gaskell's letters to friends and relatives with the same regularity as long lists of guests and social activities. But Mr. Gaskell did not trouble much about the entertainment of guests. In the letter to Mrs. Robson where Mrs. Gaskell complained that his family only saw him at meal-times[4], she added that "Wm trots off to his study, whoever is here all the same". In 1852 or 53 she wrote to Miss Fox: "Wm too busy to be agreeable to my unfortunate visitors."[5]

---

[1] Remembering Mrs. Gaskell's frequently expressed regret at her husband's neglect of family life, one can imagine a wistful note in the following description of the mill-owner's family evenings in *Mary Barton*, when they find themselves without business duties on account of the strike: "It was a pleasant thing . . . to have time for becoming acquainted with agreeable and accomplished daughters, on whose education no money had been spared, but whose fathers, shut up during a long day with calicoes and accounts, had so seldom had leisure to enjoy their daughters' talents. They were happy family evenings, now that the men of business had time for domestic enjoyments." (Chap. VI, p. 62.)

[2] This letter (now in the Brotherton Library) is only dated "Wednesday Evening", but it was evidently written in 1842, as only Marianne and "Meta" are mentioned in it, and Mrs. Gaskell writes about the possibility of her own death. Her third living daughter, Florence, was born on October 7, 1842. Furthermore, Mrs. Gaskell mentions just having finished "Miss Martineau's new romance" with its hero Toussaint. *The Hour and the Man, An historical Romance* appeared in 1841.

[3] Undated letter in the Brotherton Library. An indication of the time is given by the following passage: "letters . . . one from Tottie . . . She describes her husband as very charming, & seems very happy". ("Tottie" Fox was married in February, 1859.)   [4] Letter quoted on p. 23.

[5] Extract of letter in the Brotherton Library.

It was not always work that prevented Mr. Gaskell from enjoy-
ing the company of his family. A week before the letter quoted
above Mrs. Gaskell confided to Mrs. Robson that "William is, as
usual at this time of the year, dining out almost every day..."[1]
"Mr. Gaskell always constantly away", she wrote to C. E. Norton
on August 27, 1860.[2]

Mr. Gaskell also preferred to go off on his holidays without his
family. In August, 1850, Mrs. Gaskell wrote to "Tottie" Fox:
"It is funny how we *never* go from home together."[3] She also mentioned this fact to C. E. Norton in a letter of June 24, 1861[4], where
she wrote about Mr. Gaskell's two months holiday. She added:
"He wants a companion but wont take one of us, because he does
not wish to have any responsibility during his holidays." On February 1st, 1864, Mrs. Gaskell again told Mr. Norton about her
husband's travelling plans: "Mr. Gaskell is going to Rome on February 22 for six weeks or two months... Meta and I determined
that if we could plan it or arrange it we should go and see Rome
this winter... and now, as I said, he is going; by himself because
he prefers it."[5]

It might seem from letters such as those quoted above as if Mrs.
Gaskell willingly resigned herself to her husband's wish to spend
his holidays away from his wife. Such a conclusion would, however, be far from the truth, and to her sister-in-law and intimate
friend Mrs. Gaskell expressed her disappointment more freely.
In the letter already quoted on p. 23 she wrote:

"He does not like any of us to go with him when he goes from home, saying it does not give him so much change; ... I had got money enough
(from my writing) both to pay for his going, and for Meta's *or* mine, *or*

---

[1] Jan. 2, 1865. (Copy of letter in the Brotherton Library.) It might be con-
jectured that Mrs. Gaskell had this habit of her husband in mind when she remarked on the slight to Mrs. Wilkins in *A Dark Night's Work*, when her husband
"visited among them [the surrounding families of distinction] in a way which no
mere lawyer had ever done before; dined at their tables—he alone, not accompanied by his wife, be it observed"; (p. 7). The novel appeared in 1863, not
quite three years before the author wrote the letter to her sister-in-law.

[2] Whitehill, *op. cit.*, letter 21.

[3] Copy of letter in the Brotherton Library.

[4] Whitehill, *op. cit.*, letter 26.

[5] *Ibid.*, letter 37.

both of us, *with him* but he quite declined it, ... He *always* goes to the Edmund Potters in his holidays, wherever they take a house ... Mrs. Potter says she has often asked me (in her letters to him) to accompany him; but if she has, he has never told me of it; preferring the entire change and independence."

There is ample evidence that Mrs. Gaskell was hurt by her husband's lack of sympathy, though she sometimes reproached herself for this feeling. "I am afraid I have too often set you a bad example by being much hurt, as I sometimes am, when people I love dearly, find fault with me", she wrote to her eldest daughter.[1]

Mr. Gaskell did not encourage his wife's confidences. "Wm, I dare say kindly, wont allow me ever to talk to him about anxieties, while it would be *such a relief* often. So don't allude too much to what I've been saying in your answer", she wrote to Mrs. Nancy Robson in 1842.[2] Later in the same letter she commented on her husband's reserved nature: "... you know that dear William feeling most kindly towards his children, is yet most reserved in *expressions* of either affection or sympathy."[3]

This lack of sympathy on Mr. Gaskell's part was occasionally a real source of unhappiness for his wife. In periods of illness or depression she was naturally particularly sensitive to it, as appears from a letter which her second daughter Meta wrote to her elder sister while accompanying her mother on a journey:

---

[1] Undated letter in the Brotherton Library.

[2] Letter quoted above. (See p. 25, n. 2.) Later, Mrs. Gaskell made the same injunction not to·allude to what she had written, in any letter that Mr. Gaskell was likely to see, when writing to her daughter Marianne (letter in the Brotherton Library): "My dearest Polly ... I have had a great deal to make me very anxious this past week or fortnight, to which *don't allude in reply*, as I shall tell it you, my darling when you return and we can *talk* things over ... *Be sure and say nothing in answer*, ... I have gone *through* an affair, ... *Not in our own family*." The letter is undated. Towards the end of it Mrs. Gaskell asks her daughter to let her know "what people in London say about this terrible news about the war". In a letter to Miss Fox (copy in the Brotherton·Library) she also wrote of her "own heart chock full of private troubles and sorrows just now ... *perhaps* some day long hence, if you'll remind me of X-mas and New Year 1856 I may tell you a sad little story which only concerns me indirectly".

[3] The author voices a similar complaint in *Sylvia's Lovers* (p. 307): "Even with the most domestic and affectionate men, their emotions seem to be kept in a cell distinct and away from their actual lives."

"Mamma is wonderfully better today . . . She is *so much hurt* at Papa's never having written to her. If he is at home tomorrow eveng., when I suppose you will get this letter, do beg him to write by tomorrow evening's post—at once so that she may get a letter by Tuesday midday post. She says that she thinks he might have written to ask her if she did not want some more money (*which she does*). I told her to remember how busy Papa was—and she said something abt. his always finding time to read the papers at the Portico and that she thought he might have written to me, to tell me to get everything that money cd. buy. I said it was very different from 'if you had been dangerously ill tho' even then I think Papa would have *trusted* me to do and get everything necessary'. Whereupon she said she thought she had been dangerously ill—and I could only tell her that Mr. Butler had never thought so . . . Perhaps you had better not read Papa all that she said of his not writing . . ."[1]

Mrs. Gaskell's delicate health suffered in the climate of Manchester. She spent a considerable part of her time away from her home, and members of the congregation are said to have wondered at her long and more and more frequent absences.[2] She seems to have resigned herself to travelling without her husband's company, and the happiest time of her life was spent in Rome, whither her husband did not accompany her. About this visit to Rome in 1857 she wrote to her friends, the Storys: "It was in those charming Roman days that my life at any rate culminated. I shall never be so happy again. I don't think I was ever so happy before . . . I sometimes think that I would almost rather never have been there than have this ache of yearning for the great witch who sits with you upon her seven hills."[3]

---

[1] Undated letter in the Brotherton Library. Two sentences from it are printed in Dullemen, *op. cit.*, p. 901. Miss Dullemen, however—like Miss Haldane in some of the letters printed in her book—gives no indication either of the omissions or the changes in phrasing which she has undertaken.

[2] Chadwick, *op. cit.*, p. 287.

[3] Henry James, *William Wetmore Story and his Friends* (Edinburgh and London, 1903), I: 356, 358.

On her return from Rome Mrs. Gaskell found herself in the midst of the controversy raging over *The Life of Charlotte Brontë*. There seems no reason to suppose that Mr. Gaskell was on that occasion less "reserved in *expressions* of either affection or sympathy" than usual. His wife, however, longed particularly for sympathy about that time, as appears from a letter to C. E. Norton, June 21, 1857 (Whitehill, *op. cit.*), in which she wrote: "Many, many thanks for your letter. You can't think how kindness touches me just now, almost *pain-*

As is obvious from her stories, Mrs. Gaskell considered children the chief source of happiness for a woman, and in a letter to C. E. Norton there occurs a sentence which emphasizes this idea and at the same time implies that her own marriage had been less than ideal:

"I think an unmarried life may be to the full as happy, *in process of time* but I think there is a time of trial to be gone through with women, who naturally yearn after children. All this it is perhaps strange to write to you; but I am so perfectly sure you understand me that I have no scruple in doing it: and you will never refer I am sure to anything in your replies which I tell you, as a *brother* of my girls."[1]

Though there is no reason to conclude from the above quotations from Mrs. Gaskell's letters that her marriage was on the whole an unhappy one, it seems obvious that such statements as those about a "perfect union of tastes and affections" between husband and wife, and about Mrs. Gaskell's life as one of "unbroken hap-

---

fully." In view of this the end of *A Dark Night's Work* sounds a little pathetic: " 'Poor, poor Ellinor!' said he [Canon Livingstone], now taking her in his arms as a shelter. 'How I wish I had known of all this years and years ago! I could have stood between you and so much!' " (Pp. 165–6.) Although *A Dark Night's Work* was not published until 1863, Mrs. Gaskell obviously drew largely on her own experiences during and after her Italian journey in the composition of that short novel. Ellinor, like Mrs. Gaskell, passes through a time of trial and hardship after her Italian journey, and the accident on board ship, when the broken boiler causes a delay in the voyage home, had actually happened when Mrs. Gaskell and her party were going from Marseille to Civita Vecchia. (See Shaen, *op. cit.*, p. 140.) Ellinor keenly enjoyed her visit to Rome, which called out her "latent . . . artistic temperament". She "had not been able so completely to forget her past life for many years; it was like a renewing of her youth"; (P. 130.) Mrs. Gaskell's own visit to Rome had stimulated her in a similar manner. The carnival scene in Rome when Canon Livingstone suddenly looks up at Ellinor's party on the balcony (p. 131) is an account of Norton's and Mrs. Gaskell's meeting, as appears from Shaen, *op. cit.*, p. 140, Mrs. Gaskell's letter to Norton, June 10, 1861, (Whitehill, *op. cit.*), and a letter from Meta Gaskell to one of Norton's daughters. (See Whitfield, *op. cit.*, p. 58.) It is therefore tempting to conjecture that the character of Ellinor's second admirer and faithful helper, Canon Livingstone, was inspired by the open admiration and warm friendship of C. E. Norton, who accompanied Mrs. Gaskell and her daughters during most of their Italian tour, and with whom Mrs. Gaskell kept up a correspondence during the rest of her life.

[1] January 19, 1860. Whitehill, *op. cit.*, letter 16.

piness", have to be considerably modified to represent a true pic-- ture of the Gaskell marriage. Even if they were true of the earliest period of the marriage, they are certainly not true of the later years, when Mr. Gaskell preferred not to have his wife's company on his holidays and had grown reluctant both to talk to her about his own concerns and to let her talk to him about hers. In time Mr. and Mrs. Gaskell apparently spent less and less time together, had fewer friends in common and had more and more widely differing interests. To judge from the Manchester gossip as it was reported in a letter written by Geraldine Jewsbury to Jane Welsh Carlyle in December, 1850, Mrs. Gaskell's writing had an unfortunate effect on her marriage. Miss Jewsbury writes: "The people here are beginning mildly to be pained for Mr. 'Mary Barton'. And one lady said to me the other day, 'I don't think authoresses ought ever to marry', and then proceeded to eulogise Mr. Gaskell."[1] Too much importance should perhaps not be attached to this piece of evidence, if one is to accept the opinion of Miss Jewsbury's character to which Thomas Carlyle gave expression when he called her "that ill-natured old maid"[2], but it is worthy of notice that it was about that time that Mrs. Gaskell apparently asserted her economic independence[3], and that the more independent type of wife from Mrs. Gaskell's later works already appears in *Mr. Harrison's Confessions*, which was published in 1851.[4]

Mr. Gaskell followed the Unitarian tradition in his attitude towards women and never asserted his authority over his wife. She once wrote to Miss Fox: "I don't believe William would ever have *commanded* me."[5]

---

[1] Mrs. Alexander Ireland, *Selections from the Letters of Geraldine Endsor Jewsbury to Jane Welsh Carlyle.* London 1892. Letter 105, pp. 383-4.

[2] *Bulletin of the John Rylands Library Manchester*, Vol. 19. No. 1. January 1935., p. 112.

[3] See pp. 31 ff. It should be noted that Mrs. Gaskell had an income of her own from money inherited from her aunt Lumb (who died in 1837) long before she began to have her stories published.

[4] See p. 67.

[5] Copy of letter in the Brotherton Library. It is undated, but was probably written in 1849, as Mrs. Gaskell discusses their moving into a new house, which she fears will be too expensive for them. In 1849 the Gaskells moved into the

According to the law of the time, Mr. Gaskell had a legal right to his wife's earned income.[1] At first he seems to have made use of this right. In a letter to Miss Fox of April 26, 1850, Mrs. Gaskell wrote: "Do you know they sent me 20 £[2] for Lizzie Leigh? I stared, and wondered if I was swindling them but I suppose I am not; and Wm has composedly buttoned it up in his pocket. He has promised I may have some for my Refuge."[3] The fact that Miss Haldane quotes this passage[4] as an instance of Mr. Gaskell's legal right to his wife's earnings, has given rise to the misapprehension in several articles that Mrs. Gaskell was shocked at seeing her husband pocket her money. His composure, though, obviously refers to his failure to see any "swindling" in accepting the sum, a failure which apparently served to reassure his wife.

Later, as Mrs. Gaskell's income increased and became more regular, she apparently had charge of her own earnings. Though in 1859[5] she wrote to her eldest daughter: "we shall send your box . . . & I will put money in, when I can get it from Papa; but it is no use trying for it today", other letters show that she generally considered that she had a right to spend her own money as she chose without consulting her husband. In two undated letters to Marianne she wrote: "if you went there *I* would send you a 5 £ note (*in two halves* so I should know in time) for your expenses, so that you should not have to ask Papa for any money", and: "I wish I could have afforded to let you go to Portsmouth but you see I can't . . . [the piano] will take 4 tunings this next month, & cost *two guineas*, . . . so I must scrubble up money for that."[6] In the year of the Great Exhibition she also wrote to Marianne: "I *think* Papa will fetch you and take you to the Exhibition, so unless

---

spacious house 42 (now 84) Plymouth Grove, which was to remain in the family until the death of the last surviving unmarried daughter, Meta, in 1913.

[1] Cf. pp. 2, 8, 10, 11.

[2] Miss Haldane erroneously gives this sum as £10. The reading 20 is borne out by Mr. Shorter's copy (in the Brotherton Library) of the paying list of *Household Words*, which has the following entry under March 30, 1850: "Lizzie Leigh Ch. 1£6/13/4. April 1 sent in Registered Letter £20 for the whole bill".

[3] Copy of letter in the Brotherton Library.

[4] Elizabeth Haldane, *op. cit.*, p. 72.

[5] For discussion of date see p. 25, n. 3.

[6] Letters in the Brotherton Library.

you wish *particularly* to go before then, you need not. If you do, I will pay for you."[1] In 1859 she wrote to her sister-in-law: "I sold the right of republication to him in a hurry to get £ 100 to take Meta abroad."[2]

Letters to C. E. Norton show the same independence. On May 10, 1858, she wrote to him: "If I can muster up money (But you see I am very poor, what with doctor's bills, . . . inability to write, for want of health—) I would try and persuade Mr. Gaskell to take us three abroad", and in the same year (July 25): "Given 150 £ *and two months*—(I am republishing my Household Words Stories under the title of Round the Sofa —to get this money) and 3 people —and where can they go at the middle or end of October? Now do try and answer this."[3]

In some instances Mrs. Gaskell kept her expenditures (and those not always relatively unimportant sums) a secret from her husband. In 1865 she even bought a house without his knowledge. A letter to C. E. Norton of September 8, 1865, explains the circumstances in which this business transaction was accomplished:

"And then I did a terribly grand thing! and a secret thing too! Only you are in America and can't tell. I bought a house . . . for Mr. Gaskell to retire and for a home for my unmarried daughters. That's to say I had not money enough to pay the whole 2.600 £: but my publisher (Smith and Elder) advanced the 1000 £ on an 'equitable mortgage'. And I hope to pay him off by degrees. Mr. Gaskell is *not to know till then*, unless his health breaks down before . . . In the meantime we are furnishing it (500 £ more) and hoping to let it for 3 years; after which we hope to induce Mr. Gaskell to take possession himself. By that time I *hope* to have paid off the mortgage 1.200 £ . . ."[4]

Although the law of the time granted the husband a right to all his wife's possessions, including her earned income, he was not

---

[1] 1851. Letter in the Brotherton Library.

[2] Letter in the Brotherton Library.

[3] Whitehill, *op. cit.*, letters 10 and 11. Cf. also the letters quoted above on pp. 24 and 26 (to C. E. Norton and Mrs. Robson).

[4] Whitehill, *op. cit.*, letter 42. This letter and those quoted above show how utterly misleading are such statements as that of Hester Burton in *Barbara Bodichon* (London, 1949), p. 64: "Mrs. Gaskell never had the handling of the money she earned by her books. Her husband gave her a little pin-money when he thought she required it."

legally bound to accept this privilege; if he so desired, he could consent to the appointment of a trustee to act for his wife, and through this trustee she could then act legally as a "feme sole". I have found no evidence that any such arrangement was made in Mrs. Gaskell's case, and, as has been shown above, Mr. Gaskell made use of his right to his wife's earnings on the occasion of the payment for *Lizzie Leigh*. They seem, however, to have come to some arrangement which ensured to Mrs. Gaskell the use of her earned income at least as early as 1852. According to the paying list of *Household Words* for that year[1] the £ 10 for *The Old Nurse's Story*[2] were paid to Mrs. Shaen[3], as well as the cheques for £13/13/ and £6 respectively for *The First Cranford Dance*[4] and *Cumberland Sheep Shearers*.[5] In 1854 there is also the entry "Cheques to Mrs. Shaen" against the following items:

Feb. 25. Modern Greek Songs £5/7/
May 20. Company Manners   £8/18/6.

Most of the payments were naturally made to Mrs. Gaskell herself, and for no item during the years 1850–1858 is Mr. Gaskell or any other representative of Mrs. Gaskell than Mrs. Shaen mentioned in this list.

Mrs. Gaskell was convinced that her sex was "badly enough used and legalised *against*,'[6] and was one of those who signed the first petition for a Married Women's Property Act.[7] Though she was willing to spend a large part of her income for the benefit of her husband and daughters, as appears from her repeated offers to pay for their journeys abroad, etc., she wanted the power to make her own decisions independently of her husband. She had no intention of relinquishing her "masculine" privilege of giving expensive presents to her family. Her sense of independence in these matters had indeed developed since the time when she received £20 for *Lizzie Leigh* and was happy to tell Miss Fox that her husband had "promised I may have some for my Refuge".[8]

---

[1] Copy in the Brotherton Library.
[2] Published in the Christmas Number.
[3] See p. 53.   [4] January 15.
[5] January 22.   [6] See Chap. IX.
[7] See Chap. IX.
[8] See p. 31.

According to A. W. Ward[1] it was on Mr. Gaskell's advice that his wife began writing her first novel, *Mary Barton*. The Howitts also claimed the honour of being the promoters of this story.[2] In any case, *Mary Barton* was not Mrs. Gaskell's first literary attempt. *Sketches among the Poor* No. 1. written in collaboration with her husband, was published in 1837 and *Clopton Hall* in 1840. At least one of her short stories, *The Doom of the Griffiths* (published in 1858) had been begun "when Marianne was a baby".[3]

The importance of Mr. Gaskell's influence on his wife's writings has been much exaggerated by many writers. Mrs. Chadwick, for example, writes:

"Mrs. Gaskell never wrote anything without her husband's approval and sanction ... and it was because her writings for *Household Words* had just passed Mr. Gaskell's kind but critical inspection before they were sent out, that she wrote firmly to Dickens objecting to 'the purple patches with which he was anxious to embroider her work' ... and Mrs. Gaskell never sought or needed any other censor."[4]

The Liverpool Daily Post and Mercury goes even farther in a centenary article[5]: "Her husband was her teacher, her inspirer, her guide. He seems to have sacrificed his own chances of fame in literature to his wife's success." I have not found the slightest evidence for this extravagant statement.

Most other newspaper articles equally emphasize her husband's influence on her literary work. The *Standard* merely echoes the prevalent opinion in a centenary article[6]: "throughout her life he was

---

[1] Biographical Introduction to the Knutsford edn. The source of his statement was probably information given by Meta and Julia Gaskell.

[2] Mary Howitt, *op. cit.*, II: 28: "My husband, on the announcement of his intended 'Visits to Remarkable Places', received, in 1838, a letter from Manchester, signed E. C. Gaskell, drawing his attention to a fine old seat, Clopton Hall, near Stratford-on-Avon. It described in so powerful and graphic a manner the writer's visit as a schoolgirl to the mansion and its inmates, that, in replying, he urged his correspondent to use her pen for the public benefit. This led to the production of the beautiful story of 'Mary Barton', the first volume of which was sent in MS. to my husband, stating this to be the result of his advice."

[3] See Appendix II.

[4] *Op. cit.*, pp. 143-4.

[5] "Centenary of Mrs. Gaskell", the *Liverpool Daily Post and Mercury*, Sept. 29, 1910.

[6] September 29, 1910.

perhaps the only critic to whose judgement she was inclined to defer". It is true that Mrs. Gaskell resented Dickens' attempts to interfere with her work[1], but there is ample evidence that she often asked for and sometimes acted upon advice from other friends; She once wrote to W. S. Williams (?): "If somebody (out of my own family) would be truly interested in my poor story it would give me just the fillip I want ... Mr. Smith has had it (the MSS. of the first two vols) for a month ..."[2] And with Mr. Forster she discussed her plan of introducing a new character into *North and South*.[3] Apparently she also consulted him about *Ruth*, for in a letter of November 12, 1852, he wrote: "I don't agree with you in thinking the forgery incident an episode at all. On the contrary I think the position in which it places Benson and the Bradshaws quite essential to the drift of the story,"[4] Emily Winkworth also, who afterwards became Mrs. William Shaen, enjoyed Mrs. Gaskell's confidence in literary matters[5]. While writing *North and South* the novelist wrote in a letter to John Forster:

"I could write M. Hale[6], which Mrs. Shaen[7] has put me into spirits by liking, much to my surprise; and she, trained in German criticism is a

---

[1] For the relation between Dickens as an editor and Mrs. Gaskell, and their growing irritation with each other, see Annette B. Hopkins, "Dickens and Mrs. Gaskell" in the *Huntington Library Quarterly*, August 1946, where Miss Hopkins gives one example of Mr. Gaskell actually taking part in his wife's controversy with Dickens over *North and South*. As a result of his insistence, apparently, Dickens increased the space per issue allotted to *North and South* in *Household Words*. (In other matters Dickens was not so ready to oblige Mr. Gaskell. In the two letters to Mr. Gaskell now in the Rylands Library, Manchester, he regretfully declines to help him in his sanitary work, though he expresses his sympathy with his "kind and excellent purpose". One of these letters is dated from Tavistock House, 5 Feb., 1854, the other from Paris, 18 Dec., 1862.)

[2] Letter in the Brotherton Library, dated February 1st. The letter mentions *All the Year Round*, which was started in 1859. The novel in question must be *Sylvia's Lovers*, as Mrs. Gaskell did not publish any other full length novel between 1859 and 1863. *Sylvia's Lovers* was published that year by Smith, Elder & Co.

[3] See Appendix II.

[4] Extract of letter in the Brotherton Library.

[5] Cf. p. 53.

[6] *Margaret Hale* was the intended title for *North and South*.

[7] Miss Haldane, who quotes this letter (*op. cit.*, pp. 153–4), follows the typewritten copy of the letter in the Brotherton Library and prints Shaw for Shaen,

far severer judge than you, grunting and groaning when she does not like. She says it is good—but out of proportion to the length of the planned story, written and published—and so cram-ful of possible interest that she thinks another character would make it too much.[1] She finds faults, but not disheartening ones."[2]

And to Emily Winkworth's sister Catherine she wrote about *North and South:* "What do you think of a fire burning down Mr. Thornton's mills and house as a *help* to failure? . . . Tell me what you think."[3] She also took Charlotte Brontë into her confidence at least so far as to send her an outline of *Ruth.*[4]

Moreover she did not always confide her literary plans to her husband as is clear from a letter to her daughter Marianne: "My story . . . is going to bring me in a good price! . . . Only I don't know when they will pay me. Mr. Smith has never done yet for my C. Hill story. Don't mention that C. H. M. story to any one please[5] . . . Papa knows nothing of it . . ."[6]

According to Miss Haldane[7], Mr. Gaskell assisted his wife in collecting information for *The Life of Charlotte Brontë.* His jour-

---

adding the information that Mrs. Shaw was an American friend of Mrs. Gaskell's. The original, however, looks to me more like Shaen than Shaw. It is also to be noted that the Winkworth sisters were interested in German literature and criticism. Susanna and Emily began to take lessons in German from Mr. Gaskell in 1841 (Shaen, *op. cit.,* pp. 10–11). Both Susanna and her sister Catherine translated and edited several German works. (Miss Haldane's version of the letter contains some obvious mistakes, such as "surer" for "severer" judge, and "whom" for "when"). The only other mention of Mrs. Gaskell's friend Mrs. Shaw that Miss Haldane makes is in connection with the article about R. G. Shaw, which Mrs. Gaskell wrote in 1863. Miss Haldane, however, states that Mrs. Gaskell met Mrs. Shaw for the first time in 1855; *North and South* was published in 1854.

[1] Mrs. Gaskell followed this advice and did not use the character in question until she wrote *Sylvia's Lovers.* (See Appendix II.)

[2] Letter in the British Museum.

[3] October 15, 1854. Letter in the Brotherton Library.

[4] This is clear from one of Charlotte Brontë's letters to Mrs. Gaskell. (Letter 570 in Shorter, *The Brontës, Life and Letters.* London, 1908, II: 263.)

[5] Besides *Wives and Daughters* the following of Mrs. Gaskell's stories were published in the Corn*hill M*agazine: *Curious if True* (Feb., 1860), *Six Weeks at Heppenheim* (May, 1862), and *Cousin Phillis* (Nov.–Feb., 1864).

[6] Undated letter in the Brotherton Library.

[7] *Op. cit.,* p. 167.

ney to Haworth, to try to find proof for his wife's statements about Mrs. Robinson and Branwell Brontë in that book, has also been quoted as an instance of his interest in her work and his willingness to collaborate in every way. It is, however, worthy of notice that when the libel action was threatened, Mrs. Gaskell was still in Italy and could not go herself. As her husband, Mr. Gaskell was legally responsible, and the advertisement in *The Times* of May 26, 1857, retracting the libellous passages in the Life, was signed by William Shaen "As solicitor for and on behalf of the Rev. W. Gaskell and of Mrs. Gaskell, his wife".[1]

---

[1] To judge from a letter to C. E. Norton of June 3, 1857, Mr. Gaskell or the publishers made most of the necessary arrangements to avoid libel actions against Mrs. Gaskell without consulting her wishes. She wrote: "I found trouble enough awaiting me from the publication of my Life of C. B. or rather not 'awaiting' me, but settled without me; settled for the best, all things considered, I am sure"; (Whitehill, *op. cit.*, letter 4.)

CHAPTER III

FRIENDS OF MRS. GASKELL'S
WHO WERE INTERESTED IN THE WOMAN'S
MOVEMENT

(Fredrika Bremer, Madame Mohl, Mrs. Jameson, Elizabeth Barrett Brown-
ing, Caroline Norton, Charlotte Brontë, Richard Monckton Milnes, Florence
Nightingale, The Winkworth sisters, Mary Howitt, Charles Kingsley,
Eliza Fox.)

MRS. GASKELL's marital experience very possibly influenced
her attitude towards the woman's question to a certain extent;
it seems probable that her husband's preoccupation with his own
work, and his growing reluctance to enjoy the company of his wife
and family even during holidays, strengthened her tendency to
become her "own woman", as Charlotte Brontë expressed it.[1]
But personal experience cannot fully explain her final attitude,
for she had been married for thirteen years before she began writing her first novel, in which, as in the short stories of the period,
her conception of a wife's duties and position was entirely old-
fashioned and conventional. When, however, the sudden success
of *Mary Barton* had opened to her the doors of literary and cultural circles in London and she was brought into contact with the
topics of the day in a much more direct and personal way than
had been possible when her life and interests were chiefly confined to Manchester and its neighbourhood, that conception began
to change. Several of her new friends were deeply interested in
the woman's movement. As appears from Mrs. Gaskell's correspondence with such friends as Eliza Fox and Fredrika Bremer, the

---

[1] "Do you, who have so many friends,—so large a circle of acquaintance—
find it easy, when you sit down to write, to isolate yourself from all those ties,
and their sweet associations, so as to be your *own woman*, uninfluenced and swayed
by the consciousness of how your work may affect other minds; what blame or
what sympathy it may call forth?" (Letter from Charlotte Brontë to Mrs. Gaskell, July 9, 1853. Shorter, *op. cit.*, p. 331.)

special women problems of the time were of vital interest to them, and they tried to persuade Mrs. Gaskell to take a more active part in their efforts to enlarge the field of woman's interests and activity and to improve her legal position. It is therefore of interest to examine her relations with some of the pioneers of the Women's Rights Movement in and out of England.[1] Owing to the scarcity of the material, it is hardly possible to determine the different kind of influence each friend may have exerted on Mrs. Gaskell's ideas. What does appear from such an examination, however, is the fact that Mrs. Gaskell knew a number of advocates of women's rights, who discussed this question with her. Consequently, she had every possibility of being influenced by their views, and there can be little doubt that it was her contact with them that made her realize that the time had come for her to give up some of the traditional ideas of a woman's position and duties and strengthened her tendency to consider a morally independent woman a better ideal than the weak submissive type. She was forced to reconsider her attitude towards the woman's question, and one result of this was the marked development of her ideal of a good wife as it appears in her stories.

FREDRIKA BREMER

One of Mrs. Gaskell's foreign friends was Fredrika Bremer, the Swedish novelist, the influence of whose works can be traced in Mrs. Gaskell's writings, especially in *Wives and Daughters*.[2] Fredrika Bremer is remembered in Sweden chiefly as a pioneer of the Women's Rights Movement, but her opinions were moderate enough not to alienate Mrs. Gaskell's sympathies. According to Henrik Schück[3] she did not demand any political rights for women

---

[1] Miss Haldane, in *Mrs. Gaskell and her Friends*, gives an account of Mrs. Gaskell's friendship with Charlotte Brontë, Madame Mohl, and Florence Nightingale. In the case of other friends mentioned in the book no attempt is made to establish the beginning or extent of their friendship with Mrs. Gaskell, and in no case does she treat the attitude of these friends towards special women problems.

[2] See Appendix II.

[3] Schück och Warburg, *Illustrerad svensk litteraturhistoria*. (Tredje, fullständigt omarbetade upplagan. Utgiven av Henrik Schück. Sjätte delen. Stockholm 1930.)

but protested against the limiting of their field of activity to the home. What she sought for woman was the right to work with consequent economic independence, and, above all, a new type of education which would make all this possible.

One letter from Fredrika Bremer to Mrs. Gaskell of 1851 is quoted in Appendix II. Another letter, dated from Stockholm 29 September, 1853[1], contains an ardent appeal to Mrs. Gaskell to "work for the oppressed and neglected of our own sex". Mrs. Gaskell's *Ruth* had recently appeared, and Miss Bremer seems to have expected a work of this kind from its author, for she goes on:

"But—you have written a new Novel, perhaps it is the very thing. . . . the work I ought to do. I have worked at it before this, but only with half-opened eyes. Now and hereafter I shall work at it with full and unlimited devotion. That work—you may have guessed at part of it if you have read my former writings; you may see it more clearly still if you have patience to read through the big (too big!) work "Homes of the new world" that I have ordered to be sent to you in my name, and when you there see the strong stress I have laid on the necessity of the full development of womans mind and sphere. You will I hope see it more still in my efforts both theory and practice to come, if God permits . . .

"I wonder if England is doing something to raise the position of women to give them through education, and in after life through enlarged opportunities for work—employment for their minds and hands. It seems to me clear that no people can be greatly prosperous in the long run if it does not employ to its advantage the working powers of women, so that the greater part of them may be producents more than merely idle consuments, as I fear is the case in most nations. Yet much against the will and wish of women in general. Then they are active and want activity, and want hapiness. And if you will give happiness to a human being give a good work in which the mind is interested, that fills time and allows of some progress both in work and earthly progress. To have no work and no nobler prospects is the great woman killer in the society of our days, both high and low. I have recently seen the vivifying and ennobling power of a good labour (I mean such a one as is suited to the tastes and talents of the individuals) in young women whose life else would have been

---

[1] In the Brotherton Library. The typed copy of this letter in the same library gives the date as 1854. The figure is almost illegible in the original, but the following sentence from it proves the year to be 1853: "The day is bright and beautiful as that one I passed in your beautiful home, now nearly two years since alas!" It was in 1851, some time before her letter of Oct. 19 that year that Fredrika Bremer visited Mrs. Gaskell in Manchester.

miserable in every way and now is rich and a blessing. The situation of woman, the great wants in her education and prospects are one of the greatest questions to be noted by society; and though it may be shut up or shut out of the eyes of people in cloisters and convents for a time, it will come out and come up again till men will have to look at it, as now they must try to prevent the miasmas who make the cholera come on. The prostitutes in the lower classes, the miserable street walkers, and in the upper ones the giddy and vacant souls or the sickly and sour are, I am sure of it, the greater part products of the present state of society with regard to woman's education and prospects or rather want of both.

"Dear Elizabeth, dear sister in spirit, if I may call you so, give me your hand in sympathy and in work for the opressed or neglected of our own sex. And may the kind and strong-minded English woman look at the question in her country where all sound questions culminate and are put to their highest pit,—and from the height of the evils judge better than I the means of remedy . . .

Will you write to me? . . ."

As both Mrs. Gaskell and Miss Bremer were inveterate letter-writers[1], it seems probable that they discussed the woman's question in other letters, though none of these seem to have been preserved.

MADAME MOHL

Another foreign friend was Mme Mohl, who, though born Mary Clarke and "by descent half Irish, half Scottish", was yet "by education and residence almost wholly French".[2]

Mrs. Gaskell paid her first visit to Mme Mohl in Paris in 1854. They had met for the first time many years earlier[3], and after 1854

---

[1] Mrs. Gaskell had between thirty and forty notes and letters to answer one morning, according to a letter to Ellen Nussey, July 9, 1856. (Shorter, *op. cit.*, II: 396.)

[2] Cook, *op. cit.*, I: 19.

[3] In his introduction to *Lizzie Leigh, the Grey Woman and Other Tales* in the World's Classics edition, Mr. Shorter quotes a letter from one of Mrs. Gaskell's daughters to the effect that "In 1854 she and her eldest daughter paid a winter visit to Paris, staying there with Mrs. Salis Schwabe, at whose house she first got to know Madame Mohl . . ." Miss Haldane (*op. cit.* p. 116) and others also state that Mrs. Gaskell's acquaintance with Mme Mohl dated from 1854. The two women had, however, then known each other for some time, as appears from Mrs. Gaskell's letter to Miss Fox, December 24, 1854: "last year a Madame Mohl (English in spite of her name) whom I have known a little for many years

their acquaintance rapidly developed into warm friendship.[1] Mrs.
Gaskell frequently visited Mme Mohl in Paris, alone or in the com-
pany of her daughters[2], and they kept up a correspondence. Se-
ven letters from Mme Mohl to Mrs. Gaskell are printed in Simpson,
Letters and Recollections of Julius and Mary Mohl, the first dated
November, 1855.

Mme Mohl took a great interest in the woman's question and
wrote an article, later expanded into a book, about "society in
France from the age of chivalry, especially showing how the improved position of women in the present day is owing to that movement. She used always to extol the treatment of women in France
as compared with their position in England. Her letters at this
time are full of the subject".[3] She was often impatient with the
women themselves and occasionally willing to admit their inferiority, as in an undated letter to Miss Bonham Carter: "The great
fault I find with women is their stupidity ... In short, my observations give me a higher opinion of men."[4]

On June 7, 1860, Mme Mohl wrote to Mrs. Gaskell: "I could
make a book with the greatest ease to show that the position of
the women in France was different from elsewhere."[5] In a letter to
another friend, January 8, 1862, beginning "Dearest Minnie",
she protested against the notion that English women's conversation and culture were inferior to men's and defended mothers who
fish for husbands for their daughters, which, she said, is necessary
in a country where a brother may inherit £10 000 a year while his
sister gets £200. In blazing indignation against the way English-

---

asked us to go there three times; and three times it had to be given up. Now she
peremptorily commands us to go in February". (Copy of letter in the Brotherton Library.)

[1] Mme Mohl entertained for Mrs. Gaskell "the greatest love, respect and admiration". M. C. M. Simpson, *Letters and Recollections of Julius and Mary Mohl*
(London, 1887), p. 126.

[2] During one of Mme Mohl's visits to England Mrs. Gaskell wrote to her
daughter Marianne: "Call upon Miss Emma Weston (Mme Van der Weyers,
Portland Place) & *Mme Mohl* be *sure*." (Undated letter in the Brotherton Library).

[3] 1858–61. Simpson, *op. cit.*, p. 161.

[4] Simpson, *op. cit.*, p. 162.

[5] Simpson, *op. cit.*, p. 163.

men treated their daughters, she added: "They are his playthings; but as to thinking of their future well-being, he never does." Nor did she approve of the position of English wives: "as a sex they[1] think women inferior—they have no money, they are to obey their husband".[2]

Like Mrs. Gaskell, she disapproved of the bluestocking, though she found an excuse for her: "in England they are *not* charming when they are clever; barring the exception, they are very disagreeable, because neglect makes people disagreeable".[3] In the same letter she gave vent to her exasperation at the unquestioning acceptance of their position, which she had so often encountered in "unpushable womankind"[4]: "the ordinary misses, have a particular way of saying . . . 'Gentlemen don't like it', that always makes me long to box their base, grovelling ears . . ."

But despite her battle for women's rights, Mme Mohl herself struck at least one observer as being "eminently a woman". Elizabeth Barrett Browning characterized her in a letter to Mrs. Jameson, April 12, 1852, as "a clever shrewd woman, but most eminently and on all subjects a woman; her passions having her thoughts inside them, instead of her thoughts her passions. That's the common distinction between women and men, is it not"?.[5]

MRS. JAMESON

Naturally, Mrs. Gaskell also came in contact with some of the advocates of women's rights in England. One of these was Mrs. Jameson[6], who had published her *Characteristics of Women, moral, poetical and historical*, in 1832. In the preface to this work the authoress states that "the condition of women in society, as at present constituted, is false in itself, and injurious to them", but with

---

[1] The men in England.

[2] Simpson, *op. cit.*, pp. 188–91.

[3] Letter to "Dearest Minnie", January 5, 1869. (Simpson, *op. cit.*, p. 138.)

[4] See p. 9.

[5] Frederic G. Kenyon, *The Letters of Elizabeth Barret Browning*, edited with biographical additions. London, 1897.

[6] Anna Brownell Jameson, née Murphy, 1794–1860.

the timidity of the pioneers of women's rights she does "not choose presumptuously to fling these opinions in the face of the world, in the form of essays on morality and treatises on education", but has "rather chosen to illustrate certain positions by examples and leave my readers to deduce the moral themselves".

In the body of the book, which consists of essays analysing the woman in Shakespeare's work, there is very little trace of any "unwomanly" attitude, except in the pages about the *Merchant of Venice*, where she expresses views similar to Mme Mohl's[1]:

"A woman constituted like Portia, and placed in this age, and in the actual state of society, would find society armed against her; and instead of being like Portia, a gracious, happy, beloved, and loving creature, would be a victim, immolated in fire to that multitudinous Moloch termed Opinion ... firmness would become pride, and self-assurance; and the soft, sweet, feminine texture of the mind, settle into rigidity. Is there then no sanctuary for such a mind? Where shall it find a refuge from the world? —Where seek for strength against itself? Where, but in heaven?"[2]

But even while expressing such ideas she is relieved that Portia's love does not express itself in a way contrary to nineteenth century proprieties: "Bassanio's declaration very properly comes first."

In addition to several works on art she also published two lectures: "Sisters of Charity" (1855) and "The Community of Labour" (1856), which "did much to overcome prejudice at home".[3] As was natural for a woman with her unhappy experience of marriage[4], she took an active part in the agitation for the Petition for a Married Women's Property Bill, which Mrs. Gaskell also signed in 1856. Her activities were indeed conspicuous enough to provoke an outburst from Harriet Martineau.[5]

The earliest trace of a connection between Mrs. Gaskell and Mrs. Jameson that I have been able to find is a note[6] written during one

---

[1] See p. 43.

[2] *Characteristics of Women*, pp. 32–33.

[3] *Dictionary of National Biography*.

[4] After several years of complete neglect on the part of her husband, she lived separated from him. During his lifetime she received an annual allowance, but on his death in 1854 she found herself left almost entirely without means, as there was no provision for her in her husband's will.

[5] See p. 13.

[6] Undated. In the John Rylands Library, Manchester.

of the former's visits to London, "probably in the early days of Mrs. Gaskell's fame",[1] in which Mrs. Jameson mentions a note from Mrs. Gaskell and tries to arrange a meeting.[2] The six letters from Mrs. Gaskell to Mrs. Jameson which are printed in *Anna Jameson, Letters and Friendships*[3], all refer to a later period, after the publication of *Ruth*, on which occasion Mrs. Jameson wrote an encouraging letter to the authoress.[4] In one letter Mrs. Gaskell thanks her friend for sending her one of her lectures and *A Commonplace Book of Thoughts, Memories, and Fancies, original and selected*[5], and gives a detailed account of her difficulties with Charles Dickens over the publication of *North and South*.

Apparently Mrs. Jameson feared that Mrs. Gaskell would be hurt by her frank criticism of *The Life of Charlotte Brontë*, for in a letter to her sisters, dated May 17, 1858, she wrote: "but I cannot introduce her to Mrs. Gaskell, I am afraid—for I have expressed myself about Mrs. G. & her book about Charlotte Brontë very strongly".[6] However, in the following year she visited Mrs. Gaskell in Manchester after attending a meeting in Bradford, where papers on the employment of women were read.[7]

ELIZABETH BARRETT BROWNING

As John Kenyon remarked, "there is a relationship not very distant between *Mary Barton* and *The Cry of the Children*".[8] There was, however, no correspondence between the authors of these two works until 1853, when Mrs. Gaskell wrote to John Kenyon

---

[1] *Bulletin*, p. 145.

[2] Mrs. Jameson greatly admired Mrs. Gaskell's first novel, as appears from a letter which Elizabeth Barrett Browning wrote to Miss Mitford on Dec. 13, 1850: "Mrs. Jameson told me that since 'The Bride of Lammermoor', nothing had appeared equal to 'Mary Barton'." (Kenyon, *op. cit.*)

[3] Mrs. Steuart Erskine, *Anna Jameson, Letters and Friendships (1812–1860)*. London, 1915.

[4] Mrs. Gaskell very much regretted having lost this letter and wrote about it to Mrs. Jameson: "I should often have found it a comfort and a pleasure to read it again,—. . . because I am sure you understood what I aimed at,—." (Erskine, *op. cit.*, p. 294.)

[5] Published in 1854.   [6] Erskine, *op. cit.*, p. 299.

[7] Erskine, *op. cit.*, p. 337.

[8] *Bulletin*, p. 138, n. 2.

to ask him for a Mrs. Browning autograph.[1] Her letter of thanks apparently contained praise of Mrs. Browning's poems, for Kenyon, in a letter of June 23, 1853, announced his intention "to gratify my cousin by sending her your letter—to Florence—within a few days. I know how it will please her"![2] It did please her, according to the letter from herself to Mrs. Gaskell which it called forth. The letter, dated from Casa Guidi, Florence, July 16 (postmark 1853), expresses her admiration for Mrs. Gaskell's books. Mrs. Gaskell's reply to this was "such an interesting letter . . . simple, worthy of 'Ruth'".[3] In Mrs. Browning's next letter to Mrs. Gaskell[4] she wrote: "How it pleased me that you should care to write to me so much of yourself—." She then wrote intimately of herself, especially as a mother ("Oh, that first mother's rapture you speak of"), and ended by asking for more letters of the same kind: "I have sent you a letter of personalities because I liked yours so much—Keep the law with me henceforward even so—*an I for an I*."

Mrs. Browning had been "a little, little disappointed in 'Mary Barton'" on reading it after Mrs. Jameson's extravagant praise of it.[5] She was, however, deeply impressed by Mrs. Gaskell's treatment of the main theme of *Ruth*, "strong and healthy at once, teaching a moral frightfully wanted in English society"[3]. In her first letter to Mrs. Gaskell she expressed the same opinion: "[*Ruth*] treats of a subject scarcely ever boldly treated of except when taken up by unclean hands—I am grateful to you as a woman for having so treated such a subject."[6]

She was interested, however, not only in the special woman's question treated in *Ruth*, but also in the problem, which likewise puzzled Mrs. Gaskell, of every woman's "appointed work".[7] After expressing general admiration for Florence Nightingale in a letter to Mrs. Jameson, Feb. 24, 1855, she continued,

---

[1] Mrs. Gaskell collected autographs of contemporary and other celebrities. A large collection was deposited in the Rylands Library after the death of her last surviving daughter.

[2] *Bulletin*, p. 140.

[3] Letter from Elizabeth Barrett Browning to Mrs. Martin, Oct. 5, 1853 (Kenyon, *op. cit.*).

[4] October 7, 1853. (*Bulletin*, pp. 142–5.)   [5] See p. 45, n. 2.

[6] July 16, 1853. *Bulletin*, p. 141.   [7] See pp. 57–62.

"At the same time, I confess myself to be at a loss to see any new position for the sex, or the most imperfect solution of the 'woman's question', in this step of hers. If a movement at all, it is retrograde, a revival of old virtues! Since the siege of Troy and earlier, we have had princesses binding wounds with their hands; it's strictly the woman's part, and men understand it so, as you will perceive by the general adhesion and approbation of this late occasion of the masculine dignities. Every man is on his knees before ladies carrying lint, calling them 'angelic she's', whereas, if they stir an inch as thinkers or artists from the beaten line (involving more good to general humanity than is involved in lint), the very same men would curse the impudence of the very same women and stop there. I can't see on what ground you think you see here the least gain to the 'woman's question', so called. It's rather *the contrary*, to my mind, and, any way, the women of England must give the precedence to the *sœurs de charité*, who have magnificently won in all matters of this kind. For my own part (and apart from the exceptional miseries of the war), I acknowledge to you that I do not consider the best use to which we can put a gifted and accomplished woman is to *make her a hospital nurse*. If it is, why then woe to us all who are artists! The woman's question is at an end. The men's 'noes' carry it. For the future I hope you will know your place and keep clear of Raffaelle and criticism; and I shall expect to hear of you as an organiser of the gruel department at Greenwich, . . ."[1]

Whether or not she discussed this problem with Mrs. Gaskell does not appear from what is preserved of their correspondence, which came to an end some time before April 9, 1857, when she again wrote to Mrs. Jameson, "I hear that Mrs. Gaskell is coming, whom I am sure to like and love. I know *that* by her letters, though I was stupid or idle enough to let our correspondence go by; and by her books, which I earnestly admire. How anxious I am to see the life of Charlotte Brontë"![2]

Their meeting in Florence, however, does not seem to have been very satisfactory. Mrs. Gaskell's friend Catherine Winkworth, who accompanied her on the Italian journey, described Mrs. Browning as "very shy and silent" in a letter of April 22, 1857. In another, dated April 29, she wrote: "I really only *saw* Mrs. Browning, for she scarcely spoke. In fact the evening was not particularly brilliant. Mrs. Gaskell talked chiefly about Miss Brontë, in which I acted chorus."[3]

---

[1] Kenyon, *op. cit.*
[2] *Ibid.*
[3] Shaen, *op. cit.*, p. 171.

CAROLINE NORTON

Mrs. Gaskell also knew that indefatigable advocate of a mother's right to her children, Caroline Norton.[1] There are two letters from her to Mrs. Gaskell in the Rylands library, Manchester, both from 1859. The first of them, bearing the postmark "Fe 4", describes Tennyson's reading of Guenever and refers to two reprints of her own poems on the Burns festival which she encloses for Mrs. Gaskell. That they were already acquainted appears from the following sentence, "You will see I have corrected the expression you did not like—

'The *aggregate* of thought'".

The second letter, postmarked Ap. 24, was written while Mrs. Gaskell was in London, and expresses regret at having missed seeing her.

CHARLOTTE BRONTË

Another contemporary, whose friendship Mrs. Gaskell enjoyed for only a few years, but whose works she had read, admired and been influenced by before she met their author, was Charlotte Brontë. They met for the first time in August, 1850, but in November of the year before, Mrs. Gaskell had written to express her admiration of her writings. "Mrs. Gaskell tells me she shall keep my works as a treasure for her daughters", wrote Charlotte Brontë on Nov. 29, 1849.[2]

Mrs. Gaskell freely discussed her literary plans with Charlotte Brontë. She gave her, for instance, an outline of *Ruth* in April, 1852, and Charlotte Brontë sent the author her opinion on the way she was treating the religious problem in *North and South* on September 30, 1854.[3] She was, however, as usual, more secretive about her own plans and did not even send Mrs. Gaskell one of her own books in exchange for *The Moorland Cottage*, which was

---

[1] Cf. p. 7.

[2] Shorter, *op. cit.*, II: 90. Letter to W. S. Williams. In 1849 Mrs. Gaskell wrote to Miss Winkworth: " 'Currer Bell (aha! what will you give me for a secret?) She's a she—that I will tell you—who has sent me 'Shirley'." (Haldane, *op. cit.*, pp. 119–20.)

[3] Shorter, *op. cit.*, II: 446.

sent to her for Christmas, but instead requested W. S. Williams to send a copy of her sister Emily's *Wuthering Heights*.[1]

As is evident from *Shirley* in particular, Charlotte Brontë was interested in the woman's question, and she often discussed this problem in her letters. She seems to have given vent to some bitterness on the subject in conversations with Mrs. Gaskell. In a letter to Catherine Winkworth, August 25, 1850, quoted by Miss Haldane[2], Mrs. Gaskell wrote about her new friend: "But the poverty at home was very great ('at 19 I should have been thankful for an allowance of 1 d. a week. I asked my father, but he said what did women want with money?')."

In two letters to W. S. Williams, Charlotte Brontë pleaded for "habits of independence and industry" in daughters as well as sons, and urged him not to wish to keep them at home.[3]

In a letter to G. H. Lewes, Charlotte Brontë expressed the impatience which she felt with reviewers who judged a novel written by a woman by a special standard. He had notified her of his intention of reviewing *Shirley*, and she wrote: "I wish all reviewers believed 'Currer Bell' to be a man; they would be more just to him. You will, I know, keep measuring me by some standard of what you deem becoming to my sex; ... Come what will, I cannot, when I write, think always of myself and of what is elegant and charming in femininity; it is not on those terms, or with such ideas, I ever took pen in hand."[4] Mrs. Gaskell's comment on this is, however, not very illuminating: "Whether right or wrong her feeling was strong on this point."[5]

Generally, though, the two women thought so much alike on the woman's question that Charlotte Brontë regretted the fact that there was not enough dissimilarity of opinion between them for discussion.[6]

---

[1] January 1, 1851. Shorter, *op. cit.*, II: 188.

[2] *Op. cit.*, pp. 123–8.

[3] June 15, 1848, and July 3, 1849. Shorter, *op. cit.* I: 428, and II: 22. For a discussion of Mrs. Gaskell's appreciation of Charlotte Brontë's absolute obedience to her father, see Chap. V.

[4] *The Life of Charlotte Brontë*, p. 283.

[5] *Ibid.*, p. 292.

[6] September 20, 1851. *The Life of Charlotte Brontë*, p. 344. See below, p. 50.

Mrs. Gaskell's letters to Charlotte Brontë are now lost, as they were naturally returned to her—if her friend had kept them—along with the rest of the correspondence that was entrusted to her while she was writing the Life. From Charlotte Brontë's own letters, though, it is obvious that they discussed these problems. In a letter to Mrs. Gaskell, dated August 27 [1850], she referred to an article entitled "Woman's Mission":

"The little French book you mention shall also take its place on the list of books to be procured as soon as possible. It treats a subject interesting to all women—perhaps, more especially to single women; though, indeed, mothers, like you, study it for the sake of their daughters. The West-·minster Review is not a periodical I see regularly, but some time since I got hold of a number—for last January, I think—in which there was an article entitled 'Woman's Mission' (the phrase is hackneyed), containing a great deal that seemed to me just and sensible. Men begin to regard the position of woman in another light than they used to do; and a few men, whose sympathies are fine and whose sense of justice is strong, think and speak of it with a candour that commands my admiration. They say, however—and, to an extent, truly—that the amelioration of our condition depends on ourselves. Certainly there are evils which our own efforts will best reach; but as certainly there are other evils—deep-rooted in the foundation of the social system—which no efforts of ours can touch: of which we cannot complain; of which it is advisable not too often to think."[1]

A later article in the same Review (1851), written by Mrs. Harriet Taylor on the "Enfranchisement of Women" seems to have made a deep impression on Charlotte Brontë, as she wrote of it in two letters the next year, to Ellen Nussey and to Mrs. Gaskell.[2] To the latter she wrote:

"I have seen none, except that notable one in the Westminster on the Emancipation of Women. But why are you and I to think (perhaps I should rather say to feel) so exactly alike on some points that there can be no discussion between us? Your words on this paper express my thoughts. Well-argued it is,—clear, logical,—but vast is the hiatus of omission; harsh the consequent jar on every finer chord of the soul. What is this hiatus? I think I know; and, knowing, I will venture to say. I think the writer forgets there is such a thing as self-sacrificing love and disinterested

---

[1] The Life of Charlotte Brontë, p. 313.

[2] July 27th, 1851, and 20 Sept., 1851. In the former (Shorter, op. cit., II: 226) she corrected the impression that the article had been written by Harriet Martineau, in the latter she stated her belief that J. S. Mill was the author.

devotion. When I first read the paper, I thought it was the work of a powerful-minded, clear-headed woman, who had a hard, jealous heart, muscles of iron, and nerves of bend leather; of a woman who longed for power, and had never felt affection. To many women affection is sweet, and power conquered indifferent—though we all like influence won. I believe J. S. Mill would make a hard, dry, dismal world of it; and yet he speaks admirable sense through a great portion of his article—especially when he says, that if there be a natural unfitness in women for men's employment, there is no need to make laws on the subject; leave all careers open; let them try; those who ought to succeed will succeed, or, at least, will have a fair chance—the incapable will fall back into their right place. He likewise disposes of the 'maternity' question very neatly. In short, J. S. Mill's head is, I dare say, very good, but I feel disposed to scorn his heart. You are right when you say that there is a large margin in human nature over which the logicians have no dominion; glad am I that it is so."[1]

RICHARD MONCKTON MILNES

The *Manchester Guardian* of January 26, 1904, contained an article entitled "The Milnes of Wakefield". Its author states of Richard Monckton Milnes (afterwards Lord Houghton) that he "championed oppressed nationalities, liberty of conscience, fugitive slaves, and the rights of women". According to the Bulletin of the Rylands Library quoted above, "Mrs. Gaskell counted him as a friend from as early as 1849, when she once breakfasted at his

---

[1] *The Life of Charlotte Brontë*, p. 344.

In view of this letter it seems strange that Mrs. Gaskell later denied having read the article in question at that time. If her "words on this paper" expressed Charlotte Brontë's own opinion, she must at least have heard a summary of it. J. S. Mill wrote a letter to protest against the publication of the above passage of the Life, and in her reply of July 14, 1859, she wrote, "I knew nothing of the writer of the article in question: I had not even seen the article. Miss Brontë knew nothing either ... It seemed to me that in publishing that part of Miss Brontë's letter which gave you such acute pain that no one could receive any impression of the writer of the article in question; while to some a good deal might be learnt of Miss Brontë's state of mind and thought on such subjects ..."

In another letter to J. S. Mill, though, of August 11, 1859, she admitted that "if it were to be reedited now, I should *certainly* omit the final paragraph relating to yourself. 'In short J. S. Mill's head is I dare say, very good, but I feel disposed to scorn his heart.' It was, I see, morally wrong to have published that. But I am not so sure about the rest". (Copies of letters in the Brotherton Library.)

house".[1] Emily Winkworth wrote to her sister Catherine on May 18, 1849: "Ask Lily[2] about the breakfast at Monckton Milnes's."[3] And A. W. Ward writes about their acquaintance, "Another friend whose hospitality—none the less cordial because so catholic—was returned by the Gaskells at Manchester, was the late Lord Houghton, whom I very well remember telling me that their house made that city a quite possible place of residence for persons of literary tastes".[4]

There are four letters from Monckton Milnes to Mrs. Gaskell in the Rylands Library, Manchester. In one (1854?) he thanks her for her letter "and valuable enclosure". Another (1857) expresses his admiration of *The Life of Charlotte Brontë* and his sympathies with the author's troubles on its publication.

FLORENCE NIGHTINGALE[5]

The letter which Mrs. Gaskell wrote about Florence Nightingale to Catherine Winkworth on October 15, 1854[6], is extremely enthusiastic: ". . . She is so like a saint . . . She must be a creature of another race so high and mighty and angelic, doing things by impulse—or some divine inspiration . . . But she seems almost too holy to be talked about as a mere wonder . . ." On this occasion Florence Nightingale came home for a few days while Mrs. Gaskell was staying at Lea Hurst as Mr. and Mrs. Nightingale's guest, and the two women do not seem to have met before then, as Florence Nightingale sent Mrs. Gaskell a note beginning "Dear Madam."[7]

---

[1] P. 156.

[2] Mrs. Gaskell was called Lily by intimate friends.

[3] Shaen, *op. cit.*, p. 42.

[4] Biographical introduction to the Works of Mrs. Gaskell in the Knutsford edition, p. XXXVI.

[5] Cf. p. 14.

[6] Letter in the Brotherton Library. (Portions of it are printed in Cook, *op. cit.*, I: 8, 39, 41, 139. Miss Haldane also prints most of the letter, though with a great number of changes in the text; *Op. cit.*, pp. 98–104. Both Cook and Haldane give the date as Oct. 20. The postmark is, however, quite clear.)

[7] In the Rylands Library, Manchester. See *Bulletin*, p. 119. Mrs. Gaskell may naturally have heard much about Florence Nightingale before she actually met her and was so deeply impressed. The first evidence of her connection with the Nightingale family that I have been able to find is her visit to Lea Hurst

Nor do they ever seem to have become intimate. One letter from Mrs. Gaskell to Florence Nightingale (Dec. 31, 1858), quoted by Cook[1], expresses Mrs. Gaskell's admiration for her friend's treatise on nursing. Florence Nightingale's letter to Mrs. Gaskell, of Sept. 28, 1860[2], confines itself strictly to business about soldiers' homes, and that of Aug. 17, 1863[3], expresses admiration for the "Beautiful 'Sylvia's Lovers'".[4] For the rest, it was Parthenope Nightingale (afterwards Lady Verney) who furnished Mrs. Gaskell with news of her younger sister.

THE WINKWORTH SISTERS

Among Mrs. Gaskell's most intimate friends in Manchester were the four Winkworth sisters[5], about one of whom Mrs. Gaskell wrote to Miss Fox in 1849: "Emily Winkworth is I think the very essence of good sense."[6] Both Susanna and Catherine were specially interested in raising the standard of girls' schools, and in 1870 Catherine became Secretary of the Committee for promoting the Higher Education of Women. She read with interest—and some amusement—such books as Mill's *On the Subjection of Women*. She also attended a Women's Franchise meeting, where she thought the "ladies spoke *uncommonly* well". Both Catherine and Susanna attended a Congress of Women Workers at Darmstadt in 1872. Like Mrs. Gaskell, however, Catherine Winkworth disapproved of too much agitation for women's rights.[7] After the meeting at Darmstadt she wrote indignantly in a letter:

mentioned by Cook, and about which she wrote both to Mrs. Shaen and Catherine Winkworth. As appears from her letter to Miss Winkworth, she was, however, invited to stay alone at Lea Hurst to write *North and South* undisturbed, which indicates an acquaintance of longer standing.

[1] *Op. cit.*, I: 347.

[2] In the Rylands Library, Manchester. Quoted in the *Bulletin*, pp. 122–3.

[3] In the Rylands Library, Manchester. Quoted in the *Bulletin*, pp. 123–4.

[4] She also liked *North and South*. See Cook, *op. cit.*, I: 140.

[5] The eldest, Susanna, was born in 1820, Emily (afterwards Mrs. William Shaen) in 1822, Selina in 1825, and Catherine in 1827. There were also two brothers, William and Stephen, the latter born in 1831.

[6] Copy of letter in the Brotherton Library.

[7] Cf. Chapters IV, IX.

"I was vexed to see in a *Daily Telegraph* that we were declared to have gone in for 'Women's Rights', from the Princess downwards. There was *not a word of truth* in the statement; there was not a bit of politics talked, and Princess Alice is no more a 'Women's Rights' woman than I am!"[1]

That the friendship between the Gaskells and the Winkworths was intimate appears from the *Memorials of two Sisters*. Both Selina and Susanna stayed with Mrs. Gaskell on her holidays in England, and Catherine accompanied her on the Italian journey. The Winkworths lived in Manchester until 1850, when they moved to Alderley Edge quite near that town. Several letters from Mrs. Gaskell to the Winkworth sisters are printed in Haldane, *Mrs. Gaskell and her Friends*.

MARY HOWITT

Fredrika Bremer's translator, Mary Howitt, who took a vivid interest in the Petition for a Married Women's Property Act and desired Mrs. Gaskell's signature to it[2], met Mrs. Gaskell for the first time on a tour in the Rhine country, when Mrs. Gaskell was greatly astonished at her gay, "un-quakerish" appearance.[3] As appears from Margaret Howitt's article "Stray Notes from Mrs. Gaskell"[4], and from Mrs. Howitt's *Autobiography*, they continued to meet and to write to each other occasionally. There is, however, no evidence that they discussed any special women's problems.

CHARLES KINGSLEY

Mrs. Gaskell's ideas on social questions greatly resembled Kingsley's, and she was early an ardent admirer of his works. As early as November 26, 1849, she wrote in a letter to Miss Fox: "I mean to copy you out some lines of my *hero*, Mr. Kingsley."[5] However, he can hardly be called a personal friend of Mrs. Gaskell's, although

---

[1] See Shaen, *op. cit.*, pp. 260, 269, 275, 288, 292.

[2] See Chapter IX.

[3] Letter from Mrs. Gaskell to her sister-in-law Eliza Gaskell (in the Brotherton Library).

[4] *Good Words*, Sep., 1895.

[5] Extract of letter in the Brotherton Library.

there was some correspondence between them. When he heard of the abuse which was heaped on Mrs. Gaskell's *Ruth*, he wrote an encouraging letter to the author[1], with whom he does not then seem to have been acquainted. In 1857 he renewed their "long-interrupted acquaintance"[2] to express his admiration for *The Life of Charlotte Brontë*.[3]

His attitude to the Women's Rights Movement also resembled Mrs. Gaskell's. In 1870 he wrote on this subject to Mrs. Peter Taylor: "If I . . . might dare to give advice, it would be, not in the direction of increased activity, but in that of increased passivity . . . We shall not win by petitions . . . By pamphleteering we shall not win . . . By quiet, modest, silent, private influence, we shall win", and to J. S. Mill: "I deprecate the interference in this movement of unmarried women . . . I object, also, to the question of woman's right to vote or to labour, and above all, to woman's right to practice as physicians and surgeons, being mixed up with social, *i.e.* sexual questions."[4]

ELIZA FOX

Among the many new acquaintances that Mrs. Gaskell made during her visit to London in 1849 after the publication of *Mary Barton* was that of Eliza Fox.[5] She was the daughter of William Johnson Fox, former Unitarian minister of Chichester, who had been disowned by his brother ministers because he held the view that marriage was dissoluble, and separated from his wife on account of incompatibility of temper. He was a well-known literary critic and a promoter of political and social reform.

From the many copies of letters, covering a period of ten years

---

[1] See Chapter VIII.

[2] Letter printed in *Charles Kingsley. His Letters and Memories of his Life*, edited by his wife (London, 1901), III: 25.

[3] See p. 59.

[4] Letters printed in *Charles Kingsley. His Letters and Memories of his Life*, edited by his wife (London, 1901), IV: 65, 68.

[5] In February, 1859, she married the well-known landscape painter Fredetick Lee Bridell, and afterwards spent much time travelling abroad, which is probably the reason why she does not seem to have kept many letters from Mrs. Gaskell after that year.

(1849–59), from Mrs. Gaskell to Miss Fox in the Brotherton Library it appears that their acquaintance soon grew into intimate friendship. As early as 1849 Mrs. Gaskell declared, "I shant Miss Fox you any more", and "My dear Eliza" soon became "My dearest Tottie". They both seem to have had strong humanitarian interests, and "shared" one or two unfortunate young girls, whom they helped to emigrate.[1] Miss Fox was a successful painter, and the conflict between home duties and an artist's life puzzled both women.[2] They discussed this problem in letters, and Mrs. Gaskell wrote to Miss Fox both about her books and her family life.[3] In one letter she discussed a wife's duty to accept moral responsibility instead of trusting always to her husband's judgment.[4] It was Miss Fox who sent Mrs. Gaskell the petition for a Married Women's Property Act to be signed by her[5], and the two friends naturally discussed this kind of activity for the woman's cause.

---

[1] "Our girl (yours and mine) sails in the Royal Albert on March 4, . . . and I like the girl much, poor creature." "My and your girl is going on well *as yet* in the Refuge . . . have found a man and his wife going to the Cape, who will take loving care of her; and sail in February." (Copies of letters from Mrs. Gaskell to Miss Fox in the Brotherton Library. Nov. 26, 1849, and Jan. 2, 1850. About this time various schemes were brought forward for the relief especially of destitute sewing-women by means of emigration. The best known was one organized by Mrs. Chisholm in 1850 and carried out in the Family Colonization Loan Society, for which propaganda appeared in various articles in *Household Words*.)

[2] Cf. p. 58.

[3] Cf. pp. 24, 58, 65, Chap. IX.

[4] See p. 65.

[5] See Chap. IX.

CHAPTER IV

PROBLEMS OF WIVES AND GIRLS ENGAGED TO BE MARRIED

(Conflict between home duties and artistic duties in Mrs. Gaskell's life. Development of Mrs. Gaskell's ideal of a wife from the submissive to the independent type, from Lizzie Leigh to Right at Last. A woman's right, or duty, to break an engagement and to dissolve a marriage. New emphasis on the advantages of an intellectual, artistic wife who can understand her husband's work, over the devoted wife with interests confined to home and children.)

In her own life Mrs. Gaskell had to face the special problems that arose from her position as a wife and mother on the one hand, and a successful writer on the other. She did not treat the resulting conflict of duties in any of her stories, but from her letters to friends it appears that it constituted a real difficulty to her, which she never succeeded in overcoming to her satisfaction. She was a devoted mother, and the intellectual and moral development of her four daughters was of absorbing interest to her. Her analysis of their characters takes up a large part of her correspondence with relatives and intimate friends. But sometimes she felt a temptation to put the demands of her art in the first place. "I like to keep myself in readiness to give them [her daughters] sympathy or advice at any moment; and consequently I do not do as I am often tempted to do, shut myself up secure from any interruption", she wrote to C. E. Norton on December 12, 1860.[1] A letter to Miss Fox, probably from about the same time[2], shows clearly that Mrs. Gaskell felt her conflicting duties as a real problem, and that she hardly hoped to arrive at a satisfactory conclusion of it. She wrote:

---

[1] Whitehill, *op. cit.*, Letter 23.

[2] The letter (copy in the Brotherton Library) is dated only "Tuesday, a week ago", but the fact that "Tottie" was apparently at this time puzzling about the problem of home duties may point to the conclusion that the letter was written after her marriage, which took place in February, 1859.

"I could say so much about . . . what follows in your letter about home duties and individual life; it is just my puzzle; and I don't think I can get nearer to a solution than you have done . . . One thing is pretty clear, *Women*, must give up an artist's life, if home duties are to be paramount. It is different with men, whose home duties are so small a part of their life. However we were talking of women. I am sure it is healthy for them to have the refuge of the hidden world of Art to shelter themselves in when too much pressed upon by daily small Lilliputian arrows of peddling cares; it keeps them from being morbid as you say; and takes them into the land where King Arthur lies hidden, and soothes them with its peace. I have felt this in writing. I see others feel it in music, you in painting, so assuredly a blending of the two is desirable. (Home duties and the development of the Individual I mean), which you will say it takes no Solomon to tell you but the difficulty is where and when to make one set of duties subserve and give place to the other. I have no doubt that the cultivation of each tends to keep the other in a healthy state,—. . .

"*Thursday*. I've been reading over your note, and believe I've only been repeating in different language what you said. If Self is to be the end of exertions, those exertions are unholy, there is no doubt of *that*—and that is part of the danger in cultivating the Individual Life; but I do believe we have all some appointed work to do, whh. no one else can do so well; Wh. is *our* work; what *we* have to do in advancing the Kingdom of God; and that first we must find out what we are sent into the world to do, and define it and make it clear to ourselves (that's *the* hard part), and then forget ourselves in our work, and our work in the End we ought to strive to bring about. I never can either talk or write clearly so I'll ee'n leave it alone . . ."

Charlotte Brontë struggled with similar difficulties, and it was in *The Life of Charlotte Brontë* that Mrs. Gaskell most clearly stated the compromise which she accepted in her own life as a solution of this problem:

"Henceforward Charlotte Brontë's existence becomes divided into two parallel currents—her life as Currer Bell, the author; her life as Charlotte Brontë, the woman. There were separate duties belonging to each character—not opposing each other; not impossible, but difficult to be reconciled. When a man becomes an author, it is probably merely a change of employment to him. He takes a portion of that time which has hitherto been devoted to some other study or pursuit; he gives up something of the legal or medical profession, in which he has hitherto endeavoured to serve others, or relinquishes part of the trade or business by which he has been striving to gain a livelihood; and another merchant or lawyer, or doctor, steps into his vacant place, and probably does as well as he. But no other can take up the quiet, regular duties of the daughter, the wife, or the mother, as well as she whom God has appointed to fill that particular place: a woman's principal work in life is hardly left to her own choice; nor can she drop the domestic charges devolving on her as an individual, for the exercise of the most splendid talents that were ever bestowed. And yet she must not shrink from the extra responsibility implied by the very fact of her possessing such talents. She must not hide her gift in a napkin; it was meant for the use and service of others. In an humble and faithful spirit must she labour to do what is not impossible, or God would not have set her to do it."[1]

Indeed, throughout the *Life* Mrs. Gaskell stressed her admiration of Charlotte Brontë's acceptance of her home duties so strongly that Charles Kingsley thought the book would "shame literary people into some stronger belief that a simple, virtuous, practical home life is consistent with high imaginative genius;".[2]

She touched on the same problem when she quoted Southey's reply to Charlotte Brontë's request for advice about her literary ability. He wrote, among other things:

"Literature cannot be the business of a woman's life, and it ought not to be. The more she is engaged in her proper duties, the less leisure will she have for it, even as an accomplishment and a recreation . . . Write poetry for its own sake; . . . So written, it is wholesome both for the heart and soul; it may be made the surest means, next to religion, of soothing the mind and elevating it."[3]

It is significant that Mrs. Gaskell, so chary of direct comment in this book unless strongly moved, did give an opinion on this letter: "It is partly because I think it so admirable . . . that I have taken the liberty of inserting the above extracts from it."[4]

Further on in the same *Life* she again expressed her wholehearted approval of a woman placing home duties above any other work: "I call particular attention to the following letter of Charlotte's, dated July 10th, 1846. . . . the wholesome sense of duty in it—the sense of the supremacy of that duty which God, in placing us in families, has laid out for us, seems to deserve especial regard in these days." In the letter, Charlotte Brontë ad-

---

[1] *The Life of Charlotte Brontë*, pp. 237–8.
[2] Letter to Mrs. Gaskell, May 14, 1857; *Charles Kingsley, His Letters and Memories of his Life*, edited by his wife (London, 1901), III: 25.
[3] *The Life of Charlotte Brontë*, pp. 102–3.
[4] *Ibid.*, p. 103.

vised a friend to stay at home with her aged mother and thus to give up "*for the present*, every prospect of independency for yourself". "The right path is that which necessitates the greatest sacrifice of self-interest—which implies the greatest good to others", she declared.[1]

That Mrs. Gaskell did not doubt the supremacy of home duties even when artistic duties were concerned, is also evident a few pages further on, where she relates how Charlotte Brontë, even when inspiration had come back to her after weeks or months of inactivity, broke off in the middle of her writing to go and peel the potatoes more carefully than their aged servant could do. "This little proceeding may show how orderly and fully she accomplished her duties, even at those times when the 'possession' was upon her."[2]

Mrs. Gaskell could never reconcile herself to the idea that a woman was justified in subordinating home duties to the demands of her art. The problem worried her, not only in her own case, but also in her daughter's. Meta, her second daughter, wanted to take up drawing and painting as a profession. Mrs. Gaskell, in a letter to C. E. Norton, August 27, 1860, declared herself willing to agree to this plan, but added, "—is she to draw to give pleasure to others, or to improve herself? You see the complexity of the question, as to selfishness, Goethean theories of self development. I believe it to be *right* in all things to aim at the highest standard; but I can't quite work it out with my conscience . . ."[3]

The letters in which Mrs. Gaskell discusses the conflict between home duties and individual life all date from the time after the publication of *The Life of Charlotte Brontë*, which was published in 1857 and marks the transition in Mrs. Gaskell's authorship from the writing of novels with a purpose, such as *Mary Barton, Ruth*

---

[1] *Ibid.*, pp. 207–8.

[2] *Ibid.*, p. 214. This was one of those points where Mrs. Gaskell and Charlotte Brontë thought so exactly alike that the latter regretted that there could be no discussion between them. (See p. 50.) She once wrote about Harriet Martineau: "The manner in which she combines the highest mental culture with the nicest discharge of feminine duties filled me with admiration." (Letter to Laetitia Wheelwright, Jan. 12, 1851. Shorter, *op. cit.*, I: 190.)

[3] Whitehill, *op. cit.*

and *North and South*, to the writing for art's sake. In her early period, before she had come in such close contact both with ideas about women's rights and Goethean ideas of self development, she had probably taken the supremacy of home duties so much for granted that she did not see any reason for discussing this question, even if she dimly felt it as a personal problem. She may then even have doubted her right as a wife and mother to devote a great deal of time to the writing of books. An indication that this may have been the case is her reaction to an article on *Ruth* in the *North British Review* of May, 1853, which discusses the relative merits of married and unmarried women writers. The author entreats unmarried women, because they "are denied the most blessed enjoyments of the heart" not to strive to blight their capacity for such as remain to them by giving themselves up to those of the intellect. But in the case of married women, "with family cares upon their hands, and the moral responsibilities of their now completed life upon their consciences, to write and to print will be no mere temptation to their vanity", so he assures them that "the world will receive such works with a righteous deference". If Mrs. Gaskell had any conscientious scruples at that period about writing books, the article must have served to reassure her, and in a letter to Catherine Winkworth[1] she called the review *"delicious"* and declared that it made her "swear with delight".

In time, however, another aspect of the same problem assumed a similar importance in her eyes. After she had become a novelist of established fame, she had come to consider her duty to "aim at the highest standard" in her art as a real moral obligation. She knew that she "must not shrink from the extra responsibility" imposed on her by her talents. Her art, as well as her home duties, might demand the whole of her time. Hence her new dilemma. It seems highly probable that many of her friends who struggled with similar problems in their own lives discussed the subject with her as Charlotte Brontë had done.[2] Miss Fox's letter is proof that this was actually the case in one instance.[3] It seems probable, then, that there were three chief reasons for Mrs. Gaskell to dis-

---

[1] Quoted by Haldane, *op. cit.*, p. 68.

[2] Cf. pp. 50, 51.

[3] See p. 58.

cuss the conflict between home and artistic duties in the late 'fifties and early 'sixties: She had come to regard the demands of her
art as more important than she had previously done[1], the writing
of *The Life of Charlotte Brontë* had forced her to consider the problem as it affected that writer, whose situation in this special case
was so like her own, and letters from other friends in a similar situation gave the question a renewed interest of topicality. Charlotte
Brontë's example strengthened both her resolution not to subordinate either set of duties to the other and her hope that a reconcilia-
tion of apparently opposite demands on her time and energy would
not prove to be an impossible task. But the problem did not cease
to worry her, and her solution remained in her own eyes an unsatisfactory compromise.

The reason why Mrs. Gaskell did not try to illustrate in her
works the situation of a wife whose interests were divided between
her home and some artistic activity may have been her feeling that
she had not really solved the resulting problem in her own life.
She did, however, take up several other marriage problems in her
works. One such problem, which recurs in a number of her stories, is the question: should a wife conform to the traditional ideal
of a submissive woman who always trusts to her husband's judgment, or should she take over the responsibility for moral decisions
when her husband is too weak a character to make them, or has
ideas of right and wrong which are different from her own? This
latter problem, as it appears in Mrs. Gaskell's works, is specially
interesting because her attitude towards it shows a definite gradual
development—parallel to the development of her attitude towards
some other female problems treated in her stories. In the course
of her literary career, her ideal changed from the submissive wife
of the earliest stories to the wife of strong character, willing to accept moral responsibility, of *Right at Last* (1858), and it is worthy
of notice that the time when the first hints of this change appear
coincides with the time when the influence of some of the friends
mentioned in the preceding chapter might be expected to have
made itself felt.

In the first novel that Mrs. Gaskell wrote, *Mary Barton, a Tale*

---

[1] See letter to Norton about Meta, quoted on p. 60.

of Manchester Life, which was begun some time after the death of her only son on August 10, 1845, and published on October 14, 1848, the wife's *problems* do not appear at all. In this moralising tale, with its great number of Bible quotations in the manner of Charlotte Elizabeth's factory stories[1], Mrs. Gaskell has not yet come to question the conventional idea of "woman's sphere" and "woman's mission".

Mrs. Barton's mission in life is to do good, but, as a good wife, she can accomplish this end only by means of her influence on her husband. When she dies, "One of the good influences over John Barton's life had departed . . . One of the ties which bound him down to the gentle humanities of earth was loosened, and . . . he was a changed man. His gloom and his sternness became habitual instead of occasional".[2] The phrase, "gentle humanities", might have been quoted direct from Mrs. Sandford's or any other conventional book on "female improvement" of that time. It is noteworthy, that Mrs. Gaskell's chief objection to factory work for women in this book is that it tends to make women neglect their duties in the home.[3]

There is no hint of irony or protest in her way of reporting John Barton's views concerning a husband's authority: "Her father now began to wish Mary was married . . . He felt that he could not resume the reins he had once slackened. But with a husband it would be different."[4] On the other hand, she cannot resist making fun of the inherent feeling of superiority in the male sex and makes the little boy Charley say of his mother, "there's no good arguing with a woman".[5]

In the short stories published in the years 1847–49 there is nothing of interest in this context.[6] The first time that Mrs. Gaskell openly discusses the problem of a wife whose loyalty and obedience to her husband clashes with her own perceptions of right and wrong is in *Lizzie Leigh*.[7]

---

[1] See Appendix II.

[2] Chap. III, pp. 29–30.   [3] See Chap. VI.

[4] Chap. XI, p. 127.   [5] Chap. XXVII, p. 281.

[6] *The Sextons' Hero, Christmas Storms and Sunshine, Hand and Heart.*

[7] *Lizzie Leigh* was published in 1850 but probably written earlier. See p. 66, n. 1.

In the opening chapter we are told that

"They had been two-and-twenty years man and wife; for nineteen of those years their life had been as calm and happy as the most perfect uprightness on the one side, and the most complete confidence and loving submission on the other, could make it. Milton's famous line[1] might have been framed and hung up as the rule of their married life, for he was truly the interpreter, who stood between God and her; she would have considered herself wicked if she had ever dared even to think him austere, though as certainly as he was an upright man, so surely was he hard, stern, and inflexible."[2]

He shows this hardness, when their only daughter, who has gone out to service in Manchester, is seduced. Then "he had forbidden his weeping, heart-broken wife to go and try to find her poor sinning child, and declared that henceforth they would have no daughter".[3]

This is the point at which the conflict arises.

"But for three years the moan and the murmur had never been out of her heart; she had rebelled against her husband as against a tyrant, with a hidden, sullen rebellion, which tore up the old landmarks of wifely duty and affection, and poisoned the fountains whence gentlest love and reverence had once been for ever springing."[4]

On his death-bed, though, he whispers to his wife that he forgives their daughter, and "those last blessed words replaced him on his throne in her heart, and called out penitent anguish for all the bitter estrangement of later years".[5]

As yet Mrs. Gaskell represents it as the duty of a woman to show complete obedience to her husband, even when he is obviously wrong in his unchristian lack of charity. Mrs. Leigh has to be penitent for her secret thoughts, even though they never led to any act of open rebellion. And it should be noted that this submissiveness is represented as right only for a wife in relation to her husband, not otherwise for woman in relation to man. As long as her husband is alive Mrs. Leigh must rely on his judgment, but after his death she must and does face responsibility alone. She has the necessary strength of character; that she trusted her hus-

---

[1] "He for God only, she for God in him." *Paradise Lost*, Book IV, l. 297.
[2] P. 386.　　[3] P. 391.
[4] Pp. 386-7.　　[5] P. 387.

band in all moral questions was not out of weakness but from a sense of duty. She is not afraid of assuming responsibility for her son. The following passage does not describe a weak, helpless woman, unable to grapple with moral problems: "'I am your mother, and I dare to command you, because I know I am in the right, and that God is on my side . . .' She stood no longer as the meek, imploring, gentle mother, but firm and dignified, as if the interpreter of God's will."[1] She stands here in the same relation to her son as her husband did to her when he was "truly the interpreter, who stood between God and her".

There is interesting evidence as to Mrs. Gaskell's own attitude towards this kind of problem about the year 1850 in two letters now in the Brotherton Library. One of them, about the payment for *Lizzie Leigh*, has already been quoted on p. 31 and shows that Mrs. Gaskell's anxious conscience was reassured by the fact that her husband felt no compunction in accepting the £20 in question. The other letter was written in the preceding year:

"... You *must* come and see us in it[2], dearest Tottie, and try and make me see 'the wrong the better cause', and that it is right to spend so much ourselves on *so* purely selfish a thing as a house is, while so many are wanting —thats the haunting thought to me; at least to one of my 'Mes', for I have a great number, and that's the plague. One of my mes is, I do believe, a true Christian—(only people call her socialist and communist), another of my mes is a wife and mother, and highly delighted at the delight of every one else in the house, Meta and William most especially who are in full ecstacy . . . I try to drown myself (my *first* self) by saying it's Wm. who is to decide on all these things, and his feeling it right ought to be my rule. And so it is—only that does not quite do. Well! I must try and make the house give as much pleasure to others as I can and make it as little a selfish thing as I can. My dear! its 150 a year, and I dare say we shall be ruined; ... I long (weakly) for the old times where right and wrong did not seem such complicated matters; and I am sometimes coward enough to wish that one were back in the darkness where obedience was the only seen duty of women . . . My idea of Heaven just now is, a place where we shan't have any consciences,—and Hell vice versa . . ."

This letter shows clearly that Mrs. Gaskell still vaguely thought of a husband's sense of right and wrong as an authority, which it was a wife's duty to accept: "his feeling it right ought to be my

---

[1] P. 407.   [2] The new house.

rule". The easiest way to soothe her conscience would have been uncritically to adopt this doctrine of vicarious responsiblity, but she could not help seeing a difficulty: "only that does not quite do". Even if she had not yet come to rebel consciously and explicitly against the traditional conception of a wife's duty of submission to her husband, she had evidently begun to doubt the duty, or even the right, of a wife to delegate all moral responsibility to her husband[1], and, as her way of treating this problem in her works shows, her doubts later developed into a firm conviction that women as well as men have to judge for themselves in moral matters. To herself, though, it remained a duty rather than a privilege to assume such responsibility and independence of judgment. While she was writing *North and South* with the strong, independent character of Margaret Hale she wrote a little wistfully in a letter to Mr. Forster[2] about Charlotte Brontë's engagement to Mr. Nicholls:

"... with all his bigotry it must be charming to be loved with all the strength of his heart as she sounds to be. Mr. Shaen accuses me always of being 'too much of a woman' in always wanting to obey somebody— but I am sure that Miss Brontë would never have borne not to be well-ruled and ordered—... I mean that she would never have been happy but with an exacting, rigid, law-giving passionate man ..."

Even if this sometimes seemed to Mrs. Gaskell an ideal to be longed for, the letter to Miss Fox quoted above shows that her reason and conscience told her that such a longing was weak, cowardly, and unenlightened.

In the next two stories, *The Heart of John Middleton* and *The Moorland Cottage*—both published in 1850—we again find the portrait of a rather passive wife, representing the good influence in the life of her husband. Though Nelly in *The Heart of John*

---

[1] The fact that the ideas about a wife's duty of submission to her husband which Mrs. Gaskell expresses in this letter do not tally with the author's conviction as it appears in *Lizzie Leigh* seems to confirm A. W. Ward's theory (in his introduction to *Mary Barton* etc. in the Knutsford edn) that *Lizzie Leigh* was written before *Mary Barton*. Mrs. Chadwick also mentions this theory: "*Lizzie Leigh* is said to have been written before *Mary Barton*, although published some time afterwards." (*Op. cit.*, p. 138.)

[3] April 23, 1854. Copy of letter in the Brotherton Library.

Middleton shields her lover from the stone aimed at him, she is not otherwise described as either strong or energetic, though her moral influence is important. When the hero of the story thirsts for revenge on his enemy, there was "only my gentle, pleading Nelly to pull me back from the great gulf"[1], and at her death-bed he "learned that it is better to be sinned against than to sin".[2]

Mrs. Buxton in *The Moorland Cottage* "foresaw that . . . feelings might arise [between the two young people] which would militate against her husband's hopes and plans, and which, therefore, she ought not to allow to spring up".[3] She was "a gentle wife, who if she ruled him never showed it, or was conscious of the fact herself".[4] She "was meekly content to *be* gentle, holy, patient, and undefiled—".[5]

In 1851 that fore-runner of *Cranford, Mr. Harrison's Confessions*, was published. Here, there is no more hesitation in Mrs. Gaskell's attitude towards the "she for God in him" doctrine. The simpering, affected Miss Caroline, one of the very few entirely unsympathetic characters in Mrs. Gaskell's stories, talks of "the illness of a worshipped husband". But

"Mrs. Brouncker said—
'Please, ma'am, I don't worship my husband. I would not be so wicked.'
" 'Goodness! You don't think it wicked, do you? For my part . . . I should worship, I should adore him.' . . .
"But sturdy Mrs. Brouncker said again—
" 'I hope I know my duty better. I've not learned my Commandments for nothing. I know whom I ought to worship.' "[6]

There is no doubt as to which side enjoys Mrs. Gaskell's sympathies. Her attitude has indeed changed since she wrote *Lizzie Leigh*[7], where the "wickedness" consisted in criticizing the husband.

---

[1] P. 326.

[2] P. 334. Mrs. Gaskell was willing to change the tragic ending of this story, though her letter to that effect did not arrive until the manuscript had already gone to press, according to a letter to Mrs. Gaskell from Dickens, dated Dec. 20, 1850, now in the Rylands Library, Manchester.

[3] P. 303.   [4] P. 323.

[5] P. 383.   [6] P. 421.

[7] Cf. p. 66, n. 1.

It is not merely because of her self-delusion, but also on account of her mistaken ideal, that Mrs. Gaskell is ironical about Mrs. Rose in *Mr. Harrison's Confessions*, the widow who imagines that all her decisions are dictated by her deference to what her late husband would have wished.

In Cranford[1], full of exquisite irony though it is about the attitude of the charming old ladies towards the other sex, there is very little of interest for this chapter.

The next story of interest in this context is *Ruth*, which was published in 1853 but was planned early enough for Mrs. Gaskell to give Charlotte Brontë an outline of it in August, 1852.[2] Not only the main theme of *Lizzie Leigh*, but also the story of a wife who rebels against her husband recurs here. In fact *Lizzie Leigh* might almost be said to be a rough draft of *Ruth*, though the wife's problem is treated in a somewhat different way. The situation is the same, only intensified; we meet again the tyrannical husband in the person of Mr. Bradshaw, and his cowed wife, "thoroughly broken into submission".[3] She was, however, not completely broken, for "Mrs. Bradshaw murmured faintly at her husband when his back was turned; but if his voice was heard, or his footsteps sounded in the distance, she was mute.[4]

"And yet she looked up to her husband with a reverence, and regard, and a faithfulness of love, which his decision of character was likely to produce on a weak and anxious mind. He was a rest and a support to her, on whom she cast all her responsibilities; she was an obedient, unremonstrating wife to him; no stronger affection had ever brought her duty to him into conflict with any desire of her heart."[5]

So far the relationship between husband and wife in *Ruth* is exactly like that in *Lizzie Leigh*. The author's attitude towards it, however, has undergone a marked change. In *Lizzie Leigh* the "complete confidence and loving submission" were "the landmarks of wifely duty", the "sullen rebellion" against which called for "penitent anguish"; here it is only a "weak and anxious mind" that casts its responsibilities on somebody else.

---

[1] *Cranford* began to appear in *Household Words* on Dec. 18, 1851.
[2] See Shorter, *op. cit.*, II: 263, letter 570.
[3] P. 107.   [4] P. 147.
[5] P. 161.

Mrs. Bradshaw's obedience is not the result of a conscious principle; she has merely followed the law of least resistance, as no "stronger affection" has come into play. Before the crisis in their relationship, Mrs. Bradshaw is truly "for God in him", "for his approval or disapproval was the standard by which she measured all things".[1] She even obeys his orders to tell him everything that has been said in his absence, although this tends to isolate her from her children.

When he discovers his son's forgery, Mr. Bradshaw, like Lizzie Leigh's father, refuses to forgive his child, but Mrs. Bradshaw rebels, not only in her heart but, unlike Mrs. Leigh, openly. She refuses to go near him, and in the conflict between her duty to her husband and her love for her children she chooses her son:

"Oh! is not he cruel? I don't care. I have been a good wife till now. I know I have. I have done all he bid me, ever since we were married. But now I will speak my mind, and say to everybody how cruel he is—how hard to his own flesh and blood! If he puts poor Dick in prison, I will go too. If I'm to choose between my husband and my son, I choose my son; for he will have no friends, unless I am with him."[2]

Such a reason for rebellion, the only one which Mrs. Gaskell, the devoted mother, recognized as valid, is entirely consistent with the general pattern of her thinking. That the authority of a husband and father was the corner stone of family life was one of the most firmly rooted convictions of the Victorian age, and Mrs. Gaskell, who valued family unity and family affection above most other things[3], did not mean to evoke sympathy with wives who rebelled against their husbands on their own behalf. The only justification for such a rebellion, in Mrs. Gaskell's opinion, was a wish to protect others more helpless. Margaret Hale in *North and South* formulates this principle in her defence of her brother, who had taken part in a mutiny on board his ship: "Loyalty and obedience to wisdom and justice are fine; but it is still finer to defy arbitrary power, unjustly and cruelly used—not on behalf of our-

---

[1] P. 232.

[2] P. 284.

[3] "I could not bear my life if you and Meta did not love each other most dearly", she wrote in an undated letter to her eldest daughter, now in the Brotherton Library.

selves, but on behalf of others more helpless."[1] Consequently, the crisis in the Bradshaws' marriage had to come through one of the children.

Although Mrs. Gaskell never hesitated to end her stories tragically by a death-bed scene, she could not yet bring herself to depict a definitely unhappy marriage and resorted to her old device of making the man helpless and so calling out motherly pity in the woman.[2] Mr. Bradshaw has a stroke when he hears about his son's accident, and then, almost exactly like Mrs. Leigh, "Mrs. Bradshaw forgot all her vows of estrangement from the dead-like husband . . . and bitterly accused herself for every angry word she had spoken against him during these last few miserable days".[3]

In *Ruth* Mrs. Gaskell expressed her opinion that "similarity of opinion is not always—I think not often—needed for fulness and perfection of love".[4] In *Morton Hall*, however, published in the same year as *Ruth*, she tells a story very much to the opposite effect. The scene is set in the time of the restoration of Charles II, the hero is a partisan of the Stuarts and the heroine an ardent Puritan. There is no question here of a submissive wife. Though the husband thinks of her as "a beautiful woman to be tamed, and made to come to his beck and call", "such fierce, strong wills would quarrel the first day of their wedded life".[5] Though she loves him "with a terrible love" they quarrel fiercely over religion and politics and even over property: He

"made a deadly oath that none of them should find harbour or welcome in any house of his. She looked scornfully back at him, and said she had yet to learn in what county of England the house he spoke of was to be found; but in the house her father purchased, and she inherited, all who preached the Gospel should be welcome."[6]

Not even Mrs. Gaskell could imagine a happy ending to this marriage, so she went to the other extreme, following the pattern of

---

[1] P. 117.

[2] She used the same device in *The Moorland Cottage, Cranford, Morton Hall, North and South, The Crooked Branch,* and *Sylvia's Lovers.*

[3] P. 289.   [4] P. 262.

[5] P. 366.

[6] P. 367. For Mrs. Gaskell's attitude to economic questions in her own marriage, see pp. 31–33.

the lurid tragedies of the time, and let the wife freeze to death after being imprisoned by her husband for several years in a lunatic
asylum.

My French Master, also published in 1853, is of interest in this
connection as providing the first example in Mrs. Gaskell's stories
of a marriage where the wife—in the person of "my mother"—
has taken over the whole responsibility for the practical affairs of
the home. It is she who sees to it that her husband's agricultural
experiments do not exceed the limit they can afford, and "my
mother undertook the greater part of our education".[1] Mrs. Gaskell
is now more amused by than moralizing about Susan Dixon's
wifely submission: "She was a little awed by him, to be sure; never quite at her ease before him; but I imagine husbands do not
dislike such a tribute to their Jupiter-ship."[2] Nor does she particularly admire the grave, stately Susan de Chalabre, who "made
rather a pomp of her conjugal obedience".

In the following year, 1854, *North and South* began to appear
serially in *Household Words*. Just as Mr. Hale had one trait in common with Mr. Gaskell[3], Mrs. Hale shared Mrs. Gaskell's inability to appreciate her husband's absorption in his work[4]; Mr.
Hale has to be much from home, and "these duties were regarded
as hardships by his wife, not to be accepted as the natural conditions of his profession, but to be regretted and struggled against
by her as they severally arose. So he withdrew ... into his library".[5]

Both Mrs. Hale and the minor character Mrs. Boucher in *North
and South* are represented as bad wives who make no attempt to
sympathize with their husbands in the difficulties against which
they struggle, Mr. Hale in his religious dilemma and Mr. Boucher
in his conflict with the trade union. Mrs. Hale's unwillingness to
try to understand her husband's religious difficulties was taken
from her counterpart in *Pomfret*[6], but Mrs. Boucher has no parallel in that book. Her lack of sympathetic understanding is one
among many reasons which bring about her husband's suicide.

---

[1] P. 507. [2] P. 524.
[3] See p. 17. [4] See p. 23.
[5] P. 24.
[6] See Appendix II.

Neither Mrs. Hale nor Mrs. Boucher, however, plays an important part in the novel, and the marital situation created by their lack of insight into their husbands' needs is hardly more than touched upon; nor did Mrs. Gaskell treat the same problem at greater length until nine years later, in *Crowley Castle*.[1]

For the next two years Mrs. Gaskell was chiefly occupied with *The Life of Charlotte Brontë*[2], during the writing of which she had perforce reconsidered several problems concerning the position of women in England. She had also come into contact with the ideas of such intrepid pioneers of the woman's cause as Charlotte Brontë's intimate friend, Mary Taylor.[3]

The literary by-product of Mrs. Gaskell's preoccupation with *The Life of Charlotte Brontë* was a short story which marks the

---

[1] See p. 84 ff.

[2] Mrs. Gaskell's other literary output during that time is negligible. The few stories she did write or publish were probably earlier efforts, which she now finished or partly rewrote. The author herself assured C. E. Norton that *The Doom of the Griffiths* was such a tale from her earlier period. (See Appendix II.) Consequently, there are no new ideas concerning the position of a wife in this story. We find, in the person of Mrs. Robert Griffiths, the gentle, yielding wife, who stands in awe of her husband, "partly from his devoting much time to studies of which she could understand nothing"; Robert's stepmother in the same story is the wicked stepmother of the fairy tales, who dominates her husband but "sacrificed the show of authority for the power" (p. 218), and "sat by with a smile of triumph on her beautiful lips" (p. 219), when he carries out the evil plans she has insinuated into his mind. In the person of Nest we have the first instance in Mrs. Gaskell's stories of a woman who, though her husband's inferior in social position, is the perfect wife, and whom we find again in the Neapolitan fisherman's daughter in *My Lady Ludlow*, also published in 1858, and, later, in Osborne Hamley's wife in *Wives and Daughters*. Though this type of happy marriage is exemplified in three of Mrs. Gaskell's stories, she did not apparently consider them as typical. She writes about Robert in *The Doom of the Griffiths* that "he looked back on his wedding-day with a thankfulness which is seldom the result of unequal marriages". (P. 227.)

[3] Mrs. Gaskell did not meet Miss Taylor personally, as the latter had already emigrated to New Zealand when Mrs. Gaskell met Charlotte Brontë for the first time in 1850. They corresponded, however, and Mary Taylor gave her valuable information about their mutual friend, as appears from several references to her in the *Life*. It seems probable that Mrs. Gaskell had also seen the letter from Miss Taylor to Charlotte Brontë, dated from New Zealand April 29th, 1850, where she accused her friend of too great timidity on the subject of the woman's question in *Shirley*. (Shorter, *op. cit.* II: 131–2 quoted on p. 122.)

final stage in the gradual development of her ideas about the position and duties of a wife.[1] It was published in *Household Words* on Nov. 27, 1858, under the title of *The Sin of a Father*. When it was afterwards reprinted, this title was changed into *Right at Last*.

As has been shown above, Mrs. Gaskell had already treated a wife's problems in several of her stories. But they had always been treated as of secondary importance and not made the central theme of the story. In *Right at Last*, however, the difficulties which encounter the heroine in her marriage constitute the main theme.

Margaret[2], a strong-willed young woman, marries against her uncle's will, as she has a right to do, because she is of age; but, like Mrs. Gaskell herself, who was accused of being "too much of a woman"[3] because she longed to obey somebody all the time, Margaret does not value independence for its own sake. She implores her guardian to give his unnecessary consent to the marriage: "Let me belong to you that much! It seems so desolate at such a time to have to dispose of myself."[4]

When married, it is she who insists upon the necessary economy, trying to spare her husband the mortification which he experiences every time he cannot offer her the luxury which she has been used to. A servant robs them of a sum of money and threatens, if he is arrested, to tell the world that his master is the son of a convict— a secret which he believes that he has kept from his wife, though she has in fact known it all the time. Fearing that his wife will cease

---

[1] Another reason for Mrs. Gaskell to reconsider this kind of problem might have been her second daughter Meta's engagement which had lasted about a year before it was broken off towards the end of 1858. (See p. 79.)

[2] It seems to have been one of Mrs. Gaskell's difficulties to invent names for her characters and she often did not trouble to vary them from one story to another. Margaret in *Right at Last* shares her Christian name with Margaret Jennings in *Mary Barton*, Margaret Dawson in *My Lady Ludlow* and the two girls in *North and South* and *Libbie Marsh's Three Eras* whose surnames are as similar as Hale and Hall. There are two Hester Roses in Mrs. Gaskell's stories (in *Sylvia's Lovers* and *The Crooked Branch*), no less than five Fannys and five Bessys, not counting one Betsy and two Bettys. Mary is also one of her favourite names (five plus one Maria); there are four Ellinors or Eleanors, etc.

[3] See p. 66.

[4] P. 281.

to love him if she hears the truth, he remains in a state of helpless inactivity, unable to make up his mind to face the crisis, and

"Margaret was infinitely distressed and dismayed by the effect the robbery seemed to have had on her husband's energies. The probable loss of such a sum was bad enough; but there was something so weak and poor in character in letting it affect him so strongly as to deaden all energy and destroy all hopeful spring, that, although Margaret did not dare to define her feeling, nor the cause of it, to herself, she had the fact before her perpetually, that, if she were to judge of her husband from this morning only, she must learn to rely on herself alone in all cases of emergency."[1]

It is she who has to answer the inspector's questions; it is she who insists on following her social conscience, which tells her that it would be a wrong against the community not to let justice be done. Her husband weakly tries to persuade her to inactivity:

" 'I can refuse to prosecute.' 'Let Crawford go free, you knowing him to be guilty? . . . you cannot do this thing. You let loose a criminal upon the public . . . I don't care for poverty; and, as to shame, I should feel it twenty times more grievously, if you and I consented to screen the guilty, from any fear or for any selfish motives of our own. I don't pretend I shall not feel it, when first the truth is known . . .' "

Still, her husband cannot make up his mind to write the irretrievable refusal to the blackmailer.

" 'May *I* write it?' said Margaret.
"She wrote:—'Whatever you may do or say, there is but one course open to us. No threats can deter your master from doing his duty.
"Margaret Brown."[2]

Margaret Brown is indeed far removed from Mrs. Gaskell's first passive, submissive wives, whose only mission in life was to provide their husbands with restful homes and who considered it a crime to criticize any decisions of these "interpreters of God's will" and would never have dreamed of taking the lead in moral issues.

Mrs. Gaskell had epitomized her first ideal of a wife in the early, entirely traditional portrait of Mrs. Leigh, who lived "in the darkness where obedience was the only seen duty of women",[3] and who was never to oppose or criticize her husband, even when he acted

---

[1] P. 290.   [2] P. 298.
[3] See p. 65.

wrongly, against his wife's moral creed and Christian principles. This ideal had been modified when Mrs. Gaskell wrote *Ruth*. Mrs. Bradshaw in that novel is represented as doing right in opposing her husband when he acts in an obviously unchristian way. Finally, in *Right at Last*, Mrs. Gaskell stated her conviction that it is the duty of a woman to take over the whole responsibility and initiative, not only for her own actions, as when Margaret marries against her uncle's will, but also for her husband, if his moral courage and discernment are not sufficient.[1]

Mrs. Gaskell's way of treating this theme in her books developed gradually. The first signs of a change in her attitude towards it appeared in 1851, and it reached its final stage in 1858. As can be concluded from the evidence quoted in Chapter II and on pp. 57–65, Mrs. Gaskell's attitude towards the question of a wife's independence or submissiveness as she encountered the problem in her own life underwent a similar change in the same period. Her real opinions were faithfully reproduced in her works. It appears, however, from the letters to Miss Fox and to Forster quoted on pp. 65–6 that, far from hailing with joy the new conception of woman as free and responsible, Mrs. Gaskell was reluctant to accept it and sometimes longed for the "darkness where obedience was the only seen duty of women". This fact is one of the chief reasons why it seems probable that Mrs. Gaskell's personal marital experience was of subordinate importance to the development of her ideas, which began to change as soon as she

---

[1] Never, though, did Mrs. Gaskell approve of the "masculine", assertive woman (Cf. her letter about Barbara Bodichon quoted in Chap. IX), or the bluestocking type. Her heroines are always strictly "womanly", and her satirical portrait in *North and South* of the vicar's efficient wife, who was "not troubled with much delicacy of perception" and who "went as near as a lady could towards holding Mr. Bell by the button, while she explained the Phonetic system to him", is drawn without a trace of the almost proverbial Gaskell gentleness. Gentleness in women remained an essential virtue in her eyes. Fearing that the reader might think Margaret in *Right at Last* the hard, efficient, masculine type of which she so strongly disapproved, she hastened to correct this impression by giving the reader a glimpse of her some years after the crisis. She is then "graver; more portly; more stern, I had almost said. But, ... I saw her come to the dining-room window with a baby in her arms, and her whole face melted into a smile of infinite sweetness". (P. 299.)

had come in personal contact with some of the advocates of the new ideal. As her intimacy with them grew and the circle of these new friends became larger, their influence as well as the influence of the newspaper and magazine debate on woman's mission and sphere, to which they directed her attention, became more marked and showed itself both in her life and in her books. Entirely consistent with Mrs. Gaskell's reluctance to embrace the new ideas is the fact that she wrote stories about the problems of wives that read more like expositions of her own changing attitude than like propaganda for the abolition of a social evil. There is, indeed, a marked difference between her way of writing about such problems as affected her private life, and her more propagandic way of treating, for instance, the question of fallen women or the conditions of dressmakers' apprentices; which must be one of the reasons why the former group of problems in her works has entirely escaped the notice both of contemporary reviewers and later commentators.

Mrs. Gaskell never stressed the duty of a wife to be an independent woman, responsible for her own actions and moral decisions, more strongly than she had done in *Right at Last*. After that story she even seems to have lost interest in this particular problem. It is not treated at all in her next few stories, in which the wives are not faced with any moral conflict resulting from their marriage. The situation in *The Crooked Branch*, which was published one year after *Right at Last*, is somewhat similar to that story. The importance of legal justice is again stressed, and Hester Rose looks to her own conscience and not to her husband (as the mother of Lizzie Leigh would have done) for guidance when she decides to set truth and justice above her love for her son. But this fact is neither discussed nor emphasized. The problem, once solved, did not interest Mrs. Gaskell enough to treat it seriously in her later stories.

The old idea of a wife's duty of obedience crops up again in one place in Mrs. Gaskell's last novel, *Wives and Daughters*, but it is now considered as so preposterous as to need no explanatory remarks. Lady Cumnor, with her belief in the divine right of aristocrats, represents much that Mrs. Gaskell found deliciously absurd, and this far from submissive wife gives a young woman in the book the following advice: "You must reverence your husband, and conform to his opinion in all things. Look up to him as your head, and do nothing without consulting him."[1]

A strong influence from other works of fiction made itself felt in several of the works written in Mrs. Gaskell's later period, after she had given up writing stories with a social purpose. *Cousin Phillis*, published in 1863, which assumes its place in the long line of idylls like Goldsmith's *The Vicar of Wakefield* and Goethe's *Hermann und Dorothea*, contains a portrait of a wife who reverts to a literary tradition. Cousin Holman, the minister's practical, unintellectual, devoted wife, comes very close to Walter Scott's ideal of a wife as it appears in the person of Mrs. Butler, née Jeanie Deans, in *The Heart of Midlothian*, who "did not pretend to understand his expositions of divinity, but no minister of the Presbytery had his humble dinner so well arranged, his clothes and linen in equal good order, his fireside so neatly swept, his parlour so clean, and his books so well dusted".[2] It should, however, be noted that Mrs. Gaskell points out Cousin Holman's inability to share her husband's interests as a flaw in their otherwise happy marriage.[3]

If Mrs. Gaskell's literary treatment of the question whether a wife ought to be submissive or independent was chiefly influenced by theoretical argumentation, her way of treating the question whether a woman might be justified in breaking off an engagement, running away from her husband, or loving more than once, shows what decisive influence her personal experience—or rather the experience of one of her daughters—could have on her writing. Mary Barton had imagined herself in love with Mr. Carson before she engaged herself to Jem, but this inconstancy on the heroine's part drew down the wrath of reviewers on the author.[4]

---

[1] P. 579.   [2] Chap. XLVII.

[3] See p. 83, n. 2.

[4] "the worst thing in the whole Tale ... the character of its heroine, or rather the unnatural combination of the two elements that go to make up her character. Take away the extraneous addition, and leave us the genuine Mary Barton, the simple-hearted and faithful mistress of Jem,—such as we can suppose the first *pure* conception presented itself to the mind of the author—and nothing can be imagined more lovely and engaging. But to this is prefixed ... a character of quite another hue, which is out of harmony with it; and the discrepancy between the two involves consequences in the development of the story, which form the chief drawback on its general impression of naturalness and probability.

Mrs. Gaskell protested, as her aim had been to give a realistic picture of a young girl in spite of the contemporary tradition of a highly
idealised novel heroine.[1] In 1849 she wrote to Eliza Fox: "I am
glad you like Mary, I do: but people are angry with her just because she is not perfect."[2] However, the question had not yet
come to be of great personal importance to her; she took good care
not to repeat the mistake, and her heroines were marvels of constancy in their feelings, until her daughter's broken engagement
caused her to take up the theme in *Six Weeks at Heppenheim*.

That story was published in *The Cornhill Magazine* in May,
1862, but had actually been written more than three years earlier.
In a letter to Clement Shorter[3] Meta Gaskell gave the following
information:

"The only times that Mrs. Gaskell stayed in Germany were, during a
short tour in Rhine-land with her husband, 1839 or 1840; and during a

---

We refer of course to Mary's flirtations with Mr. Carson, and her strange ignorance of her feelings towards Jem". (The *Prospective Review*, Feb., 1849.)

Maria Edgeworth wrote to Miss Holland on Dec. 27, 1848: "Mary herself
is charming—from not being too perfect . . . Here are no such faultless nor any
such vicious monsters as the world ne'er saw—" (*Bulletin*, pp. 108-11), but the
literary fashion of the day did not tolerate any such realism in the portrait of a
novel heroine. The *Edinburgh Review*, in a review of Charlotte Brontë's *Shirley*
(January, 1850), laid down the law for novelists in this respect: "In a subordinate
character such a lapse from the elevation of moral rectitude, might have been
pardoned; but in a hero—in a man for whom our sympathies and admiration
are almost exclusively claimed—to imagine it possible, is a decided blunder
in art—as well as an inconsistency in nature."

[1] She also declared war against the type of romantic story in which the Minerva Press excelled. Mary Barton had picked up "simple, foolish, unworldly
ideas . . . from the romances which Miss Simmonds' young ladies were in the
habit of recommending to each other". Mrs. Bradshaw in *Ruth* also read the
same kind of escapist literature: "castle-building, after the manner of the Minerva
press, was the outlet by which she escaped from the pressure of her prosaic life,
as Mr. Bradshaw's wife". (P. 131.) It is no wonder, therefore, that the authoress
particularly resented that review of *Ruth* which said, "the language is often after
the Minerva press, and sentimentality is made to occupy the place of sentiment".
(The *Literary Gazette and Journal of Belles Lettres, Science, and Art*, 22 Jan.,
1853.) In a letter to Miss Fox of 1853 (copy in the Brotherton Library) Mrs.
Gaskell complained that "Spectator, Lity. Gazette, Sharpe's Mag; Colborn have
all abused it as roundly as may be. Litery. Gazette in every form of abuse".

[2] Extract of letter in the Brotherton Library.

[3] Copy of letter in the Brotherton Library.

long visit to Heidelberg in the winter of 1858-9, with two of her daughters—I think the visit lasted 13 weeks.

"She went down the Rhine in going there; and 'Six Weeks at Heppenheim' was planned and, I fancy, written at Heidelberg."

The reason for this journey appears from a letter to Mrs. Nancy Robson[1]: "I sold the right of republication[2] to him in a hurry to get £ 100 to take Meta abroad out of the clatter of tongues consequent on her breaking off her engagement..."[3]

In Thekla and Franz we find again the strong woman and the weak man: "She was the strong, good, helpful character, he the weak and vain."[4] He comes back after four years' absence, and Thekla realizes that she no longer loves him. We seem to be given a scene direct out of the Gaskell family:

"She came to ask me if I thought it her duty to marry this fellow, whose very appearance, changed for the worse ... seemed to have repelled her ... I told her, what I believe to be as true as gospel, that as she owned she did not love him any longer, now his real self had come to displace his remembrance, that she would be sinning in marrying him—doing evil that possible good might come."[5]

The narrator of the story is said to be a young man, but Mrs. Gaskell so far forgets this circumstance as to make him ask Thekla to "tell me all about it, as you would to your mother".[6]

In the earlier stories where broken engagements had occurred[7], no change in the heroine's affections had been considered possible, and they were left to grow "wan and bitter", only to find some happiness in their old age in the unselfish service of others. Nor could Lizzie Leigh or Ruth love more than once. The literary fashion of the day might demand this kind of life for a virtuous novel heroine suffering from an unhappy love affair, but it was hardly a prospect

---

[1] In the Brotherton Library. Undated.

[2] The *Household Words* stories referred to were those published in 1859 by the "rascally publisher" Sampson Low, who tried to "pass them off as new". (Letter quoted above. See n. 1.)

[3] On March 21, 1859, Mrs. Gaskell wrote to Miss Fox: "[Meta] enjoyed Heidelberg thoroughly ... and I don't think she ever thinks of her year of engagement." (Copy of letter in the Brotherton Library.)

[4] P. 362.   [5] P. 370.

[6] P. 360.

[7] *The Well of Pen-Morfa*, 1850, *Half a Lifetime Ago*, 1855.

which Mrs. Gaskell would like to contemplate for her own daughter, and Thekla, in spite of her assurance that "her heart was not like a room to let", is happily married soon after giving up her first lover.

Mrs. Gaskell's treatment of the problem in *Six Weeks at Heppenheim* shows some striking dissimilarities to her treatment of the question of a wife's submissiveness or independence. The reason she discussed it as a problem, which she had not done in *Mary Barton*, was a personal experience. This fact did not change her original ideas on the subject, but it lent a new importance to them, and she realized that she could no longer go on following the traditional literary pattern which had been enforced on her. In *Mary Barton* she had simply given a realistic description of a young girl's behaviour in a certain situation; in *Six Weeks at Heppenheim* she felt obliged to justify the course of action which she had no doubt advised her daughter to adopt in a similar situation. She had realized what harmful effects might result from a submissive acceptance of the rules enforced by unimaginative public opinion and, as usual in such a case, she did not hesitate to take up arms against mere conventions — not, be it noted, on behalf of herself but on behalf of somebody "more helpless".[1] That she considered the question of real importance is proved by her attitude towards it in the stories which she wrote after *Six Weeks at Heppenheim*. After that time, she never reverted to the conventional literary pattern which she had followed before the problem had assumed such a personal significance to her.

Never, before *Six Weeks at Heppenheim*, had any of Mrs. Gaskell's heroines broken off their engagements, and in her stories she had never contemplated the possibility of dissolving a marriage, before she wrote *The Grey Woman*, which was published the year before *Six Weeks at Heppenheim*, but apparently written either later than or at the same time as that story.[2] In *The Grey Woman* Mrs. Gaskell wrote a story which illustrates the disastrous effects of a

---

[1] See pp. 69–70.

[2] The heroine of *The Grey Woman* is German, and the scene of the first part of the story is set in Germany, and Mrs. Gaskell's "German" stories (*The Grey Woman* and *Six Weeks at Heppenheim*) were probably both inspired by her visit to that country in 1858–9. (Cf. Appendix II.)

rigid adherence to the doctrine of the indissolubility of an engagement. The heroine "had got into a net . . . and . . . did not see how
to get out of it".[1] When she tells her father that she does not want
to be married, "he seemed to feel this speech of mine as dereliction
of duty as great as if I had committed perjury".[2] She is forced to
marry, and after one year of marriage, intolerable conditions drive
her to leave her home. Characteristically for Mrs. Gaskell, the
heroine's immediate reason for this action is the thought of a child.
There are very few villains in Mrs. Gaskell's stories, but in *The
Grey Woman* she painted him in the most sinister colours. Even
though this was in keeping with the Gothic tradition in which the
whole story is conceived, it was also necessary for her to do so in
order to justify his wife's decision to run away from him. The
heroine at first tries, because he is the father of her unborn child,
to feel some love for the husband whom she fears.[3] Even after
she has discovered that he is a robber and murderer, she does not
make up her mind to leave him until he gives proof of his callous-
ness concerning the child of the man whom he has killed: "Up to
that moment, I think, I had only feared him, but his unnatural,
half-ferocious reply made me hate even more than I dreaded him."[3]
Like Thekla in *Six Weeks at Heppenheim*, but unlike the unfortunate
heroines in Mrs. Gaskell's early tales about unhappy engagements

---

[1] P. 269.

[2] P. 270.

[3] The editions which I have examined have a curious misprint in the last
paragraph but one of Portion I of this story. Smith and Elder's editions (Pocket
edition of Mrs. Gaskell's works in eight volumes, no date, *A Dark Night's Work
and other tales; Ruth and Other Tales*, Vol. VI in Novels and Tales by Mrs. Gaskell in seven volumes, 1893) print the following passage about the heroine's
waning love for her husband: ". . . my dread of his displeasure . . . conquered
my *humorous* inclination to love one who was so handsome . . .". As this reading
is obviously absurd, the same sentence in the Knutsford edition (1906) has been
changed into the more plausible "my *natural* inclination". The MS, however
(now in the Rylands Library, Manchester), has "amorous". In this MS there is
no difference in Mrs. Gaskell's handwriting between a and u, but there is no
trace of any h at the beginning of the word.

[3] P. 285. It is interesting to notice that Mrs. Gaskell implies that one of the
reasons why disasters come down upon the wife is her passivity in the early days
of her marriage: "I was young and inexperienced, and thankful to be spared any
responsibility". (P. 274.)

or marriages, the Grey Woman is not faced with a long life of hopeless grief, but marries her faithful second admirer in the end.

According to the first sentence of the manuscript of *The Grey Woman*, the story was "true as to its main facts".[1] The wife's running away from her husband probably formed an integral part of the original story, even if the justification of that action is characteristic of Mrs. Gaskell's own line of thought. The very fact that she took up this theme, however, is an indication that the question interested her at that time. After she had expressly stated her opinion that a woman was justified, under certain circumstances, in breaking off an engagement to be married, the logical consequence for her was to consider the possible justification of dissolving an unendurable marriage, and she showed her toleration of such a possibility, not only in *The Grey Woman*, but also, about the same time, in a letter to C. E. Norton, in which she wrote about George Eliot: "Miss Marianne Evans ... left Coventry, going to live in London, where she became acquainted with Mr. Lewes ... His wife left him ... & Mr. Lewes went abroad (5 years ago) with Miss Evans, who now takes the name of Mrs. Evans. All this is miserable enough,—but I believe there are many excuses—."[2]

Mrs. Gaskell's ideas concerning second love and a woman's duty not to marry a man knowing that she did not love him underwent no change in the seven remaining years of her life. Ellinor's situation in *A Dark Night's Work* (1863) is very much like that of Nest in the early story *The Well of Pen-Morfa* (1850), who is deserted by her lover on account of a misfortune which has befallen her, but unlike Nest, whose only chance of happiness is blighted when her lover deserts her, Ellinor, in the last pages of the book, is going to be happily married. In *Six Weeks at Heppenheim* Mrs. Gaskell had stigmatised a marriage begun without love as sinful, and the heroine in *Sylvia's Lovers* (1863) therefore experiences no happiness in hers except through her child: " 'I'm glad enough I've getten a baby', said Sylvia, 'but for ought else I wish I had niver been married, I do'!"[3]

Although, in her works, Mrs. Gaskell never treated the conflict

---

[1] Cf. Appendix II.

[2] October 30, 1859. Whitehill, *op. cit.*, letter 14.

[3] P. 314.

between a wife's home duties and the demands made on her time by her own professional work, she did touch on the problem of a wife's lack of interest in those of her husband's joys and worries that arose from his profession in *North and South*, and in *Crowley Castle* she contrasted two types of wives and two sets of duties, the one concerned with home and children, the other with the husband's professional career and general culture.

The question of what type of woman makes the best wife was of course far from new in English literature. Among Mrs. Gaskell's contemporaries Dickens, for instance, had already made the difference between the child-wife Dora and the intelligent, sympathetic, altogether perfect Agnes an integral part of *David Copperfield* (1849–50). Mrs. Gaskell, however, contrasted two women who were both good wives according to their lights, though one of them confined her activities to the traditional "woman's sphere", and the other developed all her intellectual and cultural possibilities to meet her husband's needs.

In her later period Mrs. Gaskell never forced her opinions on the reader, but followed the artistic principle which can be deduced from one of Mme Mohl's letters to her, asking for advice about her own manuscript: "you will give a good scratch with a pencil when you see any ungraceful testimony of opinion; for I agree with you that a thing should always be let seen, and not shown".[1] The reader must no longer look for those direct comments from the author or exhortations to the reader in which Mrs Gaskell indulged in *Mary Barton*. Nor can the author be supposed always to agree with the opinions expressed by the characters in her books. The narrator of *Cousin Phillis*, which was published in 1863, admires Cousin Holman, the devoted wife who keeps her home in perfect order but understands nothing of her husband's intellectual activities.[2] He rejects the thought of Phillis as his wife, because "she's so clever—she's more like a man than a woman—she knows Latin and Greek". His father has very similar

---

[1] July 1, 1860. Simpson, *op. cit.*, p. 164.

[2] Though the marriage is represented as on the whole a happy one, the minister "did not know what to talk about to a purely motherly woman, whose intellect had never been cultivated, and whose loving heart was entirely occupied with her husband, her child, her household affairs". (P. 216.)

ideas, though he does not give Phillis' case up as hopeless yet: "a scholar—but that can't be helped, and is more her misfortune than her fault, seeing she is the only child of a scholar—and as I said afore, once she's a wife and a mother she'll forget it all, ..."[1]

That their idea of a perfect wife was very far from Mrs. Gaskell's own at that period appears from *Crowley Castle*, which was published in the same year as *Cousin Phillis*, in the Christmas number of *All the Year Round*. It is the story of a man who is married twice, to two very different types of women. Bessy, the first wife, admires her husband unreservedly; "she felt him to be her pattern of noble, chivalrous manhood".[2] "Bessy was a daisy of an English maiden, pure and good to the heart's core and most hidden thought."[3] And yet this description is not meant to be wholly laudatory. The scope of her mind is limited to her "smaller cares and domestic talk—now about the servants, now about her mother and the Parsonage, now about the parish..."[4] She takes only "a sluggish interest in all things beyond her immediate ken".[5] When her husband returns home from his political triumphs in London she is with her sick child in the nursery and has no welcome or sympathy to give him. The child dies, and the mother is poisoned by Theresa's French maid and dies in her sleep. Not even here is there any trace of the sentimentality or moralising that might have been expected, if this had been one of the earlier tales.

While alive, Bessy seemed rather insipid; it was not until after her death that "all her innocent virtues, all her feminine homeliness, came vividly into Theresa's mind—not as wearisome, but as admirable, qualities..."[6]

Theresa, Duke's second wife, forms the most striking contrast to Bessy. As a young girl she had "a full, pretty, pouting, passionate mouth"; she was "a wilful little creature"; though habitually generous, she tyrannized over Bessy. When Duke reproached her, "her wits were called into play to refute his arguments; her head rather than her heart took the prominent part in the controversy";

She rebels as soon as she discovers her father's plans about a

---

[1] P. 200. [2] 689.

[3] P. 697. [4] P. 706.

[5] P. 707. [6] Pp. 710–11.

marriage between herself and Duke. "She intended to make her own choice, when the time came".

When her father decides to take her to Paris, "nothing could exceed Theresa's mad joy". After an unhappy secret marriage there, in which "her pride helped her to keep her woe to herself", she comes back to share Duke's and Bessy's home. "She questioned Duke about his travels, and could enter into his appreciation and judgment of foreign nations; she perceived the latent powers of his mind; she became impatient of their remaining dormant in country seclusion . . . one of the members for Sussex died; and Theresa set herself to stir up Duke to assume his place."[1]

She reproaches Bessy for the narrow sphere of her interests: "when he wants to talk to you of politics, of foreign news, of great public interests, you drag him down to your level of woman's cares".[2]

"Theresa, with her Parisian experience of the way in which women influenced politics, would have given anything for the Brownlows to have taken a house in London. She longed to see the great politicians, to find herself in the thick of the struggle for place and power"[3];

After Bessy's death she marries Duke, and for the first time he experiences what a perfect marriage is. When she goes back into the country, horror-stricken at the discovery that Victorine, her faithful maid, had poisoned Bessy in order to render her own marriage with Duke possible,

"he missed her terribly. No more pleasant *tête-à-tête* breakfasts, enlivened by her sense and wit, and cheered by her pretty caressing ways. No gentle secretary now, to sit by his side through long, long hours, never weary. When he went into society, he no longer found his appearance watched and waited for by the loveliest woman there. When he came home from the House at night, there was no one to take an interest in his speeches, to be indignant at all that annoyed him, and charmed and proud of all the admiration he had won".[4]

The days were long past when Mrs. Gaskell held up the example of such simple, obedient, passive wives as Mrs. Leigh, Mrs. Barton, and Nelly in *The Heart of John Middleton* for praise and

---

[1] P. 706.   [2] P. 707.
[3] P. 708.   [4] Pp. 714–15.

admiration. At the time when she wrote *Crowley Castle* she had
nothing but pity, condescension, contempt almost, for the "innocent virtues" of Bessy, whereas the sparkling, intelligent passionate Theresa had all her sympathy.

It is not difficult to find reasons for this new outlook. Early in
1857 Mrs. Gaskell undertook that journey to Rome, during which
her "life . . . culminated".[1] As Miss Haldane says, "a journey to
Italy has an extraordinary effect on the traveller, if it comes at the
moment in life when impressions are formed on impressionable
natures. Of this the outstanding example is Goethe, . . . in George
Eliot's case it also marked an important era in her work, and caused
her to turn from one subject to another and completely different
one".[2] In the nineteenth century there were innumerable examples
of this effect of a journey to Italy, that "well-known Italian intoxi-
cation, a Teutonic epidemic with fixed symptoms", as Klara Johansson calls it.[3] In Mrs. Gaskell's case, it meant leaving for ever
the moralizing novels with a social purpose to which she had devoted the first half of her literary career.[4] Novel writing for its

---

[1] See p. 28.

[2] Elizabeth Haldane, *George Eliot and her times. A Victorian Study* (London,
1927), p. 175.

[3] "Det bekanta italienruset, en germansk epidemi med fixa symtom." (*Det
speglade livet*, p. 86.)

[4] *Mary Barton, Ruth, North and South*. It is true that she had not completed,
or even begun, any such novels between the appearance of *North and South* in
1854, and the Italian journey in 1857, but she had had no time for any serious
novel during that period, occupied as she was with *The Life of Charlotte Brontë*.
Social conditions improved greatly in the 'fifties, partly owing to the generally
increasing prosperity resulting from the trade conditions, and partly also owing
to factory legislation. This had the natural effect of considerably decreasing the
production of novels with a social purpose. Kingsley, for instance, wrote no such
novel after *Alton Locke* (1850). Mrs. Gaskell, however, in her didactic
novels, had not confined herself to treating the conditions of factory workers,
dressmakers' apprentices, etc., but had also taken up problems of a more general
nature in *Ruth*. In her case, therefore, one cannot disregard personal reasons
for leaving off writing such novels.
In a letter to Fairbairn (printed in Whitfield, *op. cit.*, pp. 158–9) Mrs. Gaskell
wrote (probably in June, 1857) about *The Life of Charlotte Brontë*: "I have had
a preface to my (forthcoming) third edition sent to me, which I dare not insert
there; but it is for good to be lost, therefore I shall copy it out for you: 'If anybody
is displeased with any statement in this book, they are requested to believe it

own sake now appeared to her important and justified, and it seems probable that, if she had lived longer, we should have had more stories by her in the manner of *Sylvia's Lovers*, in which the writer is more interested in character study than in social conditions, or of *Wives and Daughters* in the best Austen and Bremer tradition of the domestic novel. Her books did, indeed, change from her first novel, *Mary Barton*, with its serious intensity of purpose, to the last, the sparkling delightful *Wives and Daughters*, written to amuse, not to instruct or reform.[1]

One other influence bearing in the same direction as the Italian journey is obvious. Theresa in *Crowley Castle*, had some "Parisian experience of the way in which women influenced politics". So

---

withdrawn, and my deep regret expressed for its insertion, as truth is too expensive an article to be laid before the British public. But for the future I intend to confine myself to lies (*i.e.* fiction). It is safer.' " Even if Mrs. Gaskell temporarily entertained some idea of "confining herself to lies for the future", too much weight should probably not be laid on this as a reason for her to give up writing didactic novels. It is true that she was subjected to much adverse criticism on the publication of *The Life of Charlotte Brontë*, but, to judge from her letters, she had taken the harsh criticism of *Ruth* much more to heart, which did not prevent her from beginning her third didactic novel, *North and South*, as early as the next year. Another indication that she had not found her experiences as a biographer so disheartening as has been generally assumed is the fact that her journey to France in 1864 was undertaken with the purpose of collecting material for a Life of Madame de Sévigné.

[1] One indication of this is that the Bible quotations so profusely used in *Mary Barton* to emphasize moral exhortations have almost entirely disappeared in *Wives and Daughters*. It should be noted, though, that Mrs. Gaskell did not use biblical language exclusively to point a moral but also to convey individual or specially Lancastrian characteristics of speech. In a letter to Forster about the "poet of humble life" Samuel Bamford she wrote that in his indignation "he first choked, and then broke out in beautiful broad Lancashire, and then as that hardly seemed to carry him high enough, he took to Bible language till his adversary fairly stood rebuked". (Letter of Oct. 8, 1849, printed in the *Manchester City News*, Feb. 5, 1916.) Seldom, though, did she use Scripture texts for any other than a moral purpose except in direct quotation, and Charlotte Brontë's very different use of them shocked her deeply (such as "she was blind to ecclesiastical defects: the white surplice covered a multitude of sins" in *Shirley*, Chapter XIV). In a letter to Mrs. Wm Shaen (now in the Brotherton Library) of Sept. 8, 1856, she wrote about the unpublished MS of *The Professor* that it was "disfigured by more coarseness and profanity in quoting texts of scripture disagreeably than in any of her other works".

had Mrs. Gaskell from 1854, when she made the first of her many journeys to Paris. Her experience, though, was not so much of politics as of the social life in a Parisian "salon" of the Mme Récamier tradition. Mme Mohl was the friend who initiated Mrs. Gaskell into this kind of life, and how instantly she was captivated by its charms appears from her enthusiastic description of the art of "Sabléing" given in *Company Manners* (1854).

She herself had changed, too, from the time when she was known only as "the author of Mary Barton" and it was reported from Manchester parties that "Mrs. Gaskell quietly knitted, as her way is".[1] This is how Mme Mohl remembered her after her death:

"She was a singularly happy person, and her happiness expressed itself in an inexhaustible flow of high spirits. She looked happy. Her round blue eyes were wide open in a perpetual sparkle of curiosity and interest; her little turned-up nose, spirited and commanding, seemed to be scenting clever *mots* in the air; her mouth, like a bent bow, was incessantly shooting out light arrows of wit; her upright figure, the pose of her head, her quick step, her whole air and deportment, expressed energy, vivacity, and happiness."[2]

Lord David Cecil, who substitutes inference for evidence in his information about Mrs. Gaskell's actual life in *Early Victorian Novelists*, ascribes the freshness of those of her stories which he considers readable today to her "confined life": "Cloistered like a young girl in her convent of peaceful domesticity, she never lost the young girl's eager-eyed response to the world. Mrs. Gaskell

---

[1] March 2, 1849. Henry Shaen Solly, *The Life of Henry Morley, LLD.* (London, 1898), p. 116. It should be noted that Mrs. Gaskell at an early date showed that side of her personality that Mme Mohl admired, to intimate friends, if not at large parties. Susanna Winkworth wrote of her: "When we first knew Mrs. Gaskell she had not yet become celebrated, but from the earliest days of our intercourse with her we were struck with her genius ... her high, broad, serene brow, and finely-cut mobile features, were lighted up by a constantly-varying play of expression as she poured forth her wonderful talk ... one of the most brilliant persons I ever saw ... When you were with her, you felt as if you had twice the life in you that you had at ordinary times. All her great intellectual gifts ... were so warmed and brightened by sympathy and feeling, that while actually with her, you were less conscious of her power than of her charm." (Shaen, *op. cit.*, pp. 23-24.)

[2] Kathleen O'Meara, *Madame Mohl, Her Salon and her Friends. A Study of Social Life in Paris* (London, 1885), p. 180.

had not a chance to grow blasé." The very opposite seems to be more true to facts. She can hardly be said ever to have led a confined life after her marriage, living as she did in one of the most cultured homes in Manchester, that vital centre for political Radicalism, from which so many new ideas about education and social reform emerged. It is also to be noted that even *Cranford*, the earliest of the stories to which Lord David Cecil assigns any literary value, was written after the success of *Mary Barton* had opened to her the doors of the best literary circles in London and facilitated her contact with intellectuals and reformers of all kinds. As regards the three other books in Lord David Cecil's list of approved stories,—*Sylvia's Lovers*, *Wives and Daughters*, and *Cousin Phillis*— they all belong to her last period, when she had formed the habit of spending longer and longer periods away from home, in France, Italy or Germany. By that time she had had many chances to grow blasé. It is, indeed, a remarkable fact that the more opportunities she had for growing blasé and the more she saw of the world outside Manchester and England, the more did she conform to a literary tradition, and only then did she begin to write for art's sake.[1]

There can be little doubt that Mrs. Gaskell's closer contact with intellectual and artistic circles both in England and France had influenced her conception of the perfect wife. As to the reason why she chose to discuss this question at all in *Crowley Castle*, she might naturally have been inspired by some contemporary work of

---

[1] It seems far-fetched to ascribe the change in her style to her contact with the *Cornhill*, as Sanders does (*op. cit.*, p. 110). Even though she wrote more for that periodical than for Dickens' in her last years, this, like the change in her style, was only natural, considering the more literary and artistic attitude which was the result of her closer contact with French culture as well as with literary and artistic circles in England. (For reasons why she no longer liked to write for Dickens, see Hopkins, "Dickens and Mrs. Gaskell".)

Miss Haldane writes: "Should we have had 'Cranford' or 'Pride and Prejudice' from sophisticated and travelled authoresses? One is inclined to think not." (*Op. cit.*, p. 74.) Apparently she shares Lord David Cecil's view of Mrs. Gaskell's domestic stories as a result of her "confined" life, disregarding the fact that her last novel, *Wives and Daughters*, which is the one which most resembles both her own *Cranford* and Jane Austen's books, was written at a time when she must be called a "travelled authoress".

fiction. Real life also gave her occasion to consider the problem. Apart from what she might have observed concerning the marriages of her more intimate friends, there were two among her circle of acquaintances whose marriages had attracted considerable public attention.

One was Charles Dickens, whose infatuation for Ellen Ternan led him to separate from his wife, who had never had either time or interest to spare for her husband's literary or other activities. The public were first informed of the failure of their marriage by a statement in *Household Words* on June 12, 1858. An open scandal was caused in the same summer when several English newspapers printed a far more explicit statement, including the following passage:

"Mrs. Dickens and I lived unhappily together for many years. Hardly anyone who has known us intimately can fail to have known that we are in all respects of character and temperament wonderfully unsuited to each other. I suppose that no two people, not vicious in themselves, ever were joined together who had a greater difficulty in understanding one another, or who had less in common."[1]

Four years earlier John Ruskin's marriage had been dissolved by a decree of nullity.[2] Although the statement which he wrote on that occasion was not published, his friends must have been acquainted with his very definite ideas of what a perfect wife ought to be and his consequent disappointment.[3] Before his wedding

"he fell to conjuring up visions of Effie as a keen ecclesiologist, picturing to himself how, while he drew and measured, scrambling over leads and tiles, or 'creeping into crypts on my hands and knees, and into rood-lofts and turrets by inexplicable stairs, 'Effie in the dusky nave of the church would be quietly looking over the building's early written history or, pencil in hand, making her 'own unpretending little memoranda of a capital here—an ornament there'; till a time came when he could command her services in the capacity of unpaid draughtsman, and set her to record a

---

[1] Quoted by Hesketh Pearson in *Dickens, His Character, Comedy, and Career* (New York, 1949), p. 251.

[2] In an undated letter to Miss Fox (copy in the Brotherton Library; printed in Haldane, *op. cit.*, pp. 254–6), Mrs. Gaskell wrote: "[Meta] shocks me by saying you told her Mrs. Ruskin was separated from her husband—is it true?"

[3] Whatever the truth was about Ruskin's marriage, what is of importance in this context is his own version of it and his attitude towards marriage and women, as his friends, among them Mrs. Gaskell (see p. 91, n. 2) heard it from himself.

frieze while he ascended to examine the vault. For Effie understood, of course, that 'I must go on with my *profession*', and that, although during a part of the day he would be completely hers, during another part, usually the longer, 'you will have to be *mine*—or to sit at home' ".[1]

Mrs. Gaskell had strongly emphasized the moral obligation of a wife to judge and act independently of her husband's opinions when ethical problems were involved. Yet it is a remarkable fact that in *Crowley Castle*, where she chiefly considered the intellectual and artistic qualifications of a wife, she attached no importance to her as a separate individual but exclusively regarded her as her husband's appendage or assistant. Indeed, her ideas showed such a striking conformity with the opinions which her friend Ruskin used to express on the subject that her story might well have served as a literary illustration to the lecture which he was to deliver in Manchester the year after *Crowley Castle* was published.[2]

---

[1] Peter Quennell, *John Ruskin. The Portrait of a Prophet* (London, 1949), p. 58.

[2] "Of "Queens' Gardens." Cf. p. 5. Especially in the later period of her career as a writer Mrs. Gaskell seems to have had ample opportunities of discussing various questions with Ruskin, and thus of being influenced by his points of view.

There are four letters from Ruskin to Mrs. Gaskell in the Rylands Library, Manchester, three of which are printed in the *Bulletin* (pp. 149–51). Two were written in 1857, the year when the Exhibition of the Art Treasures of the United Kingdom was opened in Manchester on May 5th. The first of these letters, dated only "Wednesday evening", was written to ask Mrs. Gaskell if she could receive the writer on the next day. The second letter, dated Oct. 2, 57, expresses regret that he forgot his appointment. The next letter (postmark 2 April, 1859) thanks Mrs. Gaskell for a wheel and praises some drawings by a young girl, which Mrs. Gaskell seems to have sent to him. In the last letter (27 Oct., 1860) he offers to look at Meta's drawings and regrets that she has not received a reply to her own letter to him. A. W. Ward quotes another letter from Ruskin to Mrs. Gaskell about *Cranford* (Feb. 21, 1865) and Mrs. Gaskell's (undated) reply to it. (Introduction to *Cranford* in the Knutsford edn, pp. XXIV and XI–XII.)

According to Miss Haldane, "Ruskin was much in touch with the little company of north country friends, Winkworths, Shaens and Gaskells". (*Op. cit.*, p. 301.) Mrs. Chadwick states that "Ruskin . . . was a frequent visitor" in the Gaskell home (*op. cit.*, p. 314), and that Meta had painting lessons from him (*op. cit.*, p. 238). She also writes that "Ruskin's home in London was open to welcome Mrs. Gaskell, and she sent many a devotee of his, with a note of introduction, which Ruskin was always glad to honour". (*Op. cit.*, p. 234.)

CHAPTER V

DAUGHTERS AND WORK FOR MIDDLE CLASS WOMEN

(Mrs. Gaskell's attitude towards her own daughters. Fathers—daughters and brothers—sisters in Mrs. Gaskell's works. Mrs. Gaskell's attitude towards education for women, proprieties, and work for middle class women.)

ONE vital problem to women in the Victorian age was occasioned by the authority of fathers over their daughters, and it appears from the biographies of the time that many daughters felt their dependence acutely. Their dilemma had been treated occasionally in literature even before the nineteenth century. One of the best known examples is Mary Wollstonecraft's *Thoughts on the Education of Daughters*, which was published as early as 1787. That Mrs. Gaskell was aware of the problem constituted by the neglected position of daughters in many families is clear from her works. It was, however, apparently not a personal problem to her.[1] In her eyes family affection was sacred. Even though she regretted her husband's reluctance to *express* his affection for his children[2], she emphasized his fondness for them when she wanted to praise him.[3] She also showed what importance she attached to family affection in a letter to her eldest daughter, in which she wrote: "I could not bear my life if you and Meta did not love each other most dearly . . . it is so dreary to see sisters grow old, (as one sometimes does,) not caring for each other."[4] Her own affection for

---

[1] Cf. Chap. II.

[2] See Chap. II, p. 27.

[3] In a letter to Emma Shaen, dated May 8th, 1854, Catherine Winkworth relates a discussion about marriage which she had with Charlotte Brontë during a visit to Mrs. Gaskell, and writes: "Thereupon Lily [Mrs. Gaskell] set off praising *her* husband for being a good sick nurse and so good to the children, and how very winning that was to the mother." (Shaen, *op. cit.*, p. 114.)

[4] Undated letter in the Brotherton Library.

her children has been recognized by all her biographers and is amply proved by her writings. Her *Diary* was entirely given up to the early years of her two eldest living daughters. Her letters to intimate friends and relatives in later years are full of analysing descriptions of her children's characters and expressions of delight over them, such as "My girls, my darlings, *are* such comforts, such happiness!".[1] A. J. C. Hare, writing about the year 1860, records the following impression of Mrs. Gaskell: "I remember that one of the points which struck me most about her at first was not only her kindness, but her extreme courtesy and deference to her own daughters."[2] Her daughters returned her affection. In a letter about her mother's death, Meta wrote to Ellen Nussey[3]: "To me it has changed the face of this world for ever . . . She *was* so sweet and dear and noble beyond words."

The only hint of any serious disagreement between parents and daughters in the letters which I have examined appears in a letter from Mrs. Gaskell to C. E. Norton, dated February 5, 1865, in which she tells him about her eldest daughter's engagement, which had been opposed for six years.[4] Mr. Norton was, however, not told whose opposition had prevented the engagement for so long, nor why this opposition was finally given up. If there were conflicts between parents and daughter, he was not told of them either. In any case, Marianne's love story can have had nothing to do with *Ruth*, which was published in 1853, and which is the only one of Mrs. Gaskell's books that contains the story of a daughter who rebels against her father.

Even if Mrs. Gaskell had no experience in her own family of a father's claim to absolute authority over his daughters, she had encountered the situation in the lives of friends. One of these was Charlotte Brontë, and Mrs. Gaskell's biography of her friend might be expected to show her attitude towards the question of a daugh-

---

[1] Letter to C. E. Norton, Jan. 19, 1860. (Whitehill, *op. cit.*, letter 16.)

[2] Augustus J. C. Hare, *The Story of my Life* (London, 1896), II: 224.

[3] Jan. 22, 1866.

[4] "opposed 1stly because they are cousins (second), and 2ndly because she is 18 months older than he—and also because he, though the son of a rich man, has *eleven* brothers and sisters, and has to make his way in that most tedious of all professions *chancery* law . . ." (Whitehill, *op. cit.*)

ter's duty of obedience to a tyrannical father. Her friend's absolute obedience to her father is indeed one of the things for which
Mrs. Gaskell expresses her admiration in *The Life of Charlotte
Brontë*. Relating Charlotte Brontë's first refusal of Mr. Nicholls'
proposal of marriage, in accordance with her father's wish, Mrs.
Gaskell writes: "thus thoughtfully for her father, and unselfishly
for herself, [she] put aside all consideration of how she should
reply, excepting as he wished!"[1], and, when describing her visit
to Haworth in September, 1853: "I could not but deeply admire
the patient docility which she displayed in her conduct towards
her father."[2] But in the same connection, she states her reaction
to have been a feeling of amusement rather than of admiration:
"He never seemed quite to have lost the feeling that Charlotte
was a child to be guided and ruled, when she was present; and
she herself submitted to this with a quiet docility that half amused,
half astonished me."[3] Mrs. Gaskell's attitude towards this question
was very different from that of another of Charlotte Brontë's
friends, Mary Taylor, who wrote to Ellen Nussey on April 19,
1856: "I can never think without gloomy anger of Charlotte's
sacrifices to the selfish old man."[4]

Towards the end of 1854, however, Mrs. Gaskell expressed
rather a different opinion as to the duty of obedience to authority.
We are told about the heroine of *North and South*:

"When they returned to town, Margaret fulfilled one of her sea-side resolves, and took her life into her own hands. Before they went to Cromer,
she had been as docile to her aunt's laws as if she were still the scared
little stranger who cried herself to sleep that first night in the Harley
Street nursery. But she had learnt, in those solemn hours of thought, that
she herself must one day answer for her own life, and what she had done
with it; and she tried to settle that most difficult problem for woman, how
much was to be utterly merged in obedience to authority, and how much
might be set apart for freedom in working."[5]

It is therefore tempting to conclude that Mrs. Gaskell's anxiety
to represent her friend in as favourable a light as possible led her

---

[1] *The Life of Charlotte Brontë*, p. 371.
[2] *Ibid.*, p. 388.   [3] *Ibid.*, p. 386.
[4] Shorter, *op. cit.*, II: 395.
[5] *North and South*, p. 443.

to exaggerate her admiration for Charlotte Brontë's submissiveness to her father.[1]

In view of the examples of Mr. Brontë's ungovernable temper given in *The Life of Charlotte Brontë*, it seems unlikely that any consideration for his feelings made Mrs. Gaskell suppress any disapproving comments on his ideas of a father's authority over his daughters, especially as no such consideration for the feelings of living persons deterred her when she denounced Mrs. Robinson's alleged behaviour in Branwell Brontë's love affair, or when she described the conditions in the Cowan Bridge School in the same *Life*.

The dependent position of daughters does not seem to have moved Mrs. Gaskell to any serious attempts at reform. She did not treat the problem at any length except in the one instance of Jemima in *Ruth*. A father's selfishness and absurd preten-

---

[1] Mrs. Gaskell sometimes suppressed information which she thought would be harmful either to her own (See Appendix II) or to her friend's reputation. The most important instance is her omission of any mention of Charlotte Brontë's love letters to M. Héger. Concerning this question she wrote to Mrs. Wm Shaen (née Emily Winkworth) when discussing *The Professor*, Charlotte Brontë's novel, which had not then been published: "I dreaded lest the Prof. should involve anything with M. Heger ... I believed him to be too good to publish those letters—but I felt that his friends might really with some justice urge him to do so,—so I awaited the arrival of the Prof. . . . with great anxiety." (Letter in the Brotherton Library.)

That she was really anxious to represent her friend in as favourable a light as possible also appears from a letter of 1856 quoted by Henry James in *William Wetmore Story and his Friends* (Edinburgh and London, 1903), I: 354: "I hope to have finished my life of Miss Brontë by the end of February, and then I should like to be off and away out of the reach of reviews, which in this case will have a double power to wound, for if they say anything disparaging of *her* I know I shall not have done her and the circumstances in which she was placed justice: that is to say that in her case more visibly than in most her circumstances made her faults, while her virtues were her own."

Mrs. Gaskell had judged correctly about the reactions of the public in the instance of Charlotte Brontë's sacrifices to her father. As late as 1867 the *British Quarterly Review* wrote (April 1, "The Works of Mrs. Gaskell"): "She had a subject in which all the world could feel an interest—a woman possessed of the highest intellectual power, whose conscientiousness and family affection withstood every temptation which extraordinary literary success throws in the way of women";

sions to authority are, however, attacked at least by implication in one of Mrs. Gaskell's earliest tales, *Lizzie Leigh*. Susan Palmer's father does not work but has to be kept by his daughter. In every emergency he is found drunk and asleep, "and useless, and worse than useless, if awake".[1] Yet Susan has to ask his permission before she gives up going out working to keep a school instead, "and, after a while, he said if I earned enough for him to have his comforts, he'd let me".[2] Daniel Robson's wife in *Sylvia's Lovers* teaches her daughter to respect her father because this is the traditional rule for a daughter's good behaviour rather than because she sees any real reasons for this rule: " 'Na, na!' said Bell, 'th' feyther's feyther, and we mun respect him. But it's dree work havin' a man i' th' house . . .".[3]

In the chapter "On Politeness and Accomplishments" in *Letters on the Improvement of the Mind*[4], Mrs. Chapone asks her readers to remember that "you will be unsafe in every step which leads to a serious attachment, unless you consult your parents, from the first moment you apprehend anything of the sort to be intended: let them be your first confidants, and let every part of your conduct, in such a case, be particularly directed by them". Ellinor in *A Dark Night's Work* has been taught to follow this rule. "If he made a regular declaration to her she would be bound to tell it to her father. He should not respect her or like her so much if she did not."[5] Margaret Hale in *North and South* is an altogether more independent character than Ellinor, and she decides not to marry Mr. Lennox without consulting anybody. But "she did not know if her father might not be displeased that she had taken upon herself to decline Mr. Lennox's proposal".[6]

In *My Diary* there are repeated references to Mrs. Gaskell's fear that she might make an idol of her children, and this risk for

---

[1] P. 408. [2] P. 402.

[3] P. 39.

[4] Mrs. Chapone's *Letters* were first published in 1777 and were frequently used in girls' schools in the first half of the nineteenth century. They were often referred to in the literature of the time. Mrs. Gaskell mentions them (see Appendix III), and in the school in Hood's "Love and Lunacy" (1834) "thus their studies they pursued: . . . Tuesday—hard dumplings, globes, Chapone's Advice".

[5] P. 32. [6] P. 37.

a mother is also mentioned several times in *Ruth*. It is therefore possible that Mrs. Gaskell had also felt another temptation mentioned in her books, namely the wish to keep her daughters at home instead of letting them marry. In the letter to Norton quoted on p. 93 she wrote, "I don't know what I should do if any one of them married". In *The Life of Charlotte Brontë* she made no comments on Mr. Brontë's preventing his daughter's marriage for so long. On the other hand, in *A Dark Night's Work*, which was published in 1863, the year when her youngest daughter, Florence, was engaged and married, with the full approval of her parents[1], she denounces the selfishness of a father who will not give up his daughter's affection to a husband: "It was the usual struggle between father and lover for the possession of love, instead of the natural and graceful resignation of the parent to the prescribed course of things; and, as usual, it was the poor girl who bore the suffering for no fault of her own."[2]

It is remarkable that in her books those young girls who assert their independence do so only after their parents' death, like the two Margarets in *North and South* and *Right at Last*. Mr. Gibson in *Wives and Daughters* is only Cynthia's step-father. Otherwise she might not have claimed the right to spend her allowance as she thinks best with so much determination. These are her words: "Mamma! it may sound very cross, but I must tell Molly, and you, and everybody, once for all, that as I don't want and didn't ask for more than my allowance, I'm not going to answer any questions about what I do with it." Most of Mrs. Gaskell's young girls unquestioningly accept their fathers' authority, and Molly Gibson in *Wives and Daughters*, Ellinor in the first part of *A Dark Night's Work*, and Phillis in *Cousin Phillis*, blindly trust and admire their fathers. John Barton regretted his daughter's growing independence, but the fact is hardly treated as a serious problem.

The only girl in Mrs. Gaskell's stories whose chief problem is manifested in her relationship with her father is Jemima in *Ruth*. She is "a wild-hearted, impetuous girl, who knew nothing of life beyond her father's house, and who chafed under the

---

[1] Florence was the only one of Mrs. Gaskell's daughters to marry in her mother's life-time. Marianne married in 1866. Meta and Julia never married.

[2] P. 46.

strict discipline enforced there".[1] When Mrs. Bradshaw murmured against her husband behind his back but was cowed into silence in his presence, Jemima "rebelled against this manner of proceeding, which savoured to her a little of deceit; but even she had not, as yet, overcome her awe of her father sufficiently to act independently of him, and according to her own sense of right".[2] Her only weapon against her father's tyranny is "the sullen reserve she assumed now ... Her actions were so submissive that they were spiritless; she did all her father desired; she did it with a nervous quickness and haste".[3] He tries to force her to be agreeable to the man whom he wants for a son-in-law and whom Jemima herself really loves, but she "felt as if she would rather be bought openly, like an Oriental daughter, where no one is degraded in their own eyes by being parties to such a contract".[4] Even after her engagement, she "dreaded her father's consideration of the whole affair as a satisfactory disposal of his daughter to a worthy man who, being his partner, would not require any abstraction of capital from the concern".[5]

In her father's words, Jemima has "grown more and more insolent—more and more disobedient every day".[6] Her case is, however, a parallel of her mother's.[7] She does not rebel openly until she has to defend somebody more helpless. In her heart "Jemima had rebelled against these hard doctrines of her father's", according to which mankind was "separated ... into two great groups, to one of which, by the grace of God, he and his belonged; while the other was composed of those whom it was his duty to try and reform".[8] When he discovers the truth about Ruth's early history and tells Jemima to "shake her off from you, as St. Paul shook off the viper—even into the fire"[9], she at last "spoke out beyond all power of restraint from her father".

It was, however, as far from the author's intentions to advocate a daughter's independence for its own sake as a wife's, when no moral issue was at stake. Jemima's conversation with Mr. Benson in Chapter XXVIII is revealing:

---

[1] P. 150. [2] P. 147. [3] P. 156.
[4] P. 167. [5] Pp. 261–2.
[6] P. 235. [7] See Pp. 68–70.
[8] P. 225. [9] P. 235.

" 'Papa says I must not go to your house—I suppose it's right to obey him?'

" 'Certainly, my dear. It is your clear duty . . .'

" 'Oh! but if I could do any good . . . I should come, duty or not, I believe it would be my duty . . . And will you tell me really and truly now if I can ever do anything for Ruth? If you'll promise me that, I won't rebel unnecessarily against papa' ";[1]

Mrs. Gaskell makes no suggestion as to the possibility of improving the position of daughters. Yet Jemima had chafed so much under her father's tyranny that her fiancé asks her if her goodness to him is "owing to the desire of having more freedom as a wife than as a daughter".[2] But the importance which Mrs. Gaskell attached to family affection led her to represent Jemima's problem as solved eventually by her discovery that her father loves her. She tells Ruth: "I have been talking to papa to-night, very seriously and quietly, and it has made me love him so much more, and understand him so much better . . . after papa had been showing me that he really loved me more than I ever thought he had done."[3]

It seems certain that no similar question had arisen in Mrs. Gaskell's own family to prompt her to take up Jemima's problem. It is also to be noted that although she first met Charlotte Brontë in 1850, and the latter then told her some of her early difficulties as the daughter of an ununderstanding father[4], she did not visit her friend at Haworth until after the publication of *Ruth*. She may naturally have had other cases from real life in mind, but one indication that she may, at least in part, have been inspired by literature when drawing the portrait of Jemima, is the name, shared by another of Mrs. Gaskell's young girls, the Jemima in *Mr. Harrison's Confessions*, who bears a certain family resemblance to the Jemima in *Ruth*, and grows sullen and irritable in the uncongenial atmosphere of a home governed by her stepmother. Mrs. Gaskell did not find it easy to invent names for her characters[5], and the fact that two of the oppressed and rebellious daughters in her tales are called Jemima may indicate an acquaintance with the unfortunate heroine in

---

[1] P. 254. [2] P. 261. [3] P. 269.

[4] Cf. Chap. III.

[5] See p. 73, n. 2.

Mary Wollstonecraft's *The Wrongs of Woman*, which was published in 1798, and the plot of which "is an accumulation of misery designed to show the injustices which a woman might endure".[1]

Fredrika Bremer's ardent plea for a daughter's right to an independent life in *Hertha* did not appear until 1856.[2] Cynthia in *Wives and Daughters*, a novel which borrowed so much from Fredrika Bremer's works[3], assumed a right to decide over her own life. It is possible that, if *Hertha* had been written a few years earlier, Mrs. Gaskell's Jemima might have been more like Cynthia in her desire for independence.

Jemima had fancied that her father cared exclusively for his son at the expense of his daughters.[4] Mrs. Gaskell, the devoted mother of four daughters (her only son died in infancy), did not accept the conviction of many parents that a brother had an undoubted right to consider himself superior to his sisters. She ridiculed this idea in many of her stories, from *Bessy's Troubles at Home* (1852), where Jem is "not going to be preached to by a girl"[5], and *The Moorland Cottage* (1850), to *Ruth* (1853) and *Lois the Witch* (1859). Mrs. Browne in *The Moorland Cottage* dotes on her son but has little love for her daughter, who sighs, "I wish I was not a woman. It must be a fine thing to be a man".[6] Her brother Ned represents the same conceited assumption of superiority that Mrs. Gaskell later held up to ridicule in the person of Farmer Robson in *Sylvia's Lovers:*

---

[1] G. B. MacCarthy, *The Later Women Novelists. 1744–1818.* (Oxford, 1947), p. 193. That Mrs. Gaskell was acquainted with at least part of the work of the first real advocate of women's rights in England appears from a letter to Miss Shaen of April 24, 1851, printed in Haldane, *op. cit.*, pp. 239–40: "If you like you may adapt a sentence out of Mary Wollstonecraft to this air." Another link with Mary Wollstonecraft is a short and obscure note written 38 years after her death by her husband, William Godwin, to Mrs. Gaskell in 1835. It is now in the Rylands Library, Manchester.

[2] The English translation actually appeared a short time before the book came out in Sweden.

[3] See Appendix II.

[4] "I always fancied he was so absorbed in Dick, he did not care much for us girls." (P. 269.)

[5] P. 519.

[6] P. 271.

"Ned, who prided himself considerably on his sex, had been sitting all the morning in his father's arm-chair, in the little book-room, 'studying', as he chose to call it . . . 'You see, Maggie, a man must be educated to be a gentleman. Now, if a woman knows how to keep a house that's all that is wanted from her. So my time is of more consequence than yours. Mamma says I'm to go to college, and be a clergyman; so I must get on with my Latin",[1]

instead of helping his sister to carry a pitcher of water. Later, his advice to Maggie is: "Be obedient, I tell you. That is what a woman has to be."[2]

Jemima's brother in *Ruth* is irritated when his sister does not take his masculine privileges as much for granted as he does himself, but asks him if his father has given him leave to see the plays he speaks of. The only reason that he condescends to give is that "many things are right for men which are not for girls".[3] To silence his sister's inopportune questioning he goes on to emphasize her inferiority as a woman: "Never you trouble your head about my business, my dear. Women can't understand the share-market, and such things. Don't think I've forgotten the awful blunders you made when you tried to read the state of the money-market aloud to my father that night when he had lost his spectacles."[4]

In *Lois the Witch*, the author has only a few contemptuous words on the subject of the general superiority of man. She says about Manasseh: "and this man esteemed a hero by most of those around him, simply because he was the only man in the family".[5] She knew, from Branwell Brontë's case, what a similar attitude in his family had led to, and wrote a word of warning in *The Life of Charlotte Brontë* about "peculiar trials in the life of an only boy in a family of girls . . . the necessity of their giving way to him in some things, is too often exaggerated into their giving way to him in all, and thus rendering him utterly selfish".[6]

Mrs. Gaskell has surprisingly little to say in her books about the education of girls, although she lived during a period when, for the first time, public attention was being directed to the deplorable state of most of the existing girls' schools. Problems

---

[1] P. 270.	[2] P. 298.
[3] P. 148.	[4] P. 230.
[5] P. 147.	[6] P. 123.

concerning chiefly the upper and middle classes, however, never excited Mrs. Gaskell's pity, and pity seems to have been her main incitement to write a propagandic novel.

The question had never been a problem to herself as a girl. The Unitarians, like the Quakers, were generally reputed to take an interest in education. Cook says about Florence Nightingale's father, for example:

"like some others of the Unitarian circle, he held views much in advance of the average opinion of his time about the intellectual education of women. The home education of his daughters . . . included a range of subjects far outside the curriculum current in 'young ladies' seminaries'; . . . Tasso and Ariosto and Alfieri . . . Mr. Nightingale added constitutional history, Latin, Greek, and mathematics. By the time Florence was sixteen, he was reading Homer with his daughters."[1]

At the age of eleven, Harriet Martineau, who also came of a Unitarian family, was sent to a school the curriculum of which included a thorough study of Latin and French, composition and arithmetic.

Mrs. Gaskell's aunt Mrs. Lumb, also a Unitarian, sent her niece for five years[2] to a school which seems to have been much in advance of the average girls' educational institution of the period, Miss Byerley's school at Stratford-on-Avon. A. S. Whitfield, who relies largely on private information for his statements and who gives the correct period of Elizabeth Stevenson's stay at the school, informs his readers that the school had a good reputation, that the fees were about £140 a year, and that Elizabeth there learnt "French, Italian, something of Latin, drawing, and dancing".[3] Mrs. Chadwick, who, however, erroneously gives the period of Elizabeth Stevenson's stay at the school as only three years[4], gives a very similar account of the teaching, and prints a school account for the year 1832 which amounts, with extras, to the sum of £74, o, 6 for six months. This was a comparatively high figure. The Taunton or Endowed Schools Commission of 1864–7 stated in their report that the average fees for girls' boarding-schools varied

---

[1] Cook, *op. cit.*, I: 12–13.
[2] Cf. p. 19, n. 1.
[3] Whitfield, *op. cit.*, p. 8.
[4] Chadwick, *op. cit.*, p. 65.

from £25 to £100 a year.[1] The standard of Miss Byerley's school was higher than that of the average girls' school of the time, in which, according to the Commission's report, "there were a want of thoroughness and of system, slovenliness and showy superficiality, inattention to rudiments and waste of time on accomplishments which were badly taught".[2]

There is also a tradition that Mr. Stevensen took an interest in his daughter's education and directed her studies during the year when she lived with him on leaving school. It is certain that Mrs. Gaskell had a familiarity with Latin writers, as appears both from her quotations[3] and her numerous other references to the classics[4], which the average Victorian education for girls did not generally confer.

Like the devoted mother she was, Mrs. Gaskell followed the development of her daughters' characters and intellects with deep interest. The first written evidence of this is to be found in her *Diary*[5], in which she wrote an account of the first manifestations of her eldest daughter's personality and her own thoughts on the education of a small child. Under March 25, 1838, she announces her intention of sending Marianne to the local infant school, "not to advance her rapidly in any branch of learning, for William and I agree in not caring for this; but to perfect her habits of obedience, to give her an idea of conquering difficulties by perseverance".

She continued to consider intellectual schooling as of secondary importance. "Ma's[6] influence is capital for her. I don't know (or

---

[1] Alicia C. Percival, *The English Miss* (London, 1939), p. 92.

[2] *The Cambridge History of English Literature*, XIV: 429. It was not until 1848 that Queen's College was founded in London to continue the classes for women which had been started at King's College on the initiative of the Governesses' Benevolent Institution and which constituted the first step towards admitting women to university examinations.

[3] See Appendix III.

[4] Parts of *Cousin Phillis* seem to have been influenced by Latin writers. As Quiller-Couch writes (*op. cit.*, p. 214) about a passage in that book: "It is England and yet pure Virgil—as purely Virgilian as the vignette, in the fourth Georgic, of the old man of Corycus."

[5] *My Diary. The early years of my daughter Marianne*. By Elizabeth Cleghorn Gaskell. Privately printed by Clement Shorter. London, May 29, 1923.

[6] Her eldest daughter Marianne.

care) a straw about *lessons;* but temper etc. is so much improved",
she wrote about her third daughter, Florence, to Miss Fox in 1853.[1]

On the other hand, Mrs. Gaskell did not undervalue the importance of knowledge and intellectual work. When Marianne had
left her school near London and was teaching her youngest sisters at home, Mrs. Gaskell wrote to her: "Yes! love, get more books
if you like them. Only remember they must do *hard* and *correct* as
well as interesting work. I mean such things as French verbs, &
geography for Flossy: the dry bones of knowledge."[2]

Mrs. Gaskell did not consider the education of her daughters
as finished when they left school. On December 10, 1860, she
wrote to C. E. Norton:

"Florence has left school—. . . being 18 in years, though not that in character, and hardly in looks. But she is having French, German and Music
lessons at home; and we are reading with her Macaulay's Biographies and
Milman's Latin Xtianity, and I don't think it is a bad thing for either
Marianne, Meta, or myself to have an *obligation* to sit and settle to a little
steady reading every day."[3]

The year before, she had reported to Miss Fox:

"Marianne . . . never reads . . . but generally does the practical and polite
and elder daughter things in the house . . . Meta . . . is working at Greek
and German; practising, drawing, teaching at the ragged school, has a
little orphan boy to teach French to, reads with Elliott every night, etc;
etc; and has always more books she wanting to read than she can get
through, being a very slow reader . . ."[4]

Julia, the youngest daughter, went to a day-school in Manchester.[5] The other daughters were all sent to boarding-schools[6] after

---

[1] Copy of letter in the Brotherton Library.

[2] Undated letter in the Brotherton Library.

[3] Whitehill, *op. cit.*, letter 23.

[4] March 21, 1859. Copy of letter in the Brotherton Library.

[5] "Julia trots off to Miss Mitchells day school every day", wrote Mrs. Gaskell
to Miss Fox on March 21, 1859. (Copy of letter in the Brotherton Library.)
Julia, who was born on Sep. 3, 1846, was then twelve years old.

[6] "Heard thro' Alice of a vacancy at Miss Martineau's which we grasped at
for Meta." (Copy of letter from Mrs. Gaskell to Miss Fox of Dec. 20, 1852, in
the Brotherton Library.)

"Flossy is gone to school at the Green's of Knutsford." (Letter of 1859 from
Mrs. Gaskell to Mrs. Nancy Robson, in the Brotherton Library.)

they had first been taught at home. On one occasion Mrs. Gaskell sent a plan of Meta's studies at home to Marianne, who was then already at school: "Two afternoons she is to draw; & she is reading Alfieri (pretty difficult Italian with Rosa, & beginning mathematics with Papa."[1]

The girls were sent to different schools according to their different abilities and characters. "Meta is going to school, to Miss Martineau's . . . I always felt that this was the only school that would do for Meta . . . she is to learn dancing, Italian, German, & music from Herman", wrote Mrs. Gaskell on one occasion[2], and about the choice of a school for Florence she wrote to Miss Fox:

"Maggie has asked Meta why we did not send Flossy to Miss Lalor's[3]; we had several reasons one of the principal of which was that we so particularly desired her to learn that different people, equally good, might act in an entirely different manner, and yet be acting quite conscientiously and each and equally striving to do the will of God."[4]

In the early nineteenth century, the first real steps were taken to extend the benefits of education to the lower classes.[5] There can be no doubt that Mrs. Gaskell was keenly interested in education. Both she and her daughter Meta taught in a ragged school[6], and the only parish work to which she willingly devoted herself in nor-

---

[1] Letter in the Brotherton Library, dated from Plymouth Grove Wednesday 19.

[2] Fragment of letter in the Brotherton Library.

[3] The school to which Marianne had gone.

[4] Copy of letter (undated) in the Brotherton Library.

[5] In 1807 the Parochial Schools Bill proposed by Whitbread had been rejected by Parliament, and Lord Brougham's Bill for promoting parish schools had met with the same fate in 1820, but in 1833 Parliament granted a sum of £20.000 for the erection of school-houses for the education of the poorer classes. A Privy Council Committee on Education was appointed, the first secretary of which was Dr. Kay, afterwards Sir James Kay-Shuttleworth, Mrs. Gaskell's friend, at whose house she first met Charlotte Brontë. Private initiative was responsible for the establishment and upkeep of Sunday schools, village schools in the country, and so-called ragged schools for the pauper children of the big towns.

[6] "*my* week at the school which took me into town from 9 till 12 every morning", she wrote to Miss Fox in 1852 or 3. (Extract of letter in the Brotherton Library.)

mal times in Manchester was the teaching of a class of girls in the Sunday school[1]. In a letter of Oct. 13, 1862[2], Lord Lansdowne expressed his conviction that an article in the *Daily News* about the "wonderfully successful effort" to establish some kind of school for girls "must have proved deeply interesting you". In her books, she sometimes expressed her conviction that a lack of education constitutes a great drawback in all classes of society. She wrote, for instance, of John Barton:

"No education had given him wisdom; and without wisdom, even love, with all its effects, too often works but harm. He acted to the best of his judgment, but it was a widely-erring judgment.

"The actions of the uneducated seem to me typified in those of Frankenstein, that monster of many human qualities, ungifted with a soul, a knowledge of the difference between good and evil.

"The people rise up to life; they irritate us, they terrify us, and we become their enemies. Then, in the sorrowful moment of our triumphant power, their eyes gaze on us with mute reproach. Why have we made them what they are; a powerful monster, yet without the inner means for peace and happiness?"[3]

One of the charms of My Lady Ludlow, in the story of that name, is the combination of a warm heart with the most rigid theoretical resistance to all reforms of the existing order of society. She thinks that "education is a bad thing, if given indiscriminately. It unfits the lower orders for their duties, the duties to which they are called by God; of submission to those placed in authority over them".[4] She is, however, suitably converted in the end.

---

[1] Cf. Chap. II.

[2] In the John Rylands Library, Manchester.

[3] *Mary Barton*, p. 167.

[4] *My Lady Ludlow*, p. 134. My Lady's opinions on the education of the poor, and her disgust at being told that a maidservant can read, write, and cast accounts, are practically identical with those of the famous philanthropist and blue-stocking Hannah Moore (1744–1833), who summed up her ideas on the subject in these words: "My plan for instructing the poor is very limited and very strict. They learn of weekdays such coarse works as may fit them for servants. I allow no writing. My object has not been to teach dogmas and opinions, but to form the lower class to habits of industry and virtue." (Quoted by Percival, *op. cit.*, p. 253.) According to Chadwick (*op. cit.*, pp. 27–8) Mrs. Gaskell's elder cousin Mary Holland of Knutsford, who is sometimes alleged to have served as

Mrs. Gaskell was well aware of the unsatisfactory standard of many middle-class schools of her time, and she commented on it in *Wives and Daughters:* "far better intellectual teaching is given to the boys and girls of labourers and workpeople than often falls to the lot of their betters in worldly estate".[1] She had no admiration for the superficial education which Lady Cumnor in *Wives and Daughters* expected a middle-class girl to have enjoyed: "music, and the use of globes, and French, and all the usual accomplishments"[2], and Mrs. Bullock in *Mr. Harrison's Confessions* is exposed as hopelessly vulgar when "she began to tell me of the money that had been spent on her [step-daughter's] education; of what each separate accomplishment had cost".[3]

Mrs. Gaskell devoted much thought to the direction of her own daughters' studies and to the choice of suitable schools for them. She strongly disapproved of the indifference to the education of their daughters which many fathers displayed. Mr. Wilkins in *A Dark Night's Work* asks Lady Holster to choose a governess for his daughter: "Only, please, choose some one who will not marry me, and will let Ellinor go on making my tea, and doing pretty much what she likes, for she is so good they need not try to make her better, only to teach her what a lady should know."[4] Later, he shows the same selfish indifference to his daughter's development:

"if her father had cared for her progress in anything, she would and could have worked hard at that study or accomplishment; but Mr. Wilkins, the ease and pleasure loving man, did not wish to make himself into the pedagogue, as he would have considered it, if he had ever questioned Ellinor with a real steady purpose of ascertaining her intellectual progress. It was quite enough for him that her general intelligence and variety of desultory and miscellaneous reading made her a pleasant and agreeable companion for his hours of relaxation".[5]

a model for Miss Jenkyns in *Cranford*, had lived in London for some time, mixing "with the best society, which included such literary people as Hallam, Miss Edgeworth, the Barbaulds, and the Aikins". In her childhood Mrs. Gaskell may well have heard Miss Holland utter many of the opinions concerning the education of "the lower orders" which she ridiculed in *My Lady Ludlow*, as well as the Blue-stocking ideas about the superiority of women over men to which Miss Jenkyns gives expression in *Cranford*.

[1] *Wives and Daughters*, p. 21.
[2] *Ibid.*, p. 137.   [3] P. 411.
[4] P. 16.   [5] P. 30.

The consequences of this neglect of Ellinor's intellect prove to be disastrous for her future happiness, as she becomes engaged to a very intellectual law student:

"It had become difficult for Ralph to contract his mind to her small domestic interests, and she had little else to talk to him about, now that he responded but curtly to all her questions about himself, . . . The books she had been reading were old classics whose place in literature no longer admitted of keen discussion; the poor whom she cared for were all very well in their way, . . . but . . . There was no talking politics with her, because she was so ignorant that she always agreed with everything he said."[1]

Mrs. Gaskell blamed Mr. Wilkins for not encouraging his daughter's studies. For more intellectually active girls, however, she seems to have considered a system of non-interference or even opposition as the best plan. Phillis in *Cousin Phillis* studies under her father's supervision, as she tells her cousin: "if he has a bit of time to spare, he comes in and reads with me—but only English; we keep Latin for the evenings, that we may have time to enjoy it"[2]. The "I" of the story is inferior to Phillis in classical learning. When her father quotes some lines of Virgil about the country, the "minister shifted his eyes to Phillis's face; it mutely gave him back the sympathetic appreciation that I, in my ignorance, could not bestow".[3] We are told that she reads "Virgil, Caesar, a Greek grammar".[4] As Mrs. Gaskell knew, Emily Brontë used to knead bread with a book propped up in front of her. Phillis has the same habit of combining household work with studies. She "sat by the dresser, peeling apples with quick dexterity of finger, but with repeated turnings of her head towards some book lying on the dresser by her . . . I had seen that the book was in a language unknown to me, and the running title was 'L'Inferno' ".[5] She complains of her difficulties over old Italian, as her father has so little time to help her, but she declines the help of Mr. Holdsworth, because she "can generally puzzle a thing out in time. And then, perhaps, I remember it better than if someone had helped me".[6]

Molly Gibson in *Wives and Daughters* would "rather be a dunce than a blue-stocking"[7], and she is far from intellectual. Her "in-

---

[1] P. 90.   [2] P. 181.   [3] P. 184.
[4] P. 185.   [5] P. 191.
[6] P. 192.   [7] P. 264.

terests were her father, Miss Eyre, her garden and pony; in a fainter degree Miss Brownings, the Cumnor Charity School, and the new gown that was to come from Miss Rose's".[1] Quite early in the book Molly's character formed itself in the image of Fredrika Bremer's Flora.[2] At first, though, Mrs. Gaskell seems to have had other plans for her. Mr. Gibson does not want a learned daughter any more than Mr. Wilkins. His instructions to the governess are:

"Don't teach Molly too much; she must sew, and read, and write, and do her sums; but I want to keep her a child, and if I find more learning desirable for her, I'll see about giving it to her myself. After all, I'm not sure that reading or writing is necessary. Many a good woman gets married with only a cross instead of her name; it's rather a diluting of motherwit, to my fancy; but, however, we must yield to the prejudices of society, Miss Eyre, and so you may teach the child to read",[3]

and Miss Eyre "taught Molly to read and write, but tried honestly to keep her back in every other branch of education".[4] Molly, however, reacts to this treatment in a very different way from Ellinor:

"It was only by fighting and struggling hard, that bit by bit Molly persuaded her father to let her have French and drawing lessons. He was always afraid of her becoming too much educated, though he need not have been alarmed; the masters who visited such small country towns as Hollingford forty years ago, were no such great proficients in their arts. Once a week she joined a dancing class in the assembly-room at the principal inn in the town, the 'Cumnor Arms'; and, being daunted by her father in every intellectual attempt, she read every book that came in her way, almost with as much delight as if it had been forbidden. For his station in life, Mr. Gibson had an unusually good library; the medical portion of it was inaccessible to Molly, being kept in the surgery, but every other book she had either read, or tried to read."[5]

Neither Mrs. Gaskell herself nor her daughters had encountered any opposition to their desire for learning, but among her closest friends in Manchester she had seen an example of intellectual daughters "fighting and struggling hard" to overcome their father's hostility to lessons. In 1846 Susanna Winkworth, who was then 26, wrote to her younger sister Emily:

---

[1] P. 80. [2] See Appendix II.
[3] P. 46. [4] P. 46. [5] P. 46.

"how my heart jumped at the idea of Mr. Martineau's teaching *anything*!
... lessons from a man who stands perhaps by himself in England as a
philosophical thinker, would be invaluable to me. The great difficulty is
to bring Papa to consent. Whether he will keep to the forbidding of all
fresh lessons except Selina's painting? But surely it is as necessary for
us as for her to have the means of supporting ourselves, and I presume
Papa would not wish to expose any of us *unnecessarily* to the chance of
having to be private governesses, because we were fit for nothing better?"[1]

Even as Mrs. Gaskell disapproved of the type of education which
aimed at "accomplishments", she also disliked the other extreme,
which produced bluestockings, and Mrs. Hepworth in *North and
South*, who believes herself efficient, although Mrs. Purkis calls
her activity "turning things upside down for very little purpose"[2]
is shown up as a mockery of what a good teacher should be, with
her enthusiasm for the Phonetic system and her insistence that
an indefinite article must be called "an adjective absolute" in the
village school.

Mrs. Hepworth's case shows in what sense Mrs. Gaskell did not
"care a straw about *lessons*".[3] She shared My Lady Ludlow's
conviction that "books do little; character much; and character is
not formed from books".[4] Maggie in *The Moorland Cottage* is a
case in point. She is a frequent visitor at Combehurst, and

"When she was on these visits, she received no regular instruction; and
yet all the knowledge, and most of the strength of her character, was derived from these occasional hours. It is true her mother had given her daily
lessons in reading, writing, and arithmetic; but both teacher and taught
felt these more as painful duties to be gone through than understood
them as means to an end . . . Mrs. Buxton did not make a set labour of
teaching. I suppose she felt that much was learned from her superinten-
dence, but she never thought of doing or saying anything with a latent
idea of its indirect effect upon the little girls, her companions. She was
simply, herself";[5]

In the stories mentioned in this chapter Mrs. Gaskell's criticism of the usual education of girls is casual and incidental; in accordance with her own rule the thing is "let seen and not shown".[6]

---

[1] Shaen, *op. cit.*, p. 19.
[2] P. 413.   [3] See p. 104.
[4] *My Lady Ludlow*, p. 135.
[5] P. 294.   [6] See p. 83.

She seems to have formulated that principle fairly late in life (Mme Mohl's letter which refers to it was written in 1860). She certainly did not adhere to it closely in her early period, when she was writ-ing her didactic novels, such as *Mary Barton*, *Ruth*, and *North and South*.

Morton Hall belongs to that earlier period, and the second part of that story[1] is unique in Mrs. Gaskell's production, in so far as it criticizes and ridicules theories of education, in much the same way as Dickens did shortly afterwards in *Hard Times*[2], where Mr. Gradgrind rigidly and consistently applies the precepts of the Uti-litarian philosophy in his school and home with disastrous results for the victims of his unwise enthusiasm. As appears from Mrs. Gaskell's discussions of schools for her daughters, she did not be-lieve in one infallible system of education for all. She distrusted all rigid systems, the fundamental mistake of which seemed to her to be that they tended to adapt the child to the system instead of the system to the child. She illustrated this in *Morton Hall*. The three old sisters Morton all believe in entirely different types of education. Each wants to subject their little niece to her own system, and they solve the difficulty by taking her in turn—one week each.

The eldest of the sisters firmly believes in that means of educa-tion so frequently used in school and home in Mrs. Gaskell's time, books of advice and admonitions concerning the morals and manners of the young, such as Lord Chesterfield's *Letters to his Son*, Mrs. Chapone's *Letters on the Improvement of the Mind*, Dr. Gregory's *A Father's Legacy to his Daughters*, and Lady Pen-nington's *A Mother's Advice to her Absent Daughters*.[3] In fact she herself is engaged in writing *The Female Chesterfield; or, Letters from a Lady of Quality to her Niece*. "And the little niece sat there in a high chair, with a flat board tied to her back, and her feet in stocks on the rail of the chair; so that she had nothing to do but listen to her aunt's letters; which were read aloud to her as they were written, in order to mark their effect on her manners."[4] Miss

---

[1] Published in *Household Words* from Nov. 19–26, 1853.

[2] Published in *Household Words* from April 1 to August 12, 1854.

[3] Chesterfield, Chapone, and Gregory are all referred to in other stories by Mrs. Gaskell. See Appendix III.

[4] P. 383.

Sophronia is something of a blue-stocking, and believes in book-learning. Her niece has become a prodigy of geographical information and is told that "little girls can learn anything they choose, even French verbs".[1] Not even Miss Sophronia's teaching is, however, quite consistent with her practice. The typical books of advice for young girls all paid lip-service to an ideal of unworldly innocence of mind, while at the same time all their advice aimed at making the girls attractive enough to catch a husband. Miss Sophronia shows the same inconsistency. She tells her niece that "to be good is better than to be pretty. We don't think about looks here", but in the same breath she tells her to go into the garden, "and take care you put your bonnet on, or you'll be all over freckles."[2]

The second sister, Miss Annabella, tries to form her niece in accordance with the ideal of womanly delicacy expressed in the eighteenth century novels of sentiment and sensibility. She herself steps direct out of one of these novels: "Her voice was very sweet and plaintive, and suited well with the kind of things she said; all about charms of nature, and tears, and grief."[3] Her room, too, is quite in character: "a spinnet in a corner to amuse herself with, and a good sofa to lie down upon".[4] Concerning the education of her niece she

"said she hoped to develop the sensibilities and to cultivate the tastes. While with her, her darling niece read works of imagination, and acquired all that Miss Annabella could impart of the fine arts. We neither of us quite knew what she was hinting at, at the time; but afterwards, by dint of questioning little miss, and using our own eyes and ears, we found that she read aloud to her aunt while she lay on the sofa. *Santo Sebastiano; or, the Young Protector*, was what they were deep in at this time; and, as it was in five volumes and the heroine spoke broken English—which required to be read twice over to make it intelligible—it lasted them a long time. She also learned to play on the spinnet";[5]

None of the sisters allow the girl to play with other children. As for exercise, "though there were exceptions, early nineteenth century schools of the more fashionable type regarded physical

---

[1] P. 383.   [2] Pp. 383–4.
[3] P. 384.   [4] P. 384.
[5] Pp. 384–5.

exercise as approaching the indecent"[1], and Miss Annabella, true to her romantic character, sends her niece into the wood to meditate—not, of course, to play. The sister who is most against natural exercise and movement in any form is, however, Miss Dorothy, whose room "had a north-east look about it, though it did face direct south".[2] She interferes with the girl for dirtying her frock on the grass in the garden, even though it is not her week; she is also the one who sees to it that the child walks "in the measured step she was taught to use in that house; where such things as running, going upstairs two steps at a time, or jumping down three, were considered undignified and vulgar".[3]

All three sisters set great store by the artificial standard of propriety which was rigidly enforced in certain classes of society. "The rules that were made for Miss Cordelia! . . . there were ever so many words she might not use; each aunt had her own set of words which were ungenteel or improper for some reason or another. Miss Dorothy would never let her say 'red'; it was always to be pink, or crimson, or scarlet . . . Miss Morton told her never to say she had got a stomach-ache, for that it was not proper to say so."[4]

The kind but simple visitors to Morton Hall represent the common-sense attitude to all these systems:

" 'Poor little miss!' said Ethelinda; 'does she never get a game of play with other little girls?' And I am sure from that time Ethelinda considered her in a diseased state from this very circumstance, and that her knowledge of geography was one of the symptoms of the disorder; for she used often to say, 'I wish she did not know so much geography! I'm sure it is not quite right'."[5]

The fault was in the systems, not in the well-meaning sisters, as Mrs. Gaskell takes care to point out: "But though I tell all these

---

[1] Percival, *op. cit.*, p. 84.

[2] P. 387.

[3] Pp. 386–7.

[4] P. 388. This was a type of affectation that Mrs. Gaskell found particularly irritating. In a letter to her daughter Marianne (now in the Brotherton Library), dated "Tuesday Morng.", she wrote: "*Don't* call Shifts Chemises. Take the pretty simple English word whenever you can."

[5] P. 385.

peculiarities of the Miss Mortons, they were good women in the main: even Miss Dorothy had her times of kindness, and really did love her little niece, though she was always laying traps to catch her doing wrong."[1]

In *Hard Times* Dickens followed up his account of an exaggeratedly Utilitarian education with a demonstration of the lasting effect for the worse on those who had been subjected to it. The ultimate results in little Miss Mannisty of the three Miss Mortons' different systems would probably have been rather more complicated, and Mrs. Gaskell did not attempt to visualize them. The girl is saved from them by the return of her relative the Colonel, who sends her to school, after which she grows up in a perfectly normal way.

In *Morton Hall* Mrs. Gaskell ridiculed some of the artificial rules of social behaviour that hedged in the middle-class girl of the nineteenth century. In the case of her own daughters, however, Mrs. Gaskell was far from indifferent to certain questions of propriety. She found it difficult to decide which families her daughter Marianne should be allowed to visit.[2] She refused to let her second daughter go to a public ball without her parents[3], and she was slightly scandalized one evening to see her dance as many as eight times with the same man.[4] But on the whole her attitude must be considered broad-minded for the time. She never thought it improper for her daughters to go about unaccom-

---

[1] P. 388.

[2] "I am puzzled about Ma how far to let her accept the 1001 invitations to dances thronging in—I have attempted to draw a rule that she may go where I go, and no where else, but I am not sure if it will do." (Letter to Miss Ann A. Shaen, Dec. 21, 1849, now in the Brotherton Library.)

[3] "Meta has been disappointed about the Richmond ball, to wh*h* Lady Crompton wanted to take her, only I *wd not let* her go to public ball without me,—I am sorry to cut her off from Ly C's *private* ball,—I almost think I shall let her travel *alone* next Wednesday." (Undated letter to Marianne in the Brotherton Library.)

[4] "Miss Meta and one of the officers are a little too thick in the dancing line, 8 times in one evng. being rather too strong, and drawing down upon the young lady a parental rebuke." (Extract of letter from Mrs. Gaskell to Miss Fox. Dec. 24, 1854, in the Brotherton Library.)

panied among the poorer population of Manchester.[1] Margaret in *North and South* shares Mrs. Gaskell's opinions on this question in contrast to the "helpless" Mrs. Shaw[2]:

"Mrs. Shaw's ideas of propriety and her own helpless dependence on others, had always made her insist that a footman should accompany Edith and Margaret, if they went beyond Harley Street . . . The limits by which this rule of her aunt's had circumscribed Margaret's independence had been silently rebelled against at the time."[3]

Mrs. Gaskell found it hard to tolerate the ideas of people who had so little sense of proportion as to consider artificial propriety in questions of real importance. When Margaret's old friend Mr. Bell in *North and South* is dying and wishes to see her, her relatives try to stop her going:

" 'You don't know where you're going. I should not mind if he had a house of his own; but in his Fellow's rooms! . . .' . . . In the suddenness of the event, Mrs. Shaw became bewildered and hysterical, and so the precious time slipped by . . . after various discussions on propriety and impropriety, it was decided that Captain Lennox should accompany Margaret, as the one thing to which she was constant was her resolution to go, alone or otherwise, by the next train, whatever might be said of the propriety or impropriety of the step."[4]

---

[1] In the letter to Norton quoted on p. 22 she wrote: "Meta laboured day and night—and going out again, after a hard hard day if she thought one little scrap of duty or kindness or enquiry had been omitted."

It might be noted, as a comparison, that Florence Nightingale was told that "it would never do . . . for a young woman in her station in life to go out in London without a servant". (Cook, *op. cit.*, I: 83.)

In the discussion between Edith and the old servant Dixon in *North and South,* it is Dixon who has Mrs. Gaskell's sympathies:

" 'I'm sure I'm always expecting to hear of her [Margaret] having met with something horrible among all those wretched places she pokes herself into. I should never dare to go down some of those streets without a servant. They're not fit for ladies.'

"Dixon . . . replied rather shortly—

" 'It's no wonder to my mind, when I hear ladies talk such a deal about being ladies—and when they're such fearful, delicate, dainty ladies too—I say it's no wonder to me there are no longer any saints on earth'." (Pp. 454–5.)

[2] In Mrs. Gaskell's stories "helpless" is an adjective that generally denotes the author's strong disapproval.

[3] P. 77.

[4] P. 438.

In *Wives and Daughters* Mrs. Gaskell makes fun of Mrs. Gibson's exaggerated caution. When Molly innocently remarks, "but there is something between Cynthia and Roger; they are more to each other than I am to Osborne, for instance", her step-mother corrects her: "You should not couple your name with that of any unmarried young man; it is so difficult to teach you delicacy, child."[1]
In one respect the rules for a novel heroine's behaviour were inherited from the eighteenth century novels of sensibility, and they were extremely strict: under no circumstances must a woman love before the man had declared himself. Nor was it quite proper for her to talk about her feelings even after the engagement. This is also a rule particularly stressed in the many books of advice concerning maidenly behaviour of the time. The chapter treating Friendship, Love and Marriage in *A Father's Legacy to his Daughters* by Dr. Gregory has the following passage on the subject:

"It is even long before a woman of delicacy dares avow to her own heart that she loves; and, when all the subterfuges of ingenuity to conceal it from herself fail, she feels violence done ... to her pride ... This, I should imagine, must always be the case, where she is not sure of a return to her attachment.

"In such a situation, to lay her heart open to any person whatever, does not appear to me consistent with the perfection of female delicacy."

Concerning this question there is an interesting change in Mrs. Gaskell's stories. Mary Barton is by far the most natural and realistic of her heroines[2], with the possible exception of Cynthia in *Wives and Daughters*. Mary realizes that she loves Jem only after his proposal of marriage. She refuses him, and it is not until the trial scene that she confesses her feelings for him, and by force of circumstance her declaration of love is public.[3] This shocked some

---

[1] P. 471.

[2] Her portrait also struck the Lancashire "poet of humble life" Samuel Bamford as perfectly realistic: "who has ever seen a group of our Lancashire factory girls or dress makers either, and could not have counted Mary?" (Letter to Mrs. Gaskell, March 9, 1849, now in the Rylands Library, Manchester. Printed in the *Bulletin*, pp. 106–7.)

[3] Mrs. Gaskell had read Goethe's *Hermann und Dorothea* at least before she wrote *North and South*. (See Appendix III.) As W. W. Whewell pointed out to her, there occurs in Goethe's poem "an incident much resembling one in

of the readers. The *Prospective Review* of February 1849 expressed disapproval in the following passage:

"Resulting from the false position in which she had placed herself towards Jem Wilson, as a sort of poetical consequent—is the unseemly rectification of it by her gratuitous declaration of love for him in the open court— a feeling which the circumstances of the time would rather have led her to suppress, and the unreserved display of which on such an occasion we regard as the worst conceived and least natural incident in the story."[1]

Mrs. Gaskell was as sensitive as Charlotte Brontë to criticisms of her sense of propriety, but unlike her more original friend, she was prepared to act on advice.[2] Her treatment of second love for a woman seems to have been influenced by the criticism of *Mary Barton*, until her daughter's experience made her reconsider this question.[3] Concerning a woman's declaration of love for a man, no such personal experience made Mrs. Gaskell return to her first pattern, and none of her heroines after Mary Barton behave in such an "unmaidenly" way. Margaret in *North and South* is deeply hurt when she is reported to have publicly shown her love for Mr. Thornton on the occasion of the strike, and Thekla in *Six Weeks at Heppenheim* is relieved to have tangible evidence, even after she has ceased to love the man, that he had first spoken of his love. Philip in *Sylvia's Lovers* defends Hester's character by telling her mother that "Our Hester's not the lass to think on a young man unless he's been a-wooing on her"[4], and Hester herself accepts the same standard for her behaviour: "It was a shame, perhaps, to have thought on it ever, when he never thought o' me; but I never be-

---

'Mary Barton'; I mean the woman's declaration of her love forced from her by despair". (Letter dated May 12, 1849, now in the Rylands Library, Manchester.)

[1] Pp. 36–57. Art. III, "Mary Barton".

[2] In *The Life of Charlotte Brontë* Mrs. Gaskell reports the following words of her friend: "I trust God will take from me whatever power of invention or expression I may have, before He lets me become blind to the sense of what is fitting or unfitting to be said!" (Chap. XXVI.) In the same chapter she writes about sensitiveness to criticism: "An author may bring himself to believe that he can bear blame with equanimity, from whatever quarter it comes; but its force is derived altogether from the character of this . . . It is this knowledge of the individual worth of the reviewer's opinion, which makes the censures of some sink so deep, and prey so heavily upon an author's heart."

[3] Cf. Chap. IV.   [4] P. 210.

lieved as any one could ha' found it out. I am just fit to sink into t' ground, what with my sorrow and my shame."[1] Charlotte Brontë had been the first to break the literary tradition in this respect, and much abuse had been heaped on her for so doing. Her example had had some effect, however, and reviewers of conventional novels were beginning to criticize some writers for their exaggerated idea of the importance of proprieties.[2] But this had no effect on Mrs. Gaskell, and all her heroines after Mary Barton consider it necessary to conceal their love until the man has declared himself. When Phillis in *Cousin Phillis* is disappointed in love, the aim of all her efforts is "to . . . keep her maidenly secret"[3], and when her secret does come out, she is "so sick with shame".[4] Because Molly's story in *Wives and Daughters* is closely patterned after that of Fredrika Bremer's Selma[5], Molly falls in love with Roger long before he has any amorous feelings for her, but Mrs. Gaskell saves Molly's honour by making her innocently unaware of the character of her own feelings until the proper time.

Mrs. Gaskell obviously thought a good education essential for a woman, and wanted her daughters to be able to form their own opinions independent of any line of thought or set of beliefs of one group of people.[6] She herself refused to accept the readymade opinions of others. "I always do want to have the *facts* if I can, on which your opinions are based", she wrote to C. E. Norton on July 4, 1864.[7] She also tried to impress her daughters with the importance of finding out the facts and reserve their judgment until they were in a position to form an independent opinion. She once wrote to her eldest daughter:

---

[1] P. 380.

[2] The *Athenaeum* of August 1, 1857, for instance, wrote in a review of Mrs. C. Hall's *A Woman's Story:* "Mrs. Hall's standard of female delicacy makes us feel how far we are gone from original propriety, when we read of a friend who refrains from some desirable vindication of Helen because she could not do it without exposing the secret of her attachment, which a true woman 'holds as sacred as her honour'."

[3] P. 243.   [4] P. 248.

[5] See Appendix II.

[6] Cf. p. 105.

[7] Whitehill, *op. cit.*

"Pray *why* do you wish a Protectionist Ministry not to come in? Papa and I want terribly to know. Before you fully make up your mind, read a paper in the Quarterly on the subject of Free Trade, (written by Mr. George Taylor) and (I think) the year 1839; and then when you come home I will read with you Mr. Cobden's speeches. But first I think we should read together Adam Smith on the Wealth of Nations, not confining ourselves as we read to the limited meaning which he affixes to the word 'wealth'. Seriously, dear, you must not become a *partizan* in politics or in anything else,—you must have a 'reason for the faith that is in you',—and not in three weeks suppose you can know enough to form an opinion about measures of state. That is one reason why so many people dislike that women should meddle with politics; they say that it is a subject requiring long patient study of many branches of science; and a logical training which few women have had,—that women are apt to take up a thing without being even able to state their reasons clearly, and yet on that insufficient knowledge they take a more violent and bigoted stand than thoughtful *men* dare to do. Have as many and as large and varied interests as you can; but do not again give a decided opinion on a subject on which you can at present know nothing . . ."[1]

Miss Dullemen, who prints an extract of this letter, comments that Mrs. Gaskell was "rather afraid of women meddling in politics", and Miss Haldane, who quotes two sentences from it, adds: "Poor Polly, the days of the emancipated young woman had not come as yet!"[2] It should be noted, however, that what Mrs. Gaskell objects to in the letter is women uncritically adopting other people's ideas instead of forming their own opinions after a careful study of the facts.

In the same way as Mrs. Gaskell did not try to stop independent thinking in her daughters, she was also quite prepared to recognize an unmarried daughter's legitimate claim for an independent life and training for a profession. While staying with the Nightingale family at Lea Hurst, she wrote in a letter to Emily Winkworth-Shaen:

"I have told Meta she may begin to prepare herself for entering upon a nurse's life of devotion when she is thirty or so, by going about among sick now, and that all the help I can give in letting her see hospitals, etc.,

---

[1] Undated letter in the Brotherton Library.

[2] Dullemen, *op. cit.*, p. 87, Haldane, *op. cit.*, p. 118. Miss Dullemen makes several changes in the text and omissions not indicated, and Miss Haldane quotes "Mr. Cobdens speech" instead of "speeches", "confusing" for "confining", and "you at present know" for "you can at present know".

if she wishes she may have. I doubt if she has purpose enough to do all this; but I have taken great care not to damp her—and if she has purpose, I will help her, as I propose, to lead such a life; tho' it is not everyone who can be Miss N."[1]

On August 27, 1860, she wrote to C. E. Norton, also about Meta: "she wished (for a time) to become a professional *artist;* . . . If she really and persistently wished it, I think, at her age[2]; I should think it right to yield, . . . and as, if she had married her life would have been apart and separate from mine, so I think she has a *right* to make it now";[3]

Employment as an artist was indeed one of the very few professional careers open to a middle class woman at that period. With the coming of the nineteenth century it ceased to be taken for granted that middle class women should work. That was one of the evils which the manufacturing system brought with it. The new middle class in the towns, such as the factory owners, with their desire to imitate the way of life of the gentry, came to feel that for the women of the family to do household work was not "genteel", and as yet no employment outside the home had come to take its place. Yet the number of women that had to earn their own living was increasing.[4] Many of these women belonged to the class which filled the ranks of factory or domestic workers, but a considerable number came from the middle classes. "Attorneys and apothecaries, tradesmen and shopkeepers, bankers' and merchants' clerks, etc. In this class more than two-thirds of the women are now obliged to earn their bread", wrote Mrs. Jameson.[5] Even if her figures are not always very accurate, it is an indisputable fact that more and more middle class women had to earn a living outside the home. Miss Young, the governess in Harriet Marti-

---

[1] Letter of October 27, 1854. Haldane, *op. cit.*, pp. 90–96.

[2] Meta was then 23 years old.

[3] Whitehill, *op. cit.*, letter 21.

[4] An article in the *Athenaeum* gave the following figures for 1851:

"So far as the Census is reliable, it seems that there were, in 1851, nearly six millions of women in Great Britain above twenty years of age, 3,435,917 married, 1,767,194 unmarried, and 795,273 widows." (Review of *Industrial and Social Position of Women, in the Middle and Lower Ranks*, July 25, 1857.)

[5] Mrs. Jameson, *Memoirs and Essays illustrative of Art, Literature, and Social Morals* (London, 1846), p. 230.

neau's *Deerbrook*[1], describes the predicament of many young women of the time:

" 'for an educated woman . . . there is in all England no chance of subsistence but by teaching . . . or by being a superior Miss Nares—the feminine gender of the tailor and the hatter'.
" 'The tutor, the tailor, and the hatter. Is this all?'
" 'All; except that there are departments of art and literature from which it is impossible to shut women out.' "[2]

Mrs. Jameson, in the work quoted above, though writing nearly ten years later, does not give a much more optimistic survey: "She might be a clerk,—or a cashier,—or an assistant in a mercantile house. Such a thing is common in France, but here in England who would employ her? Who would countenance such an innovation on all our English ideas of feminine propriety?"[3]

Not even a woman who desired work for its own sake found it easy to obtain it. "The Catholic orders", wrote Florence Nightingale, "offered me work, training for that work, sympathy and help in it, such as I had in vain sought in the Church of England . . . For women she [the Church of England] has—what? . . . I would have given her my head, my heart, my hand. She would not have them . . . You may go to the Sunday School, if you like it, she said. But she gave me no training even for that. She gave me neither work to do for her, nor education for it".[4]

The reading public did not at first welcome the apparition of the urban middle class heroes and heroines of novels. Harriet Martineau wrote of the reception of her *Deerbrook*: "It was droll to hear the daughters of dissenting ministers and manufacturers expressing disgust that the heroine came from Birmingham, and that the hero was a surgeon. Youths and maidens in those days looked for lords and ladies in every page of a new novel."[5]

Jane Austen's novels of middle class life had been published in the second decade of the nineteenth century, but they dealt with country life, and her characters came from the old class of offi-

---

[1] Published in 1839.
[2] *Deerbrook*, III: 166.
[3] Mrs. Jameson, *op. cit.*, pp. 236–7.
[4] Cook, *op. cit.*, I: 57.
[5] Martineau, *Autobiography*, II: 115.

cers, sailors, and clergymen. With the one exception of the governess, we look in vain to her books for a woman earning her own
living.

Charlotte Brontë, who championed woman's cause, notably in
Shirley, described the working woman as a teacher. Her attitude
towards work for women was, however, so cautious as to provoke
the following outburst from her impetuous friend Mary Taylor:

"I have seen some extracts from *Shirley* in which you talk of women working. And this first duty, this great necessity, you seem to think that some
women may indulge in, if they give up marriage, and don't make themselves too disagreeable to the other sex. You are a coward and a traitor.
A woman who works is by that alone better than one who does not; and a
woman who does not happen to be rich and who *still* earns no money and
does not wish to do so, is guilty of a great fault, almost a crime—a dereliction of duty which leads rapidly and almost certainly to all manner of
degradation. It is very wrong of you to *plead* for toleration of workers on
the ground of their being in peculiar circumstances, and few in number
or singular in disposition. Work or degradation is the lot of all except
the very small number born to wealth."[1]

Harriet Martineau, who disapproved of Dickens' writings in
general, attacked his "articles on behalf of his view of Woman's
position; articles in which he ignored the fact that nineteen-twen-
tieths of the women of England earn their bread, and in which he
prescribes the function of Women; viz., to dress well and look
pretty, as an adornment to the homes of men".[2]

The fact that extremely few professional careers were open to
a woman of the middle classes does not seem to have worried Mrs.
Gaskell much. She herself had married early, and she seems to
have expected her daughters to do the same. After writing to
Norton in 1860: "I don't know what I should do if any one of them

---

[1] Letter dated from New Zealand April 29, 1850. (Shorter, *op. cit.*, II: 131–
2, letter 433.) Mary Taylor had not then read Charlotte Brontë's first novel,
The Professor, which was only published posthumously in 1857, and the heroine
of which insists on continuing her work as a teacher even after her marriage. It
is worthy of notice that of all Charlotte Brontë's women characters Frances in
The Professor was Mrs. Gaskell's favourite, "the most charming woman she ever
drew", as she wrote in a letter of Sep. 8, 1856 (now in the Brotherton Library)
to Mrs. Wm Shaen (née Emily Winkworth).

[2] Martineau, *Autobiography*, II: 418–419.

married"[1], she added: "and yet it is constantly a wonder to me that no one ever gives them a chance". As they grew up without marrying, she was, however, forced to consider their prospects in life. In her early stories she stressed the importance of a woman's "natural" duties. If a woman had neither husband nor children of her own, she should take care of somebody else's children. Margaret Hale in *North and South* makes a determined effort to assert her independence of action when she wants to "make herself some duties". The charity work to which she devotes herself is, however, only mentioned in extremely vague terms. The nursing to which Ruth gives her life in the book of that name must also be classed as charity work. Miss Phillis in *Morton Hall* (1853) "used to go about trying to see after the workmen and labourers, and save what she could"[2], but she stays on the family estate and does not compete with men.

Mrs. Gaskell had evidently always considered some kind of work essential for a woman. Practically all her women characters do useful work in the home, and idle ladies, such as Mr. Thornton's sister in *North and South* and Mr. Carson's daughters in *Mary Barton*, on whose hands time weighs heavily in spite of the fancy work and music-copying which they indulge in, are treated with the contempt they deserve. Nor do the heroines of her stories consider work as an evil. In times of mental strain they take refuge in heavy work instead of going off into hysterics like the heroines of the novels of sensibility. Even the heroine of such a sentimental story as *The Heart of John Middleton* (1850) does some useful work during her last days: "her white, pale hands ever busy with some kind of work".[3]

Mrs. Gaskell voiced her opinion so explicitly and frequently that there can be no doubt that she shared John Barton's ideas when he says about his daughter:

"I'd rather see her earning her bread by the sweat of her brow, as the Bible tells her she should do, ay, though she never got butter to her bread, than be like a do-nothing lady, worrying shopmen all morning, and screeching

---

[1] See p. 97.
[2] P. 373.
[3] P. 328.

at her pianny all afternoon, and going to bed without having done a good turn to any one of God's creatures but herself."[1]

Mrs. Gaskell had no sympathy with those "ladies" who were too "genteel" to do any work, as is shown by her description in *Mary Barton* of the factory owner's wife, Mrs. Carson, who

"was . . . indulging in the luxury of a headache. She was not well, certainly . . . But it was but the natural consequence of the state of mental and bodily idleness in which she was placed . . . It would have done her more good than all the ether and sal-volatile she was daily in the habit of swallowing, if she might have taken the work of one of her own housemaids for a week; made beds, rubbed tables, shaken carpets . . ."[2]

No kind of honest work could ever be degrading, in Mrs. Gaskell's eyes. Margaret Hale, in *North and South*,

"ironed away, . . . she sat down at last, and told her mother that she was no longer Peggy the laundry-maid, but Margaret Hale the lady. She meant this speech for a little joke, and was vexed enough with her busy tongue when she found her mother taking it seriously . . . 'Oh, mamma!' said Margaret . . . 'I don't mind ironing, or any kind of work, for you and papa. I am myself a born and bred lady through it all, even though it comes to scouring a floor, or washing dishes' ".[3]

Her life when she goes to live at her cousin's forms a strong contrast to this:

"The course of Margaret's day was this; a quiet hour or two before a late breakfast; an unpunctual meal, lazily eaten by weary and half-awake people, . . . an endless number of notes to write, . . . a little play with Sholto as he returned from his morning's walk; besides the care of the

---

[1] *Mary Barton*, p. 18. This was still so new in novels as to be commented on in reviews. The *Westminster Review* wrote in its article on *Mary Barton* (April–July, 1849, pp. 48–63): "Compare Mary Barton with the Evelinas, Cecilias and Belindas which superseded the Romances of the Forest, the Children of the Abbey, and the Haunted Towers of the age which preceded theirs! Mary Barton is no heiress, nursed in the lap of luxury, living upon the produce of other people's labour, without knowing, or even the curiosity to know, how it comes to her—refined, generous, capricious, indolent—dying first of ennui, then of love, and lastly falling a prey to a fortune-hunter, or a military swindler. No; Mary Barton is one of Labour's daughters—heiress of all the struggles, vicissitudes and sufferings consequent upon the ignorance and prejudices of the society into which she is born."

[2] Pp. 196–7.   [3] P. 82.

children during the servants' dinner; a drive or callers; and some dinner or morning engagement for her aunt and cousins, which left Margaret free, it is true, but rather wearied with the inactivity of the day",[1]

Naturally, Margaret cannot stand that kind of life for long, but tells her cousin: "as I have neither husband nor child to give me natural duties, I must make myself some".[2]

It is to be noted, however, that Mrs. Gaskell was enough of a Victorian to approve of such a step only in the case of a woman who had no "natural" duties.[3] The moral of her Sunday school story *Bessy's Troubles at Home* (1853) is: "never you neglect the work clearly laid out for you by either God or man, to go making work for yourself, according to your own fancies".[4] Nor should a woman find special work for herself unless she was specially gifted. Miss Matty in *Cranford* knew her limitations: "I knew I was good for little, and that my best work was to do odd jobs quietly".

This insistence on what constitutes a woman's natural sphere is particularly noticeable in the early stories. In *Libbie Marsh's Three Eras* (1847), Libbie says to Anne:

"and more reason, therefore, as God has seen fit to keep me out of woman's natural work, I should try and find work for myself . . . as I know I'm never likely to have a home of my own, or a husband that would look to me to make all straight, or children to watch over or care for, all which I take to be woman's natural work, I must not lose time in fretting and fidgetting after marriage, but just look about me for somewhat else to do. I can see many a one misses it in this. They will hanker after what is ne'er likely to be theirs, instead of facing it out, and settling down to be old maids; and, as old maids, just looking round for the odd jobs God leaves in the world for such as old maids to do. There's plenty of such work, and there's the blessing of God on them as does it".[5]

In 1858, however, the year when Meta's engagement to be married was broken, *My Lady Ludlow* was published. "My lady herself was a pretty good woman of business, as women of business go[6]", though more from necessity than inclination, as she had been

---

[1] P. 398.   [2] P. 444.

[3] On August 4th, 1835, Mrs. Gaskell wrote in her *Diary*: "How all a woman's life, at least so it seems to me now, ought to have a reference to the period when she will be fulfilling one of her greatest and highest duties, those of a mother."

[4] Pp. 534–5.   [5] P. 473.   [6] P. 156.

left a widow. In the person of Miss Galindo, however, we meet a character who sets out to do a man's work in deliberate opposition to and competition with men. At first she earns her living in a traditional and generally approved way:

"It was the custom in those days for the wealthy ladies of the country to set on foot a repository, as it was called, in the assize-town. The ostensible manager of this repository was generally a decayed gentlewoman, . . . controlled by a committee of ladies; and paid by them in proportion to the amount of goods she sold; and these goods were the small manufactures of ladies of little or no fortune . . .
"Poor water-colour drawings, . . . paintings on velvet, and such faintly ornamental works were displayed on one side of the shop . . . But, on the other side, where the Useful Work placard was put up, there was a great variety of articles, of whose unusual excellence every one might judge . . .
"And the most delicate dainty work of all was done by Miss Galindo."[1]

For all this womanly occupation she knew much about things which were considered a man's business, for we are told about a cottager that he "was . . . won over by Miss Galindo's merry ways, and sharp insight into the mysteries of his various kinds of business (he was a mason, chimney-sweeper, and ratcatcher)".[2] But it was only through My Lady Ludlow's initiative that Miss Galindo ever took up her new profession as a clerk. Consistency was never one of Lady Ludlow's strong points, and her idea about Miss Galindo's work contrasts strangely with her opinion expressed on the occasion when women writers were discussed: "I am extremely against women usurping men's employments."[3] Miss Galindo's immediate superior, Mr. Horner, was very much against the whole plan. He thought "that Miss Galindo would be most unmanageable as a clerk". He could only "heartily wish that the idea had never come into my lady's head . . . he could . . . only urge difficulties which he hoped might prove insuperable. But every one of them Lady Ludlow knocked down. Letters to copy? Doubtless . . . 'Capability with regard to accounts?' My lady would answer for that too";[4]
Miss Galindo does not disappoint my lady's confidence in her

---

[1] P. 118.   [2] P. 119.
[3] P. 124.   [4] P. 120.

ability. When once installed as a clerk in Lady Ludlow's service she describes her relations with Mr. Horner:

"Mr. Steward Horner does not like having me for a clerk . . ., I try to make him forget I am a woman, I do everything as ship-shape as a masculine man-clerk. I see he can't find a fault—writing good, spelling correct, sums all right. And then he squints up at me with the tail of his eye, and looks glummer than ever, just because I'm a woman—as if I could help that. I have gone good lengths to set his mind at ease. I have stuck my pen behind my ear, I have made him a bow instead of a curtsey, I have whistled—not a tune, I can't pipe up that—nay, if you won't tell my lady, I don't mind telling you that I have said 'Confound it!' and 'Zounds!' I can't get any farther. For all that, Mr. Horner won't forget I am a lady, and so I am not half the use I might be."[1]

Miss Galindo, unlike the new vicar's wife in *North and South*, is far from being merely a caricature of the modern efficient professional woman. Her behaviour on the occasion of the lawyer's visit to the office met with Mrs. Gaskell's unqualified approval:

"Miss Galindo . . . was very clear-headed, and soon earned the respect of Mr. Smithson, my lady's lawyer from Warwick. Mr. Smithson knew Miss Galindo a little before, both personally and by reputation; but I don't think he was prepared to find her installed as steward's clerk, and, at first, he was inclined to treat her, in this capacity, with polite contempt. But Miss Galindo was both a lady and a spirited, sensible woman, and she could put aside her self-indulgence in eccentricity of speech and manner whenever she chose. Nay, more; she was usually so talkative, that if she had not been amusing and warm-hearted, one might have thought her wearisome occasionally. But to meet Mr. Smithson she came out daily in her Sunday gown; she said no more than was required in answer to his questions; her books and papers were in thorough order, and methodically kept; her statements of matters of fact accurate, and to be relied on. She was amusingly conscious of her victory over his contempt of a woman-clerk and his preconceived opinion of her unpractical eccentricity.

" 'Let me alone', said she, one day when she came in to sit awhile with me. 'That man is a good man—a sensible man—and I have no doubt he is a good lawyer; but he can't fathom women yet. I make no doubt he'll go back to Warwick, and never give credit again to those people who made him think me half-cracked to begin with. Oh, my dear, he did! He showed it twenty times worse than my poor dear master ever did. It was a form to be gone through to please my lady, and, for her sake, he would hear

[1] Pp. 129–30.

my statements and see my books. It was keeping a woman out of harm's way, at any rate, to let her fancy herself useful. I read the man. And, I am thankful to say, he cannot read me. At least, only one side of me. When I see an end to be gained, I can behave myself accordingly. Here was a man who thought that a woman in a black silk gown was a respectable, orderly kind of person; and I was a woman in a black silk gown. He believed that a woman could not write straight lines, and required a man to tell her that two and two made four. I was not above ruling my books, and had Cocker a little more at my fingers' ends than he had. But my greatest triumph has been holding my tongue. He would have thought nothing of my books, or my sums, or my black silk gown, if I had spoken unasked. So I have buried more sense in my bosom these ten days than ever I have uttered in the whole course of my life before. I have been so curt, so abrupt, so abominably dull, that I'll answer for it he thinks me worthy to be a man."[1]

There is no reason to suppose that Mrs. Gaskell was anxious for women to go in for professional careers. Miss Galindo's example shows, however, that she did not consider it improper for women to take up some kind of "masculine" work, provided that they did it well and kept a sense of propriety. As Mrs. Jameson had pointed out[2], women clerks were common in France. They were probably becoming less rare in England, too, but twelve years before the story of Miss Galindo's clerkship was written, there were few enough of them for Mrs. Jameson to wonder "who would countenance such an innovation on all our English ideas of feminine propriety?"

There are no more Miss Galindos in Mrs. Gaskell's stories. Hester Rose in *Sylvia's Lovers* (1863) is a shop-assistant, but we are told very little about her work. Nor does she do anything to improve her position, and Mrs. Gaskell makes no comment to indicate whether or not she means Mr. Forster's speech in Chapter XIV as an ironical comment on the way men look on a woman who earns her own living. The old Quaker says to his successors: "We have not thought it necessary to comment Hester Rose to you; if she had been a lad she would have had a third o' the business along wi' yo'. Being a woman, it's ill troubling her with a partnership; better give her a fixed salary till such time as she marries."[3] The fact that Mrs. Gaskell mentions this arrangement of

---

[1] Pp. 154–6.   [2] See p. 121.   [3] P. 151.

the Quaker brothers at all may be an indication that she considered it worthy of discussion, especially as the book belongs to a period when she had given up her habit of discussing problems in her own person as author. On the other hand, it should be remembered that when Mrs. Gaskell treated the conditions of women working for a living in her other stories, she did not pay so much attention to salaries and similar impersonal questions as to the duty of the employer to feel responsibility. Miss Galindo would, in fact, have much preferred to do her work for nothing as a personal service to My Lady Ludlow. On the whole, there seems to be little reason to suppose that Mrs. Gaskell had so far changed her attitude when she wrote *Sylvia's Lovers* as to consider the manner in which Hester Rose was provided for as of any great importance.

There are hardly more than two other professional careers for middle class women discussed in Mrs. Gaskell's books, namely those of sick-nurses and of governesses, and it is her treatment of the former only that shows any originality.

As Elizabeth Barrett Browning wrote in 1855, "since the siege of Troy and earlier, we have had princesses binding wounds with their hands; . . . Every man is on his knees before ladies carrying lint".[1] But that situation could happen only in times of war; public opinion of sick-nursing as a profession in peace time was anything but worshipful. *Eliza Cook's Journal* stated in a review of *Ruth* in March, 1853, that "the world does not mind what sort of creatures nurses are; they have only to attend on the sick and dying. Character, so it seems, does not matter there". According to Forster, Dickens' Mrs. Gamp[2] was not so much of a caricature as one would like to think. In his *Life of Charles Dickens* he writes:

"In his preface to the book he speaks of her as a fair representation at the time it was published, of the hired attendant on the poor in sickness; but he might have added that the rich were no better off, for Mrs. Gamp's original was in reality a person hired by a most distinguished friend of his own, a lady, to take charge of an invalid very dear to her."[3]

In Volume III of Harriet Martineau's *Deerbrook* (1839), Margaret nurses the cottager's family under the most nauseating circumstan-

---

[1] See Chap. III, p. 47.

[2] In *Martin Chuzzlewit*. (Jan., 1843–July, 1844.)

[3] Forster, *op. cit.*, p. 210.

ces, but she is only represented as doing this in an emergency. A "lady" could not yet think of taking up such a disgusting task as a vocation, and sick-nursing is not even mentioned among the possibilities for earning a living enumerated in the passage from *Deerbrook* quoted on p. 121, either for an educated woman or for one from the working classes. The *North British Review*, in an article on *Ruth* in May, 1853, called sick-nursing "perhaps the most painful . . . of all womanly tasks to the *lady*". According to Cook,

"The idea was widely prevalent . . . that for certain cases in hospital practice a modest woman was, from the nature of things, unsuited to act as a nurse . . . And in any case, whether women were fit or unfit by nature, it was certain that many, perhaps most, of the women actually engaged in nursing were unfit by character, and that a refined gentlewoman, who joined the profession, might thus find herself in unpleasant surroundings."[1]

Mrs. Gaskell, however, did not share such opinions, and the new element *Ruth* brought English fiction concerning the attitude towards sick-nursing was the fact that Mrs. Gaskell considered it a suitable vocation for an educated woman in normal times. It is true that in Ruth's case sick-nursing constitutes the final atonement for her early sin. Her first attempt to win back to respectability had been a failure. She could be accepted again among the "pure" only when "her humility was . . . below scorn", as *Eliza Cook's Journal* significantly expressed it in the review of *Ruth* quoted above. Mrs. Gaskell, however, definitely considered refinement and education an advantage rather than a disadvantage to a nurse. The reason may have been that she had probably seen much of the sufferings of the poor in Manchester during epidemics, when they were attended by the Mrs. Gamps of real life, whom she described in *Ruth* as "the most ignorant hirelings, too brutal to recognise the solemnity of Death".[2]

As appears from the letter to Mrs. Shaen quoted on pp. 119-20, Mrs. Gaskell was willing to let her daughter Meta become a nurse. The letter was written the year after *Ruth* appeared, and Mrs. Gaskell then realized the importance of some kind of training for this call-

---

[1] Cook, *op. cit.*, Vol. I, pp. 60–61.
[2] P. 296.

ing. It is probable that both her willingness to consent to Meta's plans and her insistence on previous training were the direct result of her contact with Florence Nightingale.[1] In *Ruth* she did not advocate any special *medical* training for nurses.[2] For her time, though, it was radical enough to consider a certain degree of education essential for a nurse. In Ruth's discussion with Jemima, the author contrasts her own opinion with that of most of her contemporaries. Ruth says,

" 'I have got a plan that makes me so happy! . . . the parish doctor . . . has asked me if I would go out as a sick nurse—he thinks he could find me employment.'

" 'You, a sick nurse!' said Jemima, involuntarily glancing over the beautiful lithe figure, and the lovely refinement of Ruth's face, . . . 'you were fitted for something better. Why, Ruth, you are better educated than I am!'

" '. . . I feel as if all my education would be needed to make me a good sick nurse.'

" 'Your knowledge of Latin, for instance', said Jemima, hitting, in her vexation at the plan, on the first acquirement of Ruth she could think of.

" 'Well!' said Ruth, 'that won't come amiss; I can read the prescriptions.'

" 'Which the doctors would rather you did not do.'

" 'Still, you can't say that any knowledge of any kind will be in my way, or will unfit me for my work.'

" 'Perhaps not. But all your taste and refinement will be in your way, and will unfit you.'

" 'You have not thought about this so much as I have, or you would not say so. Any fastidiousness I shall have to get rid of, and I shall be better without; but any true refinement I am sure I shall find of use; for don't you think that every power we have may be made to help us in any right work, whatever that is? Would you not rather be nursed by a person who spoke gently and moved quietly about, than by a loud bustling woman?' "[3]

---

[1] See Chap. III.

[2] Florence Nightingale, however, expressed her approval of the order in which Ruth proceeds in her new profession—first private nursing, then hospital work: "Miss Nightingale had said of 'Ruth': 'It is a beautiful work, and I like it *better still* than when I first read it.' She added the characteristic approving comment that Mrs. Gaskell 'had not made Ruth start at once as a hospital nurse, but arrive at it after much *other* nursing that came first.' " (A. W. Ward, Introduction to *Ruth* in the Knutsford edn.)

[3] Pp. 270-1.

Events prove Ruth to have been right in her estimation of the use to which she would be able to put her refinement and education. This is how Mrs. Gaskell describes Ruth's new work:

"she was at the call of all the invalids in the town. At first her work lay exclusively among the paupers. At first, too, there was a recoil from many circumstances, which impressed upon her the physical sufferings of those whom she tended ... she had enough self-command to control herself from expressing any sign of repugnance ... she found a use for all her powers. The poor patients themselves were unconsciously gratified and soothed by her harmony and refinement of manner, voice, and gesture ... She did not talk much about religion; but those who noticed her knew that it was the unseen banner which she was following. The low-breathed sentences which she spoke into the ear of the sufferer and the dying carried them upwards to God".[1]

That Mrs. Gaskell stressed the religious influence which a nurse might have on her patients is not surprising in a book like *Ruth*, in which the Christian attitude towards life is so strongly emphasized. It may have been partly under the influence of that novel that Miss Mary Stanley sent out a circular in 1854 "to suggest that nurses should be instructed, on the Kaiserswerth plan, in the art of administering religious comfort to patients".[2]

The originality in Mrs. Gaskell's didactic novels consists more in her introducing certain questions of topical interest in fiction than in any introduction of new ideas of her own. Although she did not uncritically adopt the ideas of others, and sometimes fought for her convictions with great courage, she was not the first to formulate the ideas, whether they referred to the duties of a wife, factory work for women, or sick nursing as a vocation. It should, however, be noted that *Ruth* was written before Florence Nightingale's efforts, both during and after the Crimean war had radically altered public opinion about sick-nursing, and popularized the idea of nursing as a suitable calling for educated women. When looking for a precedent for Ruth's nursing career it is natural, therefore, first to think of the different orders of *sœurs de charité*, with which Mrs. Gaskell was familiar, as appears from *The Poor Clare*, which was published in 1856. An institution

---

[1] Pp. 272–3.
[2] Cook, *op. cit.*, I: 443.

similar to those of the *sœurs de charité* was the one of Kaiserswerth in Germany, which Florence Nightingale visited in 1850 and 1851, and which had had some influence in England even before that time, as for instance when Mrs. Samuel Gurney worked out a scheme of home nursing based on what Elizabeth Fry—who died in 1845—had seen on a visit to that institution.[1] It became even more generally known in England in 1851, when a pamphlet, published anonymously but written by Florence Nightingale, appeared under the title *The Institution of Kaiserswerth on the Rhine, for the Practical Training of Deaconesses, under the Direction of the Rev. Pastor Fliedner, embracing the support and care of a Hospital, Infant and Industrial Schools, and a Female Penitentiary.*[2] In this pamphlet Florence Nightingale violently attacks conditions in English hospitals, calling them, in one instance, "a school, it may almost be said, for immorality and impropriety—inevitable where women of bad character are admitted as nurses, to become worse by their contact with male patients and young surgeons". She added: "We see the nurses drinking, we see the neglect at night owing to their falling asleep."[3] Although Mrs. Gaskell did not actually meet Florence Nightingale until after the publication of *Ruth*, it is possible that she had read the pamphlet, especially as she had apparently been acquainted with Florence Nightingale's parents for some time before she met their younger daughter.[4]

Sick-nursing and the special questions connected with the recruiting of that profession did not become a subject of great interest to the general public until the Crimean war, but another similar problem, that of sanitary conditions generally, had been frequently debated before that time, and much propaganda was being made in the late 'forties and early 'fifties for improved sanitary conditions. Mrs. Gaskell's "hero" Charles Kingsley, for instance, tried, by means of books and pamphlets, to show the necessity

---

[1] See Janet E. Courtney, *The Adventurous Thirties. A Chapter in the Women's Movement* (London, 1933), p. 192.

[2] That the institution was well-known in England about 1853 also appears from the review of *Ruth* in the *North British Review* of May that year, which mentions "the lowly workers of Kaiserswerth".

[3] P. 15, quoted by Cook, *op. cit.*, I: 442.

[4] See Chap. III.

for drastic reform. In her novels written with a purpose, Mrs.
Gaskell never seriously treated questions with which she was not
familiar from personal experience, and yet another incitement for
her to consider the necessity for a new attitude towards sick-nursing must not, therefore, be overlooked. When Mrs. Gaskell wrote
Ruth, her husband was beginning to take an active part in the work
for improved sanitary conditions, as is clear from a letter from
Catherine Winkworth to her sister Emily, dated Nov. 22, 1852,
in which she wrote:

"Mr. Gaskell is doing a great deal now . . . in two Committees. One is
for the better regulation of beerhouses and places of public amusement,
the other a Sanitary Committee to prepare the town for the next visit of
the cholera. Both the Dean and Canon Richson are saying everywhere
that he is the most valuable member on these Committees, . . . He clearly
feels that he has found his right place, and Lily[1] is proud that he is appreciated by people whose appreciation she cares for."[2]

The improvement of sanitary conditions was thus a subject
of great personal interest to Mrs. Gaskell at the time when she
wrote *Ruth*, and it seems likely that the description of the
cholera epidemic in that novel, and of the steps taken to mitigate
its consequences, was at least to a certain extent suggested to Mrs.
Gaskell by her husband's obvious interest in the subject at that
time.

When Miss Matty in *Cranford* is faced with the necessity of
earning her living, "teaching was, of course, the first thing that suggested itself. If Miss Matty could teach children anything, it would
throw her among the little elves in whom her soul delighted".[3]
Mrs. Gaskell herself was devoted to children, and during the period
when she was writing *Cranford* she could only consider a career

---

[1] Lily was the name by which Mrs. Gaskell was called in the family circle
and by intimate friends.

[2] Nov. 22, 1852. Shaen, *op. cit.*, p. 93. This letter seems to have been written very shortly after the time when Mrs. Gaskell wrote that part of *Ruth* which
deals with sick-nursing. The above-quoted discussion in *Ruth* of a nurse's qualifications comes immediately before the chapter concerning which Mrs. Gaskell
asked Forster's advice. (See Chap. II, p. 35.) His reply is dated 12 Nov., ten
days before Catherine Winkworth's letter.

[3] P. 139.

which meant constant intercourse with children a happy one. In another book from the same time, *Ruth*, she expresses the same conviction. The heroine of that novel regards her years as a nurse governess as a happy period:

"She sat in the room with Mary and Elizabeth during the Latin, the writing, and arithmetic lessons, which they received from masters; then she read, and walked with them, they clinging to her as to an elder sister; she dined with her pupils at the family lunch, and reached home by four. That happy home—those quiet days!"[1]

Other witnesses from the time, however, give very different evidence concerning the "happiness" of the lives of governesses and school teachers. Harriet Martineau meant to "put a governess into a novel,—a good one; and show how bad it is at best"[2], and the governess in *Deerbrook* sums up her life in the three words "I *am* solitary".[3] Mrs. Gaskell's friend, Mrs. Jameson, had been a governess for four years[4], and in *Memoirs and Essays* she assures her readers that "the occupation of a governess is sought merely through necessity, as the *only* means by which a woman not born in the servile classes *can* earn the means of subsistence".[5] She adds that "to fit a woman for a private governess, you must . . . educate her in the seclusion of a nunnery,—inure her to privation, discipline, drudgery";[6] Her final advice to a prospective governess is to "learn to live without sympathy, for you will not have it".[7]

The profession of private governessing was generally admitted to be such as nobody could be expected to adopt unless forced to do so by a harsh fate. Fredrika Bremer, who visited England in 1851, mentions the Governesses' Benevolent Institution, and states that many of those assisted by this Institution had been found in the lunatic asylums.[8] Many, she says, had no means of subsistence in their old age, and they often suffered from weak eyesight and

---

[1] P. 149.

[2] Martineau, *Autobiography*, III: 189.

[3] *Deerbrook*, III: 300.

[4] 1810–14.   [5] P. 254.

[6] P. 263.   [7] P. 289.

[8] *England om hösten 1851*, p. 142. The Institution was founded in 1843, and its Honorary Secretary, Mr. Laing, established a registry of teachers, which showed that in 1850 there were about twenty-one thousand governesses in England. (Fredrika Bremer gives their number as fifteen thousand.)

nervous complaints. A book which she wished that many would read was "S. C. Hall's charming story 'The aged Governess' ".[1] The governess was indeed beginning to get her share of the awakening humanitarian interest in the oppressed of all classes of society. The *Westminster Review* of April–July, 1850, for instance, in a review of M. Ernest Legouvé's *Histoire Morale des Femmes*, pleaded for better pay and less pity for governesses. This prevalent pity for the governess, which the writer of the article objected to as ineffective, had been aroused largely by fiction, where she had long been a favourite subject.[2]

Cranford was not the first story in which Mrs. Gaskell mentioned teaching as a profession for women. Susan Palmer in *Lizzie Leigh* does not seem to have needed any training for the teaching of small children, nor are we told anything about the work itself. In *The*

---

[1] *Ibid.*, p. 138. The correct title of the book, published in 1848, was *The Old Governess, a story.*

[2] As early as 1749, Sarah Fielding had chosen to treat the life of one in *The Governess, or the Little Female Academy*. Before the next century had begun, the two anonymous authors of *The Governess, or Courtland Abbey* (1797), and *The Governess, or Evening Amusement at a boarding school* (1800), had found the same source of inspiration. To take but a few examples from the next century, there were Maria Edgeworth's *The good governess, and other stories*, and Marguerite, Countess of Blessington's *The Governess* (1839). Jane Austen's *Emma* appeared as early as 1816. The great threat to the happiness of Jane Fairfax in that book is the fact that she may have to go out as a governess, in which case she must "retire from all the pleasures of life, of rational intercourse, equal society, peace and hope, to penance and mortification for ever". (Chap. XX.) Mrs. Ross published *The Governess; Or, Politics in Private Life*, in 1836. Harriet Martineau's *Deerbrook* has been quoted above, and Rachel MacCrindell's *The English Governess. A tale of real life* appeared in 1844. Thackeray made fun of the preposterous perfection of accomplishments which a governess had to claim for herself if she wanted a good situation, and one of the most successful characters in *Vanity Fair* (1847–8), Becky Sharp, is a governess.
Nowhere was the misery of a governess's life depicted with more intensity than in Charlotte Brontë's stories, which were all, without exception, about governesses and teachers. The outstanding example is, of course, *Jane Eyre* (1849), although Mrs. Pryor in *Shirley* is nearly crushed by her experiences as a governess, and only some of Charlotte Brontë's own letters convey a more hopeless sense of loneliness than the description of the heroine's vacation in the empty school in *Villette* (1853). *Agnes Grey* (1850) shows that Anne Brontë felt the humiliations which she had to submit to in her work almost as keenly as her more famous sister.

Moorland Cottage (1850) Mrs. Gaskell numbered the governess among the silent heroines of every-day life[1], but if one were to judge from *Mr. Harrison's Confessions*, which was published in the next year, Mrs. Gaskell held a very optimistic view of the financial side of school-keeping. The Misses Tomkinson are said to have been so poor at the time of their father's death that they had to set up a school. Then the elder sister tells Mr. Harrison that she has "saved nearly three thousand pounds".[2] It must not, however, be concluded that this represents a belief on Mrs. Gaskell's part. She was scrupulously correct when she wanted to draw attention to a special problem and made no mistake about the details of working conditions in factories, or about the laws concerning prostitutes or a mother's right of custody of her children; but those stories written only to entertain abound with small mistakes and discrepancies.[3] The amount of Miss Tomkinson's savings, therefore, shows only that Mrs. Gaskell did not, in that story, pay any special attention to school teaching as a profession.

She was not, however, unacquainted with the realities of a school teacher's or governess's life. Both her sisters-in-law taught for some time[4]; she was a friend of James and Harriet Martineau's eldest sister, to whose school in Liverpool she sent her second daughter Meta, as well as of the Misses Green, daughters of the

---

[1] Mrs. Burton told Maggie "how, though the lives of these women of old were only known to us through some striking glorious deed, they yet must have built up the temple of their perfection by many noiseless stories; how, by small daily offerings laid on the altar, they must have obtained their beautiful strength for the crowning sacrifice. And then she would turn and speak of those whose names will never be blazoned on earth—some poor maid-servant, or hard-worked artisan, or weary governess—who have gone on through life quietly, with holy purposes in their hearts, to which they gave up pleasure and ease, in a soft, still, succession of resolute days", (Pp. 295–6.)

[2] P. 431.

[3] The chronology of *Cranford* is hopeless; the elder Miss Browning in *Wives and Daughters* is called Sally, Clarinda, and Dorothy in different chapters of the book; Miss Monro in *A Dark Night's Work* remains forty years old for a considerable period; Catherine in *The Squire's Story* is stated to be her father's only child, though we afterwards read of his son and heir and her brother Nathaniel, etc., etc.

[4] "Eliza Gaskell and her sister Anne had apparently both become governesses." (Coolidge, *op. cit.*, p. 21.)

Unitarian minister of Knutsford, whose school her daughter Florence attended for some time. In 1857 she wrote to C. E. Norton:

"I like Mr. Y's marriage,—. . . and you don't understand what are our 'aristocratical feelings' when you make a sort of apology to Marianne about his marrying a governess. That does not hurt us in the least,—it would if he married an uneducated girl, a daughter of a rich *trades*person.—My dearest friends, all through my life, have been governesses, either past, present or future."[1]

One of these friends was Charlotte Brontë, and it is tempting to consider Mrs. Gaskell's growing acquaintance with the works and personality of the best-known governess in English literature as one reason for the gloomier view of a governess's or school teacher's life which we find in her later books. Before she wrote *A Dark Night's Work*, which appeared in 1863, she had published *The Life of Charlotte Brontë*, and that book could not have been written if its author had not been well aware of the hardships her friend had had to put up with in her capacity as teacher. She had also then come to be better acquainted with Mrs. Jameson, whose experiences seem to have been even worse than Charlotte Brontë's.[2]

It is true that Miss Monro in *A Dark Night's Work* has a quiet life and is treated like a friend when she becomes governess to Ellinor, in much the same way as Mrs. Prior in *Shirley*, but, like Charlotte Brontë's governess, "Miss Monro had been tossed about and overworked quite enough in her life".[3] Towards the end of her life she confessed "that she was tired of the perpetual teaching in which her life had been spent during the last thirty years", and we learn that "talking aloud had become her wont in the early years of her isolated life as a governess". She had no happy memories from her early situations: "Dear! how old Mrs. Cadogan used to hate that word 'mess', and correct her granddaughters for using it right before my face, when I knew I had said it myself only the moment before! Well! those days are all over now. God be thanked!"[4]

With the curious habit of some of the Victorians to adopt for

---

[1] Whitehill, *op. cit.*, letter 8.
[2] See pp. 44–5, 135.
[3] *A Dark Night's Work*, p. 16.
[4] *Ibid.*, p. 127.

their characters names out of famous contemporary stories, Mrs. Gaskell named one of the governesses in her last book Miss Eyre.[1] She was thirty-five, "a respectable woman, the daughter of a shop-keeper in the town, who had left a destitute family".[2] Even if Miss Eyre was not expected to be a very efficient teacher, her life was not always easy. She was "sensitive and conscientious", and we are told of "her silent endurance"[3], when "Betty /the servant/ ... took up her position as censor of all Miss Eyre's sayings and doings".[4] She "buzzed about her with the teasing pertinacity of a gnat, always ready to find fault", and "made cumbrous jokes at Miss Eyre's expense";[5]. On such occasions Miss Eyre is spoken of as the "silent, trembling governess".[6]

It is only as a way out of a desperate situation that Cynthia, also in *Wives and Daughters*, tells Molly: "I think I've been long enough here, and that I had better go out as a governess."[7] Aimée, in the same work, had no reason to agree with Miss Matty in her estimation of children as "little elves in whom her soul delighted", for she "had been nothing more than a French bonne, . . . very much tyrannised over by the rough little boys and girls she had in charge."[8]

The person in *Wives and Daughters* who most dislikes her work is Clare, Mrs. Kirkpatrick, who was later to become Mrs. Gibson. She

"was rather weary of girls as a class. All the trials of her life were connected with girls in some way. She was very young when she first became a governess, and had been worsted in her struggles with her pupils, in the

---

[1] George Eliot admired Mrs. Gaskell's books, and the names Amos and Milly *Barton* in *Scenes of Clerical Life* sound reminiscent of the elder writer's first novel. The fact that the heroine in *The Mill on the Floss* was called Maggy may have been one of the reasons why Swinburne suggested "that the whole story owed much to 'Mrs. Gaskell's beautiful story of the Moorland Cottage' " (Haldane, *George Eliot and her times*, p. 168). Charlotte Brontë, who had no admiration for Jane Austen, had yet intended to call her last, unfinished book *Emma*.

[2] *Wives and Daughters*, p. 45.

[3] *Ibid.*, p. 47.

[4] *Ibid.*, pp. 46–7.

[5] P. 47.   [6] P. 47.

[7] P. 320.   [8] P. 297.

first place she ever went to ... she was constantly encountering naughty or stubborn, or over conscientious, or severe judging, or curious and observant girls".[1]

A few lines further down we read of "her dislike to girls in the abstract as 'the plague of her life' ". Consequently, it does not surprise the reader that "Mrs Kirkpatrick accepted Mr. Gibson principally because she was tired of the struggle of earning her own livelihood".[2]

She has nothing but dislike for her work: "it was such a wonderful relief to feel that she need not struggle any more for a livelihood"[3], when Mr. Gibson has proposed to her, and she asks him not to call her Clare: "I can't bear 'Clare', it does so remind me of being a governess."[4]

Mrs. Kirkpatrick never had Miss Tomkinson's bright prospects of saving three thousand pounds out of school-fees: "a speedy marriage. She looked to it as a release from the thraldom of keeping school: keeping an unprofitable school, with barely pupils enough to pay for house rent and taxes, food, washing, and the requisite masters".[5]

If she was not a very efficient private governess, one reason was the conditions under which she was expected to teach. Lady Harriet tells her mother: "you used to call Clare away from us at the most critical times of our lessons, to write your notes, or add up your accounts, and the consequence is, that I'm about she most ill-informed girl in London,"[6] and another pupil excuses her by saying that "girls are severe judges, and certainly she had had an anxious enough lifetime."[7]

Mrs. Gaskell had been converted from the belief that the life of anybody who was allowed to teach children was necessarily one of delight, but she did not devote much energy to trying to improve the position of governesses. She had not a word to say about their insufficient salaries or bare and cold rooms. Anne Brontë had something to say about such matters in *Agnes Grey*, but, like Harriet Martineau, Mrs. Jameson and Charlotte Brontë,

---

[1] Pp. 130–31.   [2] P. 131.   [3] P. 113.
[4] P. 114.   [5] P. 128.
[6] P. 99.   [7] P. 100.

Mrs. Gaskell concentrated almost exclusively on the purely personal relationship between employer and governess. The chief drawback to the life of a governess was to her, not the bad pay or the inhospitable room, nor indeed the insufficient training and knowledge of an unwilling governess, but the lack of kindness and consideration on the part of the employer.

CHAPTER VI

FACTORY WORK FOR WOMEN

(See also Appendix I.)

(Both author and contemporary reviewers conscious of the propagandic nature of Mrs. Gaskell's factory tales. Standard by which Mrs. Gaskell judged the advantages or disadvantages of factory work for women in her early stories: its effect on the home; factory work made bad wives and mothers. Immorality of women factory workers. Disapproval of independence of young girls in factories. Mrs. Gaskell's attitude towards factory work for women criticized in contemporary reviews of Mary Barton. *New reason for disapproval of factory work for women in* North and South: *the effect on women's health.)*

In 1846, Mrs. Anna Jameson wrote in her *Memoirs and Essays*[1]: "After all that has been written, sung, and said of women, one has the perception that neither in prose nor in verse has she ever appeared as the labourer." However, both Harriet Martineau and Charlotte Elizabeth had devoted a large part of their production to the problems of working women, though the stories of both can more appropriately be classed as illustrations of various theories than as fiction proper. The governess had appeared in the novel at an early date; but Harriet Martineau had bitter memories of her attempt to introduce other working middle class characters into a novel.[2] Mrs. Gaskell thought it natural for her novel heroines to work. John Forster called her "a very original writer"[3], but her claim to originality rests more on the fact that she considered factory workers as worthy heroes and heroines of fiction than on any revolutionary ideas or abstract political and social theories. She did not, in her books, devote much thought to female wage-earners from the middle classes, but the problems connected with factory work for women worried her conscience.

---

[1] Chap. V.   [2] See p. 121.

[3] John Forster, *The Life of Charles Dickens*, p. 397.

Her first novel was wholly inspired by the situation of the working classes, which had aroused her pity. In the preface to the first edition of *Mary Barton*, she wrote[1]: "I had always felt a deep sympathy with the care-worn men, who looked as if doomed to struggle through their lives between work and want; tossed to and fro by circumstances, apparently in even a greater degree than other men".

It has been said that George Eliot's was the "first important contribution by women to the problem novel with a purpose. George Eliot was the first among us to realise the full power of fiction as a vehicle more persuasive, if not more powerful, than the pulpit".[2] Such a statement is hardly fair to the author of *Mary Barton*, *Ruth*, and *North and South*. As early as 1848 she wrote to Miss Ewart about *Mary Barton*: "I do think that we must all acknowledge that there are duties connected with the manufacturing system not fully understood as yet, and evils existing in relation to it which may be remedied in some degree, although we as yet do not know how; but surely there is no harm in directing the attention to the existence of such evils."[3] In 1853 she wrote to Mrs. Jameson about *Ruth:* "I think I have put the small edge of the wedge in, if only I have made people talk and discuss the subject a little more than they did."[4]

Not only was Mrs. Gaskell herself aware of the propagandic character of such novels as *Mary Barton* and *Ruth*, but so were some reviewers, who considered them more as sermons than as novels, and even complimented the publishers on their courage in printing such controversial stories. In April, 1849, *Fraser's Magazine* contained an article called "Recent Novels" (pp. 417–32), which said of *Mary Barton:* "Had we wit and wisdom enough, we would placard its sheets on every wall, and have them read aloud from every pulpit . . . the matter puts the manner out of sight . . . we must end, complimenting Messrs. Chapman and Hall on this

---

[1] October, 1848.

[2] R. Brimley Johnson, *The Women Novelists* (London, 1918).

[3] Copy of letter in the Brotherton Library.

[4] Mrs. Steuart Erskine, *Anna Jameson, Letters and Friendships* (London, 1915), p. 294.

fresh addition to the list of noble books which their courage has
given to the English public."[1]

Mrs. Gaskell made no secret of her intention of showing up
social evils, and she evidently considered factory work for women
an evil. Even though women in factories were not her chief preoccupation while she was writing *Mary Barton*, she was familiar
with their problems. She had ample opportunities of observing
and talking to factory girls, living as she did in Manchester. Most
of the girls in the Sunday school class which she taught lived near
Lower Mosley Street, one of the poorest parts of the manufacturing town.

"She was also much interested in the elder girls at Lower Mosley Street
Sunday School, and for several years carried out a plan of having them at
her own house once a month on Sunday afternoons, when she read and
talked with them, and, as one of these old pupils expressed it, 'seemed to
divine what was in our hearts before we spoke it' ",

wrote A. Cobden Smith in 1911.[2]

When Mrs. Gaskell wrote *Mary Barton*, her ideas about factory
work for women were far from original. Concerning "woman's
sphere" and "woman's natural work", she was influenced by the
stock arguments of the time.[3] The home was to her the centre of
interest. The standard by which she judged the advantages or
disadvantages of factory work for woman was its effects on her ability to be a good wife and mother. The appalling drinking habits
of the working classes were often stated to be the result of neglected
homes. The gin shops both in London and the large manufacturing towns were innumerable. Mrs. Beecher-Stowe records her impressions of them in *Sunny Memories of Foreign Lands*, a singularly
inappropriate title for the following passage:

"The ginshops . . . thronged with men, and women, and children, drinking destruction. Mothers go there with babies in their arms, and take what

---

[1] The author of this article even objected to novels being written for entertainment at all at that time. He says about *Percy; or the Old Love and the New.
By the author of the Hen-pecked Husband*: "Most respectable and refined, all
of Percy is, no doubt—but—but—but—Rome is burning, let the fiddles be silent!"

[2] A. Cobden Smith, "Mrs. Gaskell and Lower Mosley Street". In the *Sunday School Quarterly*, January, 1911.

[3] See Appendix I.

turns the mother's milk to poison. Husbands go there, and spend the money that their children want for bread, and multitudes of boys and girls of the age of my own ... no pretence at social exhilaration, nothing but hogsheads of spirits, and people going in to drink. The number of them that I passed seemed to me absolutely appalling."[1]

Mrs. Beecher-Stowe wrote about London, but conditions were not very different in a large town like Manchester:

"In 1850 Manchester, with its 400,000 inhabitants, had 475 'publics' and 1,143 beer houses ... On Saturday night, after the workman's weekly pay had been taken, it was a revolting sight for a sensitive man to witness the ghastly scenes at the tavern doors. Drunken women by the hundred lay about higgledy-piggledy in the mud, hollow-eyed and purple-cheeked, their ragged clothing plastered with muck."[2]

Mrs. Gaskell felt strongly on the subject and often referred to it in her stories. In *Libbie Marsh's Three Eras* Anne jokingly tells Libbie that she would rather have Bob tipsy than any one else sober, but Libbie protests:

"Oh! Anne Dickson, hush! you don't know yet what it is to have a drunken husband. I have seen something of it: father used to get fuddled, and, in the long run, it killed mother, let alone—oh! Anne, God above only knows what the wife of a drunken man has to bear. Don't tell, 'said she, lowering her voice, 'but father killed our little baby in one of his bouts; mother never looked up again, nor father either, for that matter, only his was in a different way ... Oh! ... never say aught lightly of the wife's l ot whose husband is given to drink!"[3]

A well-kept home and a good-tempered wife and mother seemed to Mrs. Gaskell necessary conditions if people were to be kept out of the gin shops. She often emphasized the importance of a good home in this respect. She naturally did so in her two Sunday school stories *Hand and Heart* (1849) and *Bessy's Troubles at Home* (1852). Bessy's mother in the latter story is worried about her sons when she has to go to hospital:

"they're but young lads, and there's a deal of temptation to take them away from their homes, if their homes are not comfortable and pleasant to them.

[1] Mrs. Harriet Beecher-Stowe, *Sunny Memories of Foreign Lands* (London, 1854), p. 198.

[2] F. Wey, *A Frenchman sees the English in the 'Fifties*, 117/18, quoted by Arthur Bryant in *English Saga (1840-1940)* (London, 1940), p. 144.

[3] Pp. 472-3.

It's that, more than anything, I've been fretting about all the time I've been ill—that I've lost the power of making this house the cleanest and brightest place they know."[1]

In *Hand and Heart* Tom's uncle retires to the Spread Eagle when his neglected home and his scolding wife seem intolerable. But in the end, when Tom's example has succeeded in reforming his aunt, "Her husband is softened by the additional cleanliness and peace of his home. He does not now occasionally take refuge in a public-house, to get out of the way of noisy children, an unswept hearth, and a scolding wife".[2] Lame Harry in the same story "was supported by his daughter's earnings; but as she worked in a factory, he was much alone".[3]

Mrs. Gaskell did not believe in the possibility for a woman to be at the same time a factory worker and a good wife and mother. Mrs. Wilson in *Mary Barton* quotes her own example as a warning to Mary:

" 'If you'll believe me, Mary, there never was such a born goose at house-keeping as I were; and yet he married me! I had been in a factory sin' five years old a'most, and I knew nought about cleaning, or cooking, let alone washing and such like work. The day after we were married, he went to his work at after breakfast, and says he, 'Jenny, we'll ha' th' cold beef, and potatoes, and that's a dinner for a prince'. I were anxious to make him comfortable, God knows how anxious. And yet I'd no notion how to cook a potato. I know'd they were boiled, and know'd their skins were taken off, and that were all. So I tidied my house in a rough kind o' way, then I looked at that very clock up yonder', pointing at one that hung against the wall, 'and I seed it were nine o'clock, so, thinks I, th' potatoes shall be well boiled at any rate, and I gets 'em on th' fire in a jiffy (that's to say, as soon as I could peel 'em, which were a tough job at first), and then I fell to unpacking my boxes! and at twenty minutes past twelve, he comes home, and I had the beef ready on th' table, and I went to take the potatoes out o' th' pot; but oh! Mary, th' water had boiled away, and they were all a nasty brown mess, as smelt through all the house. He said nought, and were very gentle; but oh! Mary, I cried so that afternoon, I shall ne'er forget it; no, never. I made many a blunder at after, but none that fretted me like that.'
" 'Father does not like girls to work in factories', said Mary.
" 'No, I know he does not; and reason good. They oughtn't to go at after they 're married, that I'm very clear about. I could reckon up'

(counting with her finger), 'ay, nine men, I know, as has been driven to th' public-house by having wives as worked in factories; good folk, too, as thought there was no harm in putting their little ones out at nurse, and letting their house go all dirty, and their fires all out; and that was a place as was tempting for a husband to stay in, was it? He soon finds out gin-shops, where all is clean and bright, and where th' fire blazes cheerily, and gives a man a welcome as it were.' "[1]

Direct quotations from the characters in her books must of course not always be supposed to express the author's own opinions, though it seems safe to do so in this instance, as she so often stressed the importance of a cheerful, well-ordered home. Alice, of whose character and good sense Mrs. Gaskell obviously approves, is as much against women in factories as the young hero of *Mary Barton*, Jem: "I wish our Jem could speak a word to th' Queen, about factory work for married women. Eh! but he comes it strong when once yo get him to speak about it. Wife o' his'n will never work away fra' home."[2]

In another story from the same time, *Libbie Marsh's Three Eras* (1847), the opinion is again expressed that factory workers made bad wives. Anne says about her future husband: "he does not think I shall make him a good wife, for I know nought about house matters, wi' working in a factory".[3]

It is remarkable that in *Mary Barton* Mrs. Gaskell stresses only the disadvantages for a man to marry a factory worker. He is re-presented as conferring a favour on his wife by choosing her in spite of her work, and neither of them mentions the better finan-cial position of a household where both husband and wife might have kept their work, though this seems to have been generally taken into account by the workpeople at that time. In this respect she was of exactly the same opinion as Hickson in his Handloom Weavers' Report of 1840.[4]

But Mrs. Gaskell's disapproval of factory work for women was not confined to the case of wives and mothers, for, living as she did in the middle of a manufacturing town she did not share the common misapprehension that the majority of the women in fac-

---

[1] Chap. X, p. 120.
[2] P. 121.   [3] P. 472.
[4] See Appendix I, pp. 235–6.

tories were married.[1] John Barton is stated never to have "left off disliking a factory life for a girl, on more accounts than one"[2], and in *The Heart of John Middleton* (1850) the hero says of Nelly: "She must earn her living; was it to be as a farm-servant or by working at the mill? I knew enough of both kinds of life to make me tremble for her."[3] The author probably meant both instances as cautious allusions to the temptatiohs to immorality which were inherent in the manufacturing system according to the belief of many, including Mrs. Gaskell's intimate friend Emily Winkworth.[4] However, she refrained from any accusations of immorality against the mill-owners. It is true that the seducer in *Ruth* is the only son of a manufacturer, but Ruth herself is not a factory worker. The seduced woman in *Mary Barton*, Esther, works in a factory, but her seducer is an officer. Considering the outcry over *Mary Barton*, and later over *Ruth*, Mrs. Gaskell probably acted wisely in not openly treating Esther's fate as an evil caused by the factory system. However, one of her otherwise appreciative critics, Maria Edgeworth, objected to the story of Esther for this very reason. On December 27, 1848, she wrote in a letter to her friend and Mrs. Gaskell's elder cousin, Miss Holland[5]: "I think that some of the miserables might be left out—For instance *Esther* who is no good and does no good to Mary or anybody else—nor to the story —she might be and may be in every town of the Empire as well as at Manchester. Her faults are not the results of manufacturing wrongs from masters or evils of men—."

In one sense, Mrs. Gaskell did blame the factory system for Esther's temptations. Her fall from virtue is made possible only by the absence of all restraining authority that she enjoys. John Barton even calls the good wages of girls "the worst of factory work" for them, and all his apprehensions about his sister-in-law eventually come true. He tells Wilson about the time when she first went to the factory:

---

[1] See Appendix I, pp. 234–5.

[2] P. 32.

[3] P. 319.

[4] See Appendix I, pp. 237–8.

[5] *Bulletin*, pp. 108–11. When Miss Edgeworth wrote the letter she did not know the name of the author of *Mary Barton*, which was published anonymously.

" 'That's the worst of factory work for girls. They can earn so much when work is plenty, that they can maintain themselves anyhow. My Mary shall never work in a factory, that I'm determined on. You see Esther spent her money in dress, thinking to set off her pretty face; and got to come home so late at night, that at last I told her my mind; my missis thinks I spoke crossly, but I meant right, for I loved Esther, if it was only for Mary's sake. Says I, 'Esther, I see what you'll end at with your artificials, and your fly-away veils, and stopping out when honest women are in their beds; you'll be a street-walker, Esther, and then, don't you go to think I'll have you darken my door, though my wife is your sister.' So says she, . . . 'I'll pack up and be off now, . . .' . . . she said (and at that time I thought there was sense in what she said) 'we should be much better friends if she went into lodgings, and only came to see us now and then'."[1]

Mrs. Gaskell shared the failure of the author of *The Manufacturing Population of England*[2] to see any advantage in the increasing independence of young girls working in factories. In the end Esther herself regrets the fact that she had earned money too easily in the factory. When she tells Jem about her failure to live on the money given to her by her seducer when he leaves her, she says, "I might have done better with the money; I see now. But I did not know the value of it then. Formerly I had earned it easily enough at the factory, and as I had no more sensible wants, I spent it on dress and on eating".[3]

There is a surprising omission in Mrs. Gaskell's earlier factory tales. She makes no mention in them of the bad effects on women's health which at least some kinds of factory work were generally admitted to have.[4] Nor does she give any detailed descriptions of the work itself to show that proper precautions were not taken to prevent accidents. Mrs. Wilson in *Mary Barton* had been crippled by an accident in the factory, but this is said to have happened before the law was passed that obliged manufacturers to have guards put on all moving machinery. The reason for this omission seems to be that when Mrs. Gaskell discusses factory work for women

[1] P. 17.
[2] See Appendix I, p. 238.
[3] Pp. 158-9.
[4] See Appendix I, p. 235. Concerning the almost entire omission in Mrs. Gaskell's factory stories of any serious discussion of child labour, see Chapter IX, p. 229, n. 3.

in her early stories, the centre of interest is the home. She does not consider the effects of the work on women themselves, but only so far as it influenced the welfare of their husbands or children, or—if they were unmarried—their possibilities of becoming good wives and mothers. Her chief objection to factory work for women was therefore, in her early tales, the fact that it took the women away from the home, not the fact that it might injure their health. As regards the sanitary conditions in factories, she may also at first have accepted the arguments brought forward in the Handloom Weavers' Report of 1840[1], according to which the working conditions were more favourable in a factory than in a home where weaving and spinning were carried on. That Mrs. Gaskell was not ignorant of the actual conditions in factories appears from *Libbie Marsh's Three Eras* (1847). She knew exactly how hot the rooms were in which spinners had to work: 75 to 80 degrees, the same temperature given by Baker, in his Report of 1843.[2] The effect of these unhealthy conditions on the Dixons is, however, stated to be mental rather than bodily: "But they were fine spinners, in the receipt of good wages; and confined all day in an atmosphere ranging from seventy-five to eighty degrees. They had lost all natural, healthy appetite for simple food, and, having no higher tastes, found their greatest enjoyment in their luxurious meals."[3]

One looks in vain in Mrs. Gaskell's stories for an instance of explicit approval of factory work for women. She saw nothing but evil in this new field for woman's activities, with its consequent breaking up of the traditional forms of home life. If she had believed in the efficacy of legislation, she would probably gladly have supported the demands for the withdrawal of women workers from factories made by the Short Time Committee of 1841.[4] Considering the actual working conditions in factories at the time, her criticism seems moderate to a modern reader, but it did not seem so at the time of the publication of *Mary Barton*. Though most reviewers naturally devoted their attention to other aspects of the

---

[1] See Appendix I, p. 235.
[2] See Appendix I, p. 235.
[3] P. 453.
[4] See Appendix I, p. 234.

book, some criticized the author's attitude towards factory work for women.

The *British Quarterly Review* printed a violent attack on her in February, 1849. After telling his readers that "the labouring population engaged in the cotton manufactures of Lancashire have met with a somewhat disproportionate amount both of attention and compassion", the writer of the fourteen-page article accuses the author of *Mary Barton* of a limited experience and hasty generalisations made under the influence of Lord Ashley's speeches or Disraeli's *Sybil*. He even doubted the honesty of the writers of social novels: "More than one modern writer of fiction . . . need to be admonished, that to exhibit a caricature, which they cannot but know that the majority of their readers will accept as a portrait is nothing less than an act of dishonesty." He entirely disagreed with Mrs. Gaskell's attitude towards women factory workers, for he thought that "There are, perhaps, few employments in which female industry can be employed where the labour is so slight; compared with the drudgery of dressmakers' apprentices it is mere play; nor is there anything about it, more than other departments of female industry, which has a necessary tendency to unfit young women for the discharge of domestic duties". The article concludes with an entire condemnation of *Mary Barton:* "there is a class of misrepresentations which are mischievous, mainly because actual facts may be met with answering to them . . . It is with these that we feel inclined, . . . to class the work which has been the subject of our review".

The *Prospective Review*, also in February, 1849, was on the whole laudatory, although it expressed the opinion that Mrs. Gaskell had drawn too much attention to imperfect social conditions, and pointed out that "The mischiefs and abuses incidental to its first rapid development, especially in the employment of women and children, have exposed it to a searching scrutiny above every other branch of industry".

The *Manchester Guardian* wrote in a review of *Mary Barton*[1]: "Women must be able to enter the factories . . . *It is worse than idle* to regret that women are employed in factories."

---

[1] Feb. 28, 1849. Quoted by Dullemen, *op. cit.,* p. 196.

In a letter to a friend, Maria Edgeworth objected to the absence of a practical scheme of reform in the book: "*Emigration* is the only resource pointed out at the end of this work, and this is only an escape from the evils not a remedy nor any tendency to reparation or improvement."[1]

That, in *Mary Barton*, Mrs. Gaskell considered only the effects that factory work for women had on the home is quite consistent with the attitude towards a wife's problems that she showed in her first stories, when she uncritically adopted the ideal from the "darkness where obedience was the only seen duty of women".[2] She then saw them only as appendages to men, without any intrinsic value in themselves. But her attitude gradually changed, and she came to think of women as independent beings, whose duty it is to have a will of their own and to accept moral responsibility.[3] Thus, in 1853, the year when the story of a wife who rebels against her husband appeared in *Ruth*, Mrs. Gaskell began writing of the factory system in *North and South* from a somewhat different point of view than she had done in her first novel. In *North and South* there is no longer much insistence on the disastrous effects of factory work for women on the home. It is mentioned, but only in passing.[4] Nor does Mrs. Gaskell protest against or even comment on the fact that women preferred, to domestic service, "the better wages and greater independence of working in a mill"[5], a fact which had distressed her in *Mary Barton*. Instead, she concentrates her attention on a point which she had omitted in her earlier work, the disregard for their workers' health which many mill-owners displayed.

Bessy Higgins, who dies as a result of the unhealthful conditions under which she is obliged to work, is employed in a carding-room, which implies that she performed the work which shared with "wet spinning" a reputation for being the most dangerous in the

---

[1] Letter to Miss Holland, Dec. 27, 1848. (*Bulletin*, pp. 108–11.)

[2] See p. 65.

[3] Cf. Chap. IV.

[4] Bessy, the factory worker, says about her sister: "who has she had to teach her what to do about a house? No mother, and me at the mill till I were good for nothing but scolding her for doing badly what I didn't know how to do a bit". (P. 111.)

[5] P. 77.

textile industry. This is what she tells Margaret about her work in the factory:

" 'I think I was well when mother died, but I have never been rightly strong sin' somewhere about that time. I began to work in a carding-room soon after, and the fluff got into my lungs and poisoned me.'

" 'Fluff?' said Margaret inquiringly.

" 'Fluff', repeated Bessy. 'Little bits, as fly off fro' the cotton, when they're carding it, and fill the air till it looks all fine white dust. They say it winds round the lungs, and tightens them up. Anyhow, there's many a one as works in a carding-room, that falls into a waste, coughing and spitting blood, because they're just poisoned by the fluff.'

" 'But can't it be helped?' asked Margaret.

" 'I dunno. Some folk have a great wheel at one end o' their carding-rooms to make a draught, and carry off th' dust; but that wheel costs a deal of money—five or six hundred pound, maybe, and brings in no profit; so it's but a few of th' masters as will put 'em up; and I've heard tell o' men who didn't like working in places where there was a wheel, because they said as how it made 'em hungry, at after they'd been long used to swallowing fluff, to go without it, and that their wage ought to be raised if they were to work in such places. So between masters and men th' wheels fall through. I know I wish there'd been a wheel in our place, though.' "[1]

It has been pointed out by most of Mrs. Gaskell's critics that she showed more understanding for the mill-owner's point of view in *North and South* than in *Mary Barton*, and some have even asserted that she wrote the latter book chiefly to restore the balance in the opinions concerning the factory system which she had expressed in *Mary Barton*. It might be argued that in the passage quoted above Mrs. Gaskell divides the blame between masters and men, but it should be noted that the reason given for the workers' opposition to the introduction of safeguards is ignorance, whereas that of the masters is a wish for gain.

While Mrs. Gaskell was writing *North and South*, Dickens was at work on *Hard Times*. Apparently they discussed some factory problems connected with their stories[2], but on the whole it seems unlikely that Dickens had any influence on *North and South* in so

---

[1] Pp. 109–10.

[2] In a letter to John Forster (now in the British Museum), dated only "Sunday", Mrs. Gaskell wrote: "I wrote to Dickens, & he says he is not going to strike,—altogether his answer sets me at ease,—." In the letter from Dickens to

far as it treated factory work. It is true that they both expressed disapproval of Trades Unions, but Mrs. Gaskell naturally knew much more than Dickens both about factories and the women who worked in them, as appears, for instance, from a comparison of the disagreeable but lifelike Mrs. Boucher, or the two Higgins sisters in *North and South*, with Rachel, the factory worker in *Hard Times*, who is just another of Dickens' lifeless women saints of the same type as Agnes in *David Copperfield*. It is far more probable that Charles Kingsley's *Alton Locke* (1850) with its drastic description of the tailors' workroom in Chapter II[1], had some influence both on Mrs. Gaskell's description of the sewing-room in *Ruth*, and the risks to their health which workers had to take in carding-rooms.

It should also be noted that Mr. Gaskell was taking a special interest in sanitary questions at the time when *Ruth* and *North and South* were written, as appears both from Catherine Winkworth's letter to her sister in 1852[2], and from Dickens' letter to Mr. Gaskell on February 5, 1854.[3]

When Mrs. Gaskell wrote *Mary Barton*, she thought that evils existing in the manufacturing system might be remedied in some degree, "although we as yet do not know how".[4] Therefore her aim had only been "to give utterance to the agony which, from time to time, convulses this dumb people; the agony of suffering without the sympathy of the happy", as she wrote in the preface to *Mary Barton*. Consequently, as Maria Edgeworth pointed out, there is no practical scheme of reform in the book. When she wrote *Ruth*—which does not, however, treat factory problems— she had gone farther and hoped to insert "the small edge of the wedge" of reform.[4] In the still later *North and South*, she pointed to very special evils which might easily be remedied, instead of

---

which she refers (April 21st, 1854, printed in *The Letters of Charles Dickens.* Edited by his sister-in-law and his eldest daughter.) he had asked her to look at his story in order to see how far they were intending to treat the same material.

[1] In Chap. VIII there is also a sick girl, "coughing and expectorating", though the reader is told nothing about her early history.

[2] Quoted on p. 134.

[3] See p. 35, n. 1.

[4] See p. 143.

generally condemning all factory work for women, as she had done in *Mary Barton*, but she was still vague concerning actual schemes of reform. Noting the need of the workers for better and cheaper food, she makes Mr. Thornton in *North and South* establish a kitchen in his factory, to be run by them as their own affair. She also draws attention to the necessity of proper safeguards in the workrooms, but, typically, she nowhere demands Parliamentary interference to enforce the installation of safety devices.

North and South was first published serially in *Household Words*. A natural result of this was that reviewers showed much less interest in it when it was published in book-form in 1855 than had been the case with *Mary Barton* and *Ruth*.

The *Athenaeum*, though objecting to Mrs. Gaskell's treatment of moral problems in fiction, found Bessy one of the most successful portraits in the tale:

"Few things have been met in modern fiction more touching than the fading away of the poor girl to whom Margaret Hale attaches herself on removing from the South to a manufacturing town in Lancashire ... if they be class sympathies such as propel her to a somewhat disproportionate exposure of the trials and sufferings of the poor, her excess is a generous one, and not accompanied by that offensive caricaturing of her more 'conventional' heroes and heroines ..."[1]

Less than ten years after Mrs. Gaskell's death the author of an article entitled "Mrs. Gaskell and her Novels" in *Every Saturday*[2] expressed his conviction that the recent alterations for the better in factory conditions were partly due to Mrs. Gaskell's efforts:

"But even a cursory perusal of her works will show that Mrs. Gaskell must have deeply studied most of the questions affecting her sex, that of female labour being perhaps the most paramount ... The keenest anguish such a nature as hers could feel would arise from the fact that she could do so little in the way of actual amelioration of the condition of the factory girls she saw dying around her ... owing to the ... efforts of Mrs. Gaskell and others ... a very great and praiseworthy reform has been accomplished ... a greater rapprochement between employers and employed ... To this end the mental labors of the author of 'Mary Barton' must have largely conduced in an indirect manner."

---

[1] April 7, 1855.
[2] Feb. 28, 1874.

CHAPTER VII

DOMESTIC SERVANTS

(Domestic servants in Mrs. Gaskell's tales treated in accordance with the literary tradition. Living models for her domestic servants. Emphasis on a mistress's responsibility for her servants. Domestic servants in a factory town.)

NEEDLEWOMEN

(Actual conditions. Often treated in literature. In Mrs. Gaskell's early tales resignation under bad conditions is praised. In her later stories, her denunciations of the conditions and the responsibility of the employer and the upper classes become much stronger, owing to the influence of the current debate, especially Mayhew's articles in the Morning Chronicle.*)*

DOMESTIC SERVANTS

Mrs. Gaskell did not think factory work desirable either for married women or for young girls, but there were not many other ways open to an uneducated young woman who had to earn a living. The obvious alternatives was domestic service and sewing.

According to a long-established literary tradition, servants were used in fiction chiefly in two ways. They could either provide comic relief in a story, or serve as confidants and faithful assistants to their masters and mistresses. Most of the domestic servants in Mrs. Gaskell's tales conform to this tradition. Some, like Martha in *Cranford* and Sally in *Ruth* are of the same literary family as Dickens' Peggotty in *David Copperfield*. Others, like the determined, practical Amante in *The Grey Woman*, give the impression of female Sancho Panzas or Sam Wellers. In drawing their portraits, however, Mrs. Gaskell did not only follow a literary pattern but made use of living models as well. Thus, Sally in *Ruth* is partly drawn from the old Brontë servant "Tabby", who "claimed to be looked upon as a humble friend", although "Miss Brontë . . . found it somewhat difficult to manage, as Tabby expected to be informed of all the family concerns, and yet had grown so deaf that what was repeated to her became known to whoever might be in or about the house".[1] Sally too "had become very deaf; yet she was uneasy and jealous if she were not informed of all the family thoughts, plans, and proceedings, which often had (however private in their details) to be shouted to her at the full pitch of the voice".[2] The description of Sally's airs of superiority, as a Church of England woman condescending to serve in a dissenting household, may also have had some basis in fact, coming as it does from the pen of a Unitarian minister's wife.[3]

But Mrs. Gaskell did not use domestic servants in her books exclusively for the sake of the story. As in the case of factory workers and dressmakers, her social interest and her desire to reform imperfect conditions induced her, in a few instances, to treat the problem of domestic service in her stories from a less traditional point of view.

She had had personal experience both of devoted servants and of the difficulty of finding domestic servants of suitable character in a town like Manchester. The faithful family retainer who appears in many of her stories was a character familiar to her from real life. She wrote about one of her servants to C. E. Norton on February 5, 1865: "Hearn is still with us. Of course she is, after 22 years of service, she is as much one of the family as any one of us."[4] She was remarkably free from class prejudices and treated her servants as friends, not only in the case of Hearn. About another maid she wrote in her *Diary* on December 9, 1837: "We have lost our dear servant Betsy, who was obliged to leave us, being wanted at home in consequence of the death of a sister. But we still keep her as a friend, and she has been to stay with us several weeks in autumn." Seeking to spread this idea of servants treated like members of the family she wrote in one of the articles

---

[1] Chap. V, p. 49.

[2] Pp. 263.

[3] The Gaskells do not seem to have particularly desired their servants to be of their own religious persuasion. In a letter (now in the Rylands Library, Manchester), to Mrs. Fielden, dated from Plymouth Grove, Manchester, May 28th, Mrs. Gaskell wrote about a new servant: "Of course I shall gladly allow her to go to Church; all our servants go there, excepting a German maid, and one who is an Independent."

[4] Whitehill, *op. cit.*

on "French Life" in *Fraser's Magazine* under the heading "February, 1862":

> "I do not dislike this plan of living in a flat, especially as it is managed in Paris . . . there is the moral advantage of uniting mistresses and maids in a more complete family bond . . . French people appear to me to live in this pleasant kind of familiarity with their servants—a familiarity which does not breed contempt, in spite of proverbs."[1]

It might be mentioned in this context that Mrs. Gaskell held strong views about a mistress's responsibility for her servants, and tried to inspire her daughters with the same feeling. On one occasion her daughter Florence had trouble with a maid. Mrs. Gaskell wrote about this to her eldest daughter: "so disappointed in Margaret. She must have done something *very* bad to be turned off at a moment's notice. I hope Florence will be very careful what sort of a character she gives her. It ought to be quite *true*, but on the *kind* side of truth".[2] This letter must have been written in one of the last years of Mrs. Gaskell's life, as her third daughter was evidently no longer a child. I have found no evidence concerning Mrs. Gaskell's early attitude towards the question of a mistress's responsibility for her servants except what can be concluded from her works. As is the case concerning several other problems in her stories, Mrs. Gaskell's treatment of this subject shows a distinct development, from a simple uncommented statement of an unsatisfactory state of things towards an analysis and explicit condemnation of the attitude of mind that brought it about.

In Mrs. Gaskell's early story *Lizzie Leigh* Lizzie's mother tells her son:

> "I had a strong mind to cast it up to her, that she should ha' sent my poor lass away, without telling on it to us first; but she were in black, and looked so sad I could na' find in my heart to threep it up. But I did ask her a bit about our Lizzie. The master would have turned her away at a day's warning (he's gone to t'other place; I hope he'll meet wi' more mercy there than he showed our Lizzie—I do), and when the missus asked her should she write to us, she says Lizzie shook her head; . . . I'd got a trace of my child—the missus thought she'd gone to the workhouse to be nursed";[3]

---

[1] The Knutsford edn, Vol. 7, p. 609.
[2] Letter in the Brotherton Library.
[3] P. 397.

The author has no indignant comment here about the mistress's neglect of necessary supervision while Lizzie was still in her service or about her indifference to the girl's fate after she had left her house. Nor was Miss Simmonds in *Mary Barton* blamed for the conditions in her establishment. It would seem that the debate on social questions to which Mayhew's articles in the *Morning Chronicle* lent a renewed intensity, made Mrs. Gaskell reconsider several social problems. Mayhew wrote about maid-servants:

"Female servants are far from being a virtuous class. They are badly looked after by their mistresses as a rule, although every dereliction from the paths of propriety by them will be visited with the heaviest displeasure, and most frequently be followed by dismissal of the most summary description, without the usual month's warning, to which so much importance is usually attached by both employer and employed."[1]

Significantly, Mrs. Gaskell's expressed opinions of an employer's moral responsibility for the young girls in her service—not domestic servants in this case, but a dressmaker's apprentices—are much more explicit in *Ruth* than they had been in her earlier stories. She now denounces Mrs. Mason's attitude in no uncertain terms:

"Mrs. Mason was careless about the circumstances of temptation into which the girls intrusted to her as apprentices were thrown, but severely intolerant if their conduct was in any degree influenced by the force of these temptations. She called this intolerance 'keeping up the character of her establishment'. It would have been a better and more Christian thing if she had kept up the character of her girls by tender vigilance and maternal care."[2]

Living as she did in a large manufacturing town, Mrs. Gaskell had experienced the difficulty of finding domestic servants, which was mentioned as typical of Lancashire in official reports of the time.[3] This fact naturally induced her to inquire into the reasons

---

[1] Mayhew, *op. cit.*, p. 257.

[2] *Ruth*, p. 38.

[3] See Appendix I, p. 236. In the letter to Mrs. Fielden quoted on p. 157 n. 3, Mrs. Gaskell writes about her plan to go to Alderley and Smallwood to engage a cook. She also gives the information that the Gaskell family kept five women servants and an out-of-door man. The Hale family in *North and South* also struggle with the difficulty of finding domestic servants. Girls from a factory town, with their alleged loose morals and lack of proficiency in domestic work,

that decided most young girls in the town to choose factory work in preference to domestic work. She well knew that the position of servants was far from ideal in many households. When some of her *Household Words* stories were republished in 1859 under the title *Round the Sofa*, she wrote an introductory story, in which she tells the reader that she doubted that the discontented looking maid, Phenice, "ever received wages from the Mackenzies". In *Mary Barton* she gives an account of the objections to domestic service which she had probably often heard both from factory workers and their daughters. In her first novel, she often expresses her opinions in her own person as author, and she condemns John Barton's objections as "exaggerated", but leaves it to the reader to judge whether there is any foundation for them in reality. This method of expounding the actual facts and appealing to the consciences of those concerned always seemed to Mrs. Gaskell best suited to bring about desirable reforms. John Barton

"with his ideas and feelings towards the higher classes, . . . considered domestic servitude as a species of slavery; a pampering of artificial wants on the one side, a giving up of every right of leisure by day and quiet rest by night on the other. How far his strong exaggerated feelings had any foundation in truth, it is for you to judge. I am afraid that Mary's determination not go to service arose from far less sensible thoughts on the subject than her father's. Three years of independence of action (since her mother's death such a time had now elapsed) had little inclined her to submit to rules as to hours and associates, to regulate her dress by a mistress's ideas of propriety, to lose the dear feminine privileges of gossiping with a merry neighbour, and working night and day to help one who was sorrowful".[1]

NEEDLEWOMEN

In its review of *Mary Barton*, the *British Quarterly Review* wrote about factory work for women that "compared with the drudgery of dressmakers' apprentices it is mere play".[2] Their work had

were not generally welcomed in a Victorian middle- class home. The Hales in *North and South* "could hear of no girl to assist her; all were at work in the factories; at least, those who applied were well scolded by Dixon, for thinking that such as they could ever be trusted to work in a gentleman's house". (P. 74.)

[1] P. 32.
[2] See p. 151.

long been recognized as one of the unhealthiest and worst paid
which a woman could take up. In the general survey of oppressed
workers which was being undertaken in the first half of the nineteenth century, the needlewomen got their share of attention. The
American humanitarian writer Harriet Beecher-Stowe[1], gives an
account of the position of needlewomen, and the attempts to relieve them which had been made, in her book *Sunny Memories of
Foreign Lands* (1854), in which she tells her readers that Lord
Shaftesbury's commission of 1841 had elicited the facts that in
in London alone there were more than fifteen thousand young
people employed in the millinery and dressmaking trade and that

"during the London season, which occupied about four months of the year,
the regular hours of work were fifteen, but in many establishments they
were entirely unlimited,—the young women never getting more than six
hours for sleep, and often only two or three; that frequently they worked
all night and part of Sunday . . . the rooms in which they worked and slept
were over-crowded and deficient in ventilation; and that, in consequence
of all these causes, blindness, consumption, and multitudes of other dis-
eases carried thousands of them yearly to the grave".[2]

According to Mrs. Beecher-Stowe, however, the report for 1851
showed that in London, owing to the efforts of the Association
for the Aid of Milliners and Dressmakers, formed in 1843, "the
hours of work, speaking generally, now rarely exceed twelve,
whereas formerly sixteen, seventeen, and even eighteen hours
were not unusual".[3]

The report for 1853, however, gave a less optimistic account of
the success of the reforms:

"In this last report the committees remarked that some few houses of
business systematically persisted in exacting excessive labour from their
assistants; and they regret to state that this observation is still applicable
. . . in some establishments, . . . the principals, in cases of sickness, will

---

[1] Mrs. Beecher-Stowe (*op. cit.*, p. 336, letter dated June 3) mentions meeting
Mrs. Gaskell and Mrs. Jameson at Mrs. Milman's and goes on: "I promised her
a visit when I go to Manchester." According to A. W. Ward (Introduction to
North and South in the Knutsford edn, p. XXI) Mrs. Beecher-Stowe stayed
with the Gaskells in Manchester in 1853 and wrote to Mrs. Gaskell in May,
1856, to express her admiration for *North and South*.

[2] H. Beecher-Stowe, *op. cit.*, pp. 298–9.

[3] *Ibid.*, p. 300.

neither allow the young people an opportunity of calling in the medical officer for his advice, nor permit that gentleman to visit them at the place of business."[1]

Mrs. Gaskell had ample opportunities of observing similar conditions in Manchester. According to Mrs. Beecher-Stowe, "Although not generally known, evils scarcely less serious than those formerly prevalent in the metropolis were not uncommon in the manufacturing towns".[2] An unusually large number of ladies seem to have been anxious to improve the conditions of needleworkers in Manchester. Mrs. Beecher-Stowe writes: "In Manchester a paper, signed by three thousand ladies, was presented to the principals of the establishments, desiring them to adopt the rules of the London association."[3]

Mrs. Beecher-Stowe's picture of the working conditions of the needleworkers in England is gloomy enough, but in comparison with other contemporary sources she seems to have been given a too optimistic idea of the progress made. Lord Ashley, for instance, who was President of the Association for the Aid and Benefit of Dressmakers and Milliners, complained of the general indifference of the public, especially the clergy, many of whom he stated to be hostile to reforms in this case. Several private efforts were, however, made for the relief of needlewomen. In the eyes of many, emigration was the obvious solution of the problem, and it appears that Mrs. Gaskell early took an interest in this kind of welfare work.[4]

Even after the years of apprenticeship, the financial position of a seamstress was anything but favourable, unless she had the means to set up an establishment of her own. The reason was naturally an overstocked market. Miss Neff[5] quotes Census figures that show an increase in the number of women above twenty years of age who were engaged in dressmaking, from 151,101 in 1841 to 388,302 ten years later.

Many women from the working classes became needleworkers.

---

[1] *Ibid.*, p. 303.   [2] *Ibid.*, p. 301.
[3] *Ibid.*, p. 304.   [4] See p. 56.
[5] Wanda Fraiken Neff, *Victorian Working Women, An Historical and Literary Study of Women in British Industries and Professions 1832–1850* (London, 1929), p. 143.

In a period when there were extremely few ways open to a woman who had to earn her own living out of the home, a woman who was without education enough to become a governess and who considered herself too much of a lady to become a factory worker or a domestic servant had hardly any other alternative than needlework. Consequently, the ranks of the dressmakers' apprentices were filled from a much wider range of social classes than were those of the factory workers. "Lord Ashley stated that the daughters of poor clergymen and Nonconformist ministers, half-pay officers, or tradesmen who had suffered reverses, were crowded into these trades."[1] This was one of the reasons why, as Miss Neff points out[2], the dressmaker's apprentice, with her refinement in looks and education, was much more popular with authors than the factory worker. She instances Miss Minnifer and Miss Flinder from Thackeray's *Pendennis* (1848–50) and *The Newcomes* (1853–5) and from Dickens, Kate in *Nicholas Nickleby* (1838–9), Little Emily and Martha in *David Copperfield* (1849–50), Little Dorrit (1857–8), and Jenny Wren in *Our Mutual Friend* (1864–5). She also mentions George Eliot's Maggy in *The Mill on the Floss* (1860). All these novels except *Nicholas Nickleby* appeared too late to have had any influence on Mrs. Gaskell's first description of a dressmaker's life. In Dickens' book, however, Kate is employed in the show-room, and is altogether in a much better position than the average needleworker of the time. It seems unlikely that she had any influence on Mrs. Gaskell's idea of a dressmaker's character and working conditions.

In poetry, though, Mrs. Gaskell had come across two eloquent denunciations of the lot of sewing-women which had made a strong enough impression on her to make her quote from both in *Mary Barton*.[3] One was Thomas Hood's "The Song of the Shirt", first published in 1843; the other was Caroline Norton's *The Child of the Islands*, parts III–VII, "Spring" (1845). Both these poems try to awaken the reader's pity for "a feeble girl", "who sits working all alone" (Norton), "with eyelids heavy and red" (Hood). In Mrs. Gaskell's early tales *Mary Barton* and *Libbie Marsh's Three Eras*, the stress is also laid chiefly on the disastrous effects on the

---

[1] Neff, *op. cit.*, p. 116. [2] *Ibid.*, p. 147. [3] See Appendix III.

health and eyesight of overworked sewing-women, their loneliness, and their uncertain and insufficient earnings, whereas the moral problems resulting from these conditions were not fully treated until the authoress had her attention drawn to them by articles such as the one in the *Westminster Review* of April–July, 1850.[1]

The heroine of that Sunday school type of story *Libbie Marsh's Three Eras* (1847) is a seamstress doing plain sewing. She is conceived entirely in the tradition of vague pity for "the ruined Farmer's daughter; pale and weak", for whom "Those who have time for pity, might descry / A thousand shattered gleams of merriment gone by".[2] She is "listless and depressed, more from the state of her mind than of her body".[3] She is occupied with thoughts of her "father and mother gone, her little brother long since dead".[4] But with the happy disposition that makes her "find out she liked the gooseberries that were accessible, better than the grapes that were beyond her reach",[5] she finds her happiness in doing good to others.

In this tale, the reader's attention is not directed towards any specified evils of the trade. It was often pointed out at the time, especially by the milliners themselves, that however much they would have welcomed reforms to alleviate the lot of their apprentices, nothing could be done without the assistance of the ladies who gave their orders at the last minute so that new fashions might not come in after their orders for the season had already been given; and the only reform suggested by *Libbie Marsh's Three Eras* is an increased general benevolence and thoughtfulness on the part of the "ladies", who are stated to be "kind enough people in their way, but too rapidly twirling round on this bustling earth to have leisure to think of the little workwoman, excepting when they wanted gowns turned, carpets mended, or household linen darned".[6]

In *Mary Barton*, Mrs. Gaskell shows much more interest both in the mentality of girls who chose Libbie Marsh's work, and their actual working conditions. Mary is the daughter of a factory worker, but, like so many distressed gentlewomen, she chooses to be-

---

[1] See below, pp. 207–10.
[2] Norton, *The Child of the Islands*, "Spring", III.
[3] P. 451.   [4] P. 452.
[5] P. 458.   [6] P. 452.

come a needleworker because of the supposed gentility of the trade. She

"had early determined that her beauty should make her a lady; the rank she coveted the more for her father's abuse; the rank to which she firmly believed her lost aunt Esther had arrived. Now, while a servant must often drudge and be dirty, must be known as his servant by all who visited at her master's house, a dressmaker's apprentice must (or so Mary thought) be always dressed with a certain regard to appearances; must never soil her hands, and need never redden or dirty her face with hard labour".[1]

Mrs. Gaskell was obviously well acquainted with the labour conditions in this trade. Her books do not seem to contain any exaggerated statements about them; all her facts are confirmed by the official reports of the time. Thus

"Mary was to be a dressmaker; and her ambition prompted her unwilling father to apply at all the first establishments, to know on what terms of painstaking and zeal his daughter might be admitted into ever so humble a workwoman's situation. But high premiums were asked at all; poor man! he might have known that without giving up a day's work to ascertain the fact. He would have been indignant, indeed, had he known that if Mary had accompanied him, the case might have been rather different, as her beauty would have made her desirable as a show-woman. Then he tried second-rate places; at all the payment of a sum of money was necessary, and money he had none . . . the next day she set out herself, as her father could not afford to lose another day's work; and before night (as yesterday's experience had considerably lowered her ideas) she had engaged herself as apprentice (so called, though there were no deeds or indentures to the bond) to a certain Miss Simmonds, milliner and dressmaker . . . the workwomen were called 'her young ladies'; and . . . Mary was to work for two years without any remuneration, on consideration of being taught the business; and where afterwards she was to dine and have tea, with a small quarterly salary (paid quarterly because so much more genteel than by week), a *very* small one, divisible into a minute weekly pittance. In summer she was to be there by six, bringing her day's meals during her first two years; in winter she was not to come till after breakfast. Her time for returning home at night must always depend upon the quantity of work Miss Simmonds had to do.
"And Mary was satisfied."[2]

In *Mary Barton* Mrs. Gaskell does not accuse the head of the establishment for the undesirable conditions prevailing there. Miss Simmonds was "hasty-tempered yet kind"[3], and there is not

---

[1] *Mary Barton*, p. 33. [2] *Ibid.*, pp. 33-4. [3] P. 84.

a word of blame for her when "the dressmaker too, feeling the effect of bad times, had left off giving tea to her apprentices, setting them the example of long abstinence by putting off her own meal till work was done for the night, however late that might be".[1] Although "it was a long fast from the one o'clock dinner hour at Miss Simmonds' to the close of Mary's vigil, which was often extended to midnight", she could yet keep her health and spirits up enough to sing "a merry song over her work" in the evening.[2]

Mrs. Gaskell, who, in reviews of her books, was so often accused of unfairness to employers, did not succumb to the temptation of creating a slave-driving monster in the person of Miss Simmonds, although, according to Miss Neff, "dressmakers were more relentless toward the girls they hired than some of the most ignorant overlookers in Manchester factories".[3] Though Mary's "time for returning home at night must always depend upon the quantity of work Miss Simmonds had to do", the latter is not represented as having enforced the excessively long working-day remarked on by Government inspectors such as R. D. Grainger, who found that girl apprentices often worked twenty hours out of the twenty-four, in some places even on Sundays.[4] Mary has some time to spare "to earn a few pence by working over hours"[5], after the rent of half-a-crown a week has taken nearly all the wages which she is receiving after two unsalaried years.

Another sewing-woman in *Mary Barton* is not apprenticed to a milliner but, like Libbie Marsh, does plain sewing. With less spirit than Mary and more nearly conforming to the "gentle" ideal of a woman in the moral stories of the time, she suffers more from the work. "Plain little sensible Margaret, so prim and demure"[6], tries meekly to accept her fate, even the loss of her eyesight:

"Mary inquired—
" 'Do you expect to get paid for this mourning?'
" 'Why, I do not much think I shall. I've thought it over once or twice, and I mean to bring myself to think I sha'n't, and to like to do it as my bit towards comforting them. I don't think they can pay, and yet they're just the sort of folk to have their minds easier for wearing mourning. There's only one thing I dislike making black for, it does so hurt the eyes

---

[1] P. 114.   [2] P. 140.   [3] Neff, *op. cit.*, p. 136.
[4] See Neff, *op. cit.*, p. 119.   [5] P. 128.   [6] P. 152.

. . . I sometimes think I'm growing a little blind . . . I went to a doctor; and he did not mince the matter, but said unless I sat in a darkened room, with my hands before me, my sight would not last me many years longer. But how could I do that, Mary? . . . what I earn is a great help. For grandfather takes a day here, and a day there, for botanising or going after insects, and he'll think little enough of four or five shillings for a specimen; dear grandfather! and I'm so loath to think he should be stinted of what gives him such pleasure . . . my eye is so much worse, not hurting so much, but I can't see a bit with it.' "[1]

She resigns herself to her eventual blindness, "if it were th' Lord's will".[2] In the end, though, her eyesight is restored, and her story, like Mary's, ends in a happy marriage.

Even in her first stories, Mrs. Gaskell showed, but without emphasis, that she was aware of one more evil of the dressmaking trade. Immorality among sewing-women was proverbial, and was commented on in the reports of the Commissions of Inquiry into their conditions. In *Mary Barton* the author hints at this fact when Esther says, "I found out Mary went to learn dressmaking, and I began to be frightened for her; for it's a bad life for a girl to be out late at night in the streets, and after many an hour of weary work, they're ready to follow after any novelty that makes a little change".[3] Mary herself partly blames her trade for the difficulties in which she finds herself, after she has let herself in for an innocent flirtation with the son of a mill-owner: "Oh! how she loathed the recollection of the hot summer evening, when, worn out by stitching and sewing, she had loitered homewards with weary languor, and first listened to the voice of the tempter."[4]

Another unpleasant memory was "Sally Leadbitter's odious whispers hissing in her ear".[5] Sally is one of those realistic portraits that show that Mrs. Gaskell had no illusions about the general refinement of working-girls, even though she conformed to literary convention in so far as never to let her heroines show the least trace of vulgarity. In the person of Sally is concentrated the bad influence which Mrs. Gaskell was bound to have observed in her talks with the young Manchester girls. She, too, is apprenticed to Miss Simmonds and "was vulgar-minded to the last degree; never easy unless her talk was of love and lovers;" Although "Sally

---

[1] Pp. 52–3.   [2] P. 97.   [3] P. 160.   [4] P. 154.   [5] P. 154.

herself was but a plain, red-haired, freckled girl; never likely, one would have thought, to become a heroine on her own account . . . She had just talent enough to corrupt others. Her very good nature was an evil influence. They could not hate one who was so kind".[1]

Although the above quotations show that Mrs. Gaskell had a thorough knowledge of the conditions under which needleworkers had to live—conditions often leading to ruined health and blindness—, there is very little sign of any indignation over them in her early stories. Though she regrets the conditions, and vaguely appeals to the upper classes to show more consideration and benevolence, her attitude seems to be that the ideal for the victims is meekly to accept their fate. That was her attitude towards the wrongs of woman in general at this period. In Mrs. Gaskell's first stories, a wife's rights were, as has been shown above[2], entirely disregarded; her duty was, above all, submission to her husband. Then, under the influence of contact with the ideas of representatives of the beginning women's rights movement Mrs. Gaskell's ideas changed considerably in this respect in the period between the writing of *Mary Barton*, and that of *Ruth*. The same holds good in the case of dressmakers' apprentices; her attitude towards their conditions as well as to the moral responsibility of their employers developed to a considerable degree during the same period. In *Ruth*—published in 1853—she deliberately set out to denounce abuses which she thought it a duty to help to abolish. The reason in this case, too, must have been partly the fact that she had come to consider woman as an independent being in herself, not only as an appendage to man. But it was not the only reason.

In newspapers and magazines, needlewomen had become one of the most frequently discussed groups of workers in the social debate which was at its height about the middle of the nineteenth century. It need hardly be doubted that one of the reasons why Mrs. Gaskell chose a dressmaker's apprentice for her heroine in *Ruth* was the attention drawn to that group of women by Henry Mayhew's articles in the *Morning Chronicle* in 1849, published under the title of "London Labour and the London Poor". These

---

[1] P. 92.   [2] See Chap. IV.

articles were meant to show up the moral condition, habits, temptations, work: in short, all the naked facts of the daily life of the lower classes in London. This was something of a new departure in journalism, and the sober realism with which they presented the horrifying facts in the case of one outcast of society after another was extremely effective, and reechoed in the form of quotations and comments in the press of the day.[1] The *Westminster Review*, for instance, quoted extensively from them, among other passages the following:

"During the course of my investigation into the condition of those who are dependent upon the needle for their support, I had been so repeatedly assured that the young girls were mostly compelled to resort to prostitution to eke out their subsistence . . . I had no idea of the intensity of the privations suffered by the needle-women of London until I came to inquire into this part of the subject . . . [story of one girl]: 'I make moleskin trowsers . . . I work from six in the morning to ten at night . . . I don't make above 3 s. clear money each week . . . The trowsers work is held to be the best paid of all . . . By working from five o'clock in the morning till midnight each night I might be able to do seven in the week . . . left me 15 ¹/₂ d. to pay rent and living and buy candles with . . . I had a child, and it used to cry for food; so . . . I went into the streets . . . I then made from 3 s. to 4 s. a week, and from that time I gave up prostitution. For the sake of my child I should not like my name to be known . . .'"[2]

It is hardly possible to overestimate the influence Mayhew's articles had on the current debates in Parliament, newspapers, and magazines, dealing with the social questions of the time. They are often mentioned in pamphlets and novels too.[3]

---

[1] They were well-known in Mrs. Gaskell's circle of intimate friends. On November 17, 1850, Catherine Winkworth wrote to Emma Shaen about Kingsley's *Alton Locke:* "It is full of . . . pictures of the condition of the unprivileged, which, alas, one knows from the *Morning Chronicle*, are not over-drawn." (Shaen, *op. cit.*, p. 62).

[2] The *Westminster Review*, April–July, 1850, pp. 448–506.

[3] Kingsley makes repeated references to them. In "Cheap Clothes and Nasty" (1850) he writes: "From two articles in the 'Morning Chronicle' of Friday, Dec. 14th, and Tuesday, Dec. 18th, on the Condition of the Working Tailors, we learnt too much to leave us altogether masters of ourselves", and again, in the fourth edition of *Yeast*, Chapter VIII, which deals with the social misery which Lancelot witnesses on his wanderings: "What he saw, of course I must not say; for if I did, the reviewers would declare, as usual, one and all, that I copied out of the Morning Chronicle; and the fact that these pages, ninety-nine

Mayhew's articles were revised and published in book form on several occasions up to 1865. On pp. XXVIII–XXIX of the volume issued in 1862 we find the following harsh words about the indifference of Society to over-worked milliners' and dressmakers' apprentices:

"The present condition of . . . milliners and dressmakers, is one of the severest comments upon the heartlessness and artificialism of that society, which takes no cognizance of those who are most largely concerned in administering to its necessities. The miseries of this shamefully underpaid and cruelly overworked class of white slaves have been too often eloquently animadverted upon, to need any further denunciations of the system, under which they are hopelessly and unfeelingly condemned to labour."

Mayhew then goes on to say that "while, however, the State shrinks from the task of ameliorating their condition by any legislative interference, it is satisfactory to know that public benevolence in this wide field is not wholly unrepresented", and enumerates several organisations for the relief of women employed in various trades. At the time when *Ruth* was being written, however, the great majority of these associations were not yet in existence, and that novel was at least one of the incitements to their being founded at all.

After all the harsh criticism to which Mrs. Gaskell had been subjected in the reviews of *Mary Barton*, she always tried to treat employers with strict impartiality, and the extenuating circumstances in Mrs. Mason's case are duly stated in *Ruth:* She "was a widow, and had to struggle for the sake of the six or seven children left dependent on her exertions; thus there was some reason, and great excuse, for the pinching economy which regulated her household affairs".[1] These circumstances once stated, however, Mrs. Gaskell proceeds to lay the whole blame on the employer for the too long working day, the insufficient food, etc., and the conditions under which Mrs. Mason's apprentices have to work are much

---

hundredths of them at least, were written two years before the Morning Chronicle began its invaluable investigations, would be contemptuously put aside as at once impossible and arrogant." (*Yeast* was first published in 1848, and the fourth edn in 1859.)

[1] P. 24.

worse than those described in the earlier novel. They are also depicted with a new intensity of feeling:

"Two o'clock in the morning chimed forth the old bells of St. Saviour's. And yet more than a dozen girls still sat in the room into which Ruth entered, stitching away as if for very life, not daring to gape, or show any outward manifestation of sleepiness. They only sighed a little when Ruth told Mrs. Mason the hour of the night, as the result of her errand; for they knew that, stay up as late as they might, the work-hours of the next day must begin at eight, and their young limbs were very weary.[1]

"Mrs. Mason worked away as hard as any of them; but she was older and tougher; and, besides, the gains were hers. But even she perceived that some rest was needed. 'Young ladies! there will be an interval allowed of half an hour. Ring the bell, Miss Sutton. Martha shall bring you up some bread, and cheese, and beer. You will be so good as to eat it standing —away from the dresses—and to have your hands washed ready for work when I return. In half an hour', said she once more, very distinctly; and then she left the room.

"It was curious to watch the young girls as they instantaneously availed themselves of Mrs. Mason's absence. One fat, particularly heavy-looking damsel, laid her head on her folded arms and was asleep in a moment; refusing to be wakened for her share in the frugal supper, but springing up with a frightened look at the sound of Mrs. Mason's returning footstep, even while it was still far off on the echoing stairs . . . Some employed the time in eating their bread and cheese, . . . Others stretched themselves into all sorts of postures to relieve the weary muscles; . . . At last . . . They were told to go to bed; but even that welcome command was languidly obeyed. Slowly they folded up their work, heavily they moved about, until at length all was put away . . .

" 'OhI how shall I get through five years of these terrible nights! in that close room! and in that oppressive stillness! which lets every sound of the thread be heard as it goes eternally backwards and forwards', sobbed out Ruth, as she threw herself on her bed, without even undressing herself.

" 'Nay, Ruth, you know it won't be always as it has been tonight. We often get to bed by ten o'clock, and by and by you won't mind the closeness of the room. You're worn out tonight, or you would not have minded the sound of the needle; I never hear it . . . Most new girls get impatient at first; but it goes off and they don't care much for anything after a while. Poor child! . . .' "[2]

---

[1] This was no exaggeration of actual facts, for "Mr. R. D. Grainger, the Government inspector, found that girl apprentices began work at five or six in the morning and continued until two or three the next morning." (Neff, *op. cit.*, p. 119.) Cf. also quotations from Mrs. Beecher-Stowe above.

[2] Pp. 2–6.

As to the mental condition of these apprentices, Mrs. Gaskell speaks of "the sullen indifference which had become their feeling with regard to most events—a deadened sense of life, consequent upon their unnatural mode of existence, their sedentary days, and their frequent nights of late watching".[1]

The reason why they have to slave on the occasion quoted above is that Mrs. Mason has unnecessarily undertaken too much for fear that one dress might otherwise "fall into the hands of the rival dressmaker".[2]

There is a tone of acrimony in Mrs. Gaskell's description of a Sunday in Mrs. Mason's establishment, which was entirely absent from the passages about the dressmaker in *Mary Barton:*

"On Sundays she chose to conclude that all her apprentices had friends who would be glad to see them to dinner . . . Accordingly, no dinner was cooked on Sundays for the young work-women; no fires were lighted in any rooms to which they had access. On this morning they breakfasted in Mrs. Mason's own parlour, after which the room was closed against them through the day by some understood, though unspoken prohibition.

"What became of such as Ruth, who had no home and no friends in that large, populous, desolate town? . . .

"And last of all, Mrs. Mason returned; and, summoning her 'young people' once more into the parlour, she read a prayer before dismissing them to bed. She always expected to find them all in the house when she came home, but asked no questions as to their proceedings through the day; perhaps because she dreaded to hear that one or two had occasionally nowhere to go to, and that it would be sometimes necessary to order a Sunday's dinner, and leave a lighted fire on that day."[3]

A little further on, when Ruth is discovered to have gone on an excursion into the country alone with Mr. Bellingham, Mrs. Mason is again made the representative of that unchristian spirit of thoughtless intolerance and regard for appearances which the author made it her task to combat in this as well as in her other "social" tales:

"dropping her voice to low, bitter tones of concentrated wrath, she said to the trembling, guilty Ruth:

---

[1] P. 7.   [2] P. 5.

[3] Pp. 24–5. Here, too, Mrs. Gaskell's accuracy is proved by official reports: "Mr. Grainger . . . discovered that in some houses no meals except breakfast were provided on Sunday." (Neff, *op. cit.*, p. 121.)

" 'Don't attempt to show your face at my house again after this conduct. I saw you, and your spark too. I'll have no slurs on the character of my apprentices . . . [Ruth] knew with what severity and taunts Mrs. Mason had often treated her for involuntary failings, of which she had been quite unconscious; and now she had really done wrong, and shrank with terror from the consequences."[1]

In *Libbie Marsh's Three Eras* Mrs. Gaskell was as yet very tolerant towards the thoughtlessness of the upper classes.[2] In *Ruth* she denounces their indifference to anything but their own pleasures, and she sharply contrasts their lives with the dreary world of the poor: "the *élite* of the county danced on, little caring whose eyes gazed and were dazzled . . . the happy smoothness of the lives in which such music, and such profusion of flowers, of jewels, elegance of every description, and beauty of all shapes and hues, were every-day things".[3] After watching this kind of life from their posts in the dressing rooms, where they are stationed to mend torn skirts and catch up loose ribbons, the apprentices return home:

"The cold grey dawn was drearily lighting up the streets when Mrs. Mason and her company returned home . . . One or two houseless beggars sat on doorsteps, and shivering, slept with heads bowed on their knees, or resting against the cold hard support afforded by the wall.

"Ruth felt as if a dream had melted away, and she were once more in the actual world . . . those bright, happy people . . . Had they ever to deny themselves a wish, much less a want? . . . Here was cold, biting, mid-winter for her, and such as her—for those poor beggars almost a season of death; but to Miss Duncombe and her companions, a happy, merry time, . . . What did they know of the meaning of the word, so terrific to the poor? What was winter to them?"[4]

Miss Duncombe almost vies with Blanche Ingram in *Jane Eyre* in her haughty insolence to those beneath her in rank. When her

---

[1] Pp. 38-9. Because the fear with which Mrs. Mason inspired Ruth has often been objected to as unrealistic and exaggerated, it is of interest to note that when an attempt was made in 1855 to obtain Parliamentary interference into the conditions of dressmakers' apprentices, one of the chief difficulties which reformers came up against was the reluctance of apprentices to give evidence. They seem to have stood in such fear of their employers that they preferred to suffer in silence. (See Neff, *op. cit.*, p. 139.)

[2] Cf. above, p. 164.   [3] P. 10.   [4] P. 12.

dress is torn at the ball "she addressed Ruth. 'Make haste—don't
keep me an hour!' And her voice became cold and authoritative . . .'
'. . . Will it never be done? What a frightful time you are taking;
. . .' " Ruth , whose "noble head bent down to the occupation in
which she was engaged, formed such a contrast to the flippant,
bright, artificial girl, who sat to be served with an air as haughty
as a queen on her throne".

Then she addresses her dancing partner: "I'm ashamed to detain
you so long. I had no idea any one could have spent so much time
over a little tear. No wonder Mrs. Mason charges so much for
dressmaking, if her workwomen are so slow. . . . she gave no word
or sign of thanks to the assistant."[1]

Mayhew's articles in the *Morning Chronicle*, and the consequent
discussion in newspapers and magazines, were probably the chief
incitement for Mrs. Gaskell to take up the problems of sewing-
women in *Ruth*. When considering descriptions of working conditions like those quoted above, and the increased acerbity in
Mrs. Gaskell's references to the irresponsibility of the upper
classes, one must not, however, overlook yet another important
factor: Charles Kingsley's novel *Alton Locke* appeared in 1850.[2]
Mrs. Gaskell, who so highly admired Kingsley's earliest efforts,
can hardly have remained unmoved by the social sense in this
book, with its denunciations in Chapter II of "the great King Lais-
sez-faire" and of "those who live . . . besides such a state of things"
without trying to reform conditions, though "they are 'their
brothers' keepers', let them deny it as they will".

When concentrating on the literature of the time that advocated
reform, one might easily get the impression that all those who
thought seriously on the subject agreed as to the necessity of an
effort to improve conditions. This was, however, far from the actual situation. The Conservative hostility to reforms was, in fact,
strong enough and widespread enough to demand considerable
courage both from the authors and the publishers of such books as
Mary Barton, *Ruth*, and *Alton Locke*, and such newspaper articles

---

[1] Pp. 11–12.

[2] When writing *Alton Locke*, Kingsley, too, was probably influenced by
Mayhew's articles. Cf. p. 169, n. 3.

as Mayhew's.[1] With what hostility this kind of literature was received by a considerable part of the British public appears, for instance, from an article in the *Quarterly Review* of June–September, 1851, entitled "Revolutionary Literature" (pp. 491–543), which contains a violent attack on Kingsley and the leader of the Christian Socialist movement, F. D. Maurice, whose works the author terms "the Literature of the Poor", but is "not anxious to give . . . circulation by naming its writers, or the works of which it is composed".

A complacent belief that nobody could be held responsible for undesirable social conditions was deep-rooted. *The London Times* wrote about the East End in the 'fifties: "It is always the first to suffer . . . All full of life and happiness in brisk times, but in dull times withered and lifeless. Now their brief spring is over. There is no one to blame for this; it is the result of nature's simplest laws."[2]

---

[1] In April, 1849, *Fraser's Magazine*, in which Kingsley's *Yeast* had appeared from July to December the preceding year, complimented Mrs. Gaskell's publishers on the courage which they had shown by publishing books like *Mary Barton*. (See above pp. 143–4.)

[2] Quoted by R. H. S. Crossman in his article "The Testament of Change" in *"Ideas and Beliefs of the Victorians"*, p. 424.

CHAPTER VIII

"FALLEN" WOMEN

(Prostitution a great social problem about the middle of the nineteenth century. Examples of other "fallen" women in English literature. Mrs. Gaskell's early stories about seduced women conform entirely to literary tradition: the fallen woman either becomes a prostitute or spends her life in hopeless grief and repentance. Esther in Mary Barton *is a realistic portrait, meant to show the evils of prostitution, but there is no question of redemption for the fallen woman. Victorian attitude towards these problems: duty of silence. Mrs. Gaskell's courage in devoting a whole novel,* Ruth, *to the problem of a seduced woman. Main ideas in* Ruth: *the attitude of the "respectable" ultimately responsible for the fact of prostitution, the seduced woman's initial innocence, attack on the double moral, the seduced woman's refusal to marry her seducer, the child as the good influence in its unmarried mother's life, the seduced woman regains her self respect and is accepted again in middle class circles. The* "sources" *of* Ruth. *The reception of* Ruth.*)*

About the middle of the nineteenth century the time had become ripe for a new treatment in literature of the old theme of "woman's fall and man's desertion" and its consequence, prostitution. As Trevelyan writes in *English Social History,*

"An account of women's life at this period ought to include a reference to the great army of prostitutes ... 'the harlot's cry from street to street' made public resorts hideous at nightfall. The growing 'respectability' of the well-to-do classes in the new era diminished the numbers and position of the more fortunate 'kept mistresses', who had played a considerable part in Eighteenth Century society. But for that very reason the demand was increased for the common prostitute who could be visited in secret. The harshness of the world's ethical code, which many parents endorsed, too often drove a girl once seduced to prostitution. And the economic condition of single women forced many of them to adopt a trade they abhorred".[1]

This class of women had, of course, often been treated in literature. To take but a few examples, there are Mistress Quickly and Doll

---

[1] Pp. 490–1.

Tearsheet in Shakespeare's *Henry IV*, and Defoe's *Roxana* with the significant sub-title *The Fortunate Mistress* (1724). About twenty-five years later, the same theme was treated from the opposite point of view in Richardson's *Pamela, or Virtue Rewarded* (1740). In the second half of the same century, the seduced woman was a standard theme in the novels of sensibility. B. G. MacCarthy writes about this[1]: "The modern reader of eighteenth century fiction sometimes feels caught in a nightmare in which seduced girls, . . . clutch with their pale fingers a naked heart from which they wring streams of—tears."

From the early part of Mrs. Gaskell's own century, Effie Deans in Scott's *The Heart of Midlothian* (1818) might be mentioned. The next year, Crabbe's *Tales of the Hall* were published, interesting in this context, because they contain the story of a seduced girl whose name Mrs. Gaskell chose for the title of her own story.[2] A quarter of a century later, 1844, appeared Thomas Hood's poem "The Bridge of Sighs", which is of some importance because of the immense popularity it enjoyed.[3] There is no denunciation of the seducer in the poem, but a strong appeal to the reader for pity and tolerance for the girl who has drowned herself:

> "Alas! for the rarity
> of Christian charity . . .
> Cross her hands humbly . . .
> Owning her weakness,
> Her evil behaviour,
> And leaving, with meekness,
> Her sins to her Saviour!"

Still later, Mrs. Gaskell's "hero" Charles Kingsley[4] devoted a chapter of his first novel to the same subject. He refers to a notice in *The Times*, "one of those miserable cases, now of weekly occur-

---

[1] *Op. cit.*, pp. 37–8.

[2] In August, 1838, Mrs. Gaskell wrote to Mrs. Howitt: "We once thought of *trying* to write sketches among the poor, *rather* in the manner of Crabbe . . ." (Quoted by Ward in his Biographical Introduction to the Knutsford edn, p. XXI.)

[3] "Which of poor Hood's lyrics have an equal chance of immortality with 'The Song of the Shirt' and 'The Bridge of Sighs'." (Kingsley, *Alton Locke*, Chap. IX.)

[4] See Chap. III.

rence, of concealing the birth of a child". The seducer is here represented to be so "haggard, life-weary, shame-stricken" as to take his own life, and the letter from the seduced girl, which does not arrive until after his death, contains an eloquent accusation, very different from the meek acceptance of sin usual in the literature of the time, on the part of a "fallen" woman: "Sir—I am in prison— and where are you? Cruel man! Where were you all those miserable weeks, while I was coming nearer and nearer to my shame? Murdering dumb beasts in foreign lands. You have murdered more than them. How I loved you once! How I hate you now! But I have my revenge. *Your baby cried twice after it was born!*"[1]

Charles Dickens, who had already treated the incident of a seduced and abandoned girl who killed her child in *Dombey and Son* (1847–8), excited his readers to a high pitch of sentimental pity over the fate of little Em'ly in *David Copperfield* only three years before the publication of *Ruth*.

But Mrs. Gaskell was the first among the Victorians to make the fall and redemption of a seduced woman the main theme of a novel. Both George Eliot's *Adam Bede* (1859), with its emphatic condemnation of the seducer, and Antony Trollope's *The Vicar of Bullhampton* (1870) appeared later than *Ruth*, and show unmistakable signs of influence from that novel.[2]

---

[1] Charles Kingsley, *Yeast* (1848), Chap. XVI.

[2] In his *Autobiography* Trollope gives an account of the aim and the plot of his problem novel, which might equally well have been a summary of Mrs. Gaskell's *Ruth:* "I have introduced into *The Vicar of Bullhampton* the character of a girl whom I will call . . . a castaway. I have endeavoured to endow her with qualities that may create sympathy, and I have brought her back at last from degradation, at least to decency. I have not married her to a wealthy lover, and I have endeavoured to explain that though there was possible to her a way out of perdition, still things could not be with her as they would have been had not she fallen . . . In regard to a sin common to the two sexes, almost all the punishment and all the disgrace is heaped upon the one who in nine cases out of ten has been the least sinful . . . How is the woman to return to decency to whom no decent door is opened? Then comes the answer: it is to the severity of the punishment alone that we can trust to keep women from falling . . . life without a hope . . . is the life to which we doom our erring daughters . . . But for our erring sons we find pardon easily enough! Of course there are houses of refuge, from which it has been thought expedient to banish everything pleasant as though the only repentance to which we can afford to give a place must necessarily be one of sackcloth and ashes." (Pp. 287–91.)

Ruth was not the first "fallen" woman in Mrs. Gaskell's tales, nor even the second. *The Well of Pen-Morfa* appeared in *Household Words* from November 16 to 23, 1850, and the first of the two unconnected stories under that title is short enough to be quoted in full:

"At another house lived a woman, stern and severe-looking. She was busy hiving a swarm of bees, alone and unassisted. I do not think my companion would have chosen to speak to her; but seeing her out in her hill-side garden, she made some inquiry in Welsh, which was answered in the most mournful tone I ever heard in my life; a voice of which the freshness and 'timbre' had been choked up by tears long years ago. I asked who she was. I dare say the story is common enough; but the sight of the woman and her few words had impressed me. She had been the beauty of Pen-Morfa; had been in service; had been taken to London by the family whom she served; had come down, in a year or so, back to Pen-Morfa; her beauty gone into that sad, wild, despairing look which I saw, and she about to become a mother. Her father had died during her absence, and left her a very little money; and after her child was born, she took the little cottage where I saw her, and made a scanty living by the produce of her bees. She associated with no one. One event had made her savage and distrustful to her kind. She kept so much aloof that it was some time before it became known that her child was deformed, and lost the use of its lower limbs. Poor thing! When I saw the mother, it had been for fifteen years bedridden. But go past when you would in the night, you saw a light burning; it was often that of the watching mother, solitary and friendless, soothing the moaning child; or you might hear her crooning some old Welsh air, in hopes to still the pain with the loud monotonous music. Her sorrow was so dignified, and her mute endurance and her patient love won her such respect, that the neighbours would fain have been friends; but she kept alone and solitary. This is a most true story. I hope that woman and her child are dead now, and their souls above."[1]

This is indeed the "old tale and often told" of the ballads Mrs. Gaskell so much admired[2], with all their stark sentimentality though without their poetry. *The Well of Pen-Morfa* conforms entirely to the taste which delighted in tearful sentimentality over the sad fate of a deserted maiden[3], and the reader is expected to pity the

---

[1] Pp. 354–5.

[2] "Reading any good ballad is like eating game; and almost every thing else seems poor and tasteless after it." (*Modern Greek Songs*, p. 490.)

[3] Jane R. Coolidge, in the unfinished MS in the Brotherton Library, mentions the existence of a commonplace book of quotations compiled by Elizabeth Stevenson at the age of twenty-one. She writes about the contents: "The pages are covered with the lyrics of deserted maidens, faithful wives and lovers who have parted from their mistresses."

victim of a hard fate, but not to rebel against the conditions that brought it about. This fact, as well as the total absence of Mrs. Gaskell's later freshness of style or sense of humour, points to the conclusion that *The Well of Pen-Morfa* was an early effort, perhaps partly re-written when there began to be a continuous demand for her stories.

Another early story, *Lizzie Leigh*[1], is written in essentially the same vein. Lizzie's mother tells Susan about the early part of her life: "Her father . . . said she mun go among strangers and learn to rough it . . . in Manchester . . . That poor girl were led astray . . . the master had turned her into the street soon as he had heard of her condition—and she not seventeen!".[2] Her life takes the usual course from seduction to prostitution. She entrusts her child to Susan's care, and in the highly melodramatic scene at the child's death-bed she feels "wild despair", and violent remorse. " 'Oh, the murder is on my soul! . . . I am not worthy to touch her, I am so wicked' . . . Lizzie was old before her time; her beauty was gone; deep lines of care, and, alas! of want . . . were printed on the cheek . . . Even in her sleep she bore the look of woe and despair which was the prevalent expression of her face by day";[3] Lizzie eventually finds a refuge with her mother and devotes herself to doing good to others but, like the woman in *The Well of Pen-Morfa*, she is doomed to spend the rest of her life in grief and remorse: "every call of suffering or of sickness for help is listened to by a sad, gentle-looking woman, who rarely smiles (and when she does her smile is more sad than other people's tears), . . .— she prays always and ever for forgiveness— such forgiveness as may enable her to see her child once more . . . Lizzie sits by a little grave and weeps bitterly."[4]

Mrs. Gaskell lived in an age which considered "female chastity . . . a legal necessity"[5], and she had not yet come to question the current habit of dividing women mechanically into "innocent" and "fallen". Such a phrase as "her pure arms were round that guilty, wretched creature"[6] came naturally to her pen. Nevertheless, she asked for tolerance of, even sympathy for the "fallen"

---

[1] See p. 61, n. 1.   [2] Pp. 400–1.   [3] Pp. 409–12.   [4] P. 417.

[4] *Putnam's Monthly Magazine*, January–June, 1853.

[6] P. 409.

woman. The men in *Lizzie Leigh* apply the unthinking, mechanical classification, whereas the women take a more sympathetic and therefore more unconventional view. Lizzie's father "declared that henceforth they would have no daughter"; her eldest brother "could have struck her down in her shame"[1], and after he has fallen in love with "the sweet, delicate, modest Susan" he is convinced that she will "shrink away from him with loathing, as if he were tainted by the involuntary relationship".[2] He even thinks of the child as tainted with sin: "To think of Susan having to do with such a child!"[3] He explains to his mother: "She's never known a touch of sin; ... if she knew about my sister, it would put a gulf between us, and she'd shudder up at the thought of crossing it."[4] His mother takes up Mrs. Gaskell's own attitude: "Will, Will! if she's so good as thou say'st, she'll have pity on such as my Lizzie. If she has no pity for such, she's a cruel Pharisee, and thou'rt best without her."[4]

Not even in her earliest stories did Mrs. Gaskell agree with her "not over cleanly, though carefully whitewashed age"[5] in its identification of purity and innocence with ignorance of evil. The angelic Susan represents Mrs. Gaskell's ideal of a young woman in this story:

" '... Mother told me thou knew'st all.' His eyes were downcast in their shame.
"But the holy and pure did not lower or veil her eyes.
"She said, 'Yes, I know all—all but her sufferings. Think what they must have been!' "[6]

As the story was published in *Household Words*, it did not attract the attention of reviewers. That readers, however, were impressed by it not only as a story but also as an attempt to influence public opinion appears from a letter to Mrs. Gaskell from Leigh Hunt (1850): "... I am sure you are not the woman to be custom's slave. Witness your brave and lovely good word in behalf of the unhappiest of your sex."[7]

[1] P. 391.   [2] P. 396.   [3] P. 406.   [4] P. 398.
[5] Letter from Kingsley to Mrs. Gaskell, May 14, 1857, printed in *Charles Kingsley, His Letters and Memories of his Life*, edited by his wife (London, 1901). III: 25.
[6] P. 414.   [7] *Bulletin*, p. 127.

In her first novel, *Mary Barton*, Mrs. Gaskell again took up a case of seduction that led to prostitution, and this time in a much more realistic and less sentimental way than she had done in *Lizzie Leigh*.

The problem was one with which she must have been familiar. According to an article on prostitution in the *Westminster Review* of April–July, 1850, there were then about 700 prostitutes in Manchester, and Mrs. Gaskell was kept well acquainted with the darker sides of the lives of the outcasts of Society through such friends as Thomas Wright, the prison philanthropist, who was a frequent visitor at the Gaskells' about the time when *Mary Barton* was written.[1] It is to him that the author refers in Chapter XIV of *Mary Barton:*

" 'Sick, and in prison, and ye visited me.' Shall you, or I, receive such blessing? I know one who will. An overseer of a foundry, an aged man, with hoary hair, has spent his Sabbaths, for many years, in visiting the prisoners and the afflicted, in Manchester New Bailey; not merely advising, and comforting, but putting means into their power of regaining the virtue and the peace they had lost; becoming himself their guarantee in obtaining employment, and never deserting those who have once asked help from him."[2]

The question of "fallen" women was in the air. The proverbial immorality of dressmakers' apprentices, for instance, was stressed

---

[1] Thomas Wright (1789–1875) "was a working man in an iron foundry, who for many years devoted all his spare time—evenings and early mornings—rising at four, before his work at the foundry began at 6 A.M.—to visiting the prisoners in the gaols, and endeavouring to work upon them morally and religiously. His Christ-like sympathy and love did in many cases touch their hearts; he followed their career after their release, and may truly be said to have been the instrument of saving many souls ... At the time I began to know him (he was a frequent and always welcome visitor at the Gaskells'), about 1848, he was a beautiful white-haired old man, full of interesting experiences, and with almost as much humour as pathos", wrote Susanna Winkworth. (Shaen, *op. cit.*, p. 55, n.)

Mrs. Fletcher met him at the Gaskells' in 1851: "At Mrs. Gaskell's we had the great pleasure next day at breakfast of meeting Thomas Wright, a philanthropist of no ordinary cast of mind." (Mrs. Fletcher, *Autobiography*. Edited by the survivor of her family. Edinburgh 1875, p. 293.)

Mrs. Gaskell also made him acquainted with Watts, and took an active part in the collection of money to pay for the latter's "The Good Samaritan", painted to commemorate Wright's work. (Bulletin, p. 114 ff.)

[2] P. 155.

again and again in those official reports and newspaper articles which inspired Mrs. Gaskell to write her tales with a social purpose.[1] In her earliest novel she was indeed so much more preoccupied with bringing about a social reform than with writing fiction that she referred her readers direct to her sources: "Vide *Manchester Guardian* of Wednesday, March 18, 1846; and also the Reports of Captain Williams, prison inspector."[2]

True to the whole tendency of *Mary Barton*, Mrs. Gaskell partly blamed class differences for the existence of prostitution. Esther's seducer, an officer with the class-consciousness of his profession, has no intention of marrying the factory worker who, when abandoned, is faced with the alternative of prostitution or starvation. Esther calls attention to this connection between class differences and seduction leading to prostitution when she implores Jem to save Mary, because "she is innocent, except for the great error of loving one above her in station". This was one of those points of view which were remarked on by reviewers, by some with a certain irritation at the author's critical attitude towards the upper classes, by others with approval.[3]

In *Lizzie Leigh* Mrs. Gaskell showed that she did not consider ignorance of evil essential or even desirable for a "pure" woman, and in *Mary Barton* she drew attention to the pernicious effects of such ignorance in young girls. Mary at first "had the innocence, or the ignorance, to believe his [her would-be seducer's] intentions honourable"[4] but escapes seduction with its probable consequence, prostitution, because she comes to realize that he "meant to ruin me; for that's the plain English of not meaning to marry me".[5] But Esther is completely ignorant of the nature of her seducer's

---

[1] A wish to write for art's sake was a later stage in Mrs. Gaskell's literary career, during which period she was largely inspired by other works of fiction.

[2] P. 155. (Chap. XIV.)

[3] The *Westminster Review* wrote: "Mr. Henry Carson ... With equal power and truth is this young man's thoughtless immorality drawn—a portrait of that large number whose morals are only of, and for a class—merely conventional ... Class-morality naturally made him thoughtless of the feelings of those not of his rank; ... Esther ... Her career of degradation ... was occasioned by the class-morality on which we have before remarked." (April–July 1849. Pp. 48–63.)

[4] P. 134.   [5] P. 137.

intentions, and the quality of her ignorance is emphasized by the fact that she, like Ruth in the later novel, feels no sense of wrong during the first period of her relations with her lover: "for, mark you! he promised me marriage. They all do. Then came three years of happiness. I suppose I ought not to have been happy, but I was".[1]

The next step in Esther's degradation is occasioned by a good motive: "it was winter, cold bleak winter; and my child was so ill, so ill, and I was starving. And I could not bear to see her suffer, and forgot how much better it would be for us to die together; . . . So I went out into the street one January night—Do you think God will punish me for that?' she asked with wild vehemence".[2] There was nothing unrealistic in this. In a review of Parent-Duchatelet's *De la Prostitution dans la ville de Paris* in the *Westminster Review* of April–June, 1850, the writer states that "filial and maternal affection drive many to at least occasional prostitution, as a means, and the only means left to them, of earning bread for those dependent on them for support", and gives the following figures from an investigation into the reasons for their prostitution: of 5,183 street women in Paris, 89 had taken to prostitution to earn food for the support of their parents or children, 280 were driven by shame to fly from their homes (Lizzie Leigh's case), and 2,118 had been abandoned by their seducers and had nothing to turn to.

In her later novel, Mrs. Gaskell's attempt to prove that one false step does not necessarily destroy a woman's "purity", led her to exaggerate the nobility of Ruth's character. In *Mary Barton* she

---

[1] P. 158. In her pity for the victims of ignorance, Mrs. Gaskell never tired of pointing out that, far from being a pledge of purity, ignorance in itself was an evil. In *North and South* she instanced the extreme case of a man brought up according to the rules which the Victorian age thought it appropriate to apply to the education of "pure-minded" girls, and "of course, when this great old child was turned loose into the world, every bad counsellor had power over him. He did not know good from evil. His father had made the blunder of bringing him up in ignorance and taking it for innocence"; (P. 130).

That was also the principle on which Richard in *Ruth* was brought up, with the same fatal consequences. "Mr. Bradshaw dreaded all intimacies for his son, and wanted him to eschew all society beyond his own family", and this "unnatural life Mr. Bradshaw expected him to lead" (p. 291) makes him commit a forgery.

[2] P. 159.

wanted to attract attention to the evils of prostitution, and she had
no illusions as to the coarsening effects of Esther's kind of life, or
the disgust a prostitute herself felt for it, though she had sunk too
deep even really to want to leave it: "But it's no matter! I've done
that since, which separates us as far asunder as heaven and hell can
b e."[1]

" 'I could not lead a virtuous life if I would. I should only disgrace you.
If you will know all', said she, as he still seemed inclined to urge her, 'I
must have drink. Such as live like me could not bear life if they did not
drink. It's the only thing to keep us from suicide. If we did not drink,
we could not stand the memory of what we have been, and the thought
of what we are, for a day. If I go without food, and without shelter, I
must have my dram. Oh! you don't know the awful nights I have had in
prison for want of it', said she, shuddering, and glaring round with terri-
fied eyes, as if dreading to see some spiritual creature, with dim form, near
her.

" 'It is so frightful to see them'; whispering in tones of wildness, although so low spoken. 'There they go round and round my bed the whole
night through. My mother, carrying little Annie (I wonder how they got
together) and Mary—and all looking at me with their sad, stony eyes;
O Jem! it is so terrible! They don't turn back either, but pass behind the
head of the bed, and I feel their eyes on me everywhere. If I creep under
the clothes I still see them; and what is worse', hissing out her words with
fright, 'they see me. Don't speak to me of leading a better life—I must
have drink. I cannot pass tonight without a dram; I dare not'."[2]

This was a picture free from the tearful sentimentality of contemporary literature, and realistic enough for the writer of the above-
cited article on prostitution in the *Westminster Review* to say about
it: "The following, though in a work of fiction, is a faithful picture
of the feelings of thousands of these poor wretches."

Esther is driven by her good intentions to try to save Mary and,
if she had been Ruth, she would here have been transformed into
a guardian angel. The wish to stress the evils of prostitution, however, led Mrs. Gaskell to point out that the life Esther had led for
many years had unfitted her for any useful activity:

"With her violent and unregulated nature, rendered morbid by the course
of life she led, and her consciousness of her degradation, she cursed herself for the interference which she believed had led to this . . . How could
she, the abandoned and polluted outcast, ever have dared to hope for a

---

[1] P. 159.   [2] P. 161.

blessing, even on her efforts to do good. The black curse of Heaven rested on all her doings, were they for good or for evil . . .

"Towards the middle of the day she could no longer evade the body's craving want of rest and refreshment; but the rest was taken in a spirit vault, and the refreshment was a glass of gin . . . The time was long gone by when there was much wisdom or consistency in her projects."[1]

Her very appearance is anything but romantic: "the gauze bonnet, once pink, now dirty white, the muslin gown, all draggled, and soaking wet up to the very knees; the gay-coloured barège shawl, closely wrapped round the form, which yet shivered and shook"[2], "the glaring paint, she sharp features".[3]

"It was time for such as she to hide themselves, with the other obscene things of night, from the glorious light of day, which was only for the happy."[4] The word "happy" is significant. In *Lizzie Leigh* Mrs. Gaskell might have said "pure", but in the person of Esther she saw a victim of society, and rebelled against the attitude of the "pure" who only thought of preserving their own reputation for innocence: "To whom shall the outcast prostitute tell her tale! Who will give her help in the day of need? Hers is the lepersin, and all stand aloof dreading to be counted unclean."[5]

There were other reasons as well for pitying a woman like Esther. The law allowed prostitutes but did nothing to protect them and was indeed extremely harsh and one-sided in all the cases where they might be involved. "Prostitution in itself was no offence, prostitution accompanied by solicitation was no offence unless done to the annoyance of passengers; solicitation, however annoying, by anyone other than a common prostitute, was no offence . . . Public opinion accepted one moral code for men and one for women, and law here as elsewhere reflected public opinion."[6] Esther has to suffer under these laws when she tries to make Mary's father listen to her.

"He flung her, trembling, sinking, fainting, from him, and strode away. She fell with a feeble scream against the lamp-post, and lay there in her weakness, unable to rise. A policeman came up in time to see the close of these occurrences, and concluding from Esther's unsteady, reeling fall, that she was tipsy, he took her in her half-unconscious state to the lock-ups

---

[1] Pp. 228–9. [2] P. 123. [3] P. 124.
[4] P. 227. [5] P. 156. [6] Reiss, *op. cit.*, p. 163.

for the night, . . . The next morning she was taken up to the New Bailey. It was a clear case of disorderly vagrancy, and she was committed to prison for a month."[1]

As usual, Mrs. Gaskell's facts about social conditions are accurate. The Vagrancy Act of 1824 enacted that "every common prostitute wandering in the public streets or public highways or in any place of public resort and behaving in a riotous or indecent manner may be imprisoned for a month".[2]

It also seems certain that Thomas Wright had furnished the authoress with sufficient information to give an accurate description of the position of a woman like Esther when leaving prison:

"Esther's term of imprisonment was ended. She received a good character in the governor's books; she had picked her daily quantity of oakum, had never deserved the extra punishment of the treadmill, and had been civil and decorous in her language. And once more she was out of prison. The door closed behind her with a ponderous clang, and in her desolation she felt as if shut out of home—from the only shelter she could meet with, houseless and penniless as she was, on that dreary day."[3]

Mrs. Gaskell was obviously well aware of the legislation in these matters but, characteristically, she contented herself with pointing out the evils, and left it to others to suggest the necessary reforms. *Mary Barton* is one of those books in which she most frequently quotes the Bible[4], and it is to religion and not to any human laws or institutions that John Barton turns when trying to find a means of saving his sister-in-law. "For he now recalled her humility, her tacit acknowledgment of her lost character; and he began to marvel if there was power in the religion he had often heard of, to turn her from her ways. He felt that no earthly power that he knew of could do it, but there glimmered on his darkness the idea that religion might save her."[5]

Strong as is the treatment of the problem of the fallen woman in *Mary Barton*, that problem is but a secondary theme, and the portrait of Esther, though unusually realistic, was not essentially different from the traditional literary figure of a prostitute. She meekly accepts Society's view of herself as an outcast, she is filled

---

[1] Pp. 124–5. [2] Reiss, *op. cit.*, p. 162. [3] P. 156.
[4] See Appendix III. [5] P. 126.

with remorse and grief over her own sinful life, but makes no attempt to regain respectability. Although Maria Edgeworth, for instance, objected to the inclusion of the story of Esther in *Mary Barton*[1], her character was traditional enough generally to escape the particular notice of reviewers. Ruth, on the contrary, is the heroine of the full length novel of that name that was published five years after *Mary Barton*. She, too, is seduced but, instead of becoming a prostitute, she regains her self-respect and is readmitted into respectable middle class circles. In the writing of *Ruth* Mrs. Gaskell became one of the very first Victorian writers of fiction openly to attack the generally accepted double moral in sexual matters. She knew that she was risking much when she did so, but she had reached that stage in her development when she considered it a duty for every woman to decide for herself in questions of right and wrong. She was also firmly convinced that it was necessary openly to acknowledge the existence of social evils. To Jemima, Ruth's sin appears to be "that evil most repugnant to her womanly modesty", and at first she "would fain have ignored its existence altogether". But far from approving of this "maidenly" Victorian wish, Mrs. Gaskell found Jemima's attitude pharisaical and cowardly:

"she had never imagined that she should ever come in contact with any one who had committed open sin; . . . her conviction . . . that all the respectable, all the family and religious circumstances of her life, would hedge her in, and guard her from ever encountering the great shock of coming face to face with Vice . . . she had all a Pharisee's dread of publicans and sinners, and all a child's cowardliness—that cowardliness which prompts it to shut its eyes against the object of terror, rather than acknowledge its existence with brave faith".[2]

But Mrs. Gaskell realised that it would not be easy for her to write in opposition to the accepted standards of good taste and convention, and she stated her problem on the second page of the novel:

"The daily life into which people are born, and into which they are absorbed before they are well aware, forms chains which only one in a hundred has moral strength enough to despise, and to break when the right time comes—when an inward necessity for independent individual action arises, which is superior to all outward conventionalities."

---

[1] See p. 148.   [2] P. 225.

Mrs. Gaskell had the moral strength and decided to take up the theme. It was no easy decision. She knew from bitter experience how much criticism she could draw down upon herself by attempts at reform, even when these related to subjects which everybody was discussing openly, such as factory conditions. And she well knew how much more violent criticism would result from the use of this new theme. A woman, if she was to be considered as "pure-minded" according to Victorian standards, must know nothing about sex, and above all not show such prurience as to want to discuss anything connected with such a subject. Although it is one of the most widely known facts about the Victorian mental atmosphere that these subjects were very efficiently tabooed, modern critics of *Ruth* do not generally pay any regard to how much real courage was necessary to disregard the generally accepted standards of propriety and good taste, and Mrs. Gaskell has been much criticized for a prudish lack of realism and inability to describe passion.[1]

Other writers about the middle of the nineteenth century realized the difficulties in the path of a woman who wrote about sexual matters. Harriet Martineau, for instance, though not treating the subject from a moral angle or as a personal problem for a special individual, had to overcome strong inhibitions before she could bring herself to write about the population question, when she was writing her *Illustrations of Political Economy* in 1832.[2]

· Josephine Butler gives a good illustration, often quoted in books about women's rights, of the attitude in such circles as might be expected not to be too narrow-minded or unable to think for them-

---

[1] Lord David Cecil, who, in *Early Victorian Novelists*, criticizes Mrs. Gaskell from a purely literary point of view, accuses her of being "easily shocked", and considers *Ruth* a failure, because "Any story illustrating such a theme requires in its teller a capacity to express passion".

[2] "When the course of my exposition brought me to the Population subject, I, with my youthful and provincial mode of thought and feeling,—brought up too amidst the prudery which is found in its great force in our middle class,— could not but be sensible that I risked much ... I felt that the subject was one of science, and therefore perfectly easy to treat in itself; but I was aware that some evil associations had gathered about it,—though I did not know what they were. While writing 'Weal and Woe in Garveloch', the perspiration many a time streamed down my face, ... The misery arose from my seeing how the simplest statements and reasonings might and probably would be perverted." (Martineau, *op. cit.*, I: 200.)

selves. This is what she writes about the reactions to *Ruth* among
university people at Oxford about 1853:

"A book was published at that time by Mrs. Gaskell, and was much discussed. This led to expressions of judgment which seemed to me false—
fatally false. A moral lapse in a woman was spoken of as an immensely
worse thing than in a man; there was no comparison to be formed between
them. A pure woman, it was reiterated, should be absolutely ignorant of
a certain class of evils in the world, albeit those evils bore with a murderous
cruelty on other women. One young man seriously declared that he would
not allow his own mother to read such a book as that under discussion—a
book which seemed to me to have a very wholesome tendency, though
dealing with a painful subject. Silence was thought to be the great duty
of all on such subjects. On one occasion, when I was distressed by a bitter case of wrong inflicted on a very young girl, I ventured to speak to one
of the wisest men—so esteemed—in the university, in the hope that he
would suggest some means, not of helping her, but of bringing to a sense
of his crime the man who had wronged her. The sage, speaking kindly however, sternly advocated silence and inaction. 'It would only do harm to
open up in any way such a question as this. It was dangerous to arouse a
sleeping lion.' "[1]

In view of such prevalent attitudes, Mrs. Gaskell's courage
is indisputable when she made it "one of [her] objects to make her
readers feel how much worse he [the seducer] was in every way
than Ruth, although the world visited her conduct with so much
heavier a penalty than his".[2] In spite of the controversy to which
other problems in the novel gave rise, this was recognized by the
reading public to be the author's aim. The *Prospective Review*
stated in May, 1853, that "her object" was "to enter a protest
against the prevalent conventional morality, which treats with re-

[1] George W. and Lucy A. Johnson, ed., *Josephine E. Butler, An Autobiographical Memoir*. With Introduction by James Stuart (London, 1909), p. 31.

[2] Letter from Catherine Winkworth to Eliza Paterson in 1853. (Shaen, *op.
cit.*, p. 101.) Although Mrs. Gaskell was afterwards much pained by some people's
reactions to the book, she was from the very first perfectly aware of the risks she
was taking, and never regretted having written it. " 'An unfit subject for fiction'
is the thing they say about it; but I determined notwithstanding to speak my
mind out about it; only now I shrink with more pain than I can tell you from
what people are saying though I cld. do every jot of it over again tomorrow",
she wrote to Mrs. Robson. (Copy of letter in the Brotherton Library.) In the
same letter she expressed her conviction "that what was meant so earnestly *must*
do some good, though perhaps not all the good, or not the *very* good I meant".

volting levity the crime of the seducer, and consigns to equal ob-
liquy his innocent victim, and the hardened sinner". In July the
same year the *Gentleman's Magazine* wrote: "The most striking of
our English female novels seems to us however to be 'Ruth' . . .
the injustice of merely punishing the delinquents of one sex, however repentant . . . while . . . the actual deserter of the betrayed
woman is scarcely less welcomed by society *after* than *before* his
offence."[1]

In choosing this theme, Mrs. Gaskell was running counter not
only to public opinion, but also to the spirit of the law.

"As to what constitutes condonation, it would appear that the Courts
have held since 1857, as they held before the Matrimonial Causes Act before that year, that condonation of adultery is meritorious on the part of
a woman, but not on the part of a man. 'Forgiveness', said Sir John
Nicholl, 'on the part of the wife, especially with a large family, in the hope
of reclaiming her husband, is meritorious, while a similar forgiveness on
the part of the husband would be degrading and dishonourable'. (*Durant
v. Durant*, 1825.)"[2]

Any amendment of the laws concerning these things encountered
bitter opposition. The Poor Law Amendment Act of 1844 was the
first of a series which gave the woman herself a right to force the
father of her child to contribute to its support. When the Bastardy
Bill of 1845 was before the House of Lords one speaker asserted
that by the Act of the previous year "the Legislature thinking
itself wiser than Providence, held out a remuneration to her
[the offender] for the commission of a crime".[3] Public opinion,
like this speaker, considered it right to visit the whole punishment
in cases of immorality on one of the offenders simply because "that
was the state in which nature left it".

Mrs. Gaskell's second aim, to show the fallacy of the Victorian

---

[1] Mrs. Gaskell never ceased to feel strongly on the subject. Even in *Wives
and Daughters*, otherwise so free from polemic matter, the Gibsons' maid is
arbitrarily dismissed when discovered by her master in the act of secretly carrying
a letter to Molly, and Jenny "chose to say it was Mr. Coxe the tempter who
ought to have 'been sent packing', not Bethia, the tempted, the victim". And the
author adds: "In this view there was quite enough plausibility to make Mr. Gibson feel that he had been rather unjust." (P. 84.)

[2] Reiss, *op. cit.*, p. 54.

[3] *Ibid.*, p. 119.

classification of women as "pure" or "fallen", was equally un-popular.

When planning *Ruth*, Mrs. Gaskell was faced with a dilemma which she had not encountered in the writing of *Mary Barton*. In that book, too, she had looked to private initiative and a general change of heart to better social conditions. But the evil which she attacked were those very conditions, which could be improved, she believed, if the conscience of the people concerned was aroused, but which were not caused by the prevalent mental attitude of the general public. In *Ruth*, however, she could no longer achieve her aim by exciting the reader's pity by means of descriptions of miserable dwellings, grimy streets, hunger and sickness, except in that part of the book where she took up the cause of sewing-women. The chief cause of all the evils commonly resulting from a seduction was the rigorous attitude of the general public, and Mrs. Gaskell had to face a psychological problem. What she wanted to say, if it was to be said through the medium of a novel, could be illustrated only by an individual case, a human figure. Here two courses were open to her: she could either write a good novel with a convincing heroine, such as for instance Mary Barton, who was "charming—from not being too perfect"[1], and thus give her opponents a chance to retort that such a woman deserved her fate; or she could take every precaution against such a contingency by making her heroine conform in every detail to the accepted Victorian ideal of a young, innocent, and consequently ignorant girl, as well as to the convention that a novel heroine must have no serious faults and commit no serious moral mistakes.[2] The dilemma puzzled her. "I . . . took so much pains over writing it, that I lost my own power of judging and could not tell whether I had done it well or ill", she wrote in a letter.[3]

However, she deliberately chose to sacrifice literary interest in order to present her moral in a convincing way. The letter quoted above goes on: "I tried to make both the story and the writing as quiet as I could, in order that 'people' (my great bugbear) might not say that they could not see what the writer felt to be a very

---

[1] Maria Edgeworth's letter quoted on pp. 78, 148, 210.

[2] Cf. p. 78.

[3] Letter to Monckton Milnes of Jan. 15, 1853, quoted by Coolidge, *op. cit.*

plain and earnest truth, for romantic incidents or exaggerated writing." To her sister-in-law, Mrs. Gaskell wrote: "I could have put more power, but that I wanted to keep it quiet in tone, lest by the slightest exaggeration, or over-strained sentiment I might weaken the force of what I had to say."[1]

The plot is conventional. Like the seamstress in Caroline Norton's *The Child of the Islands*, Ruth is "a ruined farmer's daughter", apprenticed to a dressmaker, where, again like her sister in the poem, she

> "pines . . .
> For purer air; for sunbeams warm and kind; . . .
> The rural freedom, long since left behind!"

Ruth, in her perfect innocence, is all that the most conventional Victorian proprieties demanded of a young girl. Charlotte Brontë's heroines, who fell in love and confessed it before they were properly courted, shocked the reading public. Accordingly, Mrs. Gaskell took care that Ruth be guilty of no such unmaidenliness, and let her remain unaware of any tender feelings when Mr. Bellingham gives her a flower: "Yet she had no idea that any association made her camelia precious to her. She believed it was solely on account of its exquisite beauty that she touched it so carefully. Mrs. Gaskell carefully impressed her readers with the idea of the purity of Ruth's mind on this occasion; when another girl wishes that the flower had some scent, she replies: "I wish it to be exactly as it is—it is perfect. So pure!" In her anxiety to represent Ruth as a paragon of Victorian maidenly behaviour Mrs. Gaskell gives to her an intuitive but vague consciousness of having infringed the rules of propriety when she comes back from her first walk alone with Mr. Bellingham, "a thing which was, as far as reason and knowledge (*her* knowledge) went, so innocent".[2] She is not, however, allowed to have any idea of Mr. Bellingham's share in her enjoyment of the walk:

" 'How strange it is', she thought that evening, 'that I should feel as if this charming afternoon's walk were, somehow, not exactly wrong, but yet as if it were not right. Why can it be? I am not defrauding Mrs. Mason of

---

[1] Letter to Mrs. Robson quoted on p. 212.
[2] P. 28.

any of her time; . . . If I had gone this walk with Jenny, I wonder whether I should have felt as I do now. There must be something wrong in me, myself, to feel so guilty when I have done nothing which is not right; . . .' . . . She was not conscious, as yet, that Mr. Bellingham's presence had added any charm to the ramble";[1]

This confused sense of guilt would, of course, be the logical result of a girl's education according to Victorian standards, which demanded of her absolute ignorance of everything connected with sex[2], yet expected her to know by instinct when her ignorance placed her in situations not strictly proper. Echoing the apprehensions of another of Mrs. Gaskell's innocents, Miss Matty in *Cranford*[3], Ruth says about the next walk: "It seems as if it would be such a great pleasure, that it must be in some way wrong."[4]

Believing her dismissal from the dressmaking establishment irrevocable, Ruth accepts Mr. Bellingham's proposal to take her with him to London. Like the young women in the *Westminster Review* article, which seems to have inspired Mrs. Gaskell to the writing of *Ruth*[5], she does so "from pure unknowingness": "'Yes'; the fatal word of which she so little imagined the infinite consequences."[6] Again, Mrs. Gaskell stresses her innocence and her childish dependence on others—she is not yet quite sixteen—: "She was little accustomed to oppose the wishes of any one; obedient and docile by nature, and unsuspicious and innocent of any harmful consequences."[7] Moreover, "it was one of the faults of her nature to be ready to make any sacrifices for those who loved her, and to value affection almost above its price".[8]

Those pages of the novel which contain Mrs. Gaskell's analysis of Ruth's state of mind when she followed Mr. Bellingham to London, and lived with him there, were probably among those which puzzled the author and where she deliberately chose to sacrifice

---

[1] P. 29.

[2] Dr. Gregory's idea was still widely prevalent: "Virgin purity is of that delicate nature, that it cannot hear certain things without contamination." (*A Father's Legacy to his Daughters*, Edinburgh, 1821, p. 164.)

[3] "I only hope it is not improper; so many pleasant things are." (*Cranford,* Chap. IV.)

[4] P. 30.   [5] See pp. 207–10.   [6] P. 41.

[7] P. 43.   [8] P. 173.

literary interest in order to point her moral more clearly.[1] They are also those which have been most severely criticized both by modern critics and by contemporary reviewers, by the former because of the author's inability to describe passion, and by the latter because of her insistence on the heroine's essential innocence. Some refused to accept as typical the extenuating circumstances in Ruth's case, especially her essential innocence of mind even after her "fall". "It is not snow pure simplicity that slips oftenest into sin", wrote the *British Quarterly Review*.[2] *Sharpe's London Magazine* had the same objection to the book: "she has failed, because her portrait is untrue to the daily experience of actual life . . . Ruth, in her childlike purity and innocence, is not a veritable type of her class".[3]

Eliza Cook's Journal, however, accepted Mrs. Gaskell's explanation of Ruth's behaviour: "Ruth has . . . become sinful, but it is the sin of ignorance. She has not gained that consciousness which makes wrong painful"[4], and a few reviewers agreed to consider this state of mind in the heroine as true to life. The *Prospective Review* wrote: "We have no sympathy with the sentiment conveyed in Milton's familiar line: 'He for God only, she for God in him.'

"Nevertheless, we believe it to contain a truthful picture of a girl's creed, when her affections have been engaged, prior to the development of her judgment and her moral sense."[5]

With the complete ignorance of evil which was the logical result of an education in strict accordance with Victorian ideals Ruth, like Esther in *Mary Barton*, has no sense of guilt before her lover has deserted her. In fact, she is unconscious not only of having done anything wrong but also of the opinion which other people hold of her conduct. In this first phase of childish trust in and obedience to Mr. Bellingham, she makes no attempt to think for her-

---

[1] The reviewer in the *Gentleman's Magazine* (July, 1853) showed some understanding for Mrs. Gaskell's reasoning on this point: "had Ruth erred from passion rather than from ignorance, scenes must have been constructed in accordance with that view, and then we should have had the usual objectionable draggings through dangerous mazes of sentiment and suffering, which a pure writer would of course much prefer shunning altogether".

[2] April 1, 1867.   [3] Jan. 15, 1853.   [4] March, 1853.   [5] May, 1853.

self, and when a small boy is the means of revealing to her the opinion of the world, she is staggered and saddened, but still she feels no sense of sin or any wish to change her mode of life:

"Harry . . . lifted up his sturdy little right arm and hit Ruth a great blow on the face . . . 'She's a bad, naughty girl—mamma said so, she did; . . .' . . . Ruth . . . stood, white and still, with a new idea running through her mind . . . '. . . Go away, naughty woman!' said the boy . . . Ruth turned away, humbly and meekly, with bent head, and slow, uncertain steps . . . She could not put into words the sense she was just beginning to entertain of the estimation in which she was henceforward to be held. She thought he would be as much grieved as she was at what had taken place that morning; she fancied she should sink in his opinion if she told him how others regarded her; besides, it seemed ungenerous to dilate upon the sufferings of which he was the cause.

" 'I will not', thought she, 'embitter his life; I will try and be cheerful. I must not think of myself so much. If I can but make him happy, what need I care for chance speeches?' "[1]

It is of interest to see that, even at this early stage, the author makes Ruth consider Mr. Bellingham as "the cause of her sufferings", and that she regards her own life in some way as a sacrifice to him, an attitude not quite consistent with her acceptance of protection from him in the first place and unconsciousness of anything wrong in her way of life in the second. Nevertheless, the above description of her state of mind, was accepted by some contemporary reviewers as true to life, at least in individual cases.[2]

Until this moment, the essential characteristic which Mrs. Gaskell impresses on the reader as an excuse for and an explanation of Ruth's behaviour is her "childlike dependence on others".[3] Like all Mrs. Gaskell's heroines, though, she pulls herself together in a crisis and develops into an adult woman when someone is helplessly dependent on her, in this case Mr. Bellingham in his illness: "the occasion was calling out strength sufficient to meet it . . . she forced herself to eat, because his service needed her strength. She did not indulge in any tears, because the weeping she longed for would make her less able to attend upon him".[4] The realization of her "sin", however, is a slower process. Even when Mr. Bellingham deserts her, "She had no penitence, no consciousness of error

---

[1] Pp. 50–51.   [2] See p. 195.
[3] P. 56.   [4] Pp. 55–6.

or offence: no knowledge of any one circumstance but that he was gone".[1]

The conventional opinion of the world is represented by the maid who refuses to nurse Ruth in her illness: " 'no, indeed, ma'am', said the maid, drawing herself up, stiff in her virtue. 'I'm sure, ma'am, you would not expect it of me; I could never have the face to dress a lady of character again".[2] Mr. Bellingham's mother, to whom Ruth is "this creature"[2], holds the same view. To her, it seems right that the woman should bear all the blame. Her idea of propriety is hard and uncompromising: "I suppose you are not so lost to all sense of propriety as to imagine it fit or desirable that your mother and this degraded girl should remain under the same roof."[3] As usual, however, Mrs. Gaskell tried to see both sides of the question, and her wish for tolerance and understanding included even Mrs. Bellingham. She says of Mr. Benson: "He had wide-enough sympathy to understand that it must have been a most painful position in which the mother had been placed, on finding herself under the same roof with a girl who was living with her son, as Ruth was."[4]

Mr. Bellingham has some doubts about simply leaving Ruth to her fate, "though the really right never entered his head"[5], but his mother, in her own opinion, "does the thing handsomely", when she not only leaves Ruth fifty pounds, but goes to the length of giving her advice about her future way of life:

"I wish to exhort you to repentance, and to remind you that you will not have your own guilt alone upon your head, but that of any young man whom you may succeed in entrapping into vice. I shall pray that you may turn to an honest life, and I strongly recommend you, if indeed you are not 'dead in trespasses and sins', to enter some penitentiary."[6]

---

[1] P. 65.   [2] P. 74.   [3] P. 63.   [4] P. 73.   [5] P. 64.

[6] P. 64. It should be noted that, at the time when *Ruth* was published, there had as yet been very few humane attempts made to rescue "fallen" women. Henry Mayhew, in *London Labour and London Poor* (London, 1862), pp. XXXIV–XXXV, mentions twenty-three institutions in London "adapted to the rescue and reformation of fallen women, or such as have been led astray from the paths of virtue", but the large majority of them were founded as a result of articles in the press and such books as *Ruth*, which "put the small edge of the wedge in" (Letter about *Ruth* from Mrs. Gaskell to Mrs. Jameson, 1853. Erskine, *op. cit.*, p. 294). The Reformatory and Refuge Union, for instance, with the "Female

After Mr. Bellingham has left Ruth, it is the helplessness of another being that gives her strength, first that of Mr. Benson, the cripple, whose cry of pain stops her on her way to suicide, and later that of her unborn child. On the subject of the illegitimate child, Mrs. Gaskell took up a new attitude. She, who had herself written about "that first mother's rapture"[1], could not think of a baby as anything but a blessing to the mother. She herself had known no mother, and the many instances in her stories of young girls longing for their dead mothers, whose loving care would have smoothed out all difficulties, are probably autobiographical.[2] It also seems safe to assume that the perfect mother-son relationship in *Ruth*, in all its tearful sentimentality, was occasioned by regret for her only son, who died in 1845 at the age of one, a loss which constituted the great tragedy in Mrs. Gaskell's life.[3]

Mission" attached to it, was founded in 1856. Before that time, women such as Ruth were considered as criminals and treated accordingly. Concerning the path back to virtue recommended to Ruth by Mrs. Bellingham, Henry Mayhew wrote (*op. cit.*, p. XXXVI): "The almost penal character of the system pursued in many of the older penitentiaries is founded on the misconception, that the injury sustained by society in the departure from virtue of her female members, can only be atoned for by some personal mulct inflicted on the offender . . .

The impediments which the old penitentiary system of close confinement, criminal fare, and hard labour, have unfortunately presented to the rescue of fallen women is too well known to those who are accustomed to deal with this class. Frequently are the urgent entreaties of the missionary to forsake an abandoned course of life, and seek shelter in some institution, met with either rancorous denunciations against the penal system, or by polite but firm refusals to submit to the discipline, which is supposed to extend to all reformatory asylums."

[1] See p. 46.

[2] It is remarkable that in Mrs. Gaskell's stories the relationship *living* mother —daughter is not idealised, except in the early story *Lizzie Leigh*. Phillis and Sylvia in *Cousin Phillis* and *Sylvia's Lovers* have no exaggerated love for their mothers. Margaret in *North and South* finds it difficult to get on with her mother at first, and Maggie in *The Moorland Cottage* is treated by her mother as something of a Cinderella. Jemima in *Ruth* suffers from the conviction that she is not loved by either of her parents. Lastly, in *Wives and Daughters* the "separation of mother and child" is said to have "lessened the amount of affection the former had to bestow" (p. 144), and Cynthia does not think that "love for one's mother quite comes by nature". (P. 218.)

[3] "my darling's short presence in this life . . . the never ending sorrow", Mrs. Gaskell wrote to Miss Fox in a letter of April 26, 1850 (now in the Brother-

To Ruth "the strange, new, delicious prospect of becoming a mother seemed to give her some mysterious source of strength".[1] It is not difficult to see with whom the author sides in Mr. Benson's discussion with his sister Faith about the child:

> " 'Oh, I was just beginning to have a good opinion of her, but I'm afraid she is very depraved . . . she whispered, quite eagerly, 'Did he say I should have a baby?' . . . She . . . took it just as if she had a right to have a baby. She said, 'Oh, my God, I thank thee!' . . .
>
> " '. . . The sin appears to me to be quite distinct from its consequences . . . We knew her errors before, Faith.'
>
> " 'Yes, but not this disgrace—this badge of her shame!' . . .
>
> " '. . . here is the very instrument to make her forget herself, and be thoughtful for another. Teach her . . . to reverence her child; and this reverence will shut out sin,—will be purification.' . . .
>
> "I think you, Thurstan, are the first person I ever heard rejoicing over the birth of an illegitimate child. It appears to me, I must own, rather questionable morality.' . . .[2]

ton Library). Faith's warning to Ruth: "You must not make him into an idol, or God will, perhaps, punish you through him", echoes a phrase out of her *Diary*: "I pray that I may not make her [Marianne] too much of my idol." (P. 17.) This apprehension is also expressed on pp. 11, 13, and 36 of the *Diary*. The same idea appears in her poem "A Christmas Carol" (1856). The old lady in that poem tells the story of her life to some children:

"All I had left to love—with blind devotion
I almost worshipp'd him—my child, my pride!
The Lord look'd down: in mercy and compassion
Chasten'd me again; my baby died!"

[1] P. 88.

[2] Ruth's and Mr. Benson's rejoicing over the birth of an unmarried mother's child was contrary to literary tradition when the novel was written. Later, however, it influenced at least one other devoted mother in English literature, Elizabeth Barrett Browning. Some lines in the Seventh Book of *Aurora Leigh* remind the reader of the dialogue in *Ruth* quoted above:

"And *I* could be a mother in a month?
I hope it was not wicked to be glad.
I lifted up my voice and wept, and laughed,
To heaven, not her, until it tore my throat.
'Confess, confess!'—what was there to confess,
Except man's cruelty, except my wrong?
. . .
                    'Good', she cried;
'Unmarried and a mother, and she laughs.'
'These unchaste girls are always impudent.'"

"... the world's way of treatment is too apt to harden the mother's natural love into something like hatred ... as for the fathers—God forgive them! I cannot—at least, not just now.' "[1]

It is only after Ruth has lived with the Bensons for some time that she begins to have a sense of guilt for her past life. She says about her child: "I have deserved suffering, but it will be such a little innocent darling!"[2], and she refuses to be called Mrs. Hilton: "It was my mother's name ... I had better not be called by it."[3] This sense of sin grows stronger the more she sees of the Bensons' home and life. The first time she goes with them to chapel, "Ruth came to the presence of God, as one who had gone astray, and doubted her own worthiness to be called His child; she came as a mother who had incurred a heavy responsibility".[4]

Another consequence of her development from a child into a woman is her changed idea of her seducer:

" 'He did me cruel harm. I can never again lift up my face in innocence ... You, who are the father of my child!' ... that very circumstance ... changed her from the woman into the mother—the stern guardian of her child ... '... He left me to bear the burden and the shame; and never cared to learn, as he might have done, of Leonard's birth. He has no love for his child, and I will have no love for him'."[5]

As a contrast, we are shown Mr. Bellingham's complacent indifference: "Poor Ruth! and, for the first time for several years, he wondered what had become of her; though, of course, there was but one thing that could have happened, and perhaps it was as well he did not know her end, for most likely it would have made him very uncomfortable."[6] Even earlier in the novel Mrs. Gaskell had emphasized the seducer's callous contempt for his mistress: "Her beauty was all that Mr. Bellingham cared for, ... It was all he recognised of her."[7]

---

[1] Pp. 82–4.   [2] Pp. 86–7.   [3] P. 91.

[4] P. 125.   [5] P. 190.   [6] P. 193.

[7] P. 52. This insistence on the seducer's heartlessness and guilt enraged some reviewers. In a review of *Ruth* which repeatedly asked the question "why was it written?" *Sharpe's London Magazine* (Vol. II, New Series, p. 125) blamed the author for introducing into the story "a gentleman ... who is drawn as worthless and heartless as it is the erroneous and unwise habit of some to portray *gentlemen*", and attacked her "strong propensity to look at the *wrong side* of what

All Ruth's decisions are henceforward dictated by her wish for the child's good; therefore it is no temptation to her to go back to Mr. Bellingham when he asks her to become his mistress again:

"To save Leonard from the shame and agony of knowing my disgrace, I would lie down and die . . . but to go back into sin would be the real cruelty to him. The errors of my youth may be washed away by my tears . . . I should not mind his knowing my past sin, compared to the awful corruption it would be if he knew me living now, as you would have me, lost to all fear of God."[1]

Reasoning in the same way as the author of the *Westminster Review* article which probably inspired the passage in *Ruth*[2], she even refuses to be "made an honest woman again":

"I do not love you. I did once . . . I could never love you again . . . I might plead that I was an ignorant child—only I will not plead anything, for God knows all.—But this is only one piece of our great difference—. . . If there were no other reason to prevent our marriage but the one fact that it would bring Leonard into contact with you, that would be enough."[3]

---

are termed 'respectable persons' ". *Tait's Edinburgh Magazine*, however, ranged itself enthusiastically on the novelist's side: "Puritanism . . . has omitted redressing the balance by condemning equally the male offender. It is an evil among us, which needed, no less than slavery did in America, the pen of a gifted woman to challenge its consideration." ("The Story of Ruth", April, 1853, pp. 217-20.)

[1] Pp. 209-10.

[2] See below, p. 209.

[3] Pp. 210-11. In French fiction, the reading public had already come across a similar scene. The writer of an article on *Ruth* in the *Prospective Review* (May, 1853. Article IV, "Recent Works of Fiction") pointed out this fact: "George Sand, who, in her beautiful drama of Claudie, has embodied a story similar to that of Ruth." He goes on to quote the seduced girl's answer when Ronciat offers marriage to her: "pour épouser un homme, il faut jurer à Dieu de l'aimer, de l'estimer, et de le respecter toute sa vie; et quand on sent qu'on ne peut que le mépriser, c'est mentir à Dieu, c'est faire un sacrilège, je refuse". There is, however, an important difference between George Sand's and Mrs. Gaskell's ideas on this subject. Mrs. Gaskell's heroine refuses to marry as much for her child's sake as for her own, whereas Claudie says about marrying her seducer: "Tant que mon pauvre enfant a vécu, j'ai dû le vouloir à cause de lui!" (Acte premier, Scène X.) *Claudie* caused a sensation when it was performed for the first time at the théâtre de la Porte-Saint-Martin on January 11, 1851. (See Felizia Seyd, *Romantic Rebel. The Life and Times of George Sand*, New York, 1940; p. 217.)

The *North British Review* (May, 1853) found other resemblances between George Sand's and Mrs. Gaskell's works: "he decks her [Ruth's] hair with

This attitude was, however, too unconventional for most people at the time. Public opinion considered it unnatural in a mother not to grasp at the opportunity of securing conventional legitimacy for her child. The *Prospective Review*, in the article quoted on p. 201, n. 3, stated that "her rejection of Mr. Bellingham's hand . . . we have heard censured both on moral and artistic grounds". The *North British Review*, in an otherwise favourable review of *Ruth*[1], asked the author if she were "quite sure that Ruth had the right, when Mr. Donne [Mr. Bellingham] offers to marry her, and give their son all the advantages of his position, to reject his offer?" In fact, Ruth is represented as dimly fearing this very objection to her attitude: " 'He will take the child from me' . . . She had a firm conviction—not the less firm because she knew not on what it was based—that a child, whether legitimate or not, belonged of legal right to the father."[2]

---

water-lilies (a passage which has strangely reminded us by contrast of a famous description in George Sand's 'Teverino', as the trial scene in 'Mary Barton' re-called a similar one in 'Mauprat' ". (*Mauprat* was published in 1836, *Teverino* in 1846.)

It might be noted that Mrs. Gaskell knew French well, before she made her first journey to France. In his introduction to the World's Classics edition of "*Cousin Phillis and other tales, etc.*", Clement Shorter writes (pp. XVII–XVIII): "Mrs. Gaskell was very fond of French literature. In a letter . . . to one of her publishers she expresses surprise that a supposed-to-be well-educated young lady she had met knew nothing about Madame de Sévigné, 'who had been like a well-known friend to me all my life'."

[1] May, 1853.

[2] P. 202. The laws concerning the custody of legitimate children had been hotly discussed. (Cf. p. 7.) Concerning illegitimate children they do not seem to have been very explicit: "It does not appear that the law in respect of the custody of an illegitimate child has undergone much change since 1837. It is doubtful whether at Common Law the mother of an illegitimate child had ever the same right to custody as had the father of a legitimate child, but in Equity the desire of the mother of an illegitimate child to custody was primarily to be considered unless it would be detrimental to the child to do so. 'In the eyes of the law', said Slessor *L. J.*, in 1931, 'such a child is *filius nullius* and has no legal guardians . . . Yet, while the child is under the age of nurture the mother has a right to possession'." (Reiss, *op. cit.*, p. 117.)

Mrs. Gaskell was well acquainted with the legal stipulations concerning a woman's right to her children, as is clear from a passage in *Sylvia's Lovers*, when Sylvia swears never to live again with Philip as his wife. The Quaker banker then warns her: "Thee hast sworn never to forgive thy husband, nor to live with

The *Westminster Review*, in an article which compared *Ruth* un-
favourably with Charlotte Brontë's *Villette*[1], objected to "the intensity of grief with which Ruth's child is afflicted on hearing that
his mother has not been married", and assured the author that
"in our day no such brand affects the illegitimate child". It was,
however, a subject on which Mrs. Gaskell felt strongly, and she
expressed her attitude in Ruth's words:

"It is a bitter shame and a sorrow that I have drawn down upon you . . .
but, Leonard, it is no disgrace or lowering of you in the eyes of God . . .
it seems a hard and cruel thing that you should be called reproachful names
by men, and all for what was no fault of yours . . . though my sin shall
have made you an outcast in the world . . . it is only your own sin that
can make you an outcast from God."[2]

In *Ruth* Mrs. Gaskell had undertaken to show not only that the
seducer was more to be blamed than the seduced, but also that one
lapse from virtue was not irretrievable. In the novel Mrs. Pearson,
in her unimaginative repetition of the world's opinion, expresses
what Mrs. Gaskell was trying to disprove: "what could become of
her? . . . one knows they can but go from bad to worse, poor creatures"![3]

"As the world goes, a woman's fault is always painted irretrievable" wrote the *Westminster Review* in April, 1853, and as late as
April 1, 1867, the *British Quarterly Review* wrote that "society has
decreed that women who have once left the straight paths of virtue shall wander all their days outcast, branded, apart". It added:
"We may say here, once for all, that in its rigour of social law against
wantonness we believe the *world* is right." *Every Saturday* (February 28, 1874) spoke of "that social ostracism which is the ban of
all who sin", and went on to say that "even the wretched being
herself feels that humility and obscurity are the only lot in future
for her". That had been the fate of Lizzie Leigh, of the unfortunate
girl in *The Well of Pen-Morfa*, and of Esther and, as the *Westminster*

him again. Dost thee know that by the law of the land, he may claim his child;
and then thou will have to forsake it or to be forsworn?" (P. 354.) *Sylvia's
Lovers* was, however, written at a period when Mrs. Gaskell no longer wrote
books to reform social conditions, and Sylvia's problem is solved by her husband
leaving the house in despair.

[1] January–April, 1853.   [2] P. 240.   [3] P. 223.

Review wrote (January–April, 1853), "The circulating libraries have furnished ... abundance of sickly sentimentality on this subject, wherein heroines strive to atone by consumption and broken hearts, for their lapse from virtue";

In *Ruth*, however, "even the wretched being herself" does not feel "that humility and obscurity are the only lot in future for her", and the turning-point is Leonard's birth: "Deep shame made her silent and reserved on all her life before Leonard's birth; from that time she rose again in her self-respect."[1] This regaining of the seduced woman's own self-respect is the newest idea in *Ruth*, both as regards the literary tradition and Mrs. Gaskell's earlier stories, which conformed to it. Like the traditional seduced women in sentimental or moralizing novels, Ruth dies in the end, but unlike them she does not spend her remaining years after her "fall" in obscurity and hopeless repentance. An overcoming of the heroine's own sense of sin seems to have been a stumbling-block to other religious writers at the time, but here, as in so many other respects, Mrs. Gaskell's Unitarian background was an influence towards broad-mindedness.[2]

But Mrs. Gaskell had no intention of representing Ruth's way back to respectability as easy. With her customary insistence on absolute truthfulness, which, again, was a special Unitarian characteristic[3], the author set out to prove that the Bensons' first attempt to save Ruth by passing her off as a widow was necessarily a

---

[1] P. 218.

[2] The attitude towards sin among the Cross Street Chapel congregation even seems to have shocked some of their non-Unitarian friends. One of Mrs. Gaskell's closest friends in Manchester, Catherine Winkworth, wrote to Edward Herford on November 5th, 1856, about James Martineau's "deep conviction of the evil of sin", and went on: "This last, especially, is utterly unlike anything I have ever seen in other Unitarians, whose easy way of getting over the difficulty in general, by a few moments of not over-sharp repentance, and a forgiveness that really deserves no better name than good-nature, is to me one of the worst parts of their system." When writing about Mr. Gaskell's and Mr. Taylor's congregations, Susanna Winkworth found "the spirit more charitable than in other places of worship". (Shaen, *op. cit.*, pp. 162, 26.)

[3] Susanna Winkworth wrote about them: "their excellences I feel most strongly—especially their truthfulness". (Shaen, *op. cit.*, p. 148.) R. V. Holt writes that one of their characteristics was "their passion for truth". (*Op. cit.*, p. 277.)

failure, because it was founded on a lie. When the truth about Ruth's past is discovered, the world, as represented by Mr. Bradshaw, her employer, once more casts her off although, in Jemima's words, "Ruth had worked her way through the deep purgatory of repentance up to something like purity again; . . . Whatever Ruth had been, she was good, and to be respected as such, now".[1] She is accepted again as respectable only after her work as a sick-nurse during the epidemic makes an onlooker say about her: "Such a one as her has never been a great sinner; nor does she do her work as a penance, but for the love of God, and of the blessed Jesus. She will be in the light of God's countenance when you and I will be standing afar off. . . The blessing of them who were ready to perish is upon her." And "From that day forward Leonard walked erect in the streets of Eccleston, where 'many arose and called her blessed' ".[2]

The purpose of the book is summed up in Mr. Benson's words to Mr. Bradshaw in Chapter XXVII: "not every woman who has fallen is depraved; . . . Is it not time to change some of our ways of thinking and acting? . . . to every woman, who, like Ruth, has sinned, should be given a chance of self-redemption"[3], and, later, in his condemnation of Ruth's seducer: "Men may call such actions as yours youthful follies! There is another name for them with God."[4]

Further to emphasize her thesis that every wrong-doer should be given a chance for self-redemption, Mrs. Gaskell inserted the story of Mr. Bradshaw's son, who commits a forgery. She probably hoped that readers would more easily see her point in a case which was not so obscured by conventions and prudery as was seduction. She was also led by a wish to show "the right side of what are termed respectable persons".[5] Indeed, in her wish to emphasize the unconquerable love of rectitude in Mr. Bradshaw, which makes him show as little mercy to his own son as to Ruth, she succeeded a little too well; some reviewers expressed their approval of his attitude as opposed to those willing to show mercy and tolerance.[6]

---

[1] P. 227.   [2] P. 299.   [3] P. 244.   [4] P. 315.   [5] See p. 200, n. 7.

[6] Mrs. Gaskell had hesitated about drawing the parallel at all. Forster, however, encouraged her to do so: "I don't agree with you in thinking the forgery incident an episode at all. On the contrary . . . quite essential to the story." (Nov. 12, 1852. Extract of letter in the Brotherton Library.)

That the problem of prostitution worried Mrs. Gaskell is evident from her treatment of it in *Mary Barton* and in her early short stories. In her social novels, her source of inspiration was, as has been pointed out above, the debate carried an in newspapers, in Parliament, official reports, etc., on the problems of the day. Prostitution was a frequent subject for such debates, and it was attracting even more attention about 1850 than before. Henry Mayhew, whose articles in the *Morning Chronicle* had not yet appeared when *Mary Barton* was written, did not mince his words on the subject:

"Thus 'where occasional spasms of sympathy, the well-merited castigations of the press, and the voice of popular opinion had unitedly failed to shake the throne of the god of Mammon, erected on skeletons, and cemented with the blood of women and children . . . only let the solemn and fearful fact be borne in mind, that in London *alone* 1000 poor girls are yearly crushed out of life from over-toil and grinding oppression, while 15.000 are living in a state of semi-starvation. Ah! who can wonder that our streets swarm with the fallen and the lost, when *sin or starve* is the dire alternative! Who cannot track the via doloroso between the 15.000 starving and the thrice that number living by sin as a trade'."[1]

Mrs. Gaskell, with her well-known love for children, and living as she did in one of the largest manufacturing towns of the country, cannot have remained unmoved by such statements as the following:

"There is a tone of morality throughout the rural districts of England, which is unhappily wanting in the large towns and the centres of particular manufactures . . . seduction and prostitution . . . have made enormous strides in all the great towns within the last twenty years . . . compare the number of legitimate with illegitimate births. Add up the number of infanticides and the number of deaths of infants of tender years—an item more alarming than any."[2]

Anybody with a social conscience would feel obliged to inquire into the causes of this evil, and Mrs. Gaskell came to see seduction and the attitude of society towards those women who had once been seduced as the chief reason of prostitution. The logical consequence for her, the author with a social message, was the writing of *Ruth*. For the general tendency and reasoning in that book, as

---

[1] *Op. cit.*, p. XXIX.   [2] *Ibid.*, p. 255.

well as the special aspects of the problem treated there, it is tempting to point to one article in particular as its chief inspiration. The article in question is in the *Westminster and Foreign Quarterly Review* of April–July, 1850 (pp. 448–560), and is entitled "Prostitution".[1] I have found no direct proof, nor any suggestion in the work of any critic or biographer, that Mrs. Gaskell had read it but, on the other hand, there is no evidence to contradict the supposition that she did, and the resemblance between its general tendency and the ideas which Mrs. Gaskell expressed in *Ruth* is so striking that mere coincidence seems unlikely. There is no trace in Mrs. Gaskell's correspondence of any plans for writing such a work as *Ruth* before 1850; the first we hear of it is in April, 1852, in connection with a letter to Charlotte Brontë in which Mrs. Gaskell furnished her friend with an outline of the novel.[2] Moreover, it seems reasonable to assume that Mrs. Gaskell's attention was drawn to the article by virtue of the fact that the writer of the *Westminster Review* article thought her own contribution to the treatment of postitution in fiction important enough to quote a whole page from *Mary Barton* about Esther.[3] He did not, however, consider this early effort to grapple with the problem as sufficient, for the article contains a passage which must have sounded like a direct appeal to the portrayer of Esther and Lizzie Leigh:

"no ruler or writer has yet been found with nerve to face the sadness, or resolution to encounter the difficulties . . . we are aware that we shall expose ourselves to much scoffing from the vulgar and light-minded . . . much serious blame on the part of those who think that no object can justify us in compelling attention to so revolting a moral sore . . . Our divines, our philanthropists, our missionaries, nay, even our sœurs de la charité, do not shrink from entering, in person, the most loathsome abodes of sin and misery . . . it is a false and mischievous delicacy, and a culpable

---

[1] The fact that nearly three years elapsed between the publication of the *Westminster Review* article and *Ruth* (published in Jan. 1853) is not inconsistent with the theory that the article served as an incitement to Mrs. Gaskell to write the novel, as she seems sometimes to have thought of the plan for a story a long time before she actually wrote it. Concerning *North and South*, for instance, she wrote to Mrs. Jameson: "I had the plot and characters in my head long ago." (Erskine, *op. cit.*, pp. 296–7.)

[2] The letter itself is now lost, but Charlotte Brontë discussed the planned novel in her reply. (Shorter, *op. cit.*, II: 263.)

[3] From Chap. IV, "Jem's Interview with poor Esther".

moral cowardice, which shrinks from the consideration of the great social vice of Prostitution . . . It is [considered] discreditable to a woman to know of their existence".

Then the article goes on to draw up what reads like a complete plan of *Ruth*. The whole tendency of the book is expressed here:

"The swindler may repent, the drunkard may reform; society . . . welcomes back with joy . . . the lost sheep and the prodigal son. But the prostitute may *not* pause—may *not* recover: at the very first halting, timid step she may make to the right or the left, with a view to flight from her appalling doom, the whole resistless influences of the surrounding world, the good as well as the bad, close around her to hunt her back into perdition . . ."

The writer of this article emphasizes the sheer innocence and ignorance of young girls as an explanation of why so many of them were seduced—a thesis which occasioned much adverse comment in the case of *Ruth:*

"There is . . . a very general misapprehension, especially among the fair sex, as to . . . the primary circumstances of their fall from chastity . . . The causes which lead to the fall of women are various; but all of them are of a nature to move grief and compassion rather than indignation and contempt, . . .

"Many—far more than would generally be believed—fall from pure unknowingness. Their affections are engaged, their confidence secured; thinking no evil themselves, they permit caresses which in themselves, and to them, indicate no wrong, and are led on ignorantly and thoughtlessly from one familiarity to another, not conscious where those familiarities must inevitably end, till ultimate resistance becomes almost impossible; and they learn, when it is too late—what women can never learn too early or impress too strongly on their minds—that a lover's encroachments, to be repelled successfully, must be repelled and negatived at the very outset."

We find in the same article a rough draft of Ruth's own reaction to her "sin", and the almost insuperable difficulties in her way back to respectability:

"the great majority of these poor women fall, in the first instance, from causes in which vice and selfishness have no share . . . What makes it *impossible* for them to retrace their steps? . . . Clearly, that harsh, savage, unjust, unchristian public opinion which has resolved to regard a whole life of indulgence on the part of one sex as venial and natural, and a single false step on the part of the other as irretrievable and unpardonable. How few women are there who, after the first error, do not awake to repentance, agony, and shame, and would not give all they possess to be allowed to recover and recoil! They may be in love with their seducer—never with their sin . . . They yearn, with a passionate earnestness of which mere innocence can form no conception, to be permitted to recover their lost position at the expense of any penitence, however severe, after the lapse of any time, however long. But we brutally refuse to lend an ear to these entreaties. Forgetting our Master's precepts—. . . we turn contemptuously aside from the kneeling and weeping Magdalen, coldly bid her to despair, and leave her *alone with the irreparable* . . . The more shame she feels (*i.e.*, the less her *virtue* has suffered in reality), the more impossible is her recovery, because the more does she shrink from those who might have been able to redeem her.—Alas, is it not notorious that, of a hundred fathers who would fall upon the neck of the prodigal son, and hail his return with unlimited forgiveness, there is scarcely one who, obedient to the savage morality of the world, would not turn his back upon the erring and repentant daughter? When shall we learn, in judging the moral delinquencies of the two sexes, to eschew those partial balances and false weights, which are an abomination to the Lord?"

Even the problem of the abandoned woman's refusal to marry her seducer, which stirred up so much controversy in the case of *Ruth*, is discussed here:

"One only chance of restoration does society offer to the poor victim of seduction; . . . If her seducer can be induced, . . . to marry her, her fault is, not expiated, but amended and obliterated; as the phrase goes, she is 'made an honest woman again'. What a withering sarcasm upon our ethical notions is contained in that coarse expression! . . . in the cases which have come before us, . . . We have said, 'Do not let one false step lead you on to commit another, of which the punishment may last through life'."

The words "the hard-hearted, inequitable Pharisaism of society must be held responsible. In this matter 'we are very guilty concerning our sister'," call to mind such characters as Mr. Bradshaw and Mrs. Bellingham in *Ruth*.

"We have no wish to extenuate the sin or to palliate the weakness; but . . ., let us be *just*" might just as well have been written by the author of *Ruth*, and she has been almost equally blamed and praised for keeping to this attitude throughout the book.

Lastly, Mrs. Gaskell, that adoring and adored mother, cannot have been unmoved by the following paragraph in the article: "The married woman says to her, '. . . to me the consequences are a happy home and loving children, . . .; to you, the consequences are desertion, horror, and degradation, and your children shall be a terror and a curse to you . . .' " It should be noted that one of the most important ideas in Mrs. Gaskell's novel is the good influence which the child proves to be in its unmarried mother's life. In fact, all those points which stirred up controversy in the case of *Ruth*, such ideas, consequently, as were new enough to appear shocking in a work of fiction if not in a magazine article, are already emphasized in this article: the attitude of "respectable" persons is considered as one important cause of prostitution, the initial innocence of the majority of seduced girls is stressed and the double moral attacked, the seduced woman is exhorted, under certain circumstances, to refuse to marry her seducer, an appeal is made for a chance for self-redemption for the fallen, and the seduced woman is considered in her capacity as mother. As usual in the case of Mrs. Gaskell's novels with a purpose, her ideas, though she had made them her own so that they expressed her well-considered convictions, were not new. What was new, however, was her use of them in a work of fiction.

In remaining true to the general ideas thus expressed in the *Westminster Review* article, Mrs. Gaskell had, in addition to her dilemma concerning Ruth's character, the problem of a proper conclusion to the book. In *David Copperfield* (1849–50) Dickens, far from trying to show that there might still be hope for little Em'ly in her own country, saw emigration as the only possibility open to her. Mrs. Gaskell had been expressly warned against this cheap expedient, to which she too had resorted in her first novel. Maria Edgeworth, in the letter quoted on pp. 78 and 148, had written of *Mary Barton:* "Such a powerful writer as the author of Mary Barton *could* tend to this beneficial purpose by his pathetic representations and appeals to the feelings of pity and remorse—But I doubt whether this has been affected by the present tale—*Emigration* is the only resource pointed out at the end of this work, and this is only an escape from the evils not a remedy nor any tendency to reparation or improvement."[1]

---

[1] The letter is among those deposited in the John Rylands Library by the executors of Mrs. Gaskell's last surviving daughter. It was addressed to Mrs. Gaskell's cousin, Miss Mary Holland, "and was no doubt soon handed over by her to the person most interested in it". (*Bulletin*, p. 108.)

Mrs. Gaskell may have feared to give an impression of levity if she let Ruth have a long and happy life after her "sinful" youth, like Becky Sharp in Thackeray's *Vanity Fair* (1847–8) and Effie Deans in Scott's *The Heart of Midlothian* (1818). Any such tendency in the fiction of the day was strongly opposed, by the *Prospective Review* for one, which, in May 1853, in an article entitled "Recent Works of Fiction", attacked "some false tendencies, manifested in the imaginative literature of the day", expressed disgust "that authors should voluntarily select the repulsive", and condemned the "levity with which vice is not unfrequently alluded to".[1] Remembering the many deaths both in *Mary Barton* and in Mrs. Gaskell's short stories, however, one is tempted to conclude that her tendency towards melodrama was too strong for her, so that she could not resist the temptation to end *Ruth* with a tearful death-bed scene. But this ending was not received with unanimous enthusiasm by Mrs. Gaskell's fellow writers. Charlotte Brontë, who liked to end her own books with a happy marriage, protested as soon as she was told about Mrs. Gaskell's plan: "hear my protest! Why should she die"?[2] Elizabeth Barrett Browning reacted in the same way: "Was it quite impossible but that your Ruth should *die?*"[3]

As has been shown above, Mrs. Gaskell meant *Ruth* to be a novel with a purpose, to break the conspiracy of silence on the subject, and to friends such as Mrs. Jameson she expressed her satisfaction that she had set people talking.[4] The same letter, however, shows that she had not realized from what quarter criticism would come. "I am surprised to find how very many people—good kind people —and *women* infinitely more than men, really and earnestly disapprove of what I have said." But it was only to intimate friends

---

[1] When writing *Ruth*, Mrs. Gaskell knew that she would not escape the first stricture, but she was anxious to wage war against both silence and levity on the subject. Therefore, it was essential that there should be no question about Ruth's guilt. She says to her son: "You will hear me called the hardest names that ever can be thrown at women—. . . my child, you must bear it patiently, because they will be partly true. Never get confused, by your love for me, into thinking that what I did was right." (P. 239.)

[2] Shorter, *op. cit.*, II: 263.

[3] July 16, 1853. *Bulletin*, p. 141.

[4] See p. 143.

that she allowed a glimpse of the intense pain that this very fact caused her. "I anticipate so much pain from them that in several instances I have *forbidden* people to write, for their expressions of disapproval (although I have known that the feeling would exist in them) would be very painful and stinging at the time . . . I had a terrible fit of crying all Saty. night at the unkind things people were saying", she wrote to Mrs. Robson.[1] To Miss Fox she wrote in a letter dated Monday, 1853: "I *have* been *so* ill; I do believe it has been a 'Ruth' fever . . . I . . . cd not get over the hard things people said of Ruth . . . I think I must be an improper woman without knowing it, I do so manage to shock people. Now *should* you have burnt the 1st vol. of Ruth as so *very* bad? even if you had been a very anxious father of a family? Yet *two* men have; and a third has forbidden his wife to read it";[1]

Richard Cobden realzied what the reaction to *Ruth* would be, as soon as he had read the book. He wrote to Mrs. Schwabe: " 'Ruth' will be considered dangerous company for unmarried females even in a book.—But the good and brave authoress knew all this when she wrote it, and therefore is there the greater merit due to her—."[2]

The *Gentleman's Magazine* of July 1853 contained an article entitled "The Lady Novelists of Great Britain", which said about *Ruth:* "Whether it has done or will do good . . . whether . . . they will be led to study the causes which most directly lead to vice, with a view to their removal, we cannot and probably never shall know." Most other reviewers, though, expressed themselves less cautiously. The *Prospective Review* (May, 1853) thanked "our author for directing public attention to a subject fraught with such painful interest" and added that "so long as evils are ignored, and any allusion to them held to be inconsistent with good taste, no earnest conviction can be generated in the public mind"; But many of them disapproved. *Sharpe's London Magazine*, for instance, in its review of *Ruth*[3], called its power "morbid fascination" and stated its opinion that "the subject is not one for a novel—not one to treat of by the firesides, where the young should not be

---

[1] Copy of letter in the Brotherton Library.

[2] *Bulletin*, p. 118.

[3] Jan. 15, 1853.

aroused to feel an interest in vice, however garnished, but in the triumph of virtue". With a complete lack of understanding for the author's distinction between innocence and ignorance the writer of the article protested "against such a book being received into families, it would be the certain uprooting of the very *innocence* which is so frequently dwelt upon by the author with pleasure and delight".[1] Even after the first heat of the controversy had died down, *Blackwood's Edinburgh Magazine*, in the article "Modern Novelists—Great and Small" (May, 1855) called *Ruth* "a great blunder in art" because of "the mistake . . . in choosing such a heroine at all".

The Church of England was hostile to the dissenting author. The *Christian Observer*, "conducted by Members of the Established Church", published a review of *The Life of Charlotte Brontë* in July, 1857. After mentioning Mrs. Gaskell's "considerable indifference to the ninth Commandment", it goes on to inform its readers that "her taste is by no means refined; and the moral influence of her writing is, to say the least, very doubtful". *Mary Barton* and *Ruth* were equally horrifying:

"If 'Mary Barton' teaches any moral, it is that all the miseries of society are exclusively the work of the rich: according to our view, a most false and mischievous representation. And in 'Ruth', she instructs us, that a woman who has violated the laws of purity is entitled to occupy precisely the same position in society as one who has never thus offended."

By the time of the author's death, the opinion had already begun to spread that her domestic stories were her most important achievement. In 1866 the *Athenaeum* wrote (March 3), "In the interval betwixt the publication of 'Mary Barton' and 'Wives and Daughters' she once or twice . . . lost her literary way, bewildered by her desire to right that which she fancied amiss".

On the other hand, a large number of private correspondents supported the author in her attempt to "right that which she fan-

---

[1] Mrs. Gaskell herself never meant the book to be read by the very young. "Of course it is a prohibited book in *this*, as in many other households, not a book for young people, unless read with some one older (I mean to read it with Will some quiet time or other)", she wrote in an undated letter to Mrs. Robson. (Copy in the Brotherton Library.) (Her eldest daughter was 19 when *Ruth* was published.)

cied amiss". Charlotte Brontë wrote to her, when the book was as yet only planned:

"The sketch you give of your work . . . seems to me very noble; and its purpose may be as useful in practical result as it is high and just in theoretical tendency. Such a book may restore hope and energy to many who thought they had forfeited their right to both, and open a clear course for honourable effort to some who deemed that they and all honour had parted company in this world."[1]

John Forster, who read the proofs, wrote several letters about the book to the author. On January 17, 1853, he called *Ruth* "a true book beautifully thought out and written out to the end", and prophesied: "It . . . will do infinite good to all who by such means are capable of receiving it."[2]

Elizabeth Barrett Browning also expressed her admiration.[3]

Charles Kingsley, too, thought highly of *Ruth:*

"I am told, to my great astonishment, that you have heard painful speeches on account of *Ruth* . . . among all my large acquaintance I never heard, or have heard, but one unanimous opinion of the beauty and righteousness of the book, and that, above all, from real *ladies*, and really good women . . . May God bless you, and help you to write many more such books as you have already written."[4]

In a letter to Mrs. Jameson, Mrs. Gaskell told her of the regret she felt at losing her friend's comforting letter about *Ruth*[5], and Mrs. Jameson wrote again after re-reading the novel: "Yes I hope I do understand your aim—you have lifted up your voice against 'that demoralising laxity of principle' which I regard as the rotting

---

[1] Shorter, *op. cit.,* II: 263. Mrs. Gaskell placed an extract of this letter in *The Life of Charlotte Brontë* between two other letters, dated April 12th, 1852, and May 11th.

[2] Extract of letter in the Brotherton Library.

[3] Se p. 46.

[4] July 25, 1853. *Charles Kingsley. His Letters and Memories of his Life*, II: 114.

[5] March 7, 1853: "My dear Mrs. Jameson, I meant to thank you for your letter . . . it is lost! along with several other valued and comforting letters about Ruth; while every letter of reprobation and blame comes to me, straight as an arrow, . . . I should often have found it a comfort and a pleasure to read it again,—a comfort and a pleasure because I am sure you understood what I aimed at." (Erskine, *op. cit.,* p. 294.)

ulcer lying round the roots of society, and you have done it wisely and well with a mingled courage and delicacy which excites at once my gratitude and my admiration."[1]

A Manchester solicitor, Mr. D. Darbishire, expressed his "admiration of the noble object of your work . . . I believe God himself put it into your heart to write what will give strength and comfort and peace to many a weary spirit".[2]

Mrs. Green, the wife of the Unitarian minister at Knutsford, was among those who foresaw some of the unpleasantness which Mrs. Gaskell would have to bear: "I fear you will have to bear blame and disapproval from some but God will sustain you and hold you up . . . To me it seems the highest and truest morality that can be set forth by any Christian writer . . . I rejoice and glory in your courage and in your ability to do so good a work."[2]

Mrs. C. Stanley (mother of the Dean) also understood what the author had tried to achieve: "I feel quite sure that your object will be gained—that you have started new views, new feeling, new thoughts upon the subject which will tell in more ways than one knows."[3]

Mrs. Esther Hare wrote on March 12, 1853:

"Your letter pleasantly confirms the conviction I felt on reading Ruth, that your own experience of life had taught you the truths which you have so frankly expressed . . . We cannot but feel that whatever rebuke more superficial readers may cast upon you for it, the perfect truth and beauty of it will carry its own message to the hearts of many and will help them to deal more gently with their fallen fellow-creatures . . . you will have the blessed reward of restoring health to many a sorrowful broken heart, by the way in which you have spoken of the gift of the child as a blessing and redemption to the Mother."[4]

In no case did Mrs. Gaskell suggest any definite measures for the cure of the evils which she pointed out. In *Ruth* it was natural for her to remain true to the principle that made her point out the evil, and appeal to the conscience of her reader to apply the necessary remedy in each individual case. As the *Prospective Review* ex-

---

[1] Extract of letter in the Brotherton Library.
[2] *Ibid.*
[3] Copy of letter in the Brotherton Library.
[4] *Ibid.*

pressed it (May, 1853): "Our author has not attempted the impossible task of . . . establishing any general rules in reference to the evil in question; . . . she enforces the christian duty of bringing an earnest, thoughtful, and loving mind to the consideration of every individual case." And it seems clear that she was at least in some measure successful. Forty years after Mrs. Gaskell's death, Lady Ritchie[1] considered herself justified in ascribing the change in public opinion on subjects treated in *Mary Barton* and *Ruth* largely to her efforts: " 'Mary Barton' and 'Ruth' are problem stories, and their very passion and protest may have partly defeated their object; and yet what influence have they not had in the enduring convictions of the age!"[2]

---

[1] Née Anne I. Thackeray.

[2] *Blackstick Papers* (London, 1908), p. 222.

CHAPTER IX

MRS. GASKELL'S ATTITUDE TOWARDS PROTECTIVE LEGISLATION

(Utilitarianism. Carlyle. Kingsley. The Petition for a Married Women's Property Act. Mrs. Gaskell's attitude towards protective legislation as it appears in Mary Barton.*)*

A fear of legislative interference, at least in economical matters, had been characteristic of English thought ever since Adam Smith's *The Wealth of Nations*[1] became generally known. His doctrine, further elaborated by the utilitarian philosophers from Jeremy Bentham (1748–1832) to James Mill (1773–1836) and his son John Stuart Mill (1806–58), was expressed in their organ the *Westminster Review*, which was founded in 1824. They believed that political reforms must precede any legislative improvements. Competition was to them an incentive to progress. A necessary condition for national wealth was the complete freedom of the individual to make whatever bargains he thought best promoted his enlightened self-interest. It was under the influence of these ideas that Harriet Martineau, that prolific popularizer of the economic, philosophical and political creeds of her time, wrote *The Factory Controversy. A Warning against Meddling Legislation*, which was published at Manchester in 1855. The Benthamite line of thought was also characteristic of the so called Manchester School, *i.e.* the political party led by the Manchester factory owners John Bright and Richard Cobden. It was thus a logical expression of their convictions when these two political reformers and Liberals voted in Parliament against such legislative measures as the Ten Hours Bill.[2] Although "Manchester policy" was often used as a term of

---

[1] Published in 1776.

[2] Its outcome was the Factory Act of 1847, which limited the work of women and young persons in textile factories to ten hours a day and consequently made

abuse to signify a policy of self interest, it would of course be preposterous to suppose that all representatives of the Manchester
School, and especially its leaders, were indifferent to social reform.
In fact working conditions varied widely from one branch of industry to another, and also, as Fredrika Bremer had observed on
her visit to Manchester, from one factory to another, according to
the responsibility which the owner felt for his workers.[1] John
Bright, for instance, although no friend of State interference, was
renowned for the interest he took in the welfare of his "hands".
His attitude towards factory legislation, shared, like most of his
opinions, by his friend Richard Cobden, does not seem to have
changed noticeably during his political career: "In 1836 he had
already worked out his position to factory legislation . . . Writing
to a correspondent on 1 Jan., 1884, he said: 'I was opposed to all
legislation restricting the working of adults, men or women. I
was in favour of legislation restricting the labour and guarding the
health of children . . . I still hold the opinion that to limit by law
the time during which adults may work is unwise and in many
cases oppressive'."[2]

That Mrs. Gaskell, who knew both Bright and Cobden personally[3], and meant to read Cobden's Parliamentary speeches with her
eldest daughter[4], was well acquainted with their negative attitude
towards factory legislation, is obvious. It can hardly be mere coincidence that Mr. Thornton in *North and South* expresses some of

---

it impossible for any such factories to work longer hours, as the numerous
women workers were necessary in order to carry on the process. (See Trevelyan,
English Social History, p. 543.)

[1] See Appendix I.   [2] *Dictionary of National Biography*.

[3] In 1858 Mrs. Gaskell's "friend Mr. Bright" is mentioned in a letter from
D. G. Rossetti, now in the Rylands Library, Manchester. In the same library
there are two notes from Bright to Mr. Gaskell, one dated April 5, 49, the other
"Wednesday". Both refer to Mr. Gaskell's request for Bright's assistance in pro-
curing appointments for somebody. There are also several letters to Mrs. Gaskell from Cobden, with whose family she seems to have been fairly intimate.
In the letter to Miss Fox about home duties and individual life quoted on
p. 58 she wrote: "I was very nearly going to the Cobdens' for 6 days or so last
week—but did not."

[4] "when you come home I will read with you Mr. Cobden's speeches" (Undated letter from Mrs. Gaskell to her eldest daughter, now in the Brotherton
Library.).

Bright's convictions, as when he says: "We hate to have laws made for us at a distance. We wish people would allow us to right ourselves, instead of continually meddling, with their imperfect legislation. We stand up for self-government, and oppose centralisation."[1]

A violent reaction against the Benthamite philosophy, which considered man a helpless victim of economic circumstances, that "abominable heresy", as Charles Kingsley called it[2], set in with Coleridge and Carlyle. The former exposed his doctrine in such works as *Aids to Reflection* (1825), and "it is his lasting service, at the moment when the utilitarian scheme of things swept all before it, to have proclaimed the utter insufficiency of any doctrine which did not start from the postulate of duty".[3] Carlyle's influence pervaded most of the intellectual and moral life of his day. He considered the moral value of his books, which dealt chiefly with ethical questions, as more important than their artistic value, and he "insisted on the supreme need of reverence . . . not merely for what is above us, but, also, for what is on the earth, beside us and beneath us".[4] He had, however, no more faith in laws and acts of Parliament than the Utilitarians whose doctrine he abhorred. Formulas and creeds meant little to him if there was no living faith behind them. His aim was not to improve material conditions by means of legislation, but to change men's attitude towards life. In *Sartor Resartus*, a book which Mrs. Gaskell had read before

---

[1] Chapter XL, p. 354.

[2] "And so I began to look on man (and too many of us, I am afraid, are doing so) as the creature and puppet of circumstances—of the particular outward system, social or political, in which he happens to find himself. An abominable heresy, no doubt; but, somehow, it appears to me just the same as Benthamites, and economists, and high-churchmen, too, for that matter, have been preaching for the last twenty years with great applause from their respective parties." (Charles Kingsley, *Alton Locke*, Chap. IX.)

[3] *The Cambridge History of English Literature*, XI: 138. That Mrs. Gaskell had read at least some of Coleridge's poetry appears from her quotations. (See Appendix III.) She was also in a position to hear much about him personally. "Coleridge she had heard much of from her friends the Wedgwoods." (Chadwick, *op. cit.*, p. 234.) Mrs. Gaskell was related to the Wedgwoods, and Josiah Wedgwood and his brother had at one time granted the poet a pension, though Josiah later withdrew his half of it.

[4] *The Cambridge History of English Literature*, XIII: 1.

she wrote her first novel[1], he emphasized the necessity for a living faith and his own distrust of mere form and lifeless theories:

"Religion, where lies the Life-essence of Society, has been smote-at and perforated, ... till now it is quite rent into shreds ... Call ye that a Society, ... where there is no longer any Social Idea extant; not so much as the Idea of a common Home, but only of a common over-crowded Lodging-house? ... Where ... on all hands hear it passionately proclaimed: *Laissez faire;* ... eat you your wages, and sleep!

"Thus, too ... does an observant eye discern everywhere that saddest spectacle: The Poor perishing, like neglected, foundered Draught-Cattle, of Hunger and Over-work; the Rich, still more wretchedly, of Idleness, Satiety, and Over-growth ... The Soul Politic having departed ... what can follow but that the Body Politic be decently interred ... Liberals, Economists, Utilitarians enough I see marching with its bier, ... Utilitarianism spreads like a sort of Dog-madness; till the whole World-kennel will be rabid."[2]

Then Carlyle goes on to show the responsibility incurred by those who do nothing to stop the soul-killing tendencies of the time:

" 'Nevertheless', cries Teufelsdröckh, 'who can hinder it ... Wiser were it that we yielded to the Inevitable and Inexorable, ...' ... Safe himself in that 'Pinnacle of Weissnichtwo', he would consent, with a tragic solemnity, that the monster Utilitaria, held back, indeed, and moderated by nose-rings, halters, foot-shackles, and every conceivable modification of rope, should go forth to do her work;—to tread down old ruinous Palaces and Temples with her broad hoof, till the whole were trodden down, that new and better might be built!"[3]

Even in *Chartism* (1840), in which, according to Cazamian, he advocates State interference[4], he wrote: "O brother, we must if possible resuscitate some soul and conscience in us, exchange our dilettantisms for sincerities, our dead hearts of stone for living hearts of flesh"[5], and it was this part of his teaching, far more than

---

[1] This appears from the reference to this work in *Mary Barton*. (See Appendix III.) Mrs. Gaskell occasionally met Carlyle personally. (See Forster, *op. cit.* p. 408, *Shaen, op. cit.*, p. 40, Haldane, *op. cit.*, pp. 251–2, and Chadwick, *op. cit.*, p. 172.)

[2] *Sartor Resartus*, Book III, Chap. V.

[3] *Ibid.*

[4] Louis Cazamian, *Le Roman social en Angleterre (1830–1850)* (Paris, 1904), pp. 161–2.

[4] *Chartism*, Book I, Chap. IV, pp. 22–3, quoted by Cazamian, *op. cit.*, p. 163.

his advocating of protective legislation, that appealed to such of his disciples as Kingsley and Mrs. Gaskell, who, in a letter, expressed her own longing for more devotional preaching instead of controversy about doctrines.[1]

Carlyle preached the gospel of action, not that kind of action which is regulated by laws and other external restrictions, but the action which is inspired by the living faith which he hoped to see resuscitated in mankind. The final exhortation in Chapter IX in Book II of *Sartor Resartus*, "The Everlasting Yea", is "Whatsoever thy hand findeth to do, do it with thy whole might. Work while it is called Today; for the Night cometh, wherein no man can work". That was also one of Mrs. Gaskell's favourite texts. She quoted it more than once in her works[2] and preached it by implication in a large number of her stories.[3] The method which she used in her didactic novels, and by which she tried to bring about reforms, was to point out abuses and thus to arouse the consciences of those who were immediately responsible in each individual case. Consequently, she never suggested any detailed schemes of reform. She, as well as Carlyle, valued that kind of action that was inspired by the personal conviction of an individual, such as Mr. Carson's in *Mary Barton* after his final conversion, much more than a way of action forced on unwilling mill-owners by decrees of Parliament. She meant her social novels to result in action; that was, in her eyes, their only justification. She explained her principle in a letter to Mrs. Robson in 1859, in which she objected to Miss Bemond's anti slavery agitation in England:

"all the anti slavery people will attend her lectures to be convinced of what they are already convinced and to have their feelings stirred up without the natural and right outlet of stirred up feelings; the power of simple

---

[1] "oh! for some really spiritual devotional preaching instead of controversy about doctrines". (Letter to C. E. Norton, March 9, 1859. Whitehill, *op. cit.*)

[2] See Appendix III.

[3] The old servant in *Cousin Phillis* and the Methodist preacher in *The Well of Pen-Morfa* preach this text, even though they do not quote it; so does the author herself in *Bessy's Troubles at Home*, and it also expresses much of the underlying moral principle in *Libbie Marsh's Three Eras, Half a Lifetime Ago, The Poor Clare,* and *North and South;* it even in a sense gives the reason for Miss Galindo's clerkship in *My Lady Ludlow.*

and energetic *action*. I know they use any amount of *words* in reprobation of the conduct of American slave holders but I don't call the use of words *action* unless there is some definite, distinct *practical course of action* logically proposed by those words".[1]

Mrs. Gaskell saw life as a relationship between living individuals and refused under any circumstances to think of mankind in the abstract terms of legal stipulations. Characteristically, the only reservation in her admiration for Florence Nightingale was occasioned by the latter's tendency to pay more attention to mankind as a whole than to individuals. On Oct. 27, 1854, she wrote in a letter to Emily Shaen: "F. does not care for *individuals* . . . but for the whole race as being God's creatures . . . That text always jarred against me, that 'Who is my mother and my brethren?'— and there is just that jar in F. N. to me."[2]

Charles Kingsley, whose two novels with a social purpose, *Yeast* (1848) and *Alton Locke* (1850), are full of admiring references to Carlyle, must in many respects be considered as his follower. The same is true of Mrs. Gaskell in her earlier period. Her "hero" Kingsley[3], like herself, preached the doctrine that everybody must feel responsible for the social evils around him: "Those who live besides such a state of things . . . They are 'their brothers' keepers', let them deny it as they will."[4] His "Placard to the Workmen of England" (1848) ended with a warning: "But there will be no true freedom without virtue, no true science without religion, no true industry without the fear of God, and love to your fellow-citizens."[5] In the first of "Parson Lot's Letters to the Chartists",[6] he emphasized his belief that Acts of Parliament are of no avail unless accompanied by a personal striving for improvement:

---

[1] Letter in the Brotherton Library.

[2] Haldane, *op. cit.*, pp. 92–4.

[3] See Chapter III.

[4] *Alton Locke*, Chap. II.

[5] *His Letters and Memories of his Life*, I: 165.

[6] These Letters were published in the magazine *Politics for the People*, which came to an end in July, 1848, after seventeen numbers had appeared. (See Una Pope-Hennessy, *Canon Charles Kingsley, a Biography*, London 1948, pp. 78, 79, 82.) It is therefore highly probable that they contributed to Mrs. Gaskell's hero-worship of Kingsley about that time.

"I don't deny, my friends, it is much cheaper and pleasanter to be reformed by the devil than by God; for God will only reform society on the condition of our reforming every man his own self—while the devil is quite ready to help us to mend the laws and the parliament, earth and heaven, without ever starting such an impertinent and 'personal' request, as that a man should mend himself. *That* liberty of the subject he will always respect."

In his second letter he spoke of "a future of conscience, of justice, of freedom, when idlers and oppressors shall no more dare to plead parchments and Acts of Parliament for their iniquities. I say the Bible promises this, not in a few places only, but throughout".[1] In the same letter he expressly warned his readers not to overestimate the efficacy of legislative reform: "I think you have fallen into just the same mistake as the rich of whom you complain . . . the mistake of fancying that legislative reform is social reform, or that men's hearts can be changed by act of Parliament."[2]

As is clear from the preceding pages, Mrs. Gaskell had ample opportunity both to acquaint herself with and to be influenced by two lines of thought, one of which, represented by Bright and Cobden, was definitely hostile to factory legislation and all kinds of Parliamentary interference between masters and men, and the other, represented by Carlyle and, even more emphatically, by Kingsley, very unenthusiastic about legislation even if not openly hostile to it. Instead of trusting to human laws to bring about social reforms, Kingsley pointed to the teaching of the Bible as it appears "not in a few places only, but throughout". This was also Mrs. Gaskell's method. Although Mr. Thornton's dislike of State interference in his relations with his employees in *North and South* shows that Mrs. Gaskell was well acquainted with the attitude of the Manchester school towards factory legislation and management, it is Margaret who is Mrs. Gaskell's mouthpiece in that book. Her opinions are identical with Parson Lot's. She says to Thornton: "there is no human law to prevent the employers from utterly wasting or throwing away all their money, if they choose;

---

[1] Quoted from Thomas Hughes' prefatory memoir to *Alton Locke. Tailor and Poet. An Autobiography*, by Charles Kingsley. (In two vols. London and New York, 1893.)

[2] *Ibid.*

but that there are passages in the Bible which would rather imply—
. . .—that they neglected their duty as stewards if they did so".[1]

This idea, that no human law could really prevent iniquities
and bring about lasting reform, was deep-rooted in Mrs. Gaskell
and decided her attitude towards the petition for a Married Women's Property Act, which was sent to her in 1856, with a request
for her signature, by her friend Miss Fox, who was one of Barbara
Leigh Smith's supporters in her agitation for such an act. It must
not be concluded that, because Mrs. Gaskell was asked for her signature, she was considered a Women's Rights woman. Indeed, the
very opposite almost seems to have been the case, as appears from
Mary Howitt's account of the early days of the agitation in a letter
to her daughter, Jan. 8, 1856, in which she discussed the importance of the moral reputation of those women whose names were
to be associated with the petition, and objected to the signatures
of some ladies, because "These ladies hold such free opinions with
regard to marriage the people would naturally be suspicious of
the whole thing".[2] She continued: "I do think it most needful
to have an eye to the moral status of the persons supporting this
movement; and that in the fields of science and literature signatures such as those of Mrs. Somerville and Mrs. Gaskell should
be obtained."[3] Later, on March 13, 1856, she noted with satisfaction in a letter to her sister: "The petition about married women's property has already been announced in Parliament. It is
spoken of as the petition of Elizabeth Barret Browning, Anna Jameson, Mary Howitt, Mrs. Gaskell, etc."[3]

Mrs. Gaskell, with characteristic indifference to legislation,
signed without enthusiasm. In a letter accompanying the petition
she wrote to Miss Fox:

"My dearest Tottie,
    You ask for the petition back again without loss of time, so I send it
you although today certainly I shan't be able to send you a long letter, I
don't think it is very definite, and *pointed;* or that it will do much good,
—for the Turnkey's objection[4] (vide Little Dorrit) 'but if they wish to
come over her, how then can you legally tie it up' &c. will be a stronger

----

[1] *North and South*, p. 126.

[2] Mary Howitt, *op. cit.*, II: 114–16.

[3] *Ibid.*   [4] See below, p. 227.

difficulty than they can legislate for a husband can coax, wheedle, beat or tyrannize his wife out of something and no law whatever will help this that I can see. (Mr. Gaskell begs Mr. Fox to draw up a bill for the protection of *husbands* against wives who will spend all their earnings.) However our sex is badly enough used and legalised *against*, there's no doubt of *that*—so though I don't see the definite end proposed by these petitions I'll sign. I could say a good deal more, but have my own heart chock full of private troubles and sorrows just now . . ."[1]

Mrs. Gaskell was right in thinking the petition vague. After stating that "the manifold evils occasioned by the present law, by which the property and earnings of the wife are thrown into the absolute power of the husband, become daily more apparent", it pointed out that it was usual for parents to provide for their married daughters by a cumbrous machinery of trusteeship which, however, like the device for the protection of women who could afford to appeal to the Courts of Equity, was out of the reach of the lower classes. The petition particularly stressed the fact that the law deprived a mother of the power of providing for her children. It also showed that the existing law might bear unjustly upon the husband too, as it made him responsible for his wife's debts, and pointed out that in modern civilization man was no longer the only money-getting agent. It was now time that "in entering the state of marriage", women no longer passed "from freedom into the condition of a slave, all whose earnings belong to his master and not to himself". However, the petitioners did not suggest any definite changes in the law but left any such initiative in the hands of Parliament. As they expressed it in the last sentence of the petition, "your Petitioners therefore humbly pray, that your Honourable House will take the foregoing allegations into consideration, and apply such remedy as to its wisdom shall seem fit".[2]

The reason Mrs. Gaskell signed the petition at all was the fact that women were "badly . . . legalised *against*", and it is typical of the whole humanitarian group to which Mrs. Gaskell belonged that it gave its willing help to abolish oppressive laws, but did little to bring about other reforms in legislation.[3]

---

[1] Copy of letter in the Brotherton Library.

[2] Quoted from the Petition as printed in Hester Burton, *op. cit.*, pp. 70–71.

[3] Another case in point seems to be Dickens. He was, on the whole, far less accurate about the details of the imperfect social conditions, a reform of which

One reason for Mrs. Gaskell's hesitation about the petition may have been that she, with her distrust of any agitation not expected to lead to immediate action, did not think that women themselves, who were largely responsible for the agitation, were actually in a position to make the necessary reforms. This feeling was shared by many otherwise active women at the time. Charles Kingsley wrote about his wife's attitude towards the woman's question in a letter to J. S. Mill after the appearance of his *On the Subjection of Women* in 1869: "Her opinion has long been that the movement must be furthered rather by men than by the women themselves."[1]

Then, again, Mrs. Gaskell thought it admirable "to defy arbitrary power" only "on behalf of others more helpless", "not on behalf of ourselves"[2], and the petition for a Married Women's Property Act naturally seemed to her to be definitely "on behalf of ourselves". This principle, which explains the non-propagandic nature of her treatment of the wrongs of middle- class women in her books, also explains her dislike for the extremists among the advocates of women's rights. She does not seem to have known Mrs. Taylor, afterwards Mrs. John Stuart Mill, who was the author of the article on the enfranchisement of women mentioned in Chapter I, but she had met another leader of the Women's Rights Movement, Barbara Leigh Smith, afterwards Mme Bodichon, about whom she wrote to C. E. Norton:

"she is illegitimate—cousin of Hilary Carter, F. Nightingale,—and has their nature in her; ... She is—I think in consequence of her birth, a

---

he tried to bring about, and in *Oliver Twist*, although his social sense is undeniable, he was accused by such an expert as Harriet Martineau of being unable to distinguish between the old and the new poor laws. (See Martineau, *op. cit.*, I: 225.) Although, according to Cazamian (*op. cit.*, p. 298) he pronounced himself in favour of protective legislation in 1838, he, too, seems to have been chiefly interested in abolishing oppressive laws, such as those concerning imprisonment for debt, and, as F. R. Leavis writes about *Hard Times*, "Parliament for him is merely the 'national dust-yard', where the 'national dustmen' entertain one another 'with a great many noisy little fights among themselves', and appoint commissions which fill blue-books with dreary facts and futile statistics' ". (*The Great Tradition.* London 1948, pp. 245–6.)

[1] Una Pope-Hennessy, *op. cit.*, p. 256.

[2] *North and South*, p. 117.

strong fighter against the established opinions of the world,—which always goes against my—what shall I call it?—*taste* (that is not the word,) but I can't help admiring her noble bravery, and respecting—while I don't personally *like* her".[1]

Mrs. Gaskell obviously found it difficult to analyse her dislike of Mme Bodichon's activities. It seems probable that she did not so much dislike them because Mme Bodichon fought against the established opinions of the world—to which activity Mrs. Gaskell herself had devoted so much energy in *Mary Barton, Ruth,* and *North and South*—as because she made herself known as a woman openly demanding her own rights instead of fighting for "others more helpless".

The incident in *Little Dorrit* to which Mrs. Gaskell referred in her letter to Miss Fox occurs in Chapter VII. The turnkey of the Marshalsea prison wants to leave his savings to a little girl, and consults several lawyers.

" 'Supposing', he would say, stating the case with his key on the professional gentleman's waistcoat; 'suppose a man wanted to leave his property to a young female, and wanted to tie it up so that nobody else should ever be able to make a grab at it; how would you tie up that property?'
" 'Settle it strictly on herself', the professional gentleman would complacently answer.
" 'But look here', quoth the turnkey. 'Supposing she had, say a brother, say a father, say a husband, who would be likely to make a grab at that property when she came into it—how about that?'
" 'It would be settled on herself, and they would have no more legal claim on it than you', would be the professional answer.
" 'Stop a bit', said the turnkey. 'Supposing she was tenderhearted, and they came over her. Where's your law for tying it up then?'
"The deepest character whom the turnkey sounded, was unable to produce his law for tying such a knot as that. So, the turnkey thought about it all his life, and died intestate after all."

"The Turnkey's objection" was characteristic of Mrs. Gaskell's profound distrust of all legislative reform not accompanied by a striving after personal improvement on the part of the people concerned, and it is therefore surprising to find that Louis Cazamian, who is, so far as I know, the only critic who has discussed

---

[1] April 5, 1860. Whitehill, *op. cit.*

the question at all, asserts that in *Mary Barton* Mrs. Gaskell eloquently recommends protective legislation. He writes:

"Comme Dickens, Mrs. Gaskell connaît et dit leur charité les uns pour les autres [the poor]. Mais cette bienfaisance est impuissante; celle des riches même ne suffit pas; il faut que la loi intervienne. Brièvement, mais éloquemment, Mrs. Gaskell demande la législation protectrice. Les journées de travail sont trop longues; c'est pendant les deux dernières heures qu'arrivent tous les accidents (VIII, 86). Les jeunes filles commencent trop tôt à travailler; l'usine les déforme, les rend impropres à la maternité, au ménage. 'Que dirait le prince Consort, déclare une vieille, si la reine Victoria, sa femme, rentrait le soir éreintée, sale et de mauvaise humeur? Alors, pourquoi ne peut-il faire une loi qui empêche les femmes des pauvres gens de travailler aux fabriques?' (X, 124.) Appel indirect, singulièrement adroit, si l'on songe à la popularité de la reine, à son affection pour son époux."[1]

An examination of the passages in *Mary Barton* to which Cazamian refers shows, however, that it is extremely doubtful whether they can be assumed to express Mrs. Gaskell's own convictions. In her early stories, she often moralized and exhorted the reader in her own person as author, but nowhere does she recommend a legislative reform in that manner, however well acquainted she obviously was with the legislation of the time, and it is the characters in the book, not the author, that recommend legislative measures. Naturally, their opinions are often identical with Mrs. Gaskell's own, as in the cases where they disapprove of factory work for women. But this does not prove that they are so always, or even in most cases. Mrs. Wilson, for instance, who is the person in Chapter X who demands a law against married women being employed in factories, is not described either as a sympathetic character or as a person whose judgment is worth trusting. She has very vague ideas about the way laws are made:

"I say it's Prince Albert as ought to be asked how he'd like his missis to be from home when he comes in, tired and worn, and wanting some one to cheer him; and maybe, her to come in by-and-by, just as tired and down in th' mouth; and how he'd like for her never to be at home to see to th'cleaning of his house, or to keep a bright fire in his grate. Let alone his meals being all hugger-mugger and comfortless. I'd be bound, prince as he is, if his missis served him so, he'd be off to a gin-palace, or summut

---

[1] Cazamian, *op. cit.*, p. 400.

o'that kind. So why can't he make a law again poor folks' wives working in factories?"[1]

Naturally, Mrs. Gaskell herself did not share this idea of Mrs. Wilson's about the ease with which laws could be made. On the other hand, the passage shows her insight into the mentality of ignorant factory workers who believed that all their difficulties could be made to disappear by means of the least show of interest on the part of the authorities. This applies even more to Mrs. Wilson's next speech: "don't tell me it's not the Queen as makes laws; and isn't she bound to obey Prince Albert? And if he said they mustn't, why she'd say they mustn't, and then all folk would say, oh, no, we never shall do any such thing no more".[2] This passage reads far more like irony against the cheap optimism of those who expected an immediate Utopia to result from Parliamentary interference than like a sincere appeal from the author for protective legislation.

Chapter VIII, in which, according to Cazamian, Mrs. Gaskell also points out the necessity for protective legislation, contains an account of a discussion during which various friends of John Barton suggest that he recommend Parliament to pass the Short Hours Bill, to set trade free, and to allow small children to work again in factories.[3] Others want him to persuade all members of Parlia-

---

[1] P. 121.   [2] *Ibid.*

[3] Lord Althorp's Factory Act of 1833 was the first to limit the working hours of children. The Acts of 1842 and 1844 further improved their position, but as late as 1849 Fredrika Bremer was appalled by the treatment of children in English factories. (See Appendix I.) The fact that *Mary Barton* was written shortly after the acts of 1842 and 1844 were passed might explain an omission in Mrs. Gaskell's social novels otherwise difficult to account for. Public opinion had already been aroused on behalf of children in factories, and she may have thought that abuses in this respect were already on their way to being abolished altogether. Indeed, on the few occasions where she mentions child labour at all in her books she goes out of her way to point out the restrictions that existed: factory inspectors had been appointed who saw to it that no children under the legal factory age were employed. Higgins in *North and South* feels compassion for John Boucher "wi' a sickly wife, and eight childer, none on 'em factory age". (P. 144.) Mrs. Davenport in *Mary Barton* wants Barton to explain to Parliament "what a sore trial it is, this law o' theirs, keeping childer fra' factory work, whether they be weakly or strong. There's our Ben; why, porridge seems to go no way wi' him, he eats so much; . . . and th' inspector won't let him in to work

ment to wear calico shirts, as a means to relieve the trade depression. In no case does Mrs. Gaskell make any comment, but she obviously did not share all these different opinions as to the best way of improving conditions. It is, however, John Barton himself who comments with approval on a newspaper article advocating a shorter working day in factories, and it might be argued that he, the chief character of the book, expresses the author's opinions when he says that "by *far th' greater o' the accidents as comed in, happened in th' last two hours o' work*", and asserts that "Working folk won't be ground to the dust much longer. We'n a' had as much to bear as human nature can bear. So, if th' masters can't do us no good, and they say they can't, we mun try higher folk".[1] Mrs. Gaskell's letter to Mrs. Greg, quoted by Ward in his introduction to *Mary Barton* in the Knutsford edition, might be cited in support of such a theory. Mrs. Gaskell wrote: "John Barton . . . was my hero; *the* person with whom all my sympathies went, with whom I tried to identify myself all the time", but she continued: "I believed from personal observation that such men were not uncommon, and would well reward such sympathy and love as should throw light down upon their groping search after the causes of suffering, and the reason why suffering is sent, and what they can do to lighten it." The phrase "their groping search after . . . what they can do" is significant and seems to indicate that Mrs. Gaskell did not mean her identification to be one of ideas, but only one of sympathy and understanding. It will also be remembered that, at least in one instance in the novel, Mrs. Gaskell speaks of Barton's "strong exaggerated feelings".[2] In a letter to Miss Ewart in 1848, Mrs. Gaskell explained her attitude towards John Barton's opinions more clearly: "I wanted to represent the subject in the light in which some of

in th' factory, because he's not right age; though he's twice as strong as Sankey's little ritling of a lad, as works till he cries for his legs aching so, though he is right age, and better". (Chap. VIII, p. 90.) As Mrs. Gaskell makes no comment, it is difficult to conclude anything about her own attitude from this quotation. It is, however, consistent with her general distrust of protective legislation that the reader's attention is directed not only to the predicament of "Sankey's little ritling of a lad", but also to the failure of legislation to settle the difficulties in these two individual cases.

[1] Chap. VIII, p. 86.

[2] P. 32. (Concerning domestic service.)

the workmen certainly consider to be *true;* not that I dare to say is the abstract absolute truth ... my intention was simply to represent the view many of the workpeople took."[1]

Thus, there seems to be no reason to suppose that John Barton's ideas were necessarily Mrs. Gaskell's. She clearly showed that her support of legislative reform was very unenthusiastic in the case of a Married Women's Property Act, and the total absence in her works and letters of any direct appeal for any kind of protective legislation, even for children, seems to prove that on this question she unreservedly agreed with Kingsley when he warned his readers of the "mistake of fancying that legislative reform is social reform, or that men's hearts can be changed by act of Parliament".

---

[1] Copy of letter in the Brotherton Library. Printed in Haldane, *op. cit.*, p. 46.

FACTORY WORK FOR WOMEN

(Actual working conditions etc, as they appeared in the current debate, in official reports etc, about the middle of the nineteenth century.)

At the time when Mrs. Gaskell was beginning to write *Mary Barton*—or *John Barton*, as she intended to call it until the publishers suggested the change in title—the subject of the conditions of factory workers was a highly controversial one. Few had treated it in fiction[1], but Government inspectors were inquiring into the question, and newspapers and Parliament were debating it.

The eyes of the general public were opened to the terrible conditions under which a large percentage of factory workers lived and laboured by the Sadler report of 1832. The more specific problem of the conditions under which women worked was first treated in detail ten years later in the Report of the Children's Employment Commission on Mines and Collieries, which described how women were from an early age "employed in dragging trucks of coal to which they were harnessed by a chain and girdle, going on all fours, in conditions of dirt, heat and indecency, which are scarcely printable".[2] The immediate result of this Report was the Act of 1842, which excluded women from work below ground. Thus was the principle of special legislation for the employment of women accepted; but towards the end of the century, certain supporters of the Women's Rights movement protested on the grounds that women ought not to be treated like children unable to take care of themselves and without a right to dispose of their own working capacity. Two years later, however, the same principle resulted in the Factory Act of 1844, which limited work for women to twelve hours a day, and by means of certain regulations

---

[1] See Appendix II.

[2] Quoted by Reiss, *op. cit.*, p. 234.

made night work impossible. It also included sanitary regulations concerning meals, and precautions against accidents.

Work for women in the textile industries, the chief industry of Manchester, was nothing new. When work for the textile industry was carried out in the home, before the introduction of the power loom, weavers and spinners had taken the assistance of their wives and children for granted and counted on them thus to contribute to the family income—indeed, the loss of this income was one of the male weavers' most frequently repeated objections to work in the factories. The introduction of the steam loom broke up these working teams, and one man's wages did not suffice for a whole family. Most of the women workers in textile factories in the 'thirties and 'forties were therefore the wives and daughters of such weavers, simply carrying on the tradition from the time of the hand loom in the home. There were good opportunities of work for them, especially after the Factory Act of 1833 limited child labour, and consequently raised the demand for adult workers. Women were often preferred to men, because "The small amount of wages paid to women, acts as a strong inducement to employ them instead of men".[1] P. Gaskell gives the following information about textile workers in his *Manufacturing Population of England* (1833): "The individuals employed . . . are chiefly girls and young women from 16 to 22 or 23 years of age; indeed the weavers in many mills are exclusively females."[2] Women seem to have been in a majority in worsted mills, and flax mills employed women workers only.[3]

The most frequently repeated objection to factory work for women in the Victorian age was its alleged tendency to break up the unity of the family, and unfit women for household work. "Woman's sphere is the home" was the favourite argument of the Vic-

---

[1] Factory Inspectors' Report, 1843, Asunders' Report. Quoted by Ivy Pinchbeck in *Women Workers and the Industrial Revolution 1750–1850* (London, 1930), p. 188.

[2] Quoted by Pinchbeck, *op. cit.*, p. 184.

[3] "In 1833 the cotton mills employed about 60,000 adult males, 65,000 adult females, and 84,000 young persons of whom half were boys and girls of under fourteen. By 1844, of 420,000 operatives . . . 242,000 were women and girls." (Bryant, *English Saga 1840–1940*. London, 1940, p. 59.)

torians in discussions of this question, as well as of all others concerning a wider field for women's activities. The fact that most women workers in factories were single women who could not be supported at home carried no weight with those who constantly reiterated their phrase about woman's natural sphere.

Neither the women themselves nor the men workers seem to have regarded their factory work as worthy of comment until the late 'thirties and early 'forties, when a depression in the textile trade forced many mills to close down and many men found themselves without possibilities of work. From that time on, the effect of women's competition was taken into account when the distressed condition of factory workers was discussed. The argument was, however, generally concealed in phrases about women's natural place being the home. The *Manchester and Salford Advertiser* of January 8, 1842, for instance, printed an account of the reasons for which a "gradual withdrawal of all females from factories" had been demanded in 1841 by a Short Time Committee.[1] Factory work for women, said the article, was "an inversion of the order of nature and of Providence—a return to a state of barbarism, in which the woman does the work, while the man looks idly on".[2] A deputation waited on Mr. Gladstone, requesting the limitation of the number of women workers in each factory in proportion to the number of men employed there. The deputation also demanded a law to prohibit married women working in factories during the lifetime of their husbands.

Such critics of the factory system as saw nothing but evil in the employment of women in factories—such as Lord Ashley—stressed its bad influence on home life, and often exaggerated the extent to which mothers of young children worked out of the home. But

"The Report of the Factory Commission . . . showed that in the cotton factories of Lancashire, the woollen mills of the North and West, and in flax, silk, and lace mills generally, the greatest number of female operatives were aged from sixteen to twenty-one, and that there was 'prodigious diminution immediately after', during the period when most factory women married."[3]

---

[1] Attempts were being made to get the working day in factories reduced to ten hours.

[2] Quoted by Pinchbeck, *op. cit.*, p. 200.

[3] Pinchbeck, *op. cit.*, p. 197.

John Bright, who in most cases opposed factory legislation[1], stated in Parliament that "after that period, which might be termed the marriageable age, the women are to a very large extent withdrawn from factory employment, and remain at home engaged in their domestic duties".[2]

An objection to factory work for women that was frequently made about the middle of the nineteenth century was its disastrous effects on the health of the workers. Some kinds of work in which women were engaged were generally admitted to be extremely unhealthy. This applied especially to flax mills, where the method of so called wet spinning was in general use. In 1843 a factory superintendant by the name of Baker stated in a report that women worked all night in a temperature of 70° or 80°. In other cases, he had seen girls of seventeen who worked from six to ten o'clock, with only one-and-a-half hours a day for meals and rest. His report shows the necessity of the violently opposed Factory Act of 1844, which abolished the worst of these abuses. Critics of the factory system, however, often overlooked the fact that many of the disadvantages, such as the unsatisfactory sanitary conditions, were not confined to the factory, nor were at all new. Charles Kingsley showed in *Yeast* (1848) and *Alton Locke* (1850) that the poorer country population was no better off, and in a Report of Handloom Weavers of 1840 Hickson stated: "With regard to health, having seen the domestic weaver in his miserable apartment and the power loom weaver in the factory, I do not hesitate to say that the advantages are all on the side of the latter."[3]

It was often argued that the factory system led a worker to marry unwisely. The Handloom Weavers' Report quoted above stated that "a weaver would scorn to marry a servant girl ... but chooses a weaver, who earns as much, or half as much, as himself".[4] As most weavers married before they were twenty years old, they enjoyed only a few years of relative prosperity before they began

---

[1] He did not oppose legislation to limit child labour. He was famous for his regard for the well-being of his work-people, and had established a good school attached to his factory.

[2] Hansard, March 15, 1844. Quoted by Pinchbeck, *op. cit.*, p. 198.

[3] Quoted by Pinchbeck, *op. cit.*, p. 182.

[4] *Ibid.*, p. 179.

to suffer extreme poverty, when a growing family made it necessary for the wife to cease work in the factory. Hickson, in his report, had seen reason to regret the fact that factory workers did not often marry servant girls, who were supposed to make the better wives. In the same report, however, he stated that "in Lancashire profitable employment for females is abundant. Domestic servants are in consequence so scarce, that they can only be obtained from neighbouring counties".[1]

It is difficult to decide how much truth there was in the frequent assertion that factory workers were specially unfit to care for their own homes. Wanda Fraiken Neff accepts the statement as true, and instances one mill where only one out of thirteen wives could make her husband a shirt.[2] However, there is also evidence that many women who worked in factories resented the assumption that they were less able than other women to manage their homes properly. According to I. Pinchbeck[3], many women who had spent their early life in the factory testified before the Commission of 1833 that they were as competent in the home as other women. As Miss Pinchbeck points out, the standard of domestic economy was deplorably low in all working classes at that time, and, since the condition of factory workers was being examined and discussed in all its aspects in Reports and Parliamentary debates, the lack of proficiency in domestic work displayed by women factory workers may have been given a publicity out of all proportion to the standard of other classes.

There is also very conflicting evidence with regard to another of the alleged evils of the factory system. Drink, the use of laudanum, and prostitution, were repeatedly asserted to be common among the young women working in factories. Textile workers were generally better paid than workers in other types of factories, and their moral standard was consequently somewhat higher. Large numbers of girls, however, seem to have been driven to prostitution in times of unemployment. For the rest, the particular immorality ascribed

[1] *Ibid.*, p. 313.

[2] Wanda Fraiken Neff, *Victorian Working Women. An Historical and Literary Study of Women in British Industries and Professions 1832–1850* (London, 1929), p. 48.

[3] *Op. cit.*, p. 309.

to factory workers must be met with the same objection as applied in the case of their alleged lack of domestic proficiency: factory workers alone came in for a thorough scrutiny, which would probably have given very similar results if directed towards other corresponding classes of society. The Report of the Factory Commission of 1833 confirms this assumption:

"In regard to morals we find that though the statements and depositions of the different witnesses that have been examined are to a considerable degree conflicting, yet there is no evidence to shew that vice and immorality are more prevalent among these people, considered as a class, than amongst any other portion of the community in the same station, and with the same limited means of information."[1]

Grave accusations were often made against the mill- owners in this respect. Miss Neff considers them exaggerated: "industrial chiefs . . . the charges made that they frequently used the women in their mills for their amusement are probably exaggerated".[2] G. M. Trevelyan also acquits the factory system of having had disastrous effects on the moral of the workpeople: "On the whole the more regular pay and the general conditions of life in factories tended towards a higher standard of morals, although the critics of the factory system long denied it".[3]

Some contemporary writers picked out Manchester, with its large numbers of women working in textile factories, as having an especially low moral standard. Charles Kingsley is one of these. On March 28, 1856, he wrote to J. Nicholls:

"I am exceedingly pleased with what you say of the present temper of mill-owners, and, from experience of my own, I fully believe it . . . But I cannot, in justice to the working-men, forget the temper of the *nouveaux riches* of Manchester, during the forty years ending, say 1848 . . . of whom, certainly, the hardest masters and the most profligate men were to be found among those who had risen from the working classes. I fear that, some twenty years ago, the relations between the average of young masters and the girls of the factory, would not bear a close investigation; and were the unspoken cause, among brothers and sweethearts, of fearful indignation, which only found vent in political indignation, and rendered them easy

---

[1] Quoted by Pinchbeck, *op. cit.*, p. 310.
[2] *Op. cit.*, p. 56.
[3] *English Social History*, p. 491.

dupes to those who told them that their masters' interests were as much opposed to theirs, as their luxury certainly was to the morality of their female relations, . . . the manufacturing towns became sinks of unhealthiness, profligacy, ignorance, and drunkenness."[1]

His opinion about Manchester mill-owners was apparently shared by Mrs. Gaskell's friend Emily Winkworth, who lived in that town. In an unprinted review of *Mary Barton*[2] she wrote: "A limited family would be better than none at all, or than daughters demoralised in factories, (in some instances but little better than harems for their masters,) their ruin afterwards completed by the pangs of hunger."

Another objection to the factory system was occasioned by the new system of paying wages. In the days of the hand-loom, when the family formed a working team, single women who lived and worked at home were never paid separately. Consequently they enjoyed little or no independence from parental authority. In the factories every worker was naturally paid his own wages, a system which conferred considerable independence on unmarried women, many of whom left the home of their relatives and went to live by themselves. The Factory Commission of 1833 stated that factory girls usually insisted on their independence at about sixteen years of age.[3] Far from considering this new independence of women a gain, however, critics of the factory system regarded it as one of its most deplorable consequences. P. Gaskell, in his *Manufacturing Population of England* (1833) stated that the individual wage

"has led to another crying and grievous misfortune, namely, that each child ceases to view itself as a subordinate agent in the household; so far indeed loses the character and bearing of a child, that it pays over to its natural protector a stated sum for food and lodging; thus depriving itself from parental subjection and control".[4]

Mrs. Gaskell's friend Fredrika Bremer visited England in the autumn of 1849 and again two years later. She made it her business to study social conditions, especially everything concerning women's work. According to her, the treatment of children in fac-

---

[1] *Charles Kingsley, His Letters and Memories of his Life*, II: 223.
[2] In the Brotherton Library.
[3] Pinchbeck *op. cit.* p. 313.
[4] Quoted by Pinchbeck, *op. cit.*, p. 313.

tories was still intolerable as late as 1849. But she was struck with the immense improvement in the conditions of the poorer population which had taken place between 1849—the year of the cholera epidemic—and 1851: "I manufakturdistrikterna, i Liverpool, Manchester, Birmingham, överallt hörde jag samma talan av alla klasser: välståndet var allmänt där, var i stigande. Det bleka nödens anlete, som förr hade synts mig så förfärande, det såg jag ej mer så som förr."[1]

She visited factories and the welfare institutions connected with some of them, such as the industrial ragged schools. While she appreciated what was done for the children, she thought their mothers neglected: "När kommer man att upptaga i hela dess vidd vikten av mödrars inverkan på barnen? När kommer man att tänka på att i högre mening uppfostra mödrar?"[2]

In Manchester she was Mrs. Gaskell's guest and was probably assisted by her in her observations of social conditions. Her impressions were not entirely unfavourable, though she noticed some undesirable effects of factory work:

"även här skulle jag andas en lättare livsluft, även här skulle jag se ljus . . . Barnens 'klagande rop' hördes inte mera från faktorierna. Styrelsen hade satt ett slut för misshandlingen av dessa små för enskild vinningslystnad. Inga barn under tio års ålder fingo användas vid maskinerna, och även de som här användas måste hava halva dagen till skolgång.

"fabrikshusen i Manchester . . . I en av dem, som använde 1200 arbetare, såg jag i långa salar över 300 kvinnor sitta i rader, hasplande bomullsgarn. Rummen voro snygga och städade, kvinnorna ävenså. Det såg ej otrevligt ut; men den ansträngda uppmärksamhet, med vilken dessa kvinnor arbetade, syntes mig plågsam. De gåvo sig ej tid att se upp, än mindre att vända huvudet att tala. Deras liv syntes hänga vid bomullstrådarna.

"[fabrik med ryckvävstolar] . . . Så kommo de, män och kvinnor, ynglingar och flickor. De flesta voro väl klädda, sågo friska och modiga ut. Men hos många var uttrycket rått, väsendet vårdslöst och bar spår av förvildad mänsklighet . . . Man visste även i Manchester ganska väl reda på fabrikanternas karaktär som husbönder. Man nämnde med bestämdhet den goda, den vårdslösa, den elaka husbonden."[3]

[1] Fredrika Bremer, England om hösten 1851. Utgiven och kommenterad av Klara Johansson (Stockholm 1922), p. 7.
[2] Ibid., p. 11.
[3] Ibid., pp. 18–20.

Her evidence is valuable, as she may be supposed not to have been too much influenced by the current heated controversy about factory work for women. She was specially interested in all new possibilities for unmarried women to gain some independence and heartily approved of some kinds of factory work for women. This is what she wrote about a pen factory in Birmingham:

"Jag såg i stora, ljusa salar 400 unga flickor sitta var vid sin lilla pennstamp—ett behändigt och lätt arbete, särdeles passande för kvinnor. Alla voro välklädda, syntes friska och glada, många voro vackra—på det hela en syn av välstånd och trevlighet, som överträffade även den av de arbetande flickorna (the operatives) i Lowells berömda fabriker, i norra Amerika."[1]

---

[1] *Ibid.*, p. 29.

LITERARY INFLUENCES IN MRS. GASKELL'S WORKS

(Identifications of characters in Mrs. Gaskell's books with persons in real life.

North and South,
The Old Nurse's Story, Lois the Witch,
Sylvia's Lovers,
Wives and Daughters, Company Manners,
Christmas Storms and Sunshine.
Other Short Stories and Articles.
The Influence of Charlotte Elizabeth.)

In his biographical introduction to the Knutsford edition of Mrs. Gaskell's works (1906), A. W. Ward says that "she was too absolutely free from literary affectations to be guilty of even the venial sin of unconscious plagiarism—unless Charley Jones, when encouraging Mary Barton in her request by the reflection, 'we are but where we were, if we fail', is to be held to borrowed from Lady Macbeth".

In his introduction to *Sylvia's Lovers*, though, in vol. 6 of the same edition, he feels called upon to justify "the writer in one of the most beautiful unconscious plagiarisms in our literature. 'Child', said he once more, 'I ha' made thee my idol; and, if I could live my life o'er again, I would love my God more, and thee less; and then I shouldn't ha' sinned this sin against thee' ".

There can be little doubt that the above passage was inspired by Cardinal Woolsey's famous words.[1] To mention but one more similar instance, Alice, who "talked of green fields"[2] on her deathbed, cannot fail to remind the reader of Falstaff's babbling.[3]

---

[1] "Had I but served God as diligently as I have served the King, he would not have given me over in my gray hairs." (Cavendish, *Negotiations of Thomas Woolsey*, 1641, p. 113.)

[2] *Mary Barton*, end of Chap. XXII.

[3] ", and a' babbled of green fields". (Shakespeare, *King Henry V.*, II. iii.)

Examples of this kind are numerous in Mrs. Gaskell's stories, as might be expected in the case of a writer who makes such liberal use of direct quotation as she does.

It is natural that the excellent memory and comprehensive reading to which her numerous quotations bear witness should often have presented the author with models, not only for single turns of phrases but for incidents in her stories, and sometimes even for most of the plot of a novel, as well as the chief traits of some of its characters.

Three of Mrs. Gaskell's stories are set in the same small country town. Cranford in the story of that name, the Duncombe of *Mr. Harrison's Confessions*, and Hollingford in *Wives and Daughters* have all been easily identified—down to such details as individual houses and neighbouring lanes—with the Knutsford of the writer's childhood. When describing the Monkshaven of *Sylvia's Lovers*, too, Mrs. Gaskell showed the utmost fidelity to the details of topography in and around Whitby, on the east coast of England, where she had gone in search of material for her story. In her first novel, *Mary Barton. A Tale of Manchester Life*, she did not even trouble to adopt a fictitious name for the scene of action.

We have the author's own word for it that incidents in *Cranford* were such as she herself had witnessed. In a letter to John Ruskin[1] she wrote: "it is true, too, for I have seen the cow that wore the grey-flannel jacket—and I know the cat that swallowed the lace ..."

This has led commentators to assume that the characters in Mrs. Gaskell's books must also be faithful portraits of the author herself, her relatives or acquaintances. The evidence which has been brought forward to sustain this theory, however, seems very inconclusive.

In Mrs. Gaskell's case we have at least one example of a character painted from life, namely John Barton in *Mary Barton*. On this subject the novelist wrote to her friend "Tottie" Fox[2]: "Nobody and nothing was real, (I am sorry for you, but I must tell the truth) in M. Barton, but the character of John Barton; the cir-

---

[1] Quoted by A. W. Ward in his preface to *Cranford* in the Knutsford edn., vol. 2.

[2] 1849, extract of letter in the Brotherton Library, Leeds.

cumstances are different, but the character and some of the speeches, are exactly a poor man, I know."

The fact that Mrs. Gaskell admitted having had a living model in this instance lends weight to her denial in other cases. Some of her relatives and friends in Knutsford are said to have resented her putting them in a book without their permission.[1] The author, however, denied any such intention; when her daughters said that a certain character was very like so-and-so "she would reply, 'So he is, but I never meant it for him' ".[2]

The writers of a large number of articles accept A. W. Ward's opinion about the models for Miss Deborah and Miss Matty Jenkyns in *Cranford:* "It cannot be doubted that these . . . reproduced . . . Mrs. Gaskell's cousins, Miss Mary and Miss Lucy, daughters of Mr. Peter Holland of Church House, Knutsford."[3] Mrs. Chadwick considers this theory as proved: ". . . Mrs. Mary Sibylla Holland, was staying at Church House with the old aunts, the Misses Holland, and the letters that she wrote telling of the sayings of these aunts show clearly that they were the same sisters whom Mrs. Gaskell has portrayed."[4] Of the three letters which Mrs. Holland wrote on that occasion about the two old ladies, only one gives any information about their topics of conversation, and only one of their sayings is directly quoted. This one sentence, however much in character with Miss Matty's way of speaking in *Cranford*, can hardly be said "clearly to show" an identity between her and Miss Lucy. The latter is reported to have said: "Don't take ginger wine to-night, Sibyl, love; there's not much left, and Mary will not like another bottle opened, as there is no company but you."[5]

The pair of sisters from *Cranford* first appear in *Mr. Harrison's Confessions*, 1851, under the name of Tomkinson, and later in *Wives and Daughters*, here called Browning. It should be noted, though, that Miss Matty's counterpart in *Mr. Harrison's Confessions*, Miss Caroline Tomkinson, is far from possessing the gentle,

---

[1] See Chadwick, *op. cit.*, p. 16.

[2] *Ibid.*, p. 15.

[3] Introduction to *Cranford*, etc., in vol. 2 of the Knutsford edn., p. XIX.

[4] Chadwick, *op. cit.*, p. 27.

[5] Bernard Holland ed., *Letters of Mary Sibylla Holland*. (2nd edn, London, 1898.)

unselfish character which we associate with the name of Miss Matty. On the contrary, she is simpering and conceited and—sin of sins in Mrs. Gaskell's eyes—she is not even kind to children. Nor does she show any of Miss Matty's admiration for her elder sister. She accepts her sacrifices as a matter of course, while she tries to dissociate herself in the eyes of other people from her sister's abrupt manners. The latter is plainspoken to a fault, tall, gaunt and masculine-looking, but of sterling character, and is ready for every sacrifice for her beloved sister.

These were apparently the two types of character which Mrs. Gaskell had in mind when she began to write the *Cranford* sketches for *Household Words* (1851). In the first chapters, it is Miss Matty who is narrow-minded and scandalized to see a gentleman with his arm round Miss Jessie's waist, whereas Miss Jenkyns tells her to mind her own business, as that is "the most proper place in the world for his arm to be in".[1] It is Miss Jenkyns, too, who "supported Miss Jessie with a tender, indulgent firmness . . . allowing her to weep her passionate fill" at Captain Brown's funeral.[2] Mrs. Gaskell had intended to end the story after the first two chapters[3], and she only continued it because of Dickens' insistence. It is not until after the third chapter (after Miss Jenkyns' death) that Miss Matty begins to appear as the meek and undecided but thoroughly lovable heroine of the book, and her sister's character changes in retrospect from the warm-hearted, thoughtful sister into the intolerant, tyrannical law-giver.

The fact that the characters of the two sisters change from one story to another, and even from one chapter to another, in the same book, speaks against the assumption that Mrs. Gaskell had any living models in mind for them.

However, Miss Matty has a near relative in English literature. The whole tone of Jane Austen's domestic novels is strikingly like that of Mrs. Gaskell's, and it is tempting to conclude that much in Miss Matty's delightfully rambling speeches and gentle humility derives from Miss Bates in *Emma*. Jane Austen, naturally, was not the only writer before Mrs. Gaskell to have characters speaking

---

[1] *Cranford*, p. 37.   [2] *Ibid.*, p. 33.

[3] In the letter to Ruskin quoted on p. 242 she wrote: "The beginning of 'Cranford' was one paper in 'Household Words'; and I never meant to write more."

like Miss Bates. Dickens has them, and it is perhaps wise to remember what Forster says on this subject: "I told him [Dickens], on reading the first dialogue of Mrs. Nickleby and Miss Knag, that he had been lately reading Miss Bates in Emma, but I found that he had not at this time made the acquaintance of that fine writer."[1] Mrs. Gaskell, however, had both read and admired the book. In *Cumberland Sheep Shearers* she mentions "Emma's father in Miss Austen's delightful novel".[2]

Even if Mrs. Gaskell did sometimes have a living model in mind for her characters, it would seem as if there is nearly always also a literary influence at work. In the mixed character resulting from this method of composition the literary element often dominates.

The general resemblance of Mrs. Gaskell's domestic stories to Jane Austen's has often been commented on. Goldsmith, Lamb, and Mme de Sévigné, whose biography Mrs. Gaskell meant to write, have also been mentioned in this connection. Hawthorne's works have been supposed to have had some influence on such of Mrs. Gaskell's stories as *Lois the Witch*, and Maria Edgeworth's tales on her Sunday school stories. Crabbe's importance for Mrs. Gaskell's factory stories has also been emphasized. Mrs. Gaskell knew French well, and a closer examination might show some influence on her books from, for instance, George Sand's socialist novels.[3] The following pages are not meant as a study of all the literary influences on Mrs. Gaskell's works. They have been included in this study in order to point out some of Mrs. Gaskell's literary models not previously mentioned by her biographers and critics, and to support some of the statements in the preceding chapters.

NORTH AND SOUTH (1853-4)[4]

Mrs. Chadwick, who tries to identify most of the characters in Mrs. Gaskell's books with people among the authoress's relatives or acquaintances, states that Margaret Hale in *North and South* is "a more or less unconscious portrait of Elizabeth Stevenson her-

---

[1] Forster, *op. cit.*, p. 73.
[2] The Knutsford edn., vol. 3, p. 469.
[3] Cf. Chapter VIII, p. 201, n. 3.   [4] Cf. also pp. 274 and 282.

self"[1], and that "Margaret Hale has long been recognised as a prototype of Elizabeth Stevenson, and in writing this story she has undoubtedly drawn largely upon her own experiences whilst at Chelsea".[2]

Mrs. Gaskell's father gave up his work as a Unitarian minister for conscientious reasons (many years before the birth of his daughter Elizabeth), and it has therefore been taken for granted by many writers that Mr. Hale in *North and South*, who resigns his living and leaves the Church under similar circumstances, must be a portrait of the novelist's father. Lewis Melville, for instance, writes: "Mr. Hale is drawn from the authoress's father."[3] The latter's importance for his daughter's character, interests and work is rated very highly by many writers. Sarah A. Tooley, for instance, writes in a centenary article[4]: "Her literary genius came from her father ... From him she obtained her original outlook on life." This seems, however, to be an exaggeration in view of the fact that when little more than a year old, Elizabeth Stevenson was sent to live with her maternal aunt Mrs. Lumb at Knutsford, far away from her father, and only paid occasional visits to him in London, apart from the year she spent with him until his death on March 22, 1829.

Moreover, Mrs. Gaskell herself mentioned another living model for Mr. Hale. In a letter to W. Fairbairn she wrote, on the subject of his "very just criticisms on 'North and South' ":

"Mr. Hale is not a 'sceptic'; he has *doubts*, and can resolve greatly about great things, and is capable of self-sacrifice in theory; but in the details of practice he is weak and vacillating. I know a character just like his, a clergyman who has left the Church from principle; and in that did finely; but his daily life is a constant outspoken regret that he did so, although he would do it again if need be ..."[5]

According to Whitfield, "Mr. Hale ... resembles Froude in not a few features"[6], and J. A. Froude himself wrote to Mrs. Gas-

---

[1] Chadwick, *op. cit.*, p. 20.   [2] *Ibid.*, p. 96.

[3] *Victorian Novelists*, "Mrs. Gaskell" (London, 1906), pp. 204–23.

[4] "Mrs. Gaskell." (The *Unitarian Monthly*, April, 1910.)

[5] William Pole, ed., *The Life of Sir William Fairbairn, Bart.* Partly written by himself (London, 1877), pp. 460–1.

[6] Whitfield, *op. cit.*, p. 25.

kell: "It gave us *both* (I mean *C*.[1] as well as me) strange feelings to see the little dining room in Green Heys *photographed* in North and South."[2]

One more consideration which should be taken into account when discussing the theory that *North and South* was inspired by Mr. Stevenson's life, is the fact that the story, in so far as it regards Mr. Hale, has a predecessor in English literature, namely *Pomfret; or Public Opinion and Private Judgment*, which was published in three volumes in 1845.

The author of that novel, Henry Fothergill Chorley, was no stranger to Mrs. Gaskell. On May 8, 1849, her friend Emily Winkworth wrote from London to her sister Catherine to tell her about Mrs. Gaskell's visit to the capital after her sudden rise to fame as the author of *Mary Barton*. Towards the end of the letter she wrote:

"Mr. Henry Chorley, too, has given her a great dose of literary advice, really valuable, she says. So she is pursuing her studies you see as well as taking her degree. Mr. Chorley asks her whether so much advice does not puzzle her, and prophesies that her next book will be a failure, and the third a higher success than ever."[3]

Five years later they met again.[4]

The plot of *Pomfret* offers some striking resemblances to *North and South*.[5] Like Mr. Hale in *North and South*, Mr. Pomfret has

---

[1] The name of Froude's wife was Charlotte.

[2] Letter in the John Rylands Library, Manchester, dated Jan. 5. (Postmark "62".) The passage immediately preceding the sentence quoted above might refer to a discussion of Froude's own experiences when, after taking orders, he renounced orthodoxy, left his preferments, and devoted himself to literature: "I had many things to say to you which were left unsaid—partly because I could not bring myself to speak when it came to the point, and partly the most important part of it Henrietta said for me. The fear that I acted ill in that miserable business has weighed long and heavily on my mind—nor do I now feel that I understand it, though I heard all that you were able to tell H.—When I meet you again I shall perhaps feel more courage to go into the past.—"
One trait in Mr. Hale's character was copied from Mr. Gaskell's. (See Chap. I, p. 17.)

[3] Shaen, *op. cit.*, p. 39.

[4] "In the spring of 1854 . . . She renewed an acquaintanceship with Henry F. Chorley." (Whitfield, *op. cit.*, p. 50.)

[5] There is also a faint echo of *Pomfret* in *Cranford*. Mrs. Pomfret would have felt at home in that small town, where the ladies practised their famous "elegant

religious doubts and gives up his office in consequence, to take up work as a tutor. His family, like the Hales, have to leave their home. As little as Mr. Hale does Mr. Pomfret himself dare to tell his wife about his decision. In both books the daughter has to be strong for both her father and mother, though she is herself startled and estranged by her father's religious doubts. In Mr. Chorley's story, as well as in Mrs. Gaskell's, the wife never reconciles herself to her husband's "unnecessary" doubts, and dies from an illness perhaps occasioned by her departure from her old home, though she has long concealed her condition from her husband and daughter.

In *North and South* the reader is never told the exact nature of Mr. Hale's doubts. Mrs. Gaskell, like other Unitarians, showed little interest in questions of doctrine.[1] In 1859 she wrote to C. E. Norton: "oh! for some really spiritual devotional preaching instead of controversy about doctrines,—about wh^h I am more and more certain *we can never be certain* in this world".[2] The author of *Pomfret*, who came of a Quaker family with their traditional disregard for theology, tells us just as little about his hero's intellectual difficulties.

A few quotations from *Pomfret* are enough to illustrate the resemblances between that story and *North and South:*

Vol. 1, p. 13:

" 'Papa may well look pale', said Grace, ... '... walking up and down your study at three o'clock this morning? ... talking to yourself' ...

" 'Don't ... allude to my late hours before your mother ... They are unavoidable.' and he sighed again."

Vol. 1, pp. 130–1:

"But the confession was one to make the hearer tremble—so much pain, so much darkness, such a terrible sense of the discrepancy between the teacher and the speculator, were revealed. Nor was Grace thoroughly able to follow the process described; to receive, as a whole, the history of

economy", for, like them, she "practised only the elegance which was compatible with economy". (Vol. 1, p. 3.)

[1] "They hoped ... that the less attention was concentrated on abstract points of theology the more attention might be paid to the moral life." (R. V. Holt, *op. cit.*, p. 276.)

[2] Whitehill, *op. cit.*, letter 13.

doubt, unsettlement, despair, change, and resolution. She saw that her father was moved as she had never seen him: she was aware that he was no longer the serene and tranquilly-contented acquiescer in the doctrines and discipline of the Church of England that he had been . . ."

Vol. 1, pp. 135–6:

" 'We shall leave Dunwood', at length she [Grace] said, in a low voice. 'Have you thought of a shelter?'
" 'Not yet. But your mother—how shall I break it to your mother?'
" 'Shall I, then, speak to my mother?' . . .
"A silent pressure of the hand was the answer . . . 'Your calmness makes a child of me'."

Vol. 2, p. 3:

"Some one in the household must have strength; and, as her mother's health had been delicate all the Autumn, she must be that one."

Vol. 2, p. 275. [When Mrs. Pomfret hears from her daughter about her husband's decision]:

" 'You have known this long, Grace?' . . . A heavy and disconsolate flood of tears . . ."

Vol. 3, p. 259:

"Mrs. Pomfret's illness . . . I believed it to have been of long standing, and that the mind had been preying on the body. She had never recovered from that severance from Dimwood."

Vol. 3, p. 263:

"She spoke most affectionately of her husband . . . the love more strong than death must have led her to remonstrate with him on opinions she never had ceased inwardly to deplore!"

Vol. 3, p. 276:

"Throughout all her last days, Grace was admirable. That her anguish at the prospect of parting with her mother, when she was alone, was terrible, we knew; but, in the sick-chamber, she was gentle, supporting, almost cheerful,—."

In *North and South* we read that

"After tea Mr. Hale got up, and stood with his elbow on the chimney-piece, leaning his head on his hand, musing over something, and from time to time sighing deeply. Mrs. Hale went out to consult Dixon . . .
" 'Margaret!' said Mr. Hale at last, in a sort of sudden desperate way, that made her start. 'Is that tapestry thing of immediate consequence?

250

I mean, can you leave it and come into my study? I want to speak to you about something very serious to us all.'[1]

"...—and it came out with a jerk after all—'Margaret!' I am going to leave Helstone. ... Because I must no longer be a minister in the Church of England.'[2]

" 'You could not understand it all, if I told you—my anxiety, for years past, to know whether I had any right to hold my living—my efforts to quench my smouldering doubts by the authority of the Church. Oh! Margaret, how I love the holy Church from which I am to be shut out!' He could not go on for a moment or two. Margaret could not tell what to say; it seemed to her as terribly mysterious as if her father were about to turn Mahometan."[3]

" 'Margaret, I am a poor coward after all. I cannot bear to give pain. I know so well your mother's married life has not been all she hoped—all she had a right to expect—and this will be such a blow to her, that I have never had the heart, the power to tell her. She must be told though, now', said he, looking wistfully at his daughter.[4]

" 'You shall be told all, Margaret. Only help me to tell your mother. I think I could do anything but that: the idea of her distress turns me sick with dread. If I tell you all, perhaps you could break it to her to-morrow ...'

"Margaret did dislike it, did shrink from it more than from anything she had ever had to do in her life before ...

" 'It is a painful thing, but it must be done, and I will do it as well as ever I can ...'

"Mr. Hale shook his head despondingly: he pressed her hand in token of gratitude."[5]

"By seven the announcement must be made to her mother. Mr. Hale would have delayed making it till half-past six, but Margaret was of different stuff ... Mrs. Hale sat down and began to cry.[6]

"... it was an error in her father to have left her to learn his change of opinion, and his approaching change of life, from her better-informed child ...

" 'When did he tell you, Margaret?'

" 'Yesterday, only yesterday', replied Margaret, detecting the jealousy which prompted the inquiry ...

" '... I call it very unfeeling', said she [Mrs. Hale], beginning to take relief in tears. 'He has doubts, you say, and gives up his living, and all without consulting me. I daresay, if he had told me his doubts at the first I could have nipped them in the bud.'[7]

"He had a timid fearful look in his eyes; something almost pitiful to see in a man's face; but that look of despondent uncertainty, of mental and bodily languor, touched his wife's heart."[8]

---

[1] P. 37. [2] P. 38. [3] P. 39. [4] P. 41.
[5] P. 42. [6] P. 49. [7] P. 50. [8] P. 52.

"Mrs. Hale, overpowered by all the troubles and necessities for immediate household decisions that seemed to come upon her at once, became really ill, and Margaret almost felt it as a relief when her mother fairly took to her bed, and left the management of affairs to her.[1]

"Poor Margaret! All that afternoon she had to act the part of a Roman daughter, and give strength out of her own scanty stock to her father."[2]

"Margaret choked in trying to speak, and when she did it was very low. " 'I must try to be meek enough to trust. Oh, Frederick! mamma was getting to love me so! And I was getting to understand her. And now comes death to snap us asunder!'[3]

"Before the morning came all was over.

"Then Margaret rose from her trembling and despondency, and became as a strong angel of comfort to her father and brother."[4]

Naturally, the author of *Pomfret* could not help noticing how closely *North and South* followed his own story. In the review of *Wives and Daughters* in the *Athenaeum*[5], where he remarked on the likeness between Fredrika Bremer's *A Diary* and *Wives and Daughters*[6], he pointed out that "The principal characters and the leading incident in 'North and South',—the trials of the family of a clergyman who threw up his church preferment for conscience sake,— had been already presented in 'Pomfret' ".

Other contemporaries do not seem to have noticed the fact that Mrs. Gaskell's account of Mr. Hale's moral dilemma so closely followed the plot of *Pomfret*.[7] Dickens, who later objected to any

---

[1] Pp. 54–5.   [2] P. 256.   [3] P. 263.   [4] P. 264.

[5] March 3, 1866. This article is unsigned. That Chorley was the author appears, however, from the following passage in his autobiography: "Chorley's literary connection with the 'Athenaeum' down to the year 1866, . . . A fair proportion of the best works in belles-lettres issued during these years seem to have been assigned to him for review . . . Mrs. Gaskell's 'Cranford' and 'Wives and Daughters' . . . may be named." (Henry Fothergill Chorley, *Autobiography, Memoir, and Letters*. Compiled by Henry G. Hewlett. In two vols. London, 1873. Vol. 2, Chap. X, pp. 103–4.)

[6] Cf. p. 260.

[7] The religious question treated in *North and South* was in the air at the time. As Shorter points out in his preface to *North and South* in the World's Classics edn, "Tennyson had published *In Memoriam* in 1850, Charles Kingsley's *Yeast* appeared in 1851. In 1853 Francis Newman had issued his *Phases of Faith*, and . . . the Cardinal, had treated of 'Anglican Difficulties' in a series of lectures. Frederick William Robertson had been preaching eloquently at Brighton . . . and Arthur Penrhyn Stanley at Canterbury . . . Many an Anglican clergyman was questioning his position".

long discussions of Dissent in *North and South* when it was being published in *Household Words*[1], wholly approved of the choice of subject at first. He wrote to the author:

"The subject is certainly *not* too serious, so sensibly related. I have no doubt that you may do a great deal of good by pursuing it in Household Words. I strongly agree with all you say in your note; have similar reasons for giving it some anxious consideration; and shall be greatly interested in it. Pray decide to do it. Send the papers as you write them to me. Meanwhile I will think of a name for them, and bring it to bear upon yours, if I think yours improvable. I am sure you may rely on being widely understood and sympathized with."[2]

Mr. and Mrs. Pomfret in Mr. Chorley's novel are in no essential way different from Mr. and Mrs. Hale in Mrs. Gaskell's. The two girls—who both study Dante—are also remarkably alike in some respects. They bear up in a crisis better than their parents and have to give strength to them.[3] The character of Margaret in *North and South*, however, seems to derive from more than one literary model. Charlotte Brontë had revolutionized the literary fashion of her day by creating an ugly novel heroine. Mrs. Gaskell tells us that "Margaret was . . . far from regularly beautiful; not beautiful at all, was occasionally said. Her mouth was wide; no rosebud that could only open just enough to let out a 'yes' and 'no' and 'an't please you, sir' ".[4] Indeed, the utter impossibility of Margaret ever uttering the latter phrase leads one's mind at once to *Shirley*, which appeared in 1849, four years before *North and South* was begun. It seems safe to assume that Margaret would hardly have discussed labour problems, factory conditions, and other controversial topics with Mr. Thornton so freely and with

---

[1] For a discussion of his reasons, see A. B. Hopkins, "Dickens and Mrs. Gaskell", p. 369. No suggestion is made there that Dickens should have thought of any earlier treatment of this theme in English literature, and objected on that ground.

[2] Letter from Tavistock House, dated 3 May, 1853, now in the John Rylands Library, Manchester.

[3] It should be noted that the resemblance between the daughters in *Pomfret* and *North and South* is remarkable only in that part of the story which treats of their relations with their parents; where *North and South* treats of the special conditions of a factory town, Margaret Hale undoubtedly often expresses Mrs. Gaskell's own opinions.

[3] P. 21.

such a claim to intellectual equality, if Mrs. Gaskell had not admired Shirley's strong character and independent thinking.[1]

Contemporary reviewers were aware of Charlotte Brontë's influence. *Blackwood's Edinburgh Magazine* regretted it in an article called "Modern Novelists—Great and Small" (May, 1855):

"Ten years ago we professed an orthodox system of novel-making. Our lovers were humble and devoted, . . . when suddenly there stole upon the scene . . . Jane Eyre . . . No one would understand that this furious love-making was but a wild declaration of the 'Rights of Woman' in a new aspect . . . In her secret heart she longs to rush upon you, and try to grapple with you, to prove her strength and her equality . . . *North and South* is extremely clever, as a story; . . . yet here are still the wide circles in the water, showing that not far off is the identical spot where Jane Eyre and Lucy Snowe, in their wild sport, have been casting stones; here is again the desperate, bitter quarrel out of which love is to come; . . . The sober-minded who are readers of novels will feel Mrs. Gaskell's desertion a serious blow. Shall all our love-stories be squabbles after this?"

Although the opinions which Mr. Thornton expresses in *North and South* coincide with those of the group of independent factory owners in Manchester that hated State interference with their way of managing their "hands"[2], the character of the rough, plain-spoken hero is more reminiscent of Charlotte Brontë's manly ideal than is usual in Mrs. Gaskell's tales.

One more friend of Mrs. Gaskell's must be mentioned in this connection. While she was writing *North and South* she paid a visit to Florence Nightingale's parents at Lea Hurst, and the letter which she wrote from there to Catherine Winkworth[3] shows who inspired Margaret Hale with her strong desire for sensible occupation among the poor of the neighbourhood. Mrs. Gaskell wrote among other things:

"Miss Florence Nightingale who went on the 31st of August to take super-intendence of the cholera patients in the Middlesex Hospital . . . She herself was up day and night from Friday afternoon (Sept. 1) to Sunday

---

[1] That she was deeply interested in *Shirley* appears from her letters. On Dec. 21, 1849, for instance, she wrote to Miss Ann A. Shaen: "I have often meant to write to Emma, especially about Shirley." (Letter in the Brotherton Library.) She also wrote admiringly to the author herself. See p. 48.

[2] Cf. Chap. IX, pp. 218-19.

[3] Cf. Chap. III, p. 52.

afternoon, receiving the poor prostitutes as they came in, they had it the worst . . . putting on turpentine stupes, etc., all herself, to as many as she could manage, . . . She is so like a saint. Mrs. N. tells me that when a girl of 15 or so she was often missing in the evening, and Mrs. N. would take a lantern and go up into the village to find her sitting by the bedside of some one who was ill, and saying she could not sit down to a grand 7 o'clock dinner while etc. . . . Then she said life was too serious a thing to be wasted in pleasure-seeking; . . . Saturday Evening . . . I am a quarter of a mile of staircases and odd intricate passage away from everyone else in the house . . . so ought not M. Hale[1] to stand a good chance. I do think she is going on well; I have not written much, but so *well!* There's modesty for you. I have not half told you about Miss F. N. It must keep."

Like Margaret Hale, Florence Nightingale had had a struggle with her relatives before they allowed her to devote at least part of her time to her chosen work.

One character recurs in three of Mrs. Gaskell's tales. The heroine's sailor brother Frederick in *North and South* is the same type of character as "Poor Peter" in *Cranford* and William Wilson in *Mary Barton.* "Poor Peter" in particular has generally been supposed to be a portrait of Mrs. Gaskell's own brother[2], who went to sea and disappeared on a voyage to India in 1827. She does not, however, seem to have known him very well. In a letter to Clement Shorter[3], Mrs. Gaskell's eldest daughter, Mrs. Thurstan Holland, wrote:

"All I can tell you was when I was about 10 years old my mother told me that she could only just remember her brother that he went to sea. I think she said when she was quite a young girl, that she remembered coming up to a visit to her father from Knutsford to wish her brother good bye. I think she must have been about twelve years old when she paid that visit."[4]

---

[1] *Margaret Hale* was Mrs. Gaskell's own idea of a title for the book, until Dickens suggested *North and South.*

[2] "her only brother, John . . . was the original of Peter in *Cranford,* and Frederick in *North and South*", (Whitfield, *op. cit.,* p. 6).

[3] Dec. 10, 1914. Copy of letter in the Brotherton library.

[4] On the other hand, there is evidence that the brother and sister were in the habit of writing to each other. Jane R. Coolidge, in the unfinished MS in the Brotherton Library, mentions two letters from John Stevenson to his sister, one dated Dec. 5, 1826, the other July 30. In the latter, he congratulates his sister on the "very pretty story of Captain Barton" (about a narrow escape on the quicksands).

Considering how often Mrs. Gaskell's plots and characters were inspired by fiction, it seems reasonable to suppose that Fanny's sailor brother in Jane Austen's *Mansfield Park* had some share in the origin of the corresponding character in Mrs. Gaskell's work. Like him, he is kind, affectionate and cheerful. He is high-spirited, does not lack courage and makes good in his profession after several hardships.

THE OLD NURSE'S STORY (1852)

On January 1st, 1851, Charlotte Brontë wrote to W. S. Williams[1] requesting him to send a copy of her sister Emily's *Wuthering Heights* to Mrs. Gaskell, in return for the latter's *The Moorland Cottage*. It would seem that the climax of *The Old Nurse's Story*, the vision of the phantom child vainly knocking at the window pane to be let in from the dark and cold winter night, was suggested by a similar incident in *Wuthering Heights*.

This is how Emily Brontë describes Lockwood's experience when he tries while still half asleep to stop the fir-bough beating on the window:

"instead of which, my fingers closed on the fingers of a little, ice-cold hand! The intense horror of nightmare came over me: I tried to draw back my arm, but the hand clung to it, and a most melancholy voice sobbed, 'Let me in—let me in!' 'Who are you?' I asked, struggling, meanwhile, to disengage myself. 'Catherine Linton', it replied shiveringly . . . 'I'm come home: I'd lost my way on the moor!' As it spoke, I discerned, obscurely, a child's face looking through the window. Terror made me cruel; and, finding it useless to attempt shaking the creature off, I pulled its wrist on to the broken pane, and rubbed it to and fro till the blood ran down and soaked the bedclothes: still it wailed, 'Let me in!' and maintained its tenacious gripe, almost maddening me with fear. 'How can I!' I said at length. 'Let *me* go, if you want me to let you in!' The fingers relaxed, I snatched mine through the hole, hurriedly piled the books up in a pyramid against it, and stopped my ears to exclude the lamentable prayer. I seemed to keep them closed above a quarter of an hour; yet, the instant I listened again, there was the doleful cry moaning on! 'Begone!' I shouted, 'I'll never let you in, not if you beg for twenty years.' 'It is twenty years', mourned the voice: 'twenty years. I've been a waif for twenty years!' Thereat began a feeble scratching outside, and the pile of books moved

---

[1] Shorter, *op. cit.*, II: 188, letter 489.

as if thrust forward. I tried to jump up; but could not stir a limb; and so yelled aloud, in a frenzy of fright".[1]

In Mrs. Gaskell's story, Hester

"turned towards the long narrow windows, and there, sure enough, I saw a little girl, less than my Miss Rosamond—dressed all unfit to be out-of-doors such a bitter night—crying, and beating against the window panes, as if she wanted to be let in. She seemed to sob and wail, till Miss Rosamond could bear it no longer, and was flying to the door to open it, when, all of a sudden, and close upon us, the great organ pealed out so loud and thundering, it fairly made me tremble; and all the more, when I remembered me that, even in the stillness of that dead-cold weather, I had heard no sound of little battering hands on the window-glass, although the phantom child had seemed to put forth all its force; and, although I had seen it wail and cry, no faintest touch of sound had fallen upon my ears. Whether I remembered all this at the very moment, I do not know; the great organ sound had so stunned me into terror; but this I know, I caught up Miss Rosamond before she got the hall-door opened, and clutched her, and carried her away, kicking and screaming, . . .

" 'She won't let me open the door for my little girl to come in; and she'll die if she is out on the Fells all night. Cruel, naughty Hester', she said, slapping me; but she might have struck harder, for I had seen a look of ghastly terror on Dorothy's face, which made my very blood run cold".[2]

In *Wuthering Heights* Heathcliff is "as white as the wall behind him" after the vision has appeared, and "there was such anguish in the gush of grief that accompanied his raving, that my compassion made me overlook its folly".[3]

The perpetrator of the old wrong in Mrs. Gaskell's ghost story, Miss Furnivall, also cries out in agony, and she "lay at our feet stricken down by palsy—death-stricken".

LOIS THE WITCH (1859)

One more possible influence from the Brontë sisters might be mentioned in this context. In view of Mrs. Gaskell's strong love for children, it seems strange that she has not created any original child portraits. The boys and girls in her Sunday-school stories differ in no way from those in the other moralising children's tales

---

[1] Emily Brontë, *Wuthering Heights* (The World's Classics edn.), pp. 28–9.
[2] Pp. 437–8.   [3] P. 33.

of her day, and Leonard in *Ruth* is an angelic, sentimental child portrait in the worst Dickens tradition. The one startling exception is Prudence Hickson in *Lois the Witch*, that "impish child", who pinched the old Indian servant's arms black and blue, and was "deceitful, mocking, and so indifferent to the pain or sorrows of others that you could call her almost inhuman"[1], and who simulated an epileptic fit so successfully that she had a real seizure.

In all this she shows a strong family resemblance to Désirée in Charlotte Brontë's *Villette* (1853), "that possessed child", who "had a genius for simulation", and who "boasted an exquisite skill in the art of provocation, sometimes driving her bonne and her servants almost wild".[2]

Mrs. Gaskell herself must have realized the difference in originality between most of her own tales and those of her friend. She knew that reviewers were bound to see likenesses between their works, and dreaded the inevitable comparisons. "Mrs. Gaskell wrote so pitifully that it [Villette] should not clash with her Ruth, that it was impossible to refuse to defer the publication a week or two", wrote Charlotte Brontë to Ellen Nussey on January 19, 1853.[3]

SYLVIA'S LOVERS (1863)

When Mrs. Gaskell wrote *Sylvia's Lovers*, she had read and been strongly impressed by George Eliot's *Scenes from Clerical Life* and *Adam Bede*. In December, 1857, she wrote to C. E. Norton: "Read 'Scenes from Clerical Life', published in Blackwood . . . They are a discovery of my own, and I am so proud of them. *Do* read them"[4],

---

[1] P. 137.

[2] Charlotte Brontë, *Villette*, Chap. X. The resemblance may, of course, be mere coincidence. The old authorities on which Mrs. Gaskell based her story of the witchcraft persecutions at Salem mention "an old Indian female slave, called Tituba, whose tricks first infected some precocious children at Salem village with a morbid desire to dabble in the practices of sorcery". (A. W. Ward, Introduction to *Cousin Phillis*, etc., in the Knutsford edn., vol. 7, p. XXI.)

[3] Shorter, *op. cit.*, II: 301.

When writing *The Life of Charlotte Brontë*, Mrs. Gaskell naturally omitted any mention of the fact that this generosity on the part of her friend was the result of her own expressed wish.

[4] Whitehill, *op. cit.*

and on March 9, 1859: "Read ... 'Adam Bede' (you read stories from Clerical life? did you not?)"[1], and again, on Oct. 25: "Not a line of the book[2] is written yet,—I think I have a feeling that it is not worth while trying to write; while there are such books as Adam Bede & Scenes from Clerical Life—I set Janet's Repentance above all, still."

Sylvia's Lovers is strongly reminiscent of *Adam Bede*, not only in the setting in the well-kept, orderly farm-house. Sylvia's "character as undeveloped as a child's, affectionate, wilful, naughty, tiresome, charming"[3], is not very different from the equally pretty and coquettish Hetty Sorrel's "kitten"-like personality. They both have two admirers, one steady but dull, encouraged by the family, the other gay and romantic. In both books, one of them rouses the anger of his beloved by warning her against the unsteady character and doubtful intentions of his more glamorous rival. Hetty, in George Eliot's novel, comes to rely on Adam just as Sylvia does in her increasing dependence on Philip after Kinraid has disappeared.

The faithful old servant is a character familiar to all readers of Mrs. Gaskell's stories, but it can hardly be mere coincidence that in *Sylvia's Lovers* he is called Kester, like the corresponding figure in *Adam Bede*.

The character of Hester Rose in *Sylvia's Lovers* had originally been thought of in connection with *North and South*. In a letter to Forster[4], Mrs. Gaskell wrote:

"I have half considered whether another character might not be introduced into Margaret[5]—Mrs. Thornton, the mother, to have taken as a sort of humble companion & young housekeeper the orphan daughter of an old friend in humble, retired country life on the borders of Lancashire,—& this girl to be in love with Mr. Thornton in a kind of passionate despairing way,—but both jealous of Margaret; yet angry that she gives Mr. Thornton pain—I know the kind of wild wayward character that grows up in lonesome places, which has a sort of Southern capacity of hating & loving. She shd not be what people call *educated*, but with strong sense."

---

[1] Whitehill, *op. cit.*   [2] *Sylvia's Lovers.*

[3] *Sylvia's Lovers*, p. 21.

[4] April 23, 1854. Copy of letter in the Brotherton library.

[5] See p. 254, n. 1.

Hester Rose has the same feelings for Philip and Sylvia as this girl was to have had for Mr. Thornton and Margaret. With her quiet, humble self-control and Quaker-like religion she is, however, very far from being ruled by any strong, primitive passions. If Mrs. Gaskell had the Methodist preacher Dinah in *Adam Bede* in mind when she wrote *Sylvia's Lovers*, this would explain the deviation from her original idea of Hester's character.

Another possible indication that Mrs. Gaskell had George Eliot's books in mind while writing *Sylvia's Lovers* may be mentioned here. The characters of both writers make use of a large number of proverbial sayings, several of which, in George Eliot's case, were coined by the author herself.[1] In *Janet's Repentance*, that scene of clerical life which Mrs. Gaskell "set above all", one of the characters "can . . . see further through a stone wall when he's done, than other folks'll see through a glass winder". In Chapter XXI of *Sylvia's Lovers* Alice says to Philip: "If Coulson's too thick sighted to see through a board, thou'rt too blind to see through a window" . . . But Philip was as far as ever from "seeing through a glass window".[2]

---

[1] See Elizabeth S. Haldane, *George Eliot and her times. A Victorian Study* (London, 1927), p. 154.

[2] Mrs. Gaskell liked to hear new proverbs, and her retentive memory kept them, as well as other numerous quotations, for use in her stories. On a journey to Wales she learned a saying which she wrote down in *The Well of Pen-Morfa:* "The Welsh are still fond of triads, and 'as beautiful as a summer's morning at sunrise, as a white seagull on the green sea wave, and as Nest Gwynn', is yet a saying in that district." (P. 356.)

In August, 1850, Mrs. Gaskell met Charlotte Brontë for the first time. That must have been the occasion when Miss Brontë taught her the proverb about which she wrote in *The Life of Charlotte Brontë*, Chap. II, p. 7: "I remember Miss Brontë once telling me that it was a saying round about Haworth, 'Keep a stone in thy pocket seven year; turn it, and keep it seven year longer, that it may be ever ready to thine hand when thine enemy draws near."

Before the year was out, Mrs. Gaskell had used this saying in *The Heart of John Middleton*, which appeared in *Household Words* on December 28. The hero of that story says: "But I forgot not our country proverb—'Keep a stone in thy pocket for seven years; turn it, and keep it seven years more; but have it ever ready to cast at thine enemy when the time comes'." (P. 326.)

Mrs. Chadwick (*op. cit.*, p. 254) suggests another model for *Sylvia's Lovers*: "There is no doubt that *Sylvia's Lovers* owes much in the plot to *Wuthering*

WIVES AND DAUGHTERS (1864–1865),
COMPANY MANNERS (1854)

Considering the exquisite impression of freshness that *Wives and Daughters* makes on the reader, it is curious to notice how few characters and events in it are really new.

Miss Browning, who considers marriage a weakness and who says, "I don't know what I have done that any man should make me his slave", is Miss Jenkyns from *Cranford* over again, with her contempt for "the modern idea of women being equal to men" because "she knew they were superior", her protecting tyrannizing love for her sister, her consciousness of her social position as the rector's daughter, and her outspoken frankness.

Mrs. Hamley, the invalid wife, to whom her husband comes "to be soothed down and put right", who, though "quiet and passive in appearance, . . . was the ruling spirit of the house as long as she lived", is the same type as Mrs. Buxton in *The Moorland Cottage* (1850).

Nest from *The Doom of the Griffiths* (1858), the ideal wife though her husband's social inferior, who, married secretly, has to live away from him, reappears here as Aimée, Osborne Hamley's wife.

There is, however, another and more surprising reappearance of characters and events, not from Mrs. Gaskell's own books, but from those of her friend Fredrika Bremer.

H. F. Chorley wrote in the *Athenaeum* of March 3, 1866: "In 'Wives and Daughters', the group of Molly, Cynthia, and Mr. Preston, and the course of their transactions, strangely remind us of Selma, Flora, St. Orme, in the story of Stockholm life, 'A Diary' by Miss Bremer. This is noted as a coincidence, not as a charge of plagiarism." On a closer comparison between the two stories, however, the word coincidence appears singularly inadequate. Not only is the whole plot, as far as Mr. Preston is concerned, faithfully reproduced from *A Diary*[1], but both characters and epi-

---

Heights. Catherine and Sylvia, Heathcliff and Kinraid, Edgar Linton and Philip Hepburn have all something in common." I fail to detect any but the most superficial resemblance in the plots and characters of these two books.

[1] English translation, London, 1844.

sodes in *Wives and Daughters* show a marked similarity with those in *A Diary* and *The Home*.[1]

In 1851 Fredrika Bremer paid a visit to Mrs. Gaskell in Manchester. Some time later, she wrote her a letter[2] which proves that Mrs. Gaskell had then read at least one of her books: ". . . In your kind letters it is precious to me to see that my written home has been something to your living one. For such purpose, indeed, was it written."[3] From Mrs. Gaskell's *Life of Charlotte Brontë*[4], it appears that she had also read *The Neighbours*.

Commentators of Mrs. Gaskell's works have been almost as ready to find living models for the characters of *Wives and Daughters* as for those of *Cranford*. Mr. Gibson, for instance, has been identified with Dr. Holland of Knutsford for the simple reason that they were both doctors, though Mrs. Gaskell's daughter asserted that no two people could be more unlike each other.[5]

Mrs. Gaskell had a stepmother[6]; therefore it has been concluded that the sixteen-year-old Molly's despair on hearing of her father's intention to remarry must represent her own reaction.[7] But when Mr. Stevenson married again his daughter was only four years old and, as she had already at that time lived for about three years with her aunt in Knutsford, far away from her father, the event is not likely to have affected her deeply.

---

[1] *The Home, or Life in Sweden*, trans. by Mary Howitt, London, 1843 (not 1846, as the *Bulletin* states).

[2] *Bulletin*, p. 165. It is dated Fairfield, 19 Oct., 1851.

[3] Apparently Mrs. Gaskell had written to thank the author for a book which she liked particularly. This seems to have been her custom; see for instance Harriet Martineau, *Autobiography*, III: 221: " 'Deerbrook', a fruit of 1838, . . . Mrs. Gaskell in an especial manner was moved by it, and thanked her for it as a personal benefit," and Margaret Howitt, "Stray Notes from Mrs. Gaskell" (*Good Words*, Sept., 1895): "In May 1838 she writes as a stranger . . . to William and Mary Howitt to thank them for the great pleasure two of their works had given her." She wrote in the same manner to Charlotte Brontë and George Eliot.

[4] P. 387.

[5] The Rev. G. A. Payne: "Mrs. Gaskell and Knutsford" (The *Manchester Herald*, Jan. 6, 1900): "It is believed by many old inhabitants that the character of Mr. Gibson, in Wives and Daughters, was suggested to Mrs. Gaskell by her acquaintance with Dr. Peter Holland . . . I can only say that Miss Gaskell says: 'No two people could be more unlike than Dr. Gibson and Mr. Holland.' "

[6] Née Thomson.   [7] Sanders, *op. cit.*, p. 136.

Considering how very little is known about the second Mrs. Stevenson, it seems rash to identify her with Mrs. Gibson.[1] In literature, though, Mrs. Gaskell had come across a stepmother who may at least have served as a rough draft to her own Mrs. Gibson. Sophia's relations with her stepmother in *A Diary* develop in a way very similar to that between Molly and Mrs. Gibson. Sophia at first adores her new mother, but is treated with indifference by her. "Molly thought she [Clara, the future Mrs. Gibson] was the most beautiful person she had ever seen" (p. 29), but is given to understand that she has made a nuisance of herself during her visit to The Towers. The next phase in *A Diary* is open rebellion and dislike, in Molly's case her outbreak of anger and despair when she is told of her father's projected marriage. In both stories the third phase is the slow development from reluctant toleration from the stepmother's side into real though shallow affection.

Mrs. Gibson is a very successful portrait of a self-deceiving hypocrite, who always pretends to have other feelings and motives than her real ones, and whose "own words so seldom expressed her meaning". She loves to speak "in the arch manner of one possessing superior knowledge". She shares this trait, too, with Sophia's stepmother in *A Diary*. When the latter is told of Sophia's unexpected engagement, we can almost hear Mrs. Gibson in her "superior knowledge":

" 'You must not imagine, my dear Sophia, that I have not anticipated, not seen quite distinctly, how all would be, though I was not willing to say anything about it. I have foreseen everything.' "

In both stories there is one person in the home to represent something foreign, fascinating, a little mysterious: Cynthia in one, Flora in the other. Both begin the new relationship in the same way, Flora by remarking openly that she and Sophia think little of each other, which piece of frankness at once make the cousins better friends. Cynthia is no less frank to Molly: "We're all in a very awkward position together, aren't we?" (P. 215.) Selma is captivated by Flora's charm and admires and praises her singing, declaiming and drawing, just as Molly "wanted to devote herself

---

[1] Whitfield, *op. cit.*, p. 5: "Miss Thomson and her daughter are shadowed forth in the Mrs Gibson and Cynthia of *Wives and Daughters*."

to the new-comer's service" (p. 215) and "might have become jealous of all the allegiance laid at Cynthia's feet", if she "had not had the sweetest disposition in the world". (P. 227.)

Both Cynthia and Flora are singularly partial to long speeches of self-analysis, justifying their defects of character by the atmosphere of their homes during childhood.

"mamma ... never seemed to care to have me with her ... As soon as the holidays came round she was off to some great house or another. (p. 451.) ... if I had been differently brought up, I shouldn't have had the sore angry heart I have [but] ... I should always have wanted admiration and worship, and men's good opinion", (p. 525)

says Cynthia; and Flora:

'the primitive word of my mysterious character lies deeply hid in my childhood ... the influences that surrounded my cradle ... my mother was a good-natured but vain woman ... those endowments which might have subserved greater and better purposes, were pressed into the service of vanity",

St. Orme from *A Diary* steps straight into *Wives and Daughters*, under the name of Preston. In Miss Bremer's story, Flora refuses his invitation to a sledge-ride, and his face assumes "a dark expression". Cynthia refuses to dance with Mr. Preston, and his voice, "which he meant to be icily indifferent ... trembled with anger". (P. 283.)

Selma remarks that

"since St. Orme's arrival, Flora has been entirely changed ... her lively imagination always made her jump from one subject to another; but she was withal so agreeable, so amusing and amiable ... But she will not talk of this, and is equally unwilling to hear it spoken of ...,"

whereas Selma was "gentle but pale".

In *Wives and Daughters*,

"Once Molly touched on Mr. Preston's name, and found that this was a subject on which Cynthia was raw ... she ... bade Molly never name his name to her again", (p. 304), and "Molly was always gentle, but very grave and silent. Cynthia, on the contrary ... was ... too restless to hold her tongue; yet what she said was too pretty, too witty, not to be a winning and sparkling interruption ... Cynthia would not talk quietly about anything now"; (pp. 335–6).

In *A Diary*, the secret of Flora's compromising letters and early engagement comes out when Sophia surprises a meeting between St. Orme and Flora in her stepmother's house:

"I was astonished to see Flora endeavouring to disengage her hands from those of St. Orme, who with violence held them fast . . . At sight of me, St. Orme loosed his hold of Flora, and exclaimed:
" 'See, here comes, as from heaven, an angel of deliverance! Only, it is a pity that the noble deed has been achieved too late.'
"Veiling her face with her hands, Flora rushed suddenly into her inner chamber . . . She . . . cast herself on the ground with convulsive sighs and tears."

Mrs. Gaskell lets the meeting take place out of doors:

'As she turned a corner in the lonely path, she heard a passionate voice of distress; and in an instant she recognized Cynthia's tones . . . There stood Mr. Preston and Cynthia; he holding her hands tight, . . . Mr. Preston let go Cynthia's hands slowly, . . . Molly came forward and took Cynthia's arm, . . . Mr. Preston . . . said to Cynthia: 'The subject of our conversation does not well admit of a third person's presence . . . You mean that you regret that she has not been made aware of our engagement—that you promised long ago to be my wife . . .' . . . but she shrank away from him, and sobbed the more irrepressibly . . . in fact, she became hysterical, (pp. 442–3).

Flora confesses all to Sophia and Lennartson:

"This St. Orme dedicated his attentions to me five years ago . . . and acquired a certain power over me . . . I fancied I loved him. He abused my blindness, my inexperience, to seduce me into a secret epistolary correspondence, and pledge of eternal fidelity . . ."

Molly hears the same story from Cynthia:

" 'When did it all begin?' said Molly . . . 'Long ago—four or five years . . . I was only a young girl, hardly more than a child, and he was a friend to us then . . . little by little he made me tell him all my troubles. I do sometimes think he was very nice in those days . . . I liked him, and felt him as a friend all the time . . . he began to talk violent love to me, and to beg me to promise to marry him. I was so frightened, that I ran away to the others . . . I got a letter from him . . . renewing his offer, his entreaties for a promise of marriage, . . . I did not answer it at all until another letter came, entreating for a reply . . . I liked him well enough, and felt grateful to him. So I wrote and gave him my promise to marry him when I was twenty, but it was to be a secret till then." (pp. 449–53.)

In the original story, the villain threatens to show the letters to Lennartson, Flora's guardian and fiancé, who wants to fight a duel with St. Orme; in the later story it is Mr. Gibson who is to be shown the letters, and he expresses a wish to "meet Preston, and horsewhip him within an inch of his life", (p. 492). Sometimes it seems as if Mrs. Gaskell had Miss Bremer's story more in mind than her own. Thus, Flora who is stated sometimes to be more like a fury than a woman, naturally wishes for revenge:

"You have excited a terrible thirst in me. You have inspired me with desire to approximate near to you, to become your wife solely with a view to punish you and avenge myself . . . take . . . my eternal hatred."

But it is a little out of character for the indolent Cynthia to say,

"once or twice I've thought I would marry Mr. Preston out of pure revenge, and have him for ever in my power—only I think I should have the worst of it; for he is cruel in his very soul—tigerish, with his beautiful striped skin and relentless heart". (p. 455.)

That simile, too, is more likely to have been inspired by St. Orme, who invites Flora to "a *hell* of bliss' and tells her: "You will be mine or nobody's wife . . . If it is your will to have me as an enemy, why, I will deal with you accordingly", and who kisses her in the manner that "the spirits of the Abyss embrace each other".[1]

Molly is Selma, not only in her admiration and love for Cynthia. In both books she unconsciously and unselfishly loves her friend's fiancé, rejoices when she hears him praised, and implores his beloved to love him and make him happy. Thus Selma sighs, "May, oh may Flora make him happy!", and Molly speaks "with all the solemnity of an adjuration": " Cynthia! you do love him dearly, don't you?" (p. 365).

The father's influence is strong in both books, although in *A Diary* he is dead, and Selma finds it difficult to be good after his

---

[1] Rosamond Lehmann, in her preface to *Wives and Daughters*, is struck by this view of Mr. Preston in the gentle Mrs. Gaskell's book, and toys with a comparison between it and Henry James' "*glossy male tiger, magnificently marked*". She goes on: "Mrs. Gaskell . . . Henry James? . . . A far cry indeed, but there it is." The cry seems indeed to be a little too far, and it would be safer to substitute Fredrika Bremer's name for Mrs. Gaskell's in this instance.

death. It is "on account of him who had . . . presented them to her—her beloved father", that she values her pictures. In *Wives and Daughters* it is to Mr. Gibson's judgment that Molly constantly refers.

Selma goes of her own accord to get back the compromising letters for Flora, Molly is persuaded by Cynthia, but in both books the interview takes the same course from vain entreaties to sudden successful threats from the shy meek girl:

"Selma remarked his wavering, but she fancied she also saw the moment approaching when this would cease and he be obdurate to her entreaty. And suddenly she renounced the tone of a petitioner, to represent to him almost threateningly the certain consequences which would ensue to him, in the event of his abiding by his purpose. She communicated to him Flora's words and resolves for the future; she showed him Lennartson, Brenner and Felix also on the point of asserting Flora's liberty with sword in hand; she pointed out to him danger, death, and destruction, as the furies whom he would encounter on his path; and St. Orme—shuddered, . . ."

In *Wives and Daughters* Molly tries at first to reason with Mr. Preston. Then,

" 'I cannot tell about other people', said Molly; 'I only know that Cynthia does . . . as nearly hate you as anybody like her ever does hate.' . . . Molly was miserably angry with herself for her mismanagement of the affair . . . she had only made matters worse . . . 'Stop . . . I have thought of what I will do next. I give you fair warning. If I had not been foolish, I should have told my father, but Cynthia made me promise that I would not. So I will tell it all, from beginning to end, to Lady Harriet, and ask her to speak to her father. I feel sure that she will do it; and I don't think you will dare to refuse Lord Cumnor.'

"He felt at once that he should not dare"; (pp. 462–3).

In both cases a series of rumours starts. In *A Diary* "the Commercial Ladies" were "stored with gossip to such an extent that it ran over at their mouths", and "the lady of Colonel P." calls to make inquiries.

"When will the great, remarkable event be declared here? . . . The earlier this takes place, . . . the better for Flora, to silence all the evil mouths which assert that probably nothing at all will come of it. There were strange rumours in circulation for a time."

In Hollingford, too,

"All these days the buzzing gossip about Molly's meetings with Mr. Preston, her clandestine correspondence, the secret interviews in lonely places,
had been gathering strength and assuming the positive form of scandal."
(pp. 485–6.)

There, too, one of the ladies goes to tell one of the girl's relatives
what kind of things are being said. Miss Browning, though with
better intentions than "the Commercial Lady" tells Mr. Gibson a
very similar tale: "She's been carrying on a clandestine correspondence with Mr. Preston—. . . And meeting him in all sorts of
unseemly places and hours . . . All the town is talking of it." (p.
492). Miss Browning even abandons her usual benevolent attitude
to Molly and so far assumes the character of "the Commercial
Lady" as to add: "As if the poor girl who has been led away into
deceit already would scruple much at going on in falsehood",
(p. 493).

On hearing of Selma's proposed marriage, "the Commercial
Lady" inquires:

"Has not Miss Selma a fancy for a book that bears the title of 'Directions
for Economical Cookery?' I thought she might need it. Shall I purchase
it for the young lady? It costs sixteen *skilling* (sixpence)."

Mrs. Gaskell must have remembered this passage when she
wrote the description of one of Cynthia's wedding-presents,

"a collection of household account-books, at the beginning of which Lady
Cumnor wrote down with her own hand the proper weekly allowance of
bread, butter, eggs, meat, and groceries per head, with the London prices
of the articles, so that the most inexperienced housekeeper might ascertain
whether her expenditure exceeded her means, as she expressed herself in
the note which she sent with the handsome, dull present". (p. 580.)

Miss Bremer's Selma bears her trials

"with unexampled meekness but—her cheerful song is heard no more,
and her light floating gait becomes less and less elastic".

She never expresses a wish for her own happiness.

"For my part, I could wish merely . . . to . . . minister to his happiness.
May he be happy—may he be happy with Flora!"

In *Wives and Daughters,*

"Molly ... was gradually falling into low health, rather than bad health ..., the vivifying stimulant of hope—even unacknowledged hope—was gone out of her life" (p. 397). ... "Molly sat at her [Cynthia's] feet, so to speak, looking up with eyes as wistful as a dog's waiting for crumbs." (p. 398.)

When she is anxious about Roger, whose life is in danger,

"Her constant prayer 'O my lord! give her the living child, and in no wise slay it', came from a heart as true as that of the real mother in King Solomon's judgment." (p. 399.)

Selma is taken seriously ill after her successful interview with St. Orme, and only recovers slowly. During her illness, it becomes gradually clear that Lennartson's affections have transferred themselves to her. When

"Flora may ... be at rest on the subject of Selma's health, she is going to accompany her sister on a journey to Swartsjö ... Flora thinks only of cheering her own spirits ... What deep-seated egotism!"

However, this egotism is only apparent. While away, she makes up her mind to give up her beloved to Selma, and to go abroad herself.

"Like a fragment of a better being, I shall pass through life, perhaps merely to warn for the present time and point to a better future."

In *Wives and Daughters* Molly, too, passes through a serious illness, and Cynthia comes back from her seemingly heartless journey of pleasure to nurse her. She, too, writes to her fiancé to break off their engagement. At this point, though, there is a significant difference between the two stories. Mrs. Gaskell wrote her last novel at a time when she had freed herself from practically all the exaggerated sentimentalism of her earlier period, and, just as she left out the most romantic and tearful passages of *A Diary,* so also did she wisely avoid making a moralizing reformed character of Cynthia in the end. She renounces Roger only to become engaged to somebody else, who will suit her better.

According to A. W. Ward, in his introduction to *Wives and Daughters* in the Knutsford edition, Mrs. Gaskell compared Roger's scientific expedition to Charles Darwin's. But this fact hardly proves that the author had his character in mind[1] when writing *Wives and Daughters*, especially as she does not seem to have met him. She did, however, know one young man who may well have served her as a model for Roger. Her daughter Florence had engaged herself to Charles Crompton, and this is how Mrs. Gaskell described her future son-in-law in a letter to C. E. Norton of July 13, 1863[2]:

"He has almost perfect health, and perfect temper; *I* should have said not clever; but he was 4th wrangler at Cambridge and is a fellow of Trinity, and is getting on very fast in his profession; so I suppose he has those solid intellectual qualities which tell in *action*, though not in *conversation*. But his goodness is what gives me the thankfullest feeling of confidence in him . . . He is so good-principled he may be called a religious man; for I am sure the root of his life is in religion. But he has not imagination enough to be what one calls *spiritual*. It is just the same want that makes him not care for music or painting,—nor much for poetry. In these tastes Florence is his superior, although *she* is not artistic. Then he cares for science,—in which she is at present ignorant. His strong, good, *un*sensitive character is just what will, I trust, prove very grateful to her anxious, conscientious little heart."

That description might well serve as a summing up of Roger's character in *Wives and Daughters*. However, it seems probable that in this case, too, Mrs. Gaskell's novel heroes were influenced by predecessors in other works of fiction. Two of the characters in Fredrika Bremer's *The Home*, Henrik and Sternhök, bear some resemblance to Osborne and Roger Hamley in *Wives and Daughters*. Like Osborne, Henrik writes poetry. In both cases it is the mother who appreciates this, while the father is more sceptical about this occupation for a man. Henrik is "remarkable for extraordinary, almost feminine beauty; his figure was noble but slender" (pp. (35-6). Osborne "was almost effeminate in movement, though not in figure; he had the Greek features . . ." (p. 169).

They are both their mother's idol, and both die a premature death from some secret, wasting illness.

---

[1] "Roger Hamley is supposed to have been actually modelled on Darwin." (Haldane, *op. cit.*, p. 277.)

[2] Whitehill, *op. cit.*

"Sternhök ... had become early a man. All with him was muscular, firm, and powerful; his countenance was intelligent without being handsome ... Sternhök ... occupied himself very busily, partly with trying chemical experiments ... partly in the evening, and even into the night, in making astronomical observations ... The Judge took the greatest delight in his conversation, ... besides his extraordinary knowledge, he behaved always with the greatest respect towards older and more experienced persons." (p. 36.)

Roger Hamley

"was a tall powerfully-made young man, giving the impression of strength more than elegance. His face was rather square, ... the varying expressions of his face a greater range 'from grave to gay, from lively to severe', than is common with most men. To Molly ... he simply appeared 'heavy-looking, clumsy' ", (pp. 94–5).

He, too, devotes himself to scientific pursuits and is a great favourite with Mr. Gibson, and he always shows deference to his father and other older people.

In yet another case there is some resemblance between *The Home* and *Wives and Daughters*, namely, in the relationship between the Judge and his foster daughter Sara on the one hand and between Mr. Gibson and Cynthia on the other:

"The Judge was the only person before whom Sara did not exhibit the dark side of her character. His glance, his presence, seemed to have a certain power over her; besides which, she was perhaps, more beloved by him than by any other member of the family, with the exception of Petrea." (Vol. II, p. 7.)

In *Wives and Daughters* the corresponding passage runs:

"The only person of whom Cynthia appeared to be wholesomely afraid was Mr. Gibson. When he was present she was more careful in speaking, and showed more deference to her mother. Her evident respect for him, and desire to win his good opinion, made her curb herself before him; and in this manner she earned his favour as a lively, sensible girl, with just so much knowledge of the world as made her a very desirable companion to Molly." (p. 227.)

Sara asks her foster sister Petrea: "what would you say if I should leave you suddenly to go into the wide world...?" (Vol. II, p. 8), just as Cynthia tells Molly that she has formed plans to go as a governess to Russia. (p. 395.)

Mr. Gibson's stern speeches to his daughters on the occasion of their suspected or real misdemeanours are strongly reminiscent of the Judge's in *The Home:*

" 'For shame, Sara', said the Judge with severe gravity, and standing before her with a reproving glance . . . She trembled now before his eyes as she had done once before"; (Vol. II, p. 15).

In *Wives and Daughters,*

"his voice was hard and stern, his face was white and grim, and his eyes fixed Molly's with the terrible keenness of their research. Molly trembled all over", (p. 494).

The Judge thinks of the influence of Sara's actions on the innocence of his own daughter: " 'You had left the book lying on the table, and I took it, in order that I might speak with you about it, and prevent Petrea's young steps from treading this path of error without a guide.' " (Vol. II, p. 17.) So does Mr. Gibson: "There's no need to be ungenerous, Cynthia, because you've been a flirt and a jilt, even to the degree of dragging Molly's name down into the same mire." (p. 520.) What evokes Mr. Gibson's special wrath here is also Cynthia's way of flirting and not treating marriage seriously, just as the Judge is enraged, because Sara thinks of "the holiest tie on earth only as a means". (Vol. II, p. 16.)

The Judge, as well as Mr. Gibson, protests that he has given his step daughter every advantage:

"Answer me—have you had to give up any thing in this house, which, with any shew of reason, you might demand? and have we spared any possible care for your education or your accomplishments?" (*The Home*, Vol. II, p. 21.)

Mr. Gibson says to his second wife:

"Still I cannot see of what either she or you have to complain. Inasmuch as we could, I and mine have sheltered her; I have loved her; I do love her almost as if she were my own child—" (p. 521).

On another occasion

"The Judge started up, stamped on the floor, and pale with anger exclaimed with flashing eyes, 'Obdurate one! . . . I have the right of a guardian over you, and I forbid this unholy marriage!' . . . Sara . . . with an insolent expression riveted her large eyes upon him, . . . the next moment she was out of the room." (Vol. II, p. 22–23.)

Mr. Gibson

"had spoken too strongly: he knew it. But he could not bring himself to own it just at that moment . . . '. . . I asked you to tell me the full truth, in order that until he comes, and has a legal right to protect you, I may do so.' . . . But Cynthia said: '. . . you have spoken to me as you had no right to speak. I refuse to give you my confidence or accept your help . . .' . . . she tore herself away, and hastily left the room". (pp. 520–1.)

After Sara's quarrel with her step-father,

"any intercourse with the members of the family seemed to have become painful to her, whilst Petrea's tenderness and tears were received with indifference; nay, even with sternness", (Vol. II, p. 25).

In *Wives and Daughters*

"Cynthia was locked into her room, and refused to open the door. 'Open to me, please', pleaded Molly . . . 'No!' said Cynthia . . . And when Molly . . . hoped for a relenting, the same hard metallic voice . . . spoke out, '. . . Go downstairs—out of the house— anywhere away. It is the most you can do for me now' ". (p. 522.)

When Sara was leaving her home to be married, the Judge "drew her a little aside, took her hand, and pressed a banknote in it". (Vol. II, p. 26.)

"Mr. Gibson . . . called Cynthia aside . . ., and put a hundred-pound note into her hands." (p. 576.)

Here, Mrs. Gaskell's plot follows that of *The Home* very closely. Yet there is the same kind of difference as that pointed out on p. 268: In *The Home*, the Judge, with a premonition of Sara's tragic end, tells her, "you must not refuse it from your foster-father. Take it for his love's sake, you will some time need it." Mr. Gibson, in his humorous, slightly sarcastic style, protects himself from any suspicion of sentimentality in these words: "There, that's to pay your expenses to Russia and back. I hope you'll find your pupils obedient."

As has been shown above, Molly Gibson in *Wives and Daughters*, far from being "partly an unconscious portrait of the novelist"[1],

---

[1] Chadwick, *op. cit.*, p. 43. "Molly Gibson . . . whom we cannot help identifying with her creator." (Haldane, *op. cit.*, p. 274.) This kind of mistaken

is essentially the same character as Selma in Miss Bremer's story.
Cynthia, however, though most of her actions and some traits in
her character were undoubtedly suggested by Fredrika Bremer's
Flora and Sara, can uphold her claim to be "unique in Victorian
fiction".[1] Her dislike for all kinds of shams, her irresistible urge
to show up all her mother's hypocrisy, her indolent love for her
step-sister, her sense of humour, and her whimsical charm, make
her a very different person from the highly romantic and improb-
able figure of Flora.

Fredrika Bremer never entirely freed herself from the idea that
a tragically sentimental or mysterious figure was necessary in her
stories. Mrs. Gaskell, however, did, as is obvious from a comparison of the characters of her last novel with those of her earliest.
Such figures as Lizzie Leigh (1850), who in the end "sits by a little
grave and weeps bitterly", and the heroine of one story in *The
Well of Pen-Morfa* (1850) with her "sad, wild, despairing look",
are in no way different from the mother in Fredrika Bremer's
The Twins, who dies on her children's grave, or the lonely woman
in *The Solitary One*[2], all conceived entirely in the romantic, theatri-
cal novel tradition of the day.

It is not, on the whole, surprising that Mrs. Gaskell should have
found so much in Fredrika Bremer to inspire her own work. What
a contemporary reviewer wrote of the Swedish authoress also applies to those of her friend's books that are still widely read: "The
great charm of Miss Bremer's earlier work is their truth, freshness,
and domestic simplicity."[3] As appears from the letter quoted on
p. 261, Mrs. Gaskell considered that one of Fredrika Bremer's books
had been of importance for her own family life. The emphasis
that is laid on the importance of a home and a mother must have
appealed to her, as well as the highly moral and religious tone of

identifications of Mrs. Gaskell with such young girls in her books as Molly
Gibson, have probably contributed largely to the distorted picture of the author
as an essentially meek woman who uncritically accepted the ideas and moral
standards of those in authority.

[1] David Cecil, *Early Victorian Novelists.*

[2] In *Teckningar ur vardagslivet*, 1sta bandet, translated into English under
the title of *The Twins and other tales.*

[3] The article "Foreign Literature" in the *Westminster Review* of October,
1849.

some of Miss Bremer's works. Their sense of humour, too, is kindred, and the temple in the park in *The Home* that is discovered to be, in fact, a hen-house would not have been out of place in a Cranford garden. *The Home*, no more than *Cranford*, has any particular heroine, and the small joys and troubles of daily life are more essential to the story than any external events or intellectual problems. "Hovmarskalkinnan" in *The Home* with her heart of gold, gruff manner and sublime contempt for logic, has much in common with Miss Jenkyns under all her different names.[1]

There is also a strong resemblance between Ma chère mère in Fredrika Bremer's *The Neighbours*, and Mrs. Thornton in *North and South*. Emile Montégut summed up the latter's character in *Revue des deux Mondes*[2], and his characterization applies just as well to Ma chère mère: "Pour la vigueur et la résolution, elle vaut mieux qu'un homme, et elle ajoute encore à ses vertus viriles les grandes vertus féminines, l'économie, le goût du travail, le dévoument . . . cette ferme et peu gracieuse mistress Thornton."

It might also be noted here that *Company Manners*[3], that delightful recipe of how to give parties and keep the balance between material and mental entertainment, though apparently inspired wholly by the French art of what Mrs. Gaskell calls "Sabléing", is the same kind of writing as Fredrika Bremer's *Stockholm Suppers*[4], where she, too, is ironical about the kind of entertainment which consists chiefly in food and drink, those "evenings dreaded before they came, and sighed over in recollection".[5]

Mrs. Gaskell does not grudge the guests their food:

"If your friends have not dined, and it suits you to give them a dinner, in the name of Lucullus, let them dine; but take care that there shall be something besides the mere food and wine to make their fattening agreeable at the time and pleasant to remember, otherwise you had better pack up for each his portions of the dainty dish, and send it separately, in hot-water trays, so that he can eat comfortably behind a door, like Sancho Panza, and have done with it."[6]

---

[1] See pp. 243, 260.
[2] October 1, 1855.
[3] May 20, 1854, in *Household Words*.
[4] In *The Twins and other Tales*, 1844.
[5] *Company Manners*.
[6] *Company Manners*, p. 496.

Fredrika Bremer exhorts the hostess:

"Given den [kroppen] någon förfriskning, men även det lätt och i förbigående, liksom ett nöje. Sätter man sig till bords med allvarsam viktig min, kniv, gaffel och servett, för att äta—så är det ett göromål. Man äter för att leva, man lever ej för att äta, sade en vis. I viljen roa er—äten och dricken blott för att sedan hjärtligare kunna skratta."[1]

She stresses each guest's part in the entertainment; the conversation must be general:

"Varen få, men varen glada! Tänden ljusen i edra rum, men förr ändå vettets och det fina skämtets i edra huvuden! Låten glädjens lätta eldar lysa för varandra. Än en gång, varen muntra, varen goda—om I kunnen, varen kvicka! Dansen, spelen, sjungen, men allt i detta roen er! Låten intet börjas trögt, intet slutas tungt! Fläten med lätta händer oskyldiga nöjens krans—och till denna räcke var och en, anspråkslöst, sin lilla blomma fram. Konversationens nöje vare er dyrbart. Lånen eld vid varandras idéer, kasten till varandra skämtets gnistor, som lysa, men bränna ej. Låten tanke svara på tanke, känsla på känsla, leende på leende, likt melodiska ekon, eller snarare som dessa milda och granna toner, den minsta kallande knäpp framlockar ur den stämda harpan!"[2]

Mrs. Gaskell is of the same opinion:

"A little good-humoured satire is a very agreeable sauce . . . but it must be good-humoured, and the listeners must be good-humoured; above all, the conversation must be general, and not the chat, chat, chat up in a corner, by which the English so often distinguish themselves. You do not go into society to exchange secrets with your intimate friends; you go to render yourselves agreeable to every one present, and to help all to pass a happy evening."[3]

Miss Bremer was a personal friend of Mrs. Gaskell's, but the latter was already acquainted with her as a writer when they met for the first time. Her stories were widely read and appreciated in the English-speaking world, as appears from the numerous references to her in the literary magazines of the time.[4]

---

[1] Fredrika Bremer, Samlade Skrifter i urval. (Malmö, Världslitteraturens förlag. 1928.), Teckningar ur Vardagslivet. Första bandet, p. 261.

[2] Ibid., pp. 260-1.

[3] Company Manners, p. 494.

[4] Mary Howitt, op. cit., II: 22: "In England and America they [Fredrika Bremer's books] immediately met with wide recognition."

Mrs. Gaskell admired Jane Austen[1], and if she had never read about Fanny's reaction in *Mansfield Park*, when she realizes the contrast between the refinement of her adopted home and the coarseness of her own family, it is doubtful whether Molly in *Wives and Daughters* would have "felt the change of atmosphere keenly" when she returns to her old friends the Misses Browning after her stay at the Hamleys'. She

"blamed herself for so feeling even more keenly still. But she could not help having a sense of refinement, which had made her appreciate the whole manner of being at the Hall ... she became ashamed of noticing the coarser and louder tones in which they spoke, the provincialism of their pronunciation"[2],

Fanny Price in *Mansfield Park* visits her own family after growing up among her richer and more refined relatives. When she encounters her father she is "sadly pained by his language". She contrasts him with her uncle, in whose house

"there would have been a consideration of times and seasons, a regulation of subject, a propriety, an attention towards every body which there was not here. ... Everything where she now was was in full contrast to it. The elegance, propriety, regularity, harmony—and perhaps, above all, the peace and tranquillity of Mansfield, were brought to her remembrance every hour of the day, by the prevalence of every thing opposite them *here*."[3]

She, too, blamed herself for criticising and "was very anxious to be useful, and not to appear above her home, or in any way disqualified or disinclined, by her foreign education, from contributing her help to its comforts".

It might be noticed, in this context, that Margaret Hale in *North*

Obituary article in the *Athenaeum* of Jan. 13, 1866: "Her success we believe to have been instant."

In a review of Mrs. Gaskell's *Ruth* in the *North British Review* of May 1853 (pp. 151–74), Fredrika Bremer was included in a list comprising the names of Miss Austin [*sic*.], Miss Martineau and Miss Edgeworth, who are said to be the authors of "the best novels by the best unmarried female novelists". In discussion of the best contemporary writers of different countries this article states that "Miss Bremer and Mrs. Carlen [*sic*.] share the crown of Swedish novelism"';

[1] See p. 245. [2] Pp. 151–2.
[3] *Mansfield Park*, Chap. XXXIX.

and South was also, in a somewhat similar way, disappointed in
her own home when returning to it from a long stay with her aunt's
family in London.

When writing *Wives and Daughters* Mrs. Gaskell "did not outline the plot beforehand, but planned her story as she wrote"[1],
and in the end she "began to fear that it 'was getting very long on
her hands' ".[2] As it was published in the *Cornhill*, it had to be
written in instalments, which she never liked. The writing conditions, even apart from the necessity of regular instalments, were
far from ideal in one way: a considerable part of the book was
written on a journey abroad, which Mrs. Gaskell undertook in
the company of four daughters and three friends, and some chapters were written in Paris, in Mme Mohl's salon, and her amusing
but incessant chatter was proverbial.[3] The author could hardly
have had either the time or the quiet necessary for the composition
of an elaborate, original pattern. On the other hand, these conditions were favourable for a happy embroidering and embellishment
of a pattern already there.

Mrs. Gaskell's borrowings from other writers may not have been
conscious; if they had, more exact similarities in phrasing might
have been expected. She had a "marvellous memory"[4] and always
quoted freely and often inaccurately from a wide range of literature.[5]
The fact that the books from which she borrowed chiefly in *Wives
and Daughters* were such as she had read before she herself had
published anything makes it at least a possibility that the events
and characters from *A Diary* and *The Home* which she made use
of, were not realized by her to be anything but her own large stock
of material, of which she wrote to Charles Norton: "I have constantly long stories I should like to tell you, but which are too long

---

[1] Whitfield, *op. cit.*, p. 175.

[2] A. W. Ward, Introduction to *Wives and Daughters* in the Knutsford edn,
vol. 8, p. XVI.

[3] "Then, after my breakfast, which lingers long because of all this talk, I
get my writing 'Wives and Daughters' and write, as well as I can for Mme. Mohl's
talking, till 'second breakfast' about 11 . . . After breakfast no 2 I try to write
again; and very often callers come"; wrote Mrs. Gaskell to Emily Shaen in a
letter from Paris, March 27, 1863. (Haldane, *op. cit.*, p. 298.)

[4] Shaen, *op. cit.*, p. 24.

[5] Her quotations are far from always indicated by quotation marks.

and too difficult to *write*, when one can't see the impression certain words and expressions are making."[1]

CHRISTMAS STORMS AND SUNSHINE (1848)

In her early period Mrs. Gaskell highly admired Dickens, as is amply shown by her enthusiastic references to his works[2] in *Cranford*.[3] However, apart from the possible influence of Dickens mentioned on p. 245, his writings seem to have left few traces in Mrs. Gaskell's later stories.

It has been pointed out by several critics that one of her earliest efforts, *Christmas Storms and Sunshine*[4], was obviously written under Dickens's influence. The plot itself: the transformation at Christmas of a hard-hearted, mean character into one full of general benevolence and good fellowship is wholly Dickensian, down to the final exhortation: "If any of you have any quarrels, or misunderstandings, or coolnesses, or cold shoulders, or shynesses, or tiffs, or miffs, or huffs, with any one else, just make friends before Christmas,—you will be so much merrier if you do."[5] The style, with its long, merry row of nouns, is reminiscent of Dickens's *A Christmas Carol*[6] with Scrooge, who was "a squeezing, wrenching, grasping, scraping, clutching, covetous old sinner". The description of the cat and the baby, too, has a definitely Dickensian ring: "if the Hodgsons had a baby ('such a baby!—a poor, puny little thing'), Mrs. Jenkins had a cat ('such a cat! a great, nasty, miowling tom-cat, that was always stealing the milk put by for little Angel's supper').[7]

Later, when Mrs. Gaskell came to write for Dickens's periodicals, she more and more energetically resisted his attempts to "improve" her stories.[8]

---

[1] Jan., 19, 1860. Whitehill, *op. cit.*

[2] *Pickwick Papers* and *A Christmas Carol*.

[3] When the first chapters of this work appeared in *Household Words*, Dickens substituted Hood's name for his own, which upset Mrs. Gaskell so much that she wanted to stop the publication of her story altogether. Her letter to that effect, however, did not reach Dickens in time.

[4] Published in *Howitt's Journal*, 1848.   [5] P. 205.   [6] 1843.   [7] P. 194.

[8] For an account of their gradually increasing irritation with each other on this subject, see Annette B. Hopkins, "Dickens and Mrs. Gaskell".

OTHER SHORT STORIES AND ARTICLES

John Forster, writing of *Lizzie Leigh*, called Mrs. Gaskell "a very original writer".[1] It was he who, as reader for Chapman and Hall[2], realized the importance of *Mary Barton*, and it seems probable that, when writing of Mrs. Gaskell's originality, he thought chiefly of her novels with a purpose *Mary Barton* and *Ruth*, the originality of which is proved by the uproar which they caused in the press.

Her "Gothic" stories, such as *The Doom of the Griffiths* and *The Grey Woman*, were "true stories", that is to say, suggested by old tales related to or read by her.[3] The latter story appeared in *All the Year Round* in January, 1861, and for all Mrs. Gaskell's protestation that "the story I am going to relate is true as to its main facts, and as to the consequence of those facts from which this tale takes its title"[4], it is entirely in the Gothic tradition, beginning as it does with the discovery of an old manuscript about a mysterious castle with secret rooms and dark passages into which the heroine ventures at midnight, a villainous foreigner, etc.

Cranford, however personal in its inspiration, is yet conceived entirely in the Austen tradition of the domestic novel, and *Wives and Daughters*, as has been shown above, is perhaps the least original of all her novels.

One of Mrs. Gaskell's articles never pretended to be an original composition. She makes a definite statement to that effect on the first page of the article published on February 25, 1854, in *Household Words* under the title of *Modern Greek Songs*[5]: "I have lately

---

[1] *The Life of Charles Dickens*, p. 397.

[2] See Shaen, *op. cit.*, p. 39.

[3] About *The Doom of the Griffiths*, Mrs. Gaskell wrote to C. E. Norton in December, 1857: "The story, per se, is an old rubbishy one,—begun when Marianne was a baby,—the only merit whereof is that it is founded on fact . . ." (Whitehill, *op. cit.*, letter 8.)

[4] That is the first sentence in the manuscript of this tale (now in the Rylands Library, Manchester). It is left out in the printed editions. Mrs. Gaskell apparently considered it an advantage for a story to be founded on fact. Cf. n. 3.

[5] Naturally, *The Shah's English Gardener* (*Household Words*, June 19, 1852) does not pretend to be anything but the straightforward newspaper interview which it is. *Disappearances* contains stories already more or less familiar to others, which, as A. W. Ward points out in his introduction in the Knutsford edn., ap-

met with a French book ... It is called 'Chants populaires de la Grèce Moderne, par C. Fauriel'." The rest of the article consists of an account of the contents of that book with hardly any commentary from Mrs. Gaskell.

She does not give so much information concerning the source of a story published the next year, also in *Household Words*[1]: *An Accursed Race*. Sanders, among others, assumes that it was written "from information obtained on one of her trips to France".[2] The article was later[3] included in the collection called *Round the Sofa and Other Tales*. It is there purported to be a paper read by Mr. Dawson, who has compiled it "from a French book, published by one of the Academies, and rather dry in itself". A. W. Ward conjectures that this was "very possibly ... Francisque Michel's 'Histoire des races maudites de la France d'Espagne' (2 vols., Paris, 1847)".[4] There can hardly be any doubt that he is right about this source, although Mrs. Gaskell may well have got her facts from reviews of the book in English Magazines. Thus there was an article in 1848 in the *New Monthly Magazine*, entitled "The Cagots".[5] Its author sets out to "borrow from his[6] statements the following curious details", whereupon follows an enumeration of most of the facts and incidents used in Mrs. Gaskell's story, such as the special church door for the Cagots and the trick played on the congregation by the Cagot who put gravel in the key-hole of the other door. Their alleged leprosy, the curious shape of their ears, their mud habitations, are all described there, as well as the

---

pears from *The Life and Letters of Dr. Samuel Butler* (By his grandson Samuel Butler. London 1896), where Dr. Butler is asserted to have been the original teller of the story of the disappearance of the old man in Mrs. Gaskell's story. (I: 98–9.) *Traits and Stories of the Huguenots* (1853) were asserted by the author to have been told by her friends among the descendants of the Huguenots. The original version of *The Squire's Story* was well-known in Knutsford, as A. W. Ward points out in his preface (Knutsford edn, vol. 2, p. XXXII), where he refers to Henry Green, who relates the story in his *Knutsford: its Traditions and History*.

[1] August 25, 1855.   [2] Sanders, *op. cit.*, p. 62.   [3] 1859.
[4] The Knutsford edn, vol. 5, p. XVII.
[5] *The New Monthly Magazine and Humorist*. Vol. 82. Being the first part for 1848, pp. 437–41.
[6] Doctor Michel.

treachery of that friend of the Cagots who drew up the bridge so that they were all caught by their enemies. The legend about the Cagots playing at ninepins with the heads of the people of Lourdes can also be read there, with an account of the punishment meted out to offending Cagots: they were to have two ounces of flesh cut out down the whole length of the spine.

THE INFLUENCE OF CHARLOTTE ELIZABETH

In *Ruth*[1] a crisis in the heroine's life is brought about by the sudden appearance of her employer. Mrs. Mason "said to the trembling, guilty Ruth: 'Don't attempt to show your face at my house again after this conduct...' ... Ruth was left standing there, stony, sick, and pale".[2] This passage, far from original as it is, has a counterpart in *Rachel*, a novel by Charlotte Elizabeth, published in 1826. In Chapter IV we read that "They turned an angle in the walk, and Mr. and Mrs. Stanley stood before them. 'Young woman', said Mrs. Stanley coolly, 'how long have you been in my service?'—'Ten weeks, madam', answered the trembling Rachel. 'Then ... you will be pleased to ... quit the house this day; ...' Rachel stood with her eyes cast down, in mute dismay".

This similarity may be coincidence, but it is of interest to notice that Charlotte Elizabeth's descriptions of factory life[3] bear a far greater resemblance to *Mary Barton* than does, for instance, Disraeli's *Sybil*, which is so entirely unlike Mrs. Gaskell's first novel in style. Even in subject-matter the two books do not offer any striking similarities, as *Sybil* is essentially a political novel and not one about social conditions.[4] The greatest difference between

---

[1] Published in 1853.   [2] Chap. IV, p. 38.

[3] *Helen Fleetwood* (1841), *The Wrongs of Woman* (1843-4).

[4] According to A. W. Ward, it is "virtually certain that Mrs. Gaskell, before writing her own novel, had remained quite unacquainted with both 'Coningsby' or 'Sybil', of which neither she nor her husband are known ever to have made any mention". (Introduction to *Mary Barton* in the Knutsford edn, pp. LIII–LIV). Kingsley's *Yeast* and *Alton Locke* did not appear until *Mary Barton* was finished. Nor did Dickens' *Hard Times*, though *Oliver Twist* (1837–8), through its humanitarian tendency and exposure of social abuses, may have shown Mrs. Gaskell the possibilities of a novel to influence public opinion in such matters. Factory life was new material for writers, and it was used earlier

Sybil and *Mary Barton*, however, lies in the fact that in *Sybil* the workpeople are observed from outside by a member of the upper classes, whereas in *Mary Barton* the author describes everything from the point of view of the working classes themselves.

In Mrs. Gaskell's earlier stories it is tempting to see an influence from the unrelieved gloom of Charlotte Elizabeth's moralizing, pious tales with their endless Bible quotations. And some characters are remarkably similar in the books of these two writers. In *Helen Fleetwood* Mrs. Wright, who rails against religion, and her daughter Sarah, who longs for it while dying from the injuries she has sustained in her work in the factory, bear a family resemblance to Higgins and Bessy in *North and South*. The dying girl, with her long, prophetic speeches, looks to Margaret for help and comfort in Mrs. Gaskell's story, and to Helen in Charlotte Elizabeth's.[1]

With her factory stories Mrs. Gaskell has been hailed as a pioneer, and it is easy to see some reasons why Charlotte Elizabeth's similar tales did not make such a stir as *Mary Barton*, although they were actually published some five years earlier. In particular, the four parts of *The Wrongs of Woman*[2], though powerful enough in their descriptions of abuses in factories, especially the prevalent cruelty to children, must be regarded less as fiction than as illustrations of a theory in the style of Harriet Martineau's *Illustrations to Political Economy*. There are no thrilling incidents, no love interest, not the faintest sense of humour, and hardly any characterization. The same weaknesses are to be found in the long novel *Helen Fleetwood*.

---

in poetry than in novels. It might be noted that Mrs. Gaskell admired the poems of Samuel Bamford, author of *Passages in the Life of a Radical* (1840–4). Caroline Bowles (afterwards Mrs. Southey) published her *Tales of the Factories* (in verse) in 1833, Caroline Norton's poem about overworked hands, "A Voice from the Factories", appeared in 1836, and Elizabeth Barrett-Browning's "The Cry of the Children" in 1843.

[1] The situation where a young girl, dying of consumption, asks a friend to keep her sister from evil had also occurred in Charles Kingsley's *Alton Locke* (1850), Chap. VIII. The whole story of the Higgins family is, however, far more similar to *Helen Fleetwood* than to the short episode in *Alton Locke*.

[2] *Milliners and Dressmakers, The Forsaken Home, The Little Pin-Headers,* and *The Lace-Runners*.

Unlike Mrs. Gaskell, Charlotte Elizabeth did not provoke the anger of those in authority by showing an understanding for revolutionary political ideas. On the contrary, she violently attacked Socialism, that "moral Gorgon upon which whomsoever can be compelled to look must wither away".[1] Her anger is directed against the factory system as such and not, as in Mrs. Gaskell's tales, against the indifference of individuals to the suffering and misery around them. Nor did Charlotte Elizabeth take the risk of offending the factory owners of any special town, whereas Mrs. Gaskell incautiously called her book *Mary Barton; a Tale of Manchester Life.*

---

[1] Charlotte Elizabeth, *Helen Fleetwood* (London, 1841), p. 398.

MRS. GASKELL'S QUOTATIONS
FROM AND REFERENCES TO OTHER WRITERS
AND WORKS

(This list does not claim to be complete, especially as Mrs. Gaskell's quotations are far from always denoted by quotation marks. It does not include proverbs, or the works of the Brontës mentioned in *The Life of Charlotte Brontë*, or such quotations in that book as only occur in Charlotte Brontë's letters. The quotations in Part I are arranged alphabetically according to the names of the authors quoted, the rest in alphabetical order according to the titles of Mrs. Gaskell's works.

For the tracing of the quotations in *Cranford* I am indebted to the edition with an introduction and notes by E. V. Lucas, London 1899, and to the World's Classics edition with an introduction by Clement Shorter and notes by E. Limousin.)

I

Adam's opera of Richard le roi.
(*My Lady Ludlow*, p. 85.)
ADAM.

Mr. Addison's "Spectator".
(*My Lady Ludlow*, p. 29.)
ADDISON.

Addison's papers in the *Spectator*.
(*The Life of Charlotte Brontë*, p. 124.)
ADDISON.

the fable of the Boy and the Wolf;
(*Cranford*, p. 61.)
AESOP. (*Fables.*)

the grapes were sour
(*Mary Barton*, p. 33.)
AESOP. (*Fables.*)

it's rather sour grapes with me,
(*Wives and Daughters*, p. 319.)
AESOP. (*Fables.*)

"Mist clogs the sunshine.
Smoky dwarf houses

Have we round on every side."
Matthew Arnold
(*North and South*, p. 64.)
      MATTHEW ARNOLD.

consider the engagement in the same light as the Queen of Spain's legs—
facts which certainly existed, but the less said about the better.
(*Cranford*, p. 127.)
      Mme D'AULNOY in *Mémoires de la Cour d'Espagne* (done into
      Engl. by T. Brown, 1692).

Emma's father in Miss Austen's delightful novel, who required his gruel
"thin, but not too thin".
(*Cumberland Sheep Shearers*, pp. 469–470.)
      JANE AUSTEN.

Miss Austen
(*Mr. Harrison's Confessions*, p. 388.)
      JANE AUSTEN.

"Bacon's Essays" . . . his "Essay on Gardens".
(*My Lady Ludlow*, p. 47.)
      BACON.

the dictionary was Bailey's . . . she generally preferred Bailey
(*My Lady Ludlow*, p. 52.)
      NATHAN BAILEY.

a poem by Samuel Bamford, "the fine-spirited author of "Passages in the
Life of a Radical"
(*Mary Barton*, pp. 111–13.)
      SAMUEL BAMFORD.

Samuel Bamford's beautiful lines . . . Bamford's lines . . .
(*Mary Barton*, p. 236.)
      SAMUEL BAMFORD.

"we have all of us one human heart"
(*North and South*, p. 446.)
      SAMUEL BAMFORD. "*The Old Cumberland Beggar*." ("a" for
      "one".)

"we have all of us one human heart".
(*North and South*, p. 500.)
      SAMUEL BAMFORD.

we have "All of us one human heart"
(Preface to *Mabel Vaughan*.)
      SAMUEL BAMFORD.

Let China's earth, enrich'd with coloured stains,
Pencil'd with gold, and streaked with azure veins,

The grateful flavour of the Indian leaf,
Or Mocha's sunburnt berry glad receive."
>> Mrs. Barbauld.
(*North and South*, p. 81.)
>> Mrs. BARBAULD.

she herself had had to play the part of Figaro,
(*North and South*, p. 20.)
>> BEAUMARCHAIS. (*Barbier de Séville, Mariage de Figaro.*)

one of the airs out of Beaumarchais' operas
(*My Lady Ludlow*, p. 85.)
>> BEAUMARCHAIS. (*Barbier de Séville, Mariage de Figaro.*)

a sort of "A Lord and No Lord" business.
(*Cranford*, p. 88.)
>> BEAUMONT and FLETCHER. *A King and No King.* (Cf. anon.
ballad (about 1726) *The Lord and no Lord.*)

Berridge on Prayer
(*Cousin Phillis*, p. 209.)
>> BERRIDGE, JNO. (English divine, 1716-93.)

>> BEZÈ (See MAROT).

Blair's *Lectures on Belles Lettres*
(*The Life of Charlotta Brontë*, p. 68.)
>> HUGH BLAIR. (Scottish divine, 5 vols. of sermons 1777-1801.)

and he was now trying hard to read one of Blair's sermons.
(*Wives and Daughters*, p. 415.)
>> HUGH BLAIR.

even esteemed himself slightly qualified for a lawyer, from the smattering
of knowledge he had picked up from an odd volume of Blackstone
(*Mary Barton*, p. 248.)
>> Sir WILLIAM BLACKSTONE (1723-80).

"An' ye shall walk in silk attire,
An' siller hae to spare."
(*Mary Barton*, p. 97.)
>> SUSANNA BLANMIRE (1747-94). (*The Siller Crown.*)

Bollin's "Ancient History",
(*My French Master*, p. 507.)
>> BOLLIN.

Bossuet . . . "Oraison Funèbre de la Reine d'Angleterre"
(*The Life of Charlotte Brontë*, pp. 151, 158.)
>> BOSSUET.

Miss Bremer . . . the *Neighbours*
(*The Life of Charlotte Brontë*, p. 387.)
>> FREDRIKA BREMER.

his life being "a vale of tears",
(*Cranford*, p. 60.)
ROBERT BROWNING. (*Confessions.*)

some of Robert Browning's smaller poems.
(*Modern Greek Songs*, p. 490.)
ROBERT BROWNING.

"I see my way as birds their trackless way—
I shall arrive! what time, what circuit first,
I ask not: but unless God send His hail
Or blinding fire-balls, sleet, or stifling snow,
In some time—His good time—I shall arrive;
He guides me and the bird. In His good time!"
Browning's Paracelsus
(*North and South*, p. 363.)
ROBERT BROWNING. (*Paracelsus.*)

"The more Haste the Worse Speed."
Learn to win a lady's faith
Nobly, as the thing is high;
Bravely, as for life and death—
With a loyal gravity.

Lead her from the festive boards,
Point her to the starry skies,
Guard her, by your truthful words,
Pure from courtship's flatteries."
Mrs. Browning.
(*North and South*, p. 27.)
ELIZABETH BARRETT BROWNING.

"Ay sooth, we feel too strong in weal, to need Thee on that road;
But woe being come, the soul is dumb, that crieth not on 'God'."
Mrs. Browning.
(*North and South*, p. 230.)
ELIZABETH BARRETT BROWNING.

When some beloved voice that was to you
Both sound and sweetness, faileth suddenly,
And silence, against which you dare not cry,
Aches round you like a strong disease and new—
What hope? what help? what music will undo
That silence to your sense?
Mrs. Browning.
(*North and South*, p. 375.)
ELIZABETH BARRETT BROWNING.

Experience, like a pale musician, holds
A dulcimer of patience in his hand;

Whence harmonies we cannot understand,
Of God's will in His worlds, the strain unfolds
In sad, perplexed minors."
                    Mrs. Browning.
(*North and South*, p. 429.)
              ELIZABETH BARRETT BROWNING.

Oh! my God.
—Thou hast knowledge, only Thou,
How dreary 'tis for women to sit still
On winter nights by solitary fires,
And hear the nations praising them far off."
(*The Life of Charlotte Brontë*, title page of early edns.)
              ELIZABETH BARRETT BROWNING. (*Aurora Leigh*, "Father" for
              "God".)

the "little birds sang east, and the little birds sang west".
(*Ruth*, p. 180.)
              ELIZABETH BARRETT BROWNING. (*The Rime of the Duchess May*,
              last stanza.)

In the autumn days, "the saddest of the year",
(*The Doom of the Griffiths*, p. 215.)
              WILLIAM CULLEN BRYANT. (*The Death of the Flowers*, stanza I.)

she was up in the *Règne Animal*
(*Wives and Daughters*, p. 29.)
              BUFFON.

There was some French book that Molly was reading—*Le Règne Animal* . . .
(*Wives and Daughters*, p. 292.)
              BUFFON.

such as . . . "The Pilgrim's Progress"
(*Half a Lifetime Ago*, p. 247.)
              BUNYAN.

the "*Pilgrim's Progress*"
(*The Heart of John Middleton*, p. 319.)
              BUNYAN.

it was the Vanity Fair of the *Pilgrim's Progress* to her.
(*The Life of Charlotte Brontë*, p. 84.)
              BUNYAN.

"How beautiful is the land of Beulah, far over the sea, beyond the mountains!
(*Lois the Witch*, p. 179.)
              BUNYAN. (*The Pilgrim's Progress;* Cf. also Is. 62: 4.)

and longing to get away to the land o' Beulah;
(*North and South*, p. 97.)
              BUNYAN. (*The Pilgrim's Progress;* Cf. also Is. 62: 4.)

as the shepherd-boy in John Bunyan sweetly sang, "He that is low need fear no fall".
(*Ruth*, p. 262.)
BUNYAN.

stories out of the 'Pilgrim's Progress'.
(*Ruth*, p. 35.)
BUNYAN.

The Pilgrim's Progress
(*Sylvia's Lovers*, p. 211.)
BUNYAN.

Doctor Burney used to teach me music! ... And his daughter wrote a book, and they said she was but a very young lady, an nothing but a music-master's daughter;
(*My Lady Ludlow*, p. 124.)
FRANCES BURNEY.

"a man's a man for a' that, for a' that, and twice as much as a' that". ...
(*Mary Barton*, p. 173.)
BURNS. (*For a' that and a' that.*)

"That a man's a man for a' that"
(*Mary Barton*, p. 173.)
BURNS.

O Mary, canst thou wreck his peace,
Wha for thy sake wad gladly die?
Or canst thou break that heart of his,
Whose only fault is loving thee?"
Burns.
(*Mary Barton*, p. 125.)
BURNS.

"While day and night can bring delight,
Or nature aught of pleasure give;
While joys above my mind can move
For thee, and thee alone I live:

When that grim foe of joy below
Comes in between to make us part,
The iron hand that breaks our band,
It breaks my bliss—it breaks my heart."
Burns.
(*Mary Barton*, p. 321.)
BURNS.

I only want sorely to see the 'What's resisted' of Burns, ...
"What's done we partly may compute;

But know not what's resisted."
(*The Moorland Cottage*, p. 337.)
    BURNS. (*Address to the Unco Guid*.)

he's a man for a' that.
(*North and South*, p. 166.)
    BURNS. (*For a' that and a' that*.)

I ha' read a bit o' poetry about a plough going o'er a daisy, as made tears
come into my eyes,
(*North and South*, p. 310.)
    BURNS. (*To a Mountain Daisy*.)

"Should Auld Acquaintance be Forgot."
(*North and South*, p. 265.)
    BURNS.

to "gar auld claes look amaist as weel's the new".
(*Wives and Daughters*, p. 414.)
    BURNS. (*The Cottar's Saturday Night*, "gars" for "gar".)

the saying in Hudibras—
"He that's convinced against his will
Is of the same opinion still."
(*An Accursed Race*, p. 202.)
    SAMUEL BUTLER.

"Spare the rod, and spoil the child."
(*Cousin Phillis*, p. 172.)
    SAMUEL BUTLER. (*Hudibras*.)

the Puritans (who, says Butler, "Blasphemed custard through the nose".)
(*Lois the Witch*, p. 120.)
    JOSEPH BUTLER (?)

I got "Byron's Narrative"
(*The Heart of John Middleton*, p. 319.)
    JOHN BYRON. (*The Narrative* of the shipwreck of the Wager.)

Byron
(*Cranford*, p. 46.)
    LORD BYRON.

But in his pulse there was no throb,
Nor in his lips one dying sob;
Sigh, nor word, nor struggling breath
Heralded his way to death.
            Siege of Corinth.
(*Mary Barton*, p. 196.)
    LORD BYRON. (*The Siege of Corinth*.)

"The first dark day of nothingness,
The last of danger and distress."
> Byron.

(*Mary Barton*, p. 356.)
> LORD BYRON. (*The Giaour*, l. 70.)

"Revenge may have her own;
Roused discipline aloud proclaims their cause,
And injured navies urge their broken laws."
> Byron.

(*North and South*, p. 208.)
> LORD BYRON.

"What! remain to be
Dénounced—dragged, it may be, in chains."
> Werner.

(*North and South*, p. 275.)
> LORD BYRON. (*Werner*.)

her "magic of a superior mind",
(*The Poor Clare*, p. 292.)
> LORD BYRON. (Cf. *The Corsair*, Canto I, st. 8: The power of thought—the magic of the mind.)

To make a Roman holiday." Pope, or somebody else, has a line of poetry like that . . . "It's Byron, . . . I'm surprised at your lordship's quoting Byron—he was a very immoral poet."
(*Wives and Daughters*, p. 143.)
> LORD BYRON. (*Childe Harold*, Canto IV.)

the 'Prisoner of Chillon'
(*Wives and Daughters*, p. 263.)
> LORD BYRON.

your liking for Byron
(*Wives and Daughters*, p. 264.)
> LORD BYRON.

Caesar
(*Cousin Phillis*, p. 185.)
> CAESAR.

I saw, I imitated, I survived!
(*Cranford*, p. 48.)
> (Cf. Julius Caesar: Veni, vidi, vici.)

Lochiel's grandchild, who made his grandsire indignant at the luxury of his pillow of snow.
(*Curious if True*, p. 261.)
> (THOMAS CAMPBELL, *Lochiel's Warning* (?)
> DAVID CAREY, *Lochiel, or the Field of Culloden* (?) [Minerva Press, 1820.].)

Carlyle
(*The Life of Charlotte Brontë*, p. 158.)
    CARLYLE.

they might have read the opinions of that worthy Professor Teufelsdreck,
in "Sartor Resartus", to judge from the dilapidated coats and trousers,
which yet clothed men of parts and of power.
(*Mary Barton*, p. 178.)
    CARLYLE.

Mrs. Carter ... she had written "Epictetus"
(*Cranford*, p. 60.)
    Mrs. CARTER.

he can eat comfortably behind a door, like Sancho Panza,
(*Company Manners*, p. 496.)
    CERVANTES. (*Don Quixote.*)

reminding one exceedingly of Camacho's wedding.
(*Cumberland Sheep Shearers*, p. 465.)
    CERVANTES.

a tall, thin, Don Quixote-looking old man
more like my idea of Don Quixote than ever
He is very like Don Quixote
(*Cranford*, pp. 44, 46, 49.)
    CERVANTES.

"Very fine spirit, sir—quite like Don Quixote
(*Mr. Harrison's Confessions*, p. 409.)
    CERVANTES.

To Don Quixote ... Sancho Panza ... Sancho
(*The Moorland Cottage*, pp. 298, 325.)
    CERVANTES.

with a mixture of pity in one's admiration, something like what one feels
for Don Quixote
(*North and South*, p. 406.)
    CERVANTES.

"Don Quixote and Sancho Panza", said she to herself
(*Wives and Daughters*, p. 507.)
    CERVANTES.

It was a long time since she had read Mrs. Chapone,
(*Cranford*, p. 60.)
    Mrs. CHAPONE.

Mrs. Chapone's Letters
(*My Lady Ludlow*, p. 29.)
    Mrs. CHAPONE. (*Letters on the Improvement of the Mind.*)

Chatterton
(*The Life of Charlotte Brontë*, p. 250.)
> THOMAS CHATTERTON.

Bonus Bernardus non videt omnia
(*Cranford*, p. 63.)
> CHAUCER. (*Prologue of Nine Gode Wymmen* [Fairfax MS.]: Bernardus Monarkus non videt o.)

With the grace of a masculine Griselda (*The Squire's Story*, p. 541.)
> CHAUCER. (*The Clerk's Tale.*) (Cf. Chettle, Dekker, Haughton, Patient Grissil.)

Lord Chesterfield's Letters
(*Cranford*, p. 114.)
> LORD CHESTERFIELD.

(Cf. "The Female Chesterfield"
Morton Hall, p. 383.)

M. T. Ciceronis Epistolae
(*Cranford*, p. 59.)
> CICERO.

Middleton's Cicero
(*North and South*, p. 24.)
> CICERO.

the upper air bursts into life,
(*Company Manners*, p. 501.)
> COLERIDGE. (*The Rime of the Ancient Mariner.*)

eyes that looked like violets filled with dew
(*Clopton House*, p. 506.)
> (Cf. *Ancient Mariner:* I dreamt that they were filled with dew.)

the very one that suggested to Coleridge "This sycamore (oft musical with bees—Such tents the Patriarchs loved)
(*Cumberland Sheep Shearers*, p. 459.)
> COLERIDGE.

"the blue sky, that bends over all",
(*Libbie Marsh's Three Eras*, pp. 453–4.)
> COLERIDGE. (*Christabel:* For the blue sky bends . . .)

Coleridge
(*The Life of Charlotte Brontë*, p. 97.)

"and he blessed her unaware".
(*Lois the Witch*, p. 177.)
> COLERIDGE. (*Ancient Mariner.*)

as potent as that of the mariner's glittering eye. "He listened like a three-year child."
(*Mary Barton*, p. 157.)
> COLERIDGE. (*Ancient Mariner.*)

"Deeds to be hid which were not hid,
Which, all confused, I could not know,
Whether I suffered or I did,
For all seemed guilt, remorse or woe."
Coleridge.
(*Mary Barton*, p. 208.)
COLERIDGE.
Heaven blessed her unaware
(*Mary Barton*, p. 224.)
COLERIDGE. (*Ancient Mariner.*)

(even as the unholy Lady Geraldine was prevented, in the abode of Christabel) from crossing the threshold . . .
(*Mary Barton*, p. 230.)
COLERIDGE. (*Christabel.*)

"Some wishes crossed my mind and dimly cheered it,
And one or two poor melancholy pleasures,
Each in the pale unwarming light of hope,
Silvering its flimsy wing, flew silent by—
Moths in the moonbeam!"
Coleridge.
(*North and South*, p. 247.)
COLERIDGE.

("such tents the patriarchs loved")
(*Ruth*, p. 36.)
COLERIDGE.
She was fair, not pale,
(*Wives and Daughters*, p. 60.)
COLERIDGE. (*Christabel:* Her face, oh call it fair, not pale.)

I remember such a pretty line of poetry, 'Oh, call her fair, not pale!'
(*Wives and Daughters*, p. 556.)
COLERIDGE. (*Christabel.*)

the "pride which apes humility",
(*Cranford*, p. 43.)
COLERIDGE and SOUTHEY. (*The Devil's Walk.*)

with "the pride that apes humility".
(*North and South*, p. 121.)
COLERIDGE and SOUTHEY. (*The Devil's Walk.*)

Victor Cousin, the French philosopher
(*Company Manners*)
VICTOR COUSIN. (1792–1867.)

Mr. Grimshaw's life was written by Newton, Cowper's friend . . .
some of Cowper's letters . . .

the gentle and melancholy Cowper ...
(*The Life of Charlotte Brontë*, pp. 14, 92, 93.)
    WILLIAM COWPER.

"A dull rotation, never at a stay,
Yesterday's face twin image of to-day."
               Cowper.
(*North and South*, p. 396.)
    WILLIAM COWPER.

to make room for Johnnie Gilpin as my favourite poem
(*Wives and Daughters*, p. 263.)
    WILLIAM COWPER.

"my solitude requires a listener, to whom I may say, 'how sweet is solitude!'
(*Wives and Daughters*, p. 347.)
(Cf. *Wives and Daughters*, p. 615: "how sweet is friendship".)
      WILLIAM COWPER. (*Retirement*, l. 739: How sweet, how passing
      sweet, is sol.!)

"Something there was: what, none presumed to say,
Clouds lightly passing on a smiling day,—
Whispers and hints which went from ear to ear,
And mixed reports no judge on earth could clear."
               Crabbe.
"Curious conjectures he may always make,
And either side of dubious questions take."
               Ibid.
(*Mary Barton*, p. 264.)
    CRABBE.

that state which Crabbe describes—
"For when so full the cup of sorrows flows,
Add but a drop, it instantly o'erflows."
(*Mary Barton*, p. 273.)
    CRABBE.

"Yon is our quay!
Hark to the clamour in that miry road,
Bounded and narrowed by yon vessel's load;
The lumbering wealth she empties round the place,
Package and parcel; hogshead, chest, and case;
While the loud seaman and the angry hind,
Mingling in business, bellow to the wind."
               Crabbe.
(*Mary Barton*, p. 275.)
    CRABBE.

"There are, who, living by the legal pen,
Are held in honour—honourable men."
                Crabbe.
(*Mary Barton*, p. 289.)
      CRABBE.

"Show not that manner, and these features all,
The serpent's cunning, and the sinner's fall?"
                Crabbe.
(*North and South*, p. 265.)
      CRABBE.

"A wet sheet and a flowing sea,
A wind that follows fast,
And fills the white and rustling sail,
And bends the gallant mast!
And bends the gallant mast, my boy,
While, like the eagle free,
Away the good ship flies, and leaves
Old England on the lee."
              Allan Cunningham.
(*Mary Barton*, p. 282.)
      ALLAN CUNNINGHAM.

Allan Cunningham's ballad—
"It's hame, and it's hame, hame fain would I be;
Oh, hame, hame, hame, to my ain countree!"
(*Traits and Stories of the Huguenots*, p. 345.)
      ALLAN CUNNINGHAM.

"And it's hame, hame, hame,
Hame fain wad I be."
(*North and South*, p. 71.)
      ALLAN CUNNINGHAM.

L'Inferno . . .
L'Inferno—Dante! . . .
(*Cousin Phillis*, pp. 191, 209.)
      DANTE.

Dante
(*A Dark Night's Work*, pp. 52, 84.)
      DANTE.

with no "Ricordarsi di tempo felice
Nella miseria—"
(*The Life of Charlotte Brontë*, p. 295.)
        DANTE. (*Inferno;* "del" for "di".)

They only wanted a Dante to record their sufferings.
(*Mary Barton*, p. 87.)
>
> DANTE.

it was the Paradiso of Dante, . . .
(*North and South*, p. 28.)
>
> DANTE.

a good piece of Dante
(*North and South*, p. 82.)
>
> DANTE.

"E par che de la sua labbia si mova
Uno spirto suave e pien d'amore,
Chi va dicendo a l'anima: sospira!"
(*North and South*, p. 292.)
>
> DANTE. (*Paradiso*.)

described by Dr. Davy in the life of his brother.
(*The Life of Charlotte Brontë*, p. 22.)
>
> DAVY. (*Collected works of Sir Humphry Davy published with a memoir by his brother*, 1839–40.)

Mr. Day on education.
(*The Life of Charlotte Brontë*, p. 30.)
>
> THOMAS DAY.

one remembers the gouty gentleman whose cure was effected by a similar process in "Sandford and Merton", but there the heat was not carried up to torture.
(*Traits and Stories of the Huguenots*, p. 341.)
>
> THOMAS DAY.

and I'll help you if I can; that I will, right or wrong",
(*Mary Barton*, p. 249.)
>
> STEPHEN DECATUR. ("but our country, right or wrong"; in A. S. Mackenzie, *Life of D*.)

I think it is Dekker who speaks of our Saviour as "the first true gentleman that ever lived".
(*French Life*, p. 643.)
>
> DEKKER.

A castaway, lonely as Robinson Crusoe—
(*North and South*, p. 175.)
>
> DANIEL DEFOE.

Mr. Defoe, who had written a book, wherein he had named many modes of subduing apparitions, and sending them back whence they came.

(*The Poor Clare*, p. 322.)

   DANIEL DEFOE. (*True Relation of the Apparition of one Mrs. Seal.*)

De Lolme on the British Constitution
(*Cousin Phillis*, p. 231.)

   JEAN LOUIS DELOLME. (Swiss writer on Engl. constitution, 1740–1806.)

Mr. Denon
(*Cranford*, p. 101.)

   BARON DENON. (Works on Eastern travel).

the "swarry" which Sam Weller gave at Bath.
(*Cranford*, p. 24.)

   DICKENS. (*Pickwick Papers.*)

Have you seen any numbers of "The Pickwick Papers"? said he. (They were then publishing in parts.)
(*Cranford*, p. 24.)

   DICKENS.

Mr. Boz
(*Cranford*, pp. 24, 25, 27, 29, 37.)

   DICKENS.

a passage in Dickens, which spoke of a chorus in which every man took the tune he knew best, and sang it to his own satisfaction.
(*Cranford*, p. 121.)

   DICKENS. (*Pickwick Papers*, Chap. XXXII.)

a disgraced medical student of the Bob Sawyer class,
(*Mary Barton*, p. 181.)

   DICKENS. (*Pickwick Papers.*)

Dickens
(*Mr. Harrison's Confessions*, p. 388.)

too like a certain Mrs. Nickleby
(*My Lady Ludlow*, p. 48.)

   DICKENS. (*Nicholas Nickleby.*)

"Nay, I have done; you get no more of me:
And I am glad, yea glad with all my heart,
That thus so clearly I myself am free."
     Drayton.
(*North and South*, p. 340.)

   DRAYTON.

Dryden's "All for Love, or the World Well Lost", date 1686.
(*Clopton House*, p. 506.)

   DRYDEN.

Madame de Duras
(*Company Manners.*)
   Clara, Duchesse DE DURAS. (1779–1828.)

Old Poz; when I was a girl . . . I acted Lucy in "Old Poz".
(*Cranford,* p. 37.)
   Maria Edgeworth.

Miss Edgeworth's "Patronage"
(*Cranford,* p. 61.)
   Maria Edgeworth.

I have a kindness for all Susans, for Simple Susan's sake.
(*North and South,* p. 414.)
   Maria Edgeworth. (*Simple Susan.*)

that shows you've never read Miss Edgeworth's tales
I'll bring you a whole pile of Miss Edgeworth's stories,
a load of Miss Edgeworths tales
(*Wives and Daughters,* pp. 163, 164, 166.)
   Maria Edgeworth.

"the falling out of faithful friends, renewing is of love".
(*The Life of Charlotte Brontë,* p. 110.)
   Richard Edwardes. (*Amantium Irae.*)

The Pythias to your Damon
(*North and South,* p. 81.)
   Richard Edwardes. (*Damon and Pythias.*)

"her rocking it, and rating it",
(*North and South,* p. 356.)
   Richard Edwardes. (*Amantium Irae:* She rocked it, and rated
   it.)

too thick-sighted to see through a board . . . thou'rt too blind to see through
a window . . . "seeing through a glass window"
(*Sylvia's Lovers,* p. 210.)
   George Eliot. (*Janet's Repentance* in *Scenes of Clerical Life:*
   can see further through a stone wall when he's done, than other
   folks'll see through a glass winder.)

"To envy nought beneath the ample sky;
To mourn no evil deed, no hour misspent;
And like a living violet, silently
Return in sweets to Heaven what goodness lent,
Then bend beneath the chastening shower content."
   Elliott.
(*Mary Barton,* p. 34.)
   Ebenezer Elliott.

"Learned he was; nor bird, nor insect flew,
But he its leafy home and history knew:
Nor wild-flowers decked the rock, nor moss the well,
But he its name and qualities could tell"
                    Elliott.
(*Mary Barton*, p. 44.)
(Cf. *Company Manners*, p. 498: but who thinks of the leafy covert which
has been her home in life, when he sees a roasted hare?)
        EBENEZER ELLIOTT.

"My heart, once soft as woman's tear, is gnarled
With gloating on the ills I cannot cure."
                    Elliott.
(*Mary Barton*, p. 113.)
        EBENEZER ELLIOTT.

"Dixwell. Forgiveness! Oh, forgiveness, and a grave!
Mary. God knows thy heart, my father! and I shudder
To think what thou perchance hast acted.
Dixwell. Oh!
Mary. No common load of woe is thine, my father."
                Elliot's "Kerkonah".
(*Mary Barton*, p. 333.)
        EBENEZER ELLIOTT.

"On earth is known to none
The smile that is not sister to a tear."
                    Elliott.
(*North and South*, p. 176.)
        EBENEZER ELLIOTT.

"But work grew scarce, while bread grew dear,
And wages lessened, too;
For Irish hordes were bidden here,
Our half-paid work to do."
                    Corn Law Rhymes.
(*North and South*, p. 183.)
        EBENEZER ELLIOTT.

"The meanest thing to which we bid adieu,
Loses its meanness in the parting hour."
                    Elliott.
(*North and South*, p. 386.)
        EBENEZER ELLIOTT.

Emerson's Essays
(*Mary Barton*, p. 197.)
        R. W. EMERSON.

—the village Lady Bountiful
(*North and South*, p. 358.)
   FARQUAHAR. (*The Beaux' Stratagem.*)

Chants populaires de la Grèce moderne, par C. Fauriel.
(*Modern Greek Songs*, p. 471.)
   C. FAURIEL.

Dr. Ferrier
(*Cranford*, p. 110.)
   Dr. JOHN FERRIAR. (author of *Of Popular Illusions*, etc.)

Fielding
(*The Life of Charlotte Brontë*, p. 380.)
   FIELDING.

Drop, drop, slow tears!
And bathe those beautiful feet,
Which brought from heaven
The news and Prince of peace.
Cease not, wet eyes,
For mercy to entreat:

To cry for vengeance
Sin doth never cease.
In your deep floods
Drown all my faults and fears;
Nor let His eye
See sin, but through my tears.
(*Ruth*, on title-page of original edn.)
   PHINEAS FLETCHER.

an old story I had read somewhere, of a nightingale and a musician, who
strove one against the other which could produce the most admirable music, till poor Philomel dropped down dead.
(*Cranford*, p. 103.)
   JOHN FORD. (*The Lover's Melancholy.*) (Also in Crashaw's translation of Strada.)

Mr. Forster's *Life of Goldsmith*
(*The Life of Charlotte Brontë*, p. 400.)
   JOHN FORSTER. (*The Life and Times of Oliver Goldsmith.*)

the beautiful fable of Undine
(*The Doom of the Griffiths*, p. 227.)
   FRIEDRICH, Baron DE LA MOTTE FOUQUÉ. (*Undine.*)

Your beauty was the first that won the place,
And scal'd the walls of my undaunted heart,
Which, captive now, pines in a caitive case,
Unkindly met with rigour for desert:—

Yet not the less your servant shall abide,
In spite of rude repulse or silent pride."
                    William Fowler.
(*North and South*, p. 203.)
            WILLIAM FOWLER.

the air out of the "Beggar's Opera"—
"I wonder any man alive
Should ever rear a daughter!"
(*Wives and Daughters*, p. 70.)
            J. GAY.

it was a case of "first catch your hare".
(*Wives and Daughters*, p. 109.)
            HANNAH GLASSE. (*Art of Cookery:* Take your hare when it is.
            cased . . . Usually misquoted as "First catch your hare".)

I thought that there could be no more romances written on the same kind
of plot as Caleb Williams; the principal interest of which, to the superficial reader, consists in the alternation of hope and fear, that the hero may,.
or may not, escape his pursuer. It is long since I have read the story.
(*Disappearances*, p. 412.)
            WILLIAM GODWIN.

Goethe . . .
"As Goethe says, "Ye ever-verdant palaces",
(*Cranford*, p. 46.)
            GOETHE.

"My rest is gone,
My heart is sore.
Peace find I never,
And never more."
(Margaret's Song in "Faust".)
(*Mary Barton*, p. 226.)
            GOETHE.

each reminding Margaret of German idyls—of Hermann and Dorothea—
(*North and South*, p. 411.)
            GOETHE.

The *Sorrows of Werther*
(*Sylvia's Lovers*, p. 211.)
            GOETHE.

an infinite deal of nothing about the "Shakespeare and musical glasses"
of the day;
(*Company Manners*, p. 504.)
            GOLDSMITH. (*The Vicar of Wakefield*, Chapters IX, X.)

some book I once read, in which a migration from the blue bed to the brown was spoken of as a great family event.
(*Cousin Phillis*, pp. 195-6.)
>GOLDSMITH. (*The Vicar of Wakefield*, Chap. I: All our adventures were by the fireside, and all our migrations from the blue bed to the brown.)

her employment was the same as that of Beau Tibbs' wife, "just washing her father's two shirts",
(*Mary Barton*, p. 89.)
>GOLDSMITH. (*The Citizen of the World.*)

Goldsmith's "History of England"
(*My French Master*, p. 507.)
>GOLDSMITH.

The domestic changes were of much the same kind as the Vicar of Wakefield's migration from the blue bed to the brown:
(*The Shah's English Gardener*, p. 601.)
>GOLDSMITH.

those who went to mock, but remained to pray
(*Sylvia's Lovers*, p. 65.)
>GOLDSMITH. (*The Deserted Village*, l. 177: And fools, who came to scoff, remain'd to pray.)

handsome is as handsome does
(*Sylvia's Lovers*, p. 154.)
>GOLDSMITH. (Proverb quoted in *The Vicar of Wakefield.*)

"The man recovered of the bite;
The dog it was that died."
(*Wives and Daughters*, p. 152.)
>GOLDSMITH. (*Elegy on the Death of a Mad Dog.*)

the power spoken of by Goldsmith when he wrote—
"He threw off his friends like a huntsman his pack,
For he knew when he liked he could whistle them back."
(*Wives and Daughters*, p. 410.)
>GOLDSMITH.

'dragging at each remove a lengthening chain'.
(*Wives and Daughters*, p. 471.)
>GOLDSMITH. (*The Traveller*: And drags at each r. a. l. ch.)

If Lady Cumnor did not exactly shift her trumpet and take snuff there on the spot, she behaved in an equivalent manner.
(*Wives and Daughters*, p. 580.)
>GOLDSMITH. (*Retaliation*, l. 145: He shifted his trumpet, and only took snuff.)

the "Shakespeare and musical glasses" of the day.
(*Wives and Daughters*, pp. 181–2.)
GOLDSMITH. (*The Vicar of Wakefield.*)

"The Spiritual Quixote"
(*Half a Lifetime Ago*, p. 247.)
R. GRAVES. (*The Spiritual Quixote or the Summer's Ramble of Mr. Geoffrey Wildgoose.*)

in the wearied manner of the Scandinavian prophetess,—
"Leave me, leave me to repose,"
(*Cranford*, p. 43.)
THOMAS GRAY. (*The Descent of Odin.*)

those lines of Gray's . . .
"I feel the gales that from ye blow,
A momentary bliss bestow,
And breathe a second spring."
(*A Dark Night's Work*, p. 110.)
THOMAS GRAY.

dance on, "regardless of their doom".
(*Wives and Daughters*, p. 276.)
THOMAS GRAY. (*Ode on a Distant Prospect of Eton College*, l. 1.)

the refrain of Gray's Scandinavian Prophetess: "Leave me, leave me to repose!"
(*Wives and Daughters*, p. 341.)
THOMAS GRAY. (*The Descent of Odin.*)

Dr. Gregory's Advice to Young Ladies."
(*My Lady Ludlow*, p. 29.)
Dr. GREGORY.

Gerald Griffin's beautiful lines,
"To turn and look back when thou hearest
The sound of my name."
(*North and South*, p. 426.)
GERALD GRIFFIN.

Guizot
(*The Life of Charlotte Brontë*, p. 158.)
GUIZOT.

"Cast me upon some naked shore,
Where I may tracke
Only the print of some sad wracke,
If thou be there though the seas roare,
I shall no gentler calm implore."
Habington.
(*North and South*, p. 36.)
WILLIAM HABINGTON.

you look more like a delving Adam than a spinning Eve."
(*Wives and Daughters*, p. 321.)

RICHARD ROLLE DE HAMPOLE. (–1349): When Adam dalfe and Eve spane . . .

(an altered form was used by John Ball in 1381: "When Adam delved and Eve span.")

"Be the day weary or be the day long,
At length it ringeth to even-song."
(*Sylvia's Lovers*, p. 269.)

STEPHAN HAWES. (*Passetyme of Pleasure:* For though the day be never so longe
At last the belles ringeth to evensonge.)

Hayley's Cowper
(*North and South*, p. 24.)

WILLIAM HAYLEY. (*The Life of Cowper.*)

the words of Mrs. Heman's song . . .
"Ye know not what ye do,
That call the slumberer back
From the realms unseen by you,
To life's dim weary track."
(*Mary Barton*, p. 201.)

Mrs. HEMANS.

Mrs. Hemans's pathetic little poem on this subject
(*Modern Greek Songs*, p. 478.)

Mrs. HEMANS. (*The Message to the Dead.*)

"By the soft green light in the woody glade,
On the banks of moss where thy childhood played;
By the household tree, thro' which thine eye
First looked in love to the summer sky."

Mrs. Hemans.
(*North and South*, p. 19.)

Mrs. HEMANS.

"I have found that holy place of rest
Still changeless."

Mrs. Hemans.
(*North and South*, p. 218.)

Mrs. HEMANS.

Never to fold the robe o'er secret pain,
Never, weighed down by memory's clouds again,
To bow thy head! Thou art gone home!"
(*North and South*, p. 253.)

Mrs. HEMANS.

this last poem of Mrs. Hemans'?
almost as good as Mrs. Hemans'
nearly as good as Mrs. Hemans' was saying as much to the young ladies of
that day, as saying that poetry is nearly as good as Tennyson's would be
in this.
He had changed his style since the Mrs. Hemans' days.
(*Wives and Daughters*, pp. 74, 255.)
   Mrs. HEMANS.

from Shakespeare and George Herbert
(*Cranford*, p. 46.)
   GEORGE HERBERT.

those lines of George Herbert's—
"All may have,
If they dare choose, a glorious life, or grave."
(*The Moorland Cottage*, p. 296.)
   GEORGE HERBERT.

"We are the trees whom shaking fastens more."
   George Herbert.
(*North and South*, p. 85.)
   GEORGE HERBERT.

a perfect "bridal of the earth and sky".
(*Ruth*, p. 49.)
   GEORGE HERBERT. (*The Temple:* "Virtue.")

Dr. Hibbert
(*Cranford*, p. 110.)
   Dr. SAMUEL HIBBERT. (author of *Spectral Illusions*, etc.)

ever since Homer's time . . .
The little Homers of the day . . .
(*Modern Greek Songs*, pp. 480, 482.)
   HOMER.

reading Homer . . .
finished Homer . . .
(*North and South*, pp. 92, 129.)
   HOMER.

"But when the morn came dim and red,
And chill with early showers,
Her quiet eyelids closed—she had
Another morn than ours."
   Hood.
(*Mary Barton*, p. 26.)
   THOMAS HOOD.

"seam, and gusset, and band".
(*Mary Barton*, p. 77.)
      Thomas Hood. (*The Song of the Shirt.*)

"They had
Another morn than ours."
(*Mary Barton*, p. 82.)
      Thomas Hood.

"A spade, a rake, a hoe!
A pickaxe or a bill
A hook to reap, or a scythe to mow,
A flail, or what ye will—
And here's a ready hand
To ply a needful tool,
And skilled enough, by lessons rough,
In Labour's rugged school"
      Hood.
(*North and South*, p. 317.)
      Thomas Hood.

"And down the sunny beach she paces slowly,
With many doubtful pauses by the way;
Grief hath an influence so hushed and holy."
      Hood.
(*North and South*, p. 439.)
      Thomas Hood.

'It was the time of roses,
We plucked them as we went?'
(*Wives and Daughters*, p. 302.)
      Thomas Hood. (*It Was Not in the Winter;* "passed" for "went".)

Horace
(*Cousin Phillis*, p. 212.)
      Horace.

Horace
(*A Dark Night's Work*, p. 28.)
      Horace.

the maxim of "Get money, my son—honestly if you can; but get money".
(*North and South*, p. 263.)
      Horace. (*Epistles* I, 1, 66: Si posses recte, si non, quocumque
      modo reme.)

how are you getting on with Huber?
(*Wives and Daughters*, p. 171.)
      Huber. (H. François, Genevese naturalist, *Observations on Bees.*
      —1831.)

(H. Joh. Nepomuk: Germ. philosopher 1830–79.)
(H. Ludw. Ferd. Germ.-French littérateur 1764–1804.)

some one began to speak of Les Misérables,—and Mr. E.—, like a prosperous merchant as he is, objected to the socialist tendency of the book.
(*French Life*, p. 621.)
VICTOR HUGO.

Victor Hugo
(*The Life of Charlotte Brontë*, p. 154.)

Mr. Hunter, in his Life of Oliver Heywood . . .
In the life of Oliver Heywood
(*The Life of Charlotte Brontë*, pp. 10. 17.)
HUNTER.

I could not help remembering Mrs. Inchbald's pretty description of Dorriford's anxiety in feeding Miss Milner; she compares it, if I remember rightly, to that of a tender-hearted boy, caring for his darling bird, the loss of which would embitter all the joys of his holidays.
(*Six Weeks at Heppenheim*, p. 384.)
Mrs. INCHBALD.

the Tales of the Alhambra.
(*North and South*, p. 104.)
WASHINGTON IRVING. (*Legends of the Alhambra.*)

the "Seven Champions"
(*The Heart of John Middleton*, p. 319.)
R. JOHNSON. (*The Famous Historie of the Seven Champions of Christendom.*)

a Seven Champions of Christendom.
(*Sylvia's Lovers*, p. 398.)
R. JOHNSON.

Dr. Johnson
(*Cranford*, pp. 24, 25, 27, 29, 48, 49, 50, 161.)
SAMUEL JOHNSON.

'Rasselas' . . .
conversations between Rasselas and Imlac, . . .
(*Cranford*, p. 24.)
SAMUEL JOHNSON. (*Rasselas.*)

the *Rambler*
(*Cranford*, pp. 25, 37.)
SAMUEL JOHNSON. (*The Rambler.*)

a Johnsonian sentence
(*Cranford*, p. 31.)
SAMUEL JOHNSON.

the grand Latinized Johnsonian style
(*Cranford*, p. 57.)
      Samuel Johnson.

Peter was "surveying mankind from China to Peru",
(*Cranford*, p. 122.)
      Samuel Johnson. (*The Vanity of Human Wishes.*)

Johnson's Dictionary
(*Cranford*, p. 153.)
      Samuel Johnson.

the awkward habit which I do not think he could have copied from Dr.
Johnson, . . .—of trying always to retrace his steps on the exact boards
on which he had trodden . . .
(*Curious if True*, p. 265.)
      Samuel Johnson.

Dr. Johnson's famous speech to one who offered presumptuous and in-
judicious praise—
(*The Life of Charlotte Brontë*, p. 232.)
      Samuel Johnson.

we had a great Johnson in my lady's room, but, where lexicographers
differed, she generally preferred Bailey.
(*My Lady Ludlow*, p. 52.)
      Samuel Johnson.

there's a "Shakespeare" in the surgery-library: I'll take it away and put
'Johnson's Dictionary' instead.
(*Wives and Daughters*, p. 60.)
      Samuel Johnson.

"sick for home she stood in tears",
(*The Life of Ch. Brontë*, p. 65.)
      Keats. (*Ode to a Nightingale.*)

"There was a listening fear in her regard,
As if calamity had but begun;
As if the vanward clouds of evil days
Had spent their malice, and the sullen rear
Was, with its stored thunder, labouring up."
              Keats' "Hyperion".
(*Mary Barton*, p. 235.)
      Keats.

the evening hymn she had so often sung in Barfourd church—
"Glory to Thee, my God, this night";
(*Lois the Witch*, pp. 148–9.)
      Thomas Ken.

the Evening Hymn—
"Glory to Thee, my God, this night,
For all the blessings of the light!"
(*Lois the Witch*, p. 193.)
        THOMAS KEN.

that she might "dread the grave as little as her bed";
(*Sylvia's Lovers*, p. 66.)
        THOMAS KEN. (Evening Hymn, *Glory to Thee*. ["my" for
        "her"].)

"Sleep on, my love, in thy cold bed,
Never to be disquieted!
My last Good Night—thou wilt not wake
Till I thy fate shall overtake."
        Dr. King.
(*North and South*, p. 280.)
        HENRY KING. (*The Exequy*.)

there were all the stages and conditions of being that sing forth their farewell to the departing crusaders in the "Saint's Tragedy".
(*Cumberland Sheep Shearers*, p. 463.)
        CHARLES KINGSLEY.

"dark, and cold, and rugged is the North".
(*The Life of Charlotte Brontë*, p. 231.)
        CHARLES KINGSLEY(?)

her time for "being good" over and gone
(*Sylvia's Lovers*, p. 427.)
she . . . "tried to be good".
(*Wives and Daughters*, p. 132.)
        (Cf. KINGSLEY, *A Farewell to C. E. G.*: Be good, sweet maid,
        and let who can be clever;)

Klopstock's *Messiah*
(*Sylvia's Lovers*, p. 211.)
        KLOPSTOCK.

Through cross to crown! And though thy spirit's life
Trials untold assail with giant strength,
Good cheer! good cheer! Soon ends the bitter strife,
And thou shalt reign in peace with Christ at length!
        Kosegarten.
(*North and South*, p. 230.)
        KOSEGARTEN.

the fable of the lap-dog and the donkey;
(*Wives and Daughters*, p. 54.)
        LA FONTAINE. (*Fables*.)

their eager minds "browsed undisturbed among the wholesome pasturage of English literature", as Charles Lamb expresses it ...
which Charles Lamb speaks of in his *Essay on Old China* ...
(*The Life of Charlotte Brontë*, pp. 35, 393.)
      CHARLES LAMB.

"I lov'd him not; and yet, now he is gone,
I feel I am alone.
I check'd him while he spoke; yet would he speak,
Alas! I would not check.
For reasons not to love him once I sought,
And wearied all my thought."
      W. S. Landor.
(*Mary Barton*, p. 138.)
      WALTER SAVAGE LANDOR.

"The mermaid sat upon the rocks
All day long,
Admiring her beauty and combing her locks
And singing a mermaid song.

And hear the mermaid's song you may,
As sure as sure can be,
If you will but follow the sun all day,
And souse with him into the sea."
      W. S. Landor.
(*Mary Barton*, p. 146.)
      WALTER SAVAGE LANDOR.

"Thought fights with thought; out springs a spark of truth
From the collision of the sword and shield."
      W. S. Landor.
(*North and South*, p. 118.)
      WALTER SAVAGE LANDOR.

"Where are the sounds that swam along
The boyant air when I was young;
The last vibration now is o'er,
And they who listen are no more;
Ah! let me close my eyes and dream."
      W. S. Landor.
(*North and South*, p. 407.)
      WALTER SAVAGE LANDOR.

Law's Serious Call ... Law's *Serious Call*
(*Sylvia's Lovers*, pp. 64, 211.)
      WILLIAM LAW. (*Serious Call to a Devout and Holy Life*, 1729.)
when Greek meets Greek
(*Cumberland Sheep Shearers*, p. 461.)

NATHANIEL LEE. (*The Rival Queens:* When Greeks joyn'd Greeks.
Constantly misquoted as When Greek meets G.)

Mr. Lewes' review on "Recent Novels"
(*The Life of Charlotte Brontë*, p. 239.)
GEORGE HENRY LEWES.

to talk about Liebig . . .
He brought out Liebig, . . . agricultural chemistry . . .
He would not have admitted your Liebig,
(*Mr. Harrison's Confessions*, pp. 398, 411, 412.)
LIEBIG.

Tho' lost to Site, To Memory Dear
(*The Crooked Branch*, p. 439.)
GEORGE LINLEY. (Song attributed to George Linley: *Tho' lost
to sight, to mem'ry dear . . .*)
Vae victis!
(*Wives and Daughters*, p. 96.)
LIVY. (*History*, V, XLVIII, 9.)

She was faithful as Evangeline.
(*Disappearances*, p. 415.)
LONGFELLOW. (*Evangeline.*)

Evangeline
(*North and South*, pp. 411, 460.)
LONGFELLOV. (*Evangeline.*)

Lord Lyttelton's *Advice to a Lady*
(*The Life of Charlotte Brontë*, p. 26.)
GEORGE LYTTELTON.

Magnall's Questions
(*Wives and Daughters*, p. 617.)
Miss RICHMAL MANGNALL. (questions and answers on general
knowledge.)

a capital novel by Manzoni, 'I Promessi Sposi'.
(*Cousin Phillis*, p. 211.)
MANZONI.

"Pseaumes de David, mis en Rime françoise, par Clément Marot et Théo-
dore de Bèze",
(*Traits and Stories of the Huguenots*, p. 345.)
CLÉMENT MAROT.

"My brain runs this way and that way; 'twill not fix
On aught but vengeance."
(*Mary Barton*, p. 196.)
MARLOWE. (*The Massacre at Paris.*)

But let us jump (like Dr. Faustus) out of Lancashire into Greece.
(*Modern Greek Songs*, p. 479.)
MARLOWE. (*Dr. Faustus*.)

Mrs. Marsh's Story of the Deformed.
(*The Life of Ch. Brontë*, p. 387.)
Mrs. MARSH. (Anne Caldwell.)
(*Two Old Men's Tales. The Deformed, and The Admiral's Daughter*.)

Miss Martineau
(*The Life of Charlotte Brontë*, pp. 288, 375, 376.)
HARRIET MARTINEAU.

Deerbrook
(*The Life of Charlotte Brontë*, p. 288.)
HARRIET MARTINEAU.

Miss Martineau's *Letters*
(*The Life of Charlotte Brontë*, p. 329.)
(HARRIET MARTINEAU and Mr. ATKINSON: *Letters on the Nature and Development of Man*.)

copses sufficiently high to make a "green thought in a green shade"
(*Cumberland Sheep Shearers*, p. 456.)
(Cf. *Ruth*, p. 30: the elmtrees met overhead and made a green shade, *Morton Hall*, p. 365: the branches nearly met overhead, and made a green gloom.)
ANDREW MARVELL. (*The Garden:* Annihilating all that's made
To a green thought in a green shade.)

such books as *Mason on Self-Knowledge*,
(*Sylvia's Lovers*, p. 64.)
MASON, JNO. (*Self-Knowledge*.)

Mayor's Spelling-book
(*Sylvia's Lovers*, p. 115.)
MAYOR.

Ménage
(*Company Manners*.)
MÉNAGE. (French savant and critic, 1613–92.)

Middleton's Cicero
(*North and South*, p. 24.)
MIDDLETON.

My idea is that Hugh Miller mentions it somewhere, as a blind woman, going from house to house, giving death to all whom she touches . . .
(*Modern Greek Song's*, p. 489.)
HUGH MILLER.

"Thou stand'st here arraign'd,
That with presumption impious and accurs'd,
Thou hast usurp'd God's high prerogative,
Making thy fellow mortal's life and death
Wait on thy moody and diseased passions;
That with a violent and untimely steel
Hath set abroach the blood, that should have ebbed
In calm and natural current: to sum all
In one wild name—a name the pale air freezes at,
And every cheek of man sinks in with horror—
Thou art a cold and midnight murderer."
　　　　　　—Milman's "Fazio".
(*Mary Barton*, p. 303.)
　　　　HENRY HART MILMAN.

Ellinor was not wisest, best,
(*A Dark Night's Work*, p. 163.)
　　　　MILTON. (*Paradise Lost*, Book VIII, l. 547: Wisest, virtuousest,
　　　　discreetest, best;)

"Paradise Lost" and "Regained"
(*Half a Lifetime Ago*, p. 247.)
　　　　MILTON.

Milton's "Paradise Lost".
(*The Heart of John Middleton*, p. 319.)
　　　　MILTON.

Milton's famous line might have been framed and hung up as the rule of
their married life, for he was truly the interpreter, who stood between
God and her;
(*Lizzie Leigh*, p. 386.)
　　　　MILTON. (*Paradise Lost*, bk. IV, l. 297: he for God only, she for
　　　　God in him.)

"wisest, best"
(*Mary Barton*, p. 48.)
　　　　MILTON. (*Paradise Lost*, Book VIII, l. 547: Wisest, virtuousest,
　　　　discreetest, best;)

who was doomed only to "stand and wait";
(*The Moorland Cottage*, p. 383.)
(Cf. *Ruth*, p. 248: "you may have to stand and wait".)
　　　　MILTON. (*On his Blindness:* They also serve who only stand and
　　　　wait.)

Paradise Lost
(*Sylvia's Lovers*, p. 211.)
　　　　MILTON.

his poems—would they sell, and bring him in money? In spite of Milton, he thought they might.
(*Wives and Daughters*, p. 255.)
MILTON.

"to sport with Amaryllis in the shade, or or with the tangles of Neaera's hair";
(*Wives and Daughters*, p. 337.)
MILTON. (*Lycidas*.)

Molière
(*Company Manners*, p. 492.)
MOLIÈRE.

Montaigne's idea, "playing on a flute by the side of his daughter's bed, in order to waken her in the morning".
(*Traits and Stories of the Huguenots*, p. 346.)
MONTAIGNE.

Francis Moore's astrological predictions;
(*Cranford*, p. 92.)
FRANCIS MOORE.

The veiled prophet in Laila Rookh
(*Cranford*, p. 122.)
THOMAS MORE.

like apples o' Sodom, pleasant to look at, but ashes to eat.
(*Sylvia's Lovers*, p. 133.)
(Cf. *North and South*, p. 41: the mocking way in which over-fond wishes are too often fulfilled—Sodom apples as they are)
THOMAS MORE. (*Lalla Rookh, The Fire-Worshippers*, 1, l. 279: Like dead Sea-fruits, that tempt the eye, but turn to ashes on the lips.)

Lindley Murray's Grammar
(*My French Master*, p. 507.)
LINDLEY MURRAY.

Miss Brontë agreed with me in liking Mr. Newman's "Soul",
(*The Life of Charlotte Brontë*, p. 310.)
FRANCIS WILLIAM NEWMAN. (*The Soul: Her Sorrows and her Aspirations: An Essay towards the Natural History of the Soul as the basis of Theology*.)

Newton's "Principia"
(*Mary Barton*, p. 44.)
NEWTON.

There was no "rattling the bones over the stones", of the pauper's funeral.
(*Mary Barton*, p. 76.)

THOMAS NOEL. (1799–1861.) (*Rhymes and Roundelays: The Pauper's Drive:*
Rattle his bones over the stones;
He's only a pauper, whom nobody owns!)
"A life of self-indulgence is for us,
A life of self-denial is for them;
For us the streets, broad-built and populous,
For them unhealthy corners, garrets dim,
And cellars where the water-rat may swim!
For us green paths refreshed by frequent rain,
For them dark alleys where the dust lies grim!
Not doomed by us to this appointed pain—
God made us rich and poor—of what do these complain?"
> Mrs. Norton's "Child of the Islands".

(*Mary Barton*, p. 99.)
> CAROLINE NORTON.

The rich man dines, while the poor man pines,
And eats his heart away;
"They teach us lies", he sternly cries,
"Would *brothers* do as they?"
> The Dream.

(*Mary Barton*, p. 363.)
> CAROLINE NORTON.

"This is the soliloquy of one who was once a clergyman in a country parish, like me; it was written by Mr. Oldfield, minister of Carsington, in Derbyshire, 'a hundred and sixty years ago, or more . . .
When thou canst no longer continue in thy work without dishonour to God, discredit to religion, foregoing thy integrity, wounding conscience, spoiling thy peace, and hazarding the loss of thy salvation: in a word, when the conditions upon which thou must continue (if thou wilt continue) in thy employments are sinful, and unwarranted by the word of God, thou mayest, yea, thou must believe that God will turn thy very silence, suspension, deprivation, and laying aside, to His glory, and the advancement of the Gospel's interest. When God will not use thee in one kind, yet He will in another. A soul that desires to serve and honour Him shall never want opportunity to do it; nor must thou so limit the Holy One of Israel, as to think He hath but one way in which He can glorify Himself by thee. He can do it by thy silence as well as by thy preaching; thy laying aside as well as thy continuence in thy work. It is not pretence of doing God the greatest service, or performing the weightiest duty, that will excuse the least sin, though that sin capacitated or gave us the opportunity for doing that duty. Thou wilt have little thanks, O my soul! if when thou art charged with corrupting God's worship, falsifying thy vows, thou pretendest a necessity for it in order to a continuance in the ministry'.'
(*North and South*, pp. 39–40.)
> Mr. OLDFIELD.

"There's no place like home", as the poet says. "Mid pleasures and pa-
laces though I may roam", it begins, ...
(*Wives and Daughters*, p. 470.)
JOHN HOWARD PAYNE. (*Home, Sweet Home.*)

"I remember Mr. Gray's bringing me 'Philidor on Chess' ...
(*My Lady Ludlow*, p. 183.)
F. A. D. PHILIDOR.

Plato's Republic
(*North and South*, p. 129.)
PLATO.

the wail was heard, "Great Pan is dead".
(*The Life of Charlotte Brontë*, p. 254.)
PLUTARCH. (*De Defectu Oraculorum.*)

rebel against Aristides being always called the Just.
(*North and South*, p. 75.)
PLUTARCH.

'the feast of reason, and the flow of soul'.
(*Cranford*, p. 28.)
ALEXANDER POPE. (*Imitations of Horace*, II, Sat. I, l. 128.)

"fool, rush in where angels fear to tread",
(*The Moorland Cottage*, p. 321.)
ALEXANDER POPE. (*Essay on Criticism* l. 625: For fools ...)

Mr. Bellingham's "blood of all the Howards" rose ...
(*Ruth*, p. 33.)
ALEXANDER POPE. (*An Essay on Man*, l. 215.)

"A crust of bread and liberty",
(*Sylvia's Lovers*, p. 308.)
ALEXANDER POPE. (*Imitations of Horace*, Book 11, Sat. 6, l. 218.)

"from grave to gay, from lively to severe",
(*Wives and Daughters*, p. 95.)
ALEXANDER POPE. (*An Essay on Man*, Ep. IV, l. 379.)

Pope, or somebody else, has a line of poetry like that.
(*Wives and Daughters*, p. 143.)
ALEXANDER POPE.

He spoke such pretty broken English, I could not help thinking of
Thaddeus of Warshaw and the Hungarian Brothers and Santo Sebastiani;
(*Cranford*, p. 94.)
(Cf. *Morton Hall*, p. 478: "Santo Sebastiano; or The Young Protector.")
JANE PORTER. (*Thaddeus of Warshaw.*)
ANNA MARIA PORTER. (*Don Sebastian or the House of Braganza,*
the heroes of which are the Hungarian Brothers.)

"Touch us gently, gentle Time!
We've not proud or soaring wings,
Our ambition, our content,
Lies in simple things;
Humble voyagers are we
O'er life's dim unsounded sea;
Touch us gently, gentle Time!"
                                    Barry Cornwall.
(*Mary Barton*, p. 371.)
              B. W. PROCTER (= Barry Cornwall).

the proverb, "When the devil was sick, the devil a monk would be",
(*Ruth*, p. 291.)
              RABELAIS. (*Gargantua and Pantagruel*, Book IV, Chap. 24, trans.
              by P. A. Motteux: The devil was sick, the devil a monk would be;
              The devil was well, and the devil a monk he'd be.)

told me stories that sounded so very much like Baron Munchausen's,
(*Cranford*, p. 160.)
              R. E. RASPE.

M. de Retz
(*French Life.*)
              Cardinal DE RETZ.

Richardson's novels
(*The Life of Charlotte Brontë*, p. 126.)
              RICHARDSON.

Sir Charles Grandison
(*Wives and Daughters*, p. 40.)
              RICHARDSON.

was the famous maxim of Rochefoucault true with them; for in the mis-
fortunes of their friends they seemed to see some justification of their own.
(*Sylvia's Lovers*, p. 219.)
              ROCHEFOUCAULT.

'never less alone than when alone',
(*Wives and Daughters*, p. 472.)
              SAMUEL ROGERS. (*Human Life*, 1. 755.)

"Mine be a cot beside a hill",
(*North and South*, p. 32.)
              SAMUEL ROGERS. (*A Wish*, "the hill" for "a hill".)

Sir Samuel Romilly's account of his father and grandfather . . .
(*Traits and Stories of the Huguenots*, p. 345.)
              Sir SAMUEL ROMILLY.

"Wooed and married and a'."
(*North and South*, p. 9.)

ALEXANDER ROSS. (*The Fortunate Shepherdess:* Marri'd an' woo'd an' a'.)

She borrowed her words from the infamous Jean-Jacques Rousseau ... if not her words, she borrowed her principles.
(*My Lady Ludlow*, p. 70.)
JEAN JACQUES ROUSSEAU.

Rousseau ...
"I'm afraid that Rousseau and Mr. Gray are birds of a feather", replied Miss Galindo, ...
(*My Lady Ludlow*, p. 125.)
JEAN JACQUES ROUSSEAU.

my character as a gay Lothario,
(*Mr. Harrison's Confessions*, p. 442.)
NICHOLAS ROWE. (*The Fair Penitent.*)

"Of what each one should be, he sees the form and rule,
And till he reach to that, his joy can ne'er be full."
Rückert.
(*North and South*, p. 396.)
RÜCKERT.

"Like a bark upon the sea,
Life is floating over death;
Above, below, encircling thee,
Danger lurks in every breath,

Parted art thou from the grave
Only by a plank most frail;
Tossed upon the restless wave,
Sport of every fickle gale.

Let the skies be ever so clear,
And so calm and still the sea,
Shipwreck yet has he to fear
Who life's voyager will be."
Rückert.
(*Mary Barton*, p. 272.)
RÜCKERT.

Ruskins works
(*A Dark Night's Work*, p. 52.)
RUSKIN.

Modern Painters ... the *Seven Lamps* ...
The Stones of Venice
(*The Life of Charlotte Brontë*, pp. 310, 330.)
RUSKIN.

Madame de Sablé
(*Company Manners.*)
    Mme DE SABLÉ. (1599–1678.)

If she was not the rose, ... she had been near it.
(*Cranford*, p. 95.)
although she was not the rose, she lived near the rose.
(*Wives and Daughters*, p. 487.)
    allusion to a passage in the Gulistan by the Persian poet SA'DI
    (d. A. D. 1292), transl. by Francis Gladwin.

I remembered what St. Simon says, how the king, weary of noise and
grandeur, found out a little narrow valley within a few miles of his
magnificent and sumptuous Versailles.
(*French Life*, p. 629.)
    ST. SIMON. (*Mémoires.*)

"My heart revolts within me, and two voices
Make themselves audible within my bosom."
    Wallenstein.
(*North and South*, p. 148.)
    SCHILLER.

with eyes that "looked like violets filled with dew",
(*Clopton House*, p. 506.)
    WALTER SCOTT. (Cf. *The Lord of the Isles:* The dew that on the
    violet lies. See also Coleridge.)

Miss Jessie sang "Jock of Hazeldean".
(*Cranford*, p. 33.)
    WALTER SCOTT. (*Jock of Hazeldean.*)

Sir Walter Scott's writings . . .
Kenilworth . . .
Scott . . .—*Old Mortality*
(*The Life of Charlotte Brontë*, pp. 79, 80, 148.)
    WALTER SCOTT.

The plan on which he has collected these "Chants populaires" resembles
that of Sir Walter Scott, in his Border Minstrelsy."
(*Modern Greek Songs*, p. 471.)
    WALTER SCOTT.

deep in one of Sir Walter Scott's novels
Molly had been in the very middle of the *Bride of Lammermoor*, . . . her
mind quite full of "Ravenswood" and "Lucy Ashton".
(*Wives and Daughters*, pp. 80, 81.)
    WALTER SCOTT.

Molly's hero was not to eat more than Ivanhoe, when he was Friar Tuck's guest;
(*Wives and Daughters*, p. 170.)
> WALTER SCOTT. (*Ivanhoe.*)

Madame de Sévigné
(*Company Manners.*)
> Mme DE SÉVIGNÉ.

Madame de Sévigné . . .
Madame de Sévigné's *Letters*
(*French Life.*)

SHAKESPEARE

An Accursed Race:
p. 198.   in the spirit of Shylock.—(*The Merchant of Venice.*)

Company Manners:
p. 497.   as "a merry heart goes all the way",—(*The Winter's Tale*, IV, 3;
"day" for "way".)
p. 498.   "the simplicity of Venus' doves",—(*A Midsummer Night's Dream,*
I, 1.)

Cranford:
p. 28.   the 'plumed wars'—(*Othello*, III, 3: the plumèd troop, and the
big wars.)
p. 46.   Shakespeare.
p. 121.   As somebody says, that was the question.—(*Hamlet*, III, 1.)

Cumberland Sheep Shearers:
p. 457.   the "fat and scant of breath" quotation;—(*Hamlet*, V, 2.)

A Dark Night's Work:
p. 46.   As woe-begone . . . as Ophelia.—(*Hamlet.*)
p. 77.   Autolycus's song.—(*The Winter's Tale.*)

Disappearances:
p. 414.   the Dogberrys of the time.—(*Much Ado about Nothing.*)
p. 416.   an untamed *Katherine* of a bride.—(*The Taming of the Shrew.*)

The Doom of the Griffiths:
p. 210.   He says himself—or Shakespeare says it for him, which is much
the same thing—
"At my nativity
The front of heaven was full of fiery shapes
Of burning cressets . . .
. . . I can call spirits from the vasty deep.
and few among the lower orders in the principality would think of asking
Hotspur's irreverant question in reply.—(*King Henry IV.*)

French Life.
p. 628.   the "nimble" air—for that epithet of Shakespeare's exactly fits
the clear brisk air of St. Germain.
p. 633.   in King Cambyses' vein;—(*King Henry IV*, II, 4.)

The Heart of John Middleton:
p. 334. I learned that it is better to be sinned against than to sin.—
(*King Lear*, II, 1: a man more sinned against than sinning.)

Libbie Marsh's Three Eras:
p. 476. "under the greenwood tree"—(*As You Like It*, II, 5.)

The Life of Charlotte Brontë:
p. 24. Juliet's "But trust me, gentlemen, I'll prove more true
Than those that have more cunning to be strange".—(*Romeo and Juliet.*)
p. 85. Shakespeare
p. 212. she "wrote them down an ass";—(*Much Ado About Nothing*, IV.
2: to write me down an ass.)

Lois the Witch:
p. 182. the same kind of skill which Antony used in his speech to the
Romans after Caesar's murder.—(*Julius Caesar.*)

Mary Barton:
p. 173. It was Hyperion to a Satyr.—(*Hamlet*, I, 2.)
p. 180. a hasty quotation from the fat knight's well-known speech in
Henry IV.—(*King Henry IV.*)
p. 216. his mother's milk was yet in him—(*Twelfth Night*, I, 5: one
would think his mother's milk were scarce out of him.)
p. 245. still she talked of green fields,—(*King Henry V*, II, 3: a' babbled
of green fields.)
p. 277. this young Sir Oracle's speech—(*The Merchant of Venice*, I, 1:
As who should say, "I am Sir Oracle)
p. 321. Fear no more the heat o' th' sun
Nor the Furious winter's rages;
Thou thy worldly task hast done,
Home art gone and ta'en thy wages."
Cymbeline.

Modern Greek Songs:
p. 481. as flat as Hamlet without the part of Hamlet. (*Hamlet.*)

My Lady Ludlow:
p. 47. Shakespeare's musk-rose.
p. 65. I had not forgotten Christopher Sly.—(*The Taming of the Shrew.*)

North and South:
p. 9. Titania—(*A Midsummer Night's Dream.*)
p. 11. The course of true love in Edith's case had run remarkably smooth.
—(*A Midsummer Night's Dream*, I, 2: The course of true love never did
run smooth.)
p. 223. "For never anything can be amiss
When simpleness and duty tender it."
—Midsummer Night's Dream.

p. 414. You would think it romantic to be walking with a person "fat and scant o' breath" if I were Hamlet, Prince of Denmark.—(*Hamlet*, V, 2.)

p. 415. like the Hamlet you compare yourself to.—(*Hamlet*.)

Ruth:

p. 71. "It blesseth him that gives and him that takes."—(*The Merchant of Venice*, III, 1.)

p. 148. Shakespeare's plays.

p. 182. the smart gentleman's arrival "fluttered the Volscians in Corioli" —(*Coriolanus*, V: Flutter'd your Volscians in C.)

p. 311. Ruth "home must go and take her wages".—(*Cymbeline*, IV, 2: Home art gone and ta'en thy wages.)

Six Weeks at Heppenheim:

p. 376. "Methinks the lady doth protest too much",—(*Hamlet*, III, 2.)

The Squire's Story:

The Dogberries and Verges of those days—(*Much Ado About Nothing*.)

Sylvia's Lovers:

p. 333. "at heaven's gate"—(*Sonnets*, 29.)

p. 54. without fear of "the heat o' th' sun or the coming winter's rages", —(*Cymbeline*, IV, 2: Fear no more the heat o' the sun,
                                      Nor the furious winter's rages.)

p. 56. the piece of rosemary to be thrown into the grave "for remembrance"—(*Hamlet*, V, 19.)

Wives and Daughters:

p. 46. this "hidden worm i'th' bud"—(*Twelfth Night*, III: like a worm i' the bud.)

p. 60. there's a 'Shakespeare' in the surgery-library.

p. 60. her eyes were load-stars (p. 333. say at once 'her eyes are load-stars', and have done with it!)—(*A Midsummer Night's Dream*, I, 1: Your eyes are loadstarres. Cf. also Shelley, *The Revolt of Islam:* whose eyes were loadstars of delight, etc.)

p. 120. she had cast herself on the ground—that natural throne for violent sorrow— —(*King John*, III, 1: Constance "seats herself on the ground": Here I and sorrows sit, Here is my throne)

p. 146. her course of true love will run smooth.—(*A Midsummer Night's Dream*, I, 2: The course of true love never did run smooth.)

p. 333. an alliance as that of Romeo and Juliet.—(*Romeo and Juliet*.)

p. 336. the world was out of joint, and Molly had failed in her mission to set it right, (p. 396. the world was out of joint, and, if she were born to set it right, ... p. 514. She seemed to consider herself born to set the world to rights.)—(*Hamlet*, V.)

p. 467. There was a little flavour or "protesting too much" about this.— (*Hamlet*, III, 2: Methinks the lady doth protest too much.)

p. 557. "some must watch, while some must sleep, so runs the world away".—(*Hamlet*, III, 2.)

Frankenstein, that monster of many human qualities, ungifted with a soul, a knowledge of the difference between good and evil.
(*Mary Barton*, p. 167.)
    MARY SHELLEY. (*Frankenstein.*)

"The steps of the bearers, heavy and slow,
The sobs of the mourners, deep and low."
    Shelley.
(*North and South*, p. 306.)
    P. B. SHELLEY. (*The Sensitive Plant*, III, 7.)

Shelley's friend
(*The Well of Pen-Morfa*, p. 353.)

"Only the actions of the just
Smell sweet and blossom in the dust."
(*Wives and Daughters*, p. 219.)
    JAMES SHIRLEY. (*The Contention of Ajax and Ulysses.*)

a few words, which have power to stir the heart "as with the sound of a trumpet",
(*The Life of Charlotte Brontë*, p. 232.)
    SIDNEY. (*The Defence of Poesy:* I never heard the old song of Percy and Douglas that I found not my heart moved more than with a trumpet.) (Cf. Bible: sound of the trumpet.)

M. Jules Simon, whose deep study of the workwoman (l'ouvrière) in France . . .
(*French Life*, p. 655.)
    JULES SIMON. (1814–96.)

"The three black graces, Law, Physic, and Divinity, as the song calls them.
Wives and Daughters, p. 402.)
    HORACE and JAMES SMITH. (*Punch's Holiday.*)

Peregrine Pickle
(*Sylvia's Lovers*, p. 398.)
    SMOLLETT.

the play of Œdipus Tyrannus
(*The Doom of the Griffiths*, p. 220.)
  SOPHOCLES.

I have longed, like Southey, in the "Doctor", to come out with some inter-
minable nonsensical word (Aballibogibouganorribo was his, I think) . . .
(*Company Manners*, p. 507.)
  SOUTHEY. (*The Doctor.*)

nearly as scrupulous as Miss Tyler, of cleanly memory;
(*Cranford*, p. 18.)
  SOUTHEY. (in his fragment of autobiography he mentions the
  extreme cleanliness of his aunt, Miss Tyler.)

Southey's poems . . .
Mr. C. C. Southey's life of his Father . . .
(*The Life of Charlotte Brontë*, pp. 79, 102.)
  SOUTHEY.

"Oh, had he lived,
Replied Rusilla, never penitence
Had equalled his! full well I knew his heart,
Vehement in all things. He would on himself
Have wreaked such penance as had reached the height
Of fleshy suffering,—yea, which, being told,
With its portentous rigour should have made
The memory of his fault, o'erpowered and lost
In shuddering pity and astonishment,
Fade like a feeble horror."
    Southey's "Roderick".
(*Mary Barton*, p. 345.)
  SOUTHEY.

"I was used
To sleep at nights as sweetly as a child—
Now, if the wind blew rough, it made me start,
And think of my poor boy tossing about
Upon the roaring seas. And then I seemed
To feel that it was hard to take him from me
For such a little fault."
    Southey.
(*North and South*, p. 113.)
  SOUTHEY.

The "Three Bears".
(*Wives and Daughters*, p. 35.)
  SOUTHEY. (*The Doctor.*)

"The saddest bird a season finds to sing."
Southwell.
(*North and South*, p. 253.)
SOUTHWELL.

"the pure wells of English undefiled",
(*Cranford*, p. 28.)
EDMUND SPENSER. (*The Faerie Queene:* Dan Chaucer, well of English undefyled.)

The false Duessa
(*The Life of Charlotte Brontë*, p. 142.)
EDMUND SPENSER. (*The Faerie Queene.*)

the lion accompanied Una through the wilderness and the danger;
(*Mary Barton*, p. 238.)
EDMUND SPENSER. (*The Fairie Queene.*)

"Which when his mother saw, she in her mind
Was troubled sore, ne wist well what to ween."
Spenser.
(*North and South*, p. 196.)
EDMUND SPENSER.

to separate the Una from the Duessa
(*North and South*, p. 351.)
EDMUND SPENSER. (*The Fairie Queene.*)

as unharmed as Una herself . . .
choosing the false Duessa! . . .
(*Wives and Daughters*, p. 612.)
EDMUND SPENSER. (*The Fairie Queene.*)

Madame de Staël
(*Cranford*, p. 101.)
Mme DE STAËL.

like the aspect of Palestine, from Stanley's account;
(*French Life*, p. 678.)
HENRY MORTON STANLEY?

"a polite education in itself"
(*Wives and Daughters*, p. 593.)
(Cf. STEELE, The *Tatler* No. 49: "to love her is a liberal education".)

Sterne's "Sentimental Journey" where he feeds a donkey with maccaroons—
(*Company Manners*, p. 510.)
STERNE.

It is Sterne, I think, who says, 'Thine own and thy mother's friends forsake not'.
(*Wives and Daughters*, p. 345.)
  STERNE.

Mrs. Stowe ... *Uncle Tom's Cabin*
(*The Life of Charlotte Brontë*, p. 386.)
  HARRIET BEECHER-STOWE.

"Sturm's Reflections", translated from a German book
(*My Lady Ludlow*, p. 29.)
  CHRISTOPHER CHRISTIAN STURM. (–1786.)

the *Mémoires de Sully*
(*Wives and Daughters*, p. 542.)
  SULLY. (1560–1641.)

which go far to make the "art of polite conversation".
(*Wives and Daughters*, p. 262.)
  SWIFT. (*Polite Conversation.*)

the Lilliputian darts ...
(*Wives and Daughters*, p. 346.)
  SWIFT. (*Gulliver's Travels.*)

much as Mr. Gulliver might have hearkened to a lecture from a Lilliputian.   ·
(*My Lady Ludlow*, p. 148.)
  SWIFT. (*Gulliver's Travels.*)

To parody a line out of Fairfax's Tasso—
His strong idea wandered through her thought.
(*North and South*, p. 209.)
  TORQUATO TASSO. (Edward Fairfax translated *Gerusalemne Liberata* in 1600.)

The cedar spreads his dark-green layers of shade.
(*Cranford*, p. 49.)
  TENNYSON. (*The Gardener's Daughter.* "A" for "Tne".)

Black as ash-buds in March.
(*Cranford*, p. 49.)
  TENNYSON. (*The Gardener's Daughter:* more black than ash-buds in the front of March.)

"Locksley Hall"
(*Cranford*, p. 49.)
  TENNYSON.

Where falls not hail, or rain, or any snow,
Nor ever wind blows loudly; but it lies

Deep-meadow'd, happy, fair with orchard lawns,
And bowery hollows crowned with summer sea . . .
> TENNYSON. (*The Idylls of the King*, "The Passing of Arthur",
> ll. 424 ff.)

"where never wind blows loudly" . . .
(*French Life*, pp. 658, 660.)
> TENNYSON. ("The Passing of Arthur", l. 425.)

the "days that were no more".
(*The Life of Charlotte Brontë*, p. 97.)
> TENNYSON. (*The Princess*, IV, 21, "are" for "were".)

the old moan of the Moated Grange—
"Why comes he not", she said,
"I am aweary, aweary,
I would that I were dead".
(*Mary Barton*, p. 155.)
> TENNYSON. (*Mariana:* "He cometh not", She said . . .)

"Whose faith is fixed and cannot move—,
She darkly feels him great and wise,
She dwells on him with faithful eyes,
'I cannot understand: I love'."
(*The Moorland Cottage*, p. 327.)
> TENNYSON. (*In Memoriam.*)

Helstone is like a village in a poem—in one of Tennyson's poems.
(*North and South*, p. 16.)
> TENNYSON.

"Unwatch'd the garden bough shall sway,
The tender blossom flutter down,
Unloved that beech will gather brown,
The maple burn itself away;

Unloved the sun-flower, shining fair,
Ray round with flames her disk of seed,
And many a rose carnation feed
With summer spice the humming air;
. . .

Till from the garden and the wild
A fresh association blow
And year by year the landscape grow
Familiar to the stranger's child;

As year by year the labourer tills
His wonted glebe, or lops the glades;

And year by year our memory fades
From all the circle of the hills."
Tennyson.
(*North and South*, p. 58.)
TENNYSON. (*In Memoriam*.)

"stiller than chiselled marble".
(*North and South*, p. 202.)
TENNYSON. (*A Dream of Fair Women*.)

"the days that are no more".
(*North and South*, p. 411.)
TENNYSON. (*The Princess*, IV, 21.)

Then the still small voice whispered, and he spake—
(*Ruth*, p. 100.)
TENNYSON. (*The Two Voices*, 1: a still small voice spake unto me.
Cf. Kings, 19: 12: after the fire a still small voice.)

To be nearly as good as Mrs. Hemans was saying as much to the young
ladies of that day, as saying that poetry is nearly as good as Tennyson's
would be in this.
(*Wives and Daughters*, p. 74.)
TENNYSON.

it might have been the "moated grange";
(*Wives and Daughters*, p. 92.)
TENNYSON. (*Mariana*.)

Oh for thy voice to soothe and bless!
What hope of answer, or redress?
Behind the veil! Behind the veil!—
Tennyson.
(*Sylvia's Lovers*, title page. (World's Classics edn.)
TENNYSON. (*In Memoriam*.)

William Makepeace Thackeray . . . *Vanity Fair* . . .
Vanity Fair . . .
Vanity Fair . . . Mr. Thackeray . . .
Esmond . . .
Mr. Thackeray . . . Thackeray . . .
(*The Life of Charlotte Brontë*, pp. 231, 259, 287, 352, 364, 376, 380.)
TRACKERAY.

I read . . . 'Vanity Fair' . . .
Thackeray . . .
(*Mr. Harrison's Confessions*, pp. 446, 388.)
THACKERAY.

He declared his mother should never have a gown made again by such a
tyrant—such a Mrs. Brownrigg;
(*Ruth*, p. 29.)

THACKERAY. (*Elizabeth Brownrigge*, attributed to Thackeray, pbd anonymously in *Fraser's Magazine*, Aug.–Sep., 1832.)

"Rule Britannia"
(*Sylvia's Lovers*, p. 389.)
JAMES THOMSON.

Thomson's Seasons
(*North and South*, p. 24.)
JAMES THOMSON.

"That doubt and trouble, fear and pain,
And anguish, all, are shadows vain,
That death itself shall not remain;

That weary deserts we may tread,
A dreary labyrinth may thread,
Thro' dark ways underground be led;

Yet, if we will one Guide obey,
The dreariest path, the darkest way
Shall issue out in heavenly day;

And we, on divers shores now cast,
Shall meet, our perilous voyage past,
All in our Father's house at last!"
R. C. Trench.
(*North and South*, p. 106.)
R. C. TRENCH.

"So on those happy days of yore
Oft as I dare to dwell once more,
Still must I miss the friends so tried,
Whom Death has severed from my side.

But ever when true friendship binds,
Spirit it is that spirit finds;
In spirit then our bliss we found,
In spirit yet to them I'm bound."
Uhland.
(*North and South*, p. 410.)
UHLAND.

Crawford was a kind of Admirable Crichton
(*Right at Last*, p. 283.)
Sir THOMAS URQUHART. (Narrative of James Crichton's career, 1652.)

the old tune of "Life, let us cherish";
(*Ruth*, p. 133.)
J. M. USTERI. (Swiss poet, –1827.)

Appealing from Philip drunk to Philip sober
(*Wives and Daughters*, p. 393.)
VALERIUS MAXIMUS.

"As angels in some brighter dreams
Call to the soul when man doth sleep,
So some strange thoughts transcend our wonted themes,
And into glory peep."
Henry Vaughan.
(*North and South*, p. 156.)
HENRY VAUGHAN.

"Fais ce que dois, advienne que pourra."
(*North and South*, pp. 209, 301.)
VAUVENARGUES.

Casimir de la Vigné's poem on the "Death of Joan of Arc".
(*The Life of Charlotte Brontë*, p. 151.)
CASIMIR DE LA VIGNÉ.

dum memor ipsemei, dum spiritus regit artus,
(*Cranford*, p. 59.)
VIRGIL. (*Aeneid*, IV, 336.)

Virgil has hit the enduring epithets . . .
Virgil . . .
the Georgics . . .
the first Georgic . . .
(*Cousin Phillis*, pp. 184, 211, 212, 185, 233, 238.)
VIRGIL.

a certain rare folio edition of Virgil . . .
the Virgil . . .
(*A Dark Night's Work*, p. 124.)
VIRGIL.

Fine fellow, that Virgil! "Arma virumque cano, Trojae qui primus ab oris."
(*The Moorland Cottage*, p. 297.)
VIRGIL.

he is all for Æneas and filial piety
(*My Lady Ludlow*, p. 73.)
VIRGIL.

Margaret ran, swift as Camilla.
(*North and South*, p. 60.)
VIRGIL. (*Aeneid*, VII, 808 ff.)

Voiture
(*Company Manners*.)
VOITURE.

"When a man talks to you in a way that you don't understand about a thing which he does not understand, them's metaphysics." You remember the clown's definition, don't you, Manning?
(*Cousin Phillis*, p. 204.)
      VOLTAIRE. ("Quand celui à qui l'on parle ne comprend pas et celui qui parle ne se comprend pas, c'est de la métaphysique.")

Voltaire . . . his Henriade . . .
(*French Life*, pp. 607, 608.)
      VOLTAIRE. (*La Henriade.*)

among her Boulogne schoolbooks Le Siècle de Louis XIV.
(*Wives and Daughters*, p. 292.)
      VOLTAIRE.

a page of Voltaire
(*Wives and Daughters,* p. 307.)

Walker's Pronouncing Dictionary
(*Disappearances*, p. 410.)
      WALKER.

I would have every imaginary dinner sent up on the "Original" Mr. Walker's plan; each dish separately . . .
(*Company Manners*, p. 497.)
      THOMAS WALKER. (Author of a weekly periodical, *The Original*, 1835.)

"I ask Thee for a thoughtful love,
Through constant watching wise,
To meet the glad with joyful smiles,
And to wipe the weeping eyes;
And a heart at leisure from itself
To soothe and sympathise."
          Anon.
(*North and South*, p. 46.)
      ANNA LETITIA WARING.

"There are briars besetting every path,
Which call for patient care;
There is a cross in every lot,
And an earnest need for prayer."
          Anon.
(*North and South*, p. 141.)
      ANNA LETITIA WARING.

'For Satan finds some mischief still
For idle hands to do', you know, my lady.
(*My Lady Ludlow*, p. 122.)
      ISAAC WATTS. (*Divine Songs for Children.*)

'Satan finds some mischief still for idle tongues to do.'
(*Wives and Daughters*, p. 493.)
> Isaac Watts. (*Divine Songs for Children;* "hands" for "tongues".)

Our God, our help in ages past (*Sylvia's Lovers*, p. 271.)
> Isaac Watts. (Psalm XC.)

as Dr. Whitaker says, the people of this district are "strong religionists";
(*The Life of Charlotte Brontë*, pp. 16–17.)
> Whitaker.

"To think
That all this long interminable night,
Which I have passed in thinking on two words—
'Guilty'—'Not Guilty!'—like one happy moment
O'er many a head hath flown unheeded by;
O'er happy sleepers dreaming in their bliss
Of bright to-morrows—or far happier still,
With deep breath buried in forgetfulness.
O all the dismallest images of death
Did swim before my eyes!"
> Wilson.

(*Mary Barton*, p. 298.)
> Wilson.

thou'rt a sight for sair een!
(*Sylvia's Lovers*, p. 199.)
> John Wilson. (*Noctes Ambrosianae.*)

"I can like of the wealth, I must confess,
Yet more I prize the man though moneyless;
I am not of their humour yet that can
For title or estate affect a man;
Or of myself one body deign to make
With him I loathe, for his possessions' sake."
> Wither's "Fidelia".

(*Mary Barton*, p. 125.)
> George Wither. (*Fidelia.*)

the minister and his family were all "exercised in spirit"
(*Cousin Phillis*, p. 195.)
> (Cf. Wordsworth, *Charles Lamb:* exercised in prayer,
> *The Excursion:* exercised in good, . . . exercised in pain)

I have read in some book of poetry—
"A maid whom there were none to praise,
And very few to love".
(*Cousin Phillis*, p. 232.)
> Wordsworth. (*She Dwelt Among the Untrodden Ways.*)

all the solemnity with which the old Manx laws were read once a year on the Tinwald Mount.
(*Cranford*, p. 18.)

(Cf. WORDSWORTH, *Once on the top of Tynwald's formal mound.*)

Do you know what a "master's cupboard" is? Mr. Wordsworth could have told you; ay, and have shown you one at Rydal Mount, too.
(*Cumberland Sheep Shearers*, p. 458.)
WORDSWORTH.

; reminding one of Wordsworth's lines—
"In that fair clime, the lonely herdsman stretched
On the soft grass through half the summer's day", etc.
(*Cumberland Sheep Shearers*, p. 470.)
WORDSWORTH. (*The Excursion*, 4.)

"stretched in indolent repose"
(*The Doom of the Griffiths*, p. 219.)
WORDSWORTH. (*The Excursion* 4: lulled his indolent repose . . . the lonely herdsman stretched.)

the "sweet hour of prime"
(*Libbie Marsh's Three Eras*, p. 463.)
(Cf. WORDSWORTH, *The Excursion* 6: In the prime hour of sweetest scents and airs.)

heaven, "which is our home".
(*Libbie Marsh's Three Eras*, p. 468.)
(Cf. WORDSWORTH, *Ode on Intimations of Immortality* 65: God, who is our home.)

It has been common to all, from the Chaldean shepherds, the "lonely herdsman stretched on the green sward through half a summer's day".
(*The Life of Charlotte Brontë*, p. 58.)
WORDSWORTH. (*The Excursion* 4.)

Wordsworth's and Southey's poems
(*The Life of Charlotte Brontë*, p. 79.)

my soul cleaveth unto thee
(*Lois the Witch*, p. 155.)
WORDSWORTH. (*Grieve for the world forsaken:* Give him a soul that cleaveth unto Thee.)

she "caught the trick of grief and sighed".
(*Mary Barton*, p. 110.)
WORDSWORTH. (*The Excursion* 1.)

,the mysteriously beautiful lines of Wordsworth seemed to become sunclear to him:
"And she shall lean her ear

In many a secret place
Where rivulets dance their wayward round,
And beauty born of murmuring sound
Shall pass into her face."
(*The Moorland Cottage*, p. 310.)

> WORDSWORTH. (*Lines composed a few miles above Tintern Abbey*,
> l. 27 ff.)

one whose voice "like winds in summer sighing", I knew to be my dear Sophy's.
(*Mr. Harrison's Confessions*, p. 421.)

> (Cf. WORDSWORTH, Lyre', though.... winds that sigh)

"Who ask not if Thine eye
Bear them; who, in love and truth,
Where no misgiving is, rely
Upon the genial sense of youth."
(*Ruth*, p. 99.)

> WORDSWORTH. (*Ode to Duty*, 11.)

("Oh, mercy! to myself I said,
If Lucy should be dead!")
(*Ruth*, p. 146.)

> WORDSWORTH. (*Strange fits.*)

"morn or dusky eve"
(*Ruth*, p. 206.)

> (Cf. WORDSWORTH, *Devot. Incit.*: from morn to eve ["dusky"
> frequent in Wordsworth].)

she believed him to be
"A child whom all that looked on, loved".
(*Ruth*, p. 217.)

> WORDSWORTH. (Six months to six years added he remained 'A
> Child whom every eye that looked on loved;)

some strange instinct or tempter "close at his ear"
(*Sylvia's Lovers*, p. 282.)

> WORDSWORTH. (*The Prelude* VI, 630: close upon our ears.)

"I have no wrong, where I can claim no right,
Naught ta'en me fro', where I have nothing had,
Yet of my woe I cannot so be quite:
Namely, since that another may be glad
With that, that thus in sorrow makes me sad."
                    Wyatt.
(*North and South*, p. 349.)

> Sir THOMAS WYATT.

Captain James read Arthur Young's "Tours"
(*My Lady Ludlow*, p. 175.)

> ARTHUR YOUNG. (*Tour in Ireland*, 1780.)

("what ardently we wish we long believe")
(*The Crooked Branch*, p. 436.)

> EDWARD YOUNG. (*Night Thoughts*, Night VII, l. 1233, "soon" for "long".)

ANONYMOUS

an epitaph on Mrs. Mary Hand . . . in the churchyard of Stratford-on-
Avon—
"What faults you saw in me,
Pray strive to shun; And look at home; there's
Something to be done."
(*An Accursed Race*, p. 209.)

"As Joseph was a walking he heard an angel sing,
'This night shall be born our heavenly King.
He neither shall be born in housen nor in hall,
Nor in the place of Paradise, but in an ox's stall.
He neither shall be clothed in purple nor in pall,
But all in fair linen, as were babies all":
"He neither shall be rocked in silver nor in gold,
But in a wooden cradle that rocks on the mould' ",
(*Christmas Storms and Sunshine*, p. 200.)—Christmas Carol.

"A Lord and No Lord"
(*Cranford*, p. 88.)—*The Lord and no Lord* (ballad abt 1726).

"where nae men should be"
(*Cranford*, p. 104.)—*Our Goodman cam hame at e'en* (Old Scottish song).

"Tibbie Fowler", and the line—
"Set her on Tintock Tap,
The wind will blow a man till her."
(*Cranford*, p. 124.)—Scottish song.

Ah! vous dirai-je, maman?
(*Cranford*, p. 139.)—(In *Les Amours de Silvandre*, collection of French
songs published in 1780.)

"The March of the Men of Harlech", "Tri chant o'bunnan" (Three
hundred pounds), . . . "Pennillion", or a sort of recitative stanzas,
(*The Doom of the Griffiths*, p. 250.)

Ganelan de Hauteville planned to betray Roland the brave and the twelve
peers of France, at Roncevaux;
(*French Life*, p. 628.)—(*Chanson de Roland.*)

a greater choice of deaths than that offered to Fair Rosamond
(*French Life*, p. 669.)—Popular legend (told in a ballad by Deloncy included in Percy's *Reliques*.)

the rhyme, inscribed on the under part of one of the seats in the Sedilia of Whalley Abbey . . .
"Who mells wi' what another does
Had best go home and shoe his goose."
(*The Life of Charlotte Brontë*, p. 29.)

Scottish ballads . . . "The Bonnie House of Airlie." . . . "Carlisle Yetts",
(*The Life of Charlotte Brontë*, p. 379.)—Scottish ballads.

"Oh! 'tis hard, 'tis hard to be working
The whole of the live-long day,
When all the neighbours about one
Are off to their jaunts and play.

There's Richard he carries his baby,
And Mary takes little Jane,
And lovingly they'll be wandering
Through field and briery lane."
—Manchester Song.
(*Mary Barton*, p. 13.)

"Yon are the golden hills o'heaven,
Where ye sall never win."
Something about a ship and a lover that should hae been na lover, the ballad was.
(*Mary Barton*, p. 39.)—*The Daemon Lover* (in *The Oxford Book of Ballads*):
'O yon are the hills o' Heaven", he said, "Where you will never win".

a complete Lancashire ditty . . .
The Oldham Weaver
Oi'm a poor cotton wayver . . . etc. (48 lines.)
(*Mary Barton*, pp. 41–2.)

The charming Rosamond with her purple jar.
(*Mary Barton*, p. 67.)—*The Legend of Fair Rosamond*. (?) (Ballad.)

How little can the rich man know
Of what the poor man feels,
When Want, like some dark demon foe,
Nearer and nearer steals! . . . etc. (12 lines.)
Manchester Song.
(*Mary Barton*, p. 256.)

"Barbara Allen",
(*Mary Barton*, p. 139.)—*Barbare Allen's Cruelty. In The Oxford of Ballads.*)

"Mournful is't to say Farewell,
Though for few brief hours we part;
In that absence, who can tell
What may come to wring the heart!"
                    Anonymous.
(*Mary Barton*, p. 186.)

"Oh, sad and solemn is the trembling watch
Of those who sit and count the heavy hours
Beside the fevered sleep of one they love!
Oh, awful is it in the hushed midnight,
While gazing on the pallid, moveless form,
To start and ask, "Is it now sleep or death?"
                    Anonymous.
(*Mary Barton*, p. 256.)

the Adam Bells, and Clyme o' the Cloughs, or perhaps still more the
Robin Hoods of Greece.
(*Modern Greek Songs*, p. 481.)—Heroes of ballads.

the old lines—'I've a hundred captains in England', he said, 'As good as
ever was he'... Chevy Chase
(*North and South*, p. 88.)—*Chevy Chase.*

"There's iron, they say, in all our blood,
And a grain or two perhaps is good;
But his, he makes me harshly feel,
Has got a little too much of steel."
                    Anon.
(*North and South*, p. 93.)

"Trust in that veilèd hand, which leads
None by the path that he would go;
And always be for change prepared,
For the world's law is ebb and flow."
                    From the Arabic.
(*North and South*, p. 133.)

,like Leezie Lindsay's gown o' green satin in the ballad, "kilted up to her
knee",
(*North and South*, p. 176.)—*Lizzy Lindsay* (ballad): "She has kilted her
coats o' green satin, she has kilted them up to the knee."

the song of the miller who lived by the river Dee:—
"I care for nobody—
Nobody cares for me."
(*North and South*, p. 224.)

"Truth will fail thee never, never!
Though thy bark be tempest-driven,

Though each plank be rent and riven,
Truth will bear thee on for ever!"
                    Anon.
(*North and South*, p. 286.)

"Then proudly, proudly up she rose,
Tho' the tear was in her e'e;
'Whatever ye say, think what ye may,
Ye's get nae word frae me!"
                    Scotch ballad.
(*North and South*, p. 327.)

"My own, my father's friend!
I cannot part with thee!
I ne'er have shown, thou ne'er hast known,
How dear thou art to me."
                    Anon.
(*North and South*, p. 434.)

"Here we go, up, up, up;
And here we go down, down, downee!"
                    Nursery Song.
(*North and South*, p. 445.)

"Bear up, brave heart! we will be calm and strong;
Sure, we can master eyes, or cheek, or tongue,
Nor let the smallest tell-tale sign appear
She ever was, and is, and will be dear."
                    Rhyming Play.
(*North and South*, p. 454.)

"For joy or grief, for hope or fear
For all hereafter, as for here,
In peace or strife, in storm or shine."
                    Anon.
(*North and South*, p. 461.)

Queen Eleanor herself, when she presented the bowl to Fair Rosamond,
had not a more relentless purpose stamped on her demeanor . . .
(*Ruth*, p. 101.)—*The Legend of Fair Rosamond*. (Ballad by Deloney in
Percy's *Reliques*.)

and the old song of Barbary Allen would keep running in my head, and I
thought I were Barbary, and he were young Jemmy Gray,
(*Ruth*, p. 118.)—Ballad. (In *Barbara Allen*, Scottish ballad in Percy's
Reliques, the man's name is John Grehme, in *Barbara Allen's Cruelty* in
The Oxford Book of Ballads, it is Jemmy Grove.)

Gelert does not howl for nothing.
(*Ruth*, p. 57.)—Welsh legend.

the old refrain:
"On revient, on revient toujours,
A ses premiers amours."
(*Ruth*, p. 164.)

"Weel may the keel row, the keel row, the keel row,
Weel may the keel row that my laddie's in"
"Weel may the Keel row",
his own country song . . . "Weel may the keel row, the keel row", etc.
the old Newcastle song
(*Sylvia's Lovers*, pp. 17, 186, 366.)—Jacobite song.

"Long may ye live,
Happy may ye be,
And blest with a num'rous
Pro-ge-ny."
(*Sylvia's Lovers*, p. 296.)—Verse in frequent use at Knutsford weddings.
(See M. Howitt, "Stray Notes from Mrs. Gaskell".)

Norroway over the foam.
(*Sylvia's Lovers*, p. 184.)—*Sir Patrick Spens*. (Scottish ballad.)

in the mist of treasures as great as those fabled to exist on Tom Tiddler's
ground.
(*Sylvia's Lovers*, p. 405.)— Rhyming game: "I'm on Tom Tiddler's
ground, picking up gold and silver."

the Moorish maiden's cry for "Gilbert, Gilbert".
(*Traits and Stories of the Huguenots*, p. 341.)—Ballad about Gilbert Be-
ket.

the old lines:—
"Love me not for comely grace
For my pleasing eye and face;
No, nor for my constant heart—

For these may change, and turn to ill,
And thus true love may sever;
But love me on, and know not why,
So hast thou the same reason still
To dote upon me for ever."
(*Wives and Daughters*, p. 216.)—Anon. in *The Oxford Book of Engl. Verse*
from John Wilbye's Second Set of Madrigals, 1609.

that little French ballad . . .
The refrain is—Tu t'en repentiras, Colin,
          Tu t'en repentiras,
          Car, si tu prends une femme,
          Tu t'en repentiras.
(*Wives and Daughters*, p. 265.)

III

THE HOLY BIBLE and THE BOOK OF COMMON PRAYER

An Accursed Race:

p. 199. they were in fact descendants of Gehazi, servant of Elisha (second book of Kings, fifth chapter, twenty-seventh verse), who had been accursed by his master for his fraud upon Naaman, and doomed, he and his descendants, to be lepers for evermore.— 2 *Kings* 5: 27.

p. 205. Abraham and his nomadic people; and, the forty years' wandering in the wilderness.—*Ex.*

p. 208. Uzziah the leper (twenty-sixth chapter of the second book of Chronicles.)—2 *Chron.* 26.

Bessy's Troubles at Home:

p. 515. I must leave it in God's hands, He raiseth up and He bringeth low.—1 *Sam.* 2: 7 (Lord maketh poor, . . . he bringeth low); Ps. 145: 14 (raiseth up all those that be bowed down).

Christmas Storms and Sunshine:

p. 205. That old angelic song, heard so many years ago by the shepherds, keeping watch by night, on Bethlehem Heights.—*Luke* 2: 8.

Cousin Phillis:

p. 173. Judas Iscariot.—*Gospels.*

p. 174. wallowing in the mire.—2 *Peter* 2: 22 (sow . . . wallowing in m.)

p. 185. the folio volumes of Matthew Henry's Bible.—Matthew Henry's *Bible Commentaries.*

p. 179. Was I like Abraham's steward, when Rebekah gave him to drink at the well? I thought Isaac had not gone the pleasantest way to work in winning him a wife.—*Ge.* 24; 25.

p. 188. Whether we eat or drink, or whatsoever we do, let us do all to the glory of God.—1 *Co.* 10: 31 (Whether therefore ye . . .).

p. 198. as if they had been St. Peter and St. Paul;—*Gospels; Acts.*

p. 224. them that went down in ships upon the great deep,—*Ps.* 107: 23 (they that go down to the sea in ships). *Amos* 7: 4 (the great deep).

p. 224. Servants, obey in all things your masters according to the flesh.— *Col.* 3: 22.

p. 234. Whatsoever thine hand findeth to do, do it with all thy might.— *Ecc.* 9: 10 ("thy" for "thine"; with thy might).

p. 237. "harvest of the first fruits", as the minister called it. *Ex.* 22: 29 (to offer the first of thy ripe fruits).

p. 241. either to herself, or to any one that is hers, as the Bible says.—

p. 252. quoting . . . from the Book of Job . . . to take for his text, . . . "Behold, thou hast instructed many; but now it is come upon thee, and thou faintest, it toucheth thee, and thou art troubled." —*Job* 4: 3, 5.

p. 252. The Lord giveth and the Lord taketh away. Blessed be the name of the Lord.—*Job* 1: 21 (gave . . . hath taken).

p. 253. My sins I confess to God. But if they were scarlet.—*Is.* 1: 18 (Though your sins be as scarlet . . .).

Cranford:

p. 28. Debōrah . . . the Hebrew prophetess.—*Judges* 4: 4.

p. 30. God's will be done!—*Lord's Prayer.*

p. 35. Though He slay me, yet will I trust in Him.—*Job* 13: 15.

p. 61. Herod, Tetrach of Idumea.—*Mat.* 14: 1.

p. 62. David and Goliath—1 *Sam.* 17.

p. 62. An Apollyon and Abaddon—*Rev.* 9: 11.

p. 67. Queen Esther and King Ahasuerus—*Esther* 1, 2.

p. 83. as poor as Job—*Job.*

p. 95. the Witch of Endor—1 *Sam.* 28: 7.

p. 107. Samson and Solomon—*Judges;* 1 *Kings.*

The Crooked Branch:

p. 443. a pretty story i' the Gospel about the Prodigal, who'd to eat the pigs' vittle at one time, but ended i' clover in his father's house— *Luke* 15.

p. 459. The very stones . . . rise up against such a sinner.—Cf. *Job* 20: 27 (earth shall rise up against him).

p. 460. like the Prodigal i' th' Gospels—*Luke* 15.

p. 462. But the broken-hearted go home, to be comforted of God.— 2 *Co.* 1: 4 (comforted of God); *Mat.* 5: 4 (Blessed are they that mourn: for they shall be comforted).

Crowley Castle:

p. 699. Some one waited fourteen years, did he not?—*Ge.* 29.

p. 709. nigh unto death—*Phil.* 2: 27.

p. 720. his place in Parliament knew him no more.—*Job* 7: 10 (neither shall his place know him any more).

Cumberland Sheep Shearers:

pp. 462-3. there were the "Old men and maidens, young men and children" of the Psalmist;—*Ps.* 148: 12 (young men and maidens, old men . . .).

A Dark Night's Work:

p. 36. he was thankful he was not as other men.—*Luke* 18: 11.

p. 39. the wisdom of Solomon—*Kings.*

p. 49. a thorn in her father's side—2 *Cor.* 12: 7.

p. 56. an unconscious Rechabite in practice—*Jer.* 35.

p. 66. they were not rending their garments and crying aloud.—*Jer.* 36: 24 (rent their garments). *Lev.* 10: 6 (rend your clothes). 2 *Chron.* 34: 27 (rend thy c.).

p. 71. "standing afar off"—*Luke* 18: 13.

p. 80. Ellinor was "hardening her heart".—*Ex.* 14: 7 (harden hearts). *Ex.* 8: 15 (hardened his heart), etc.

p. 107. the Day o' Judgment

The Doom of the Griffiths:

p. 111. his "old familiar friend".—*Job* 19: 14 (familiar friends). *Ps.* 41: 9 (familiar friend).

p. 211. The mark of Cain—*Gen.* 4.

French Life:

p. 633. My Martha-like troubles.—*Luke* 10.

The Grey Woman:

p. 262. The sins of the fathers are visited on their children.—*Ex.* 34: 7 (visiting the iniquity of the fathers upon the children).

Half a Lifetime Ago:

p. 266. As it says in the Bible, "Nought but death shall part thee and me!"—*Ruth* 1: 17 (if ought but death part thee and me).

The Half-Brothers:

p. 350. God's will be done—*Lord's Prayer.*

Hand and Heart:

p. 454. 'Silver and gold have I none, but such as I have give I unto thee!' —*Acts* 3: 6 (give I thee).

p. 459. "Let not thy left hand know what thy right hand doeth"—*Mat.* 6: 3.

p. 459. in His hands, who is a Father to the fatherless, and defendeth the cause of the widow.—*Ps.* 146: 9.

p. 466. go "from strength to strength—*Ps.* 84: 7.

The Heart of John Middleton:

p. 313. When I first came to read, and learnt about Ishmael, I thought I must be of his doomed race, . . .—*Gen.* 16.

p. 317. like the great gourd-tree of the prophet Jonah.—*Jonah.*

p. 321. go down to Gehenna.

p. 324. I longed and yearned for the second coming of Christ,—*Rev.* 22.

p. 324. our Saviour's words on the Cross—*Gospels.*

p. 324. the publican and sinner—*Mat.* 9: 11 (Why eateth your master with publicans and sinners?).

p. 324. as Pharaoh, as the King Agag.—1. *Sam.* 15.

p. 330. Jael and Sisera—*Judges* 4.

p. 331. There is a God in Heaven, and in His house are many mansions —*John* 14: 2 (In my father's house are many mansions).

Libbie Marsh's Three Eras:

p. 456. the widow's mite—*Mark* 12: 42.

p. 465. "Our Father"—*Lord's Prayer.*

p. 471. the fourteenth chapter of St. John's Gospel.—*John* 14.

p. 471. 'flesh is grass' Bible says—*Is.* 40: 6; 1. *Peter* 1: 24.

p. 471. "Father's house"—*John* 14: 2.

The Life of Charlotte Brontë:

p. 77. to leave "her times in His hands".—*Ps.* 31: 15 (My times are in thy hand).

p. 231. as the Athenians of old, and like them "spending their time in nothing else, but either to tell or to hear some new thing",—*Acts* 17: 21.

p. 264. "lama sabachthani"—*Mark* 15: 34.

p. 264. let him pray with the Publican rather than judge with the Pharisee. —*Luke* 18.

p. 286. the "big Babylon"—*Da.* 4: 30 (great B).

p. 308. staff in hand,—*Ex.* 12: 11.

p. 387. as Scripture told us—to have their lines fall in pleasant places;— *Ps.* 16: 6 (lines fallen . . .).

Lizzie Leigh:

p. 388. Prodigal Son.—*Luke* 15.

p. 398. she's a cruel Pharisee.

p. 403. Mary Magdalen—*Mat.* 27; *Mark* 15. *Luke* 8, 24, *John* 19, 20.

p. 403. But thou'rt not a Pharisee.

p. 407. who was lost and is found—*Luke* 15: 24 (he was . . .).

p. 417. as the lost piece of silver—found once more—*Luke* 15: 8-10.

Lois the Witch:

p. 120. 'Inasmuch as ye did not unto one of the least of these, my breth-ren, ye did it not unto me.'—*Mat.* 25: 45.

p. 120. Satan hath many powers, and, if it be the day when he is permit-ted to go about like a roaring lion, he will not stick at trifles, but make his work complete.
(Cf. p. 160: "Satan is of a truth let loose.")—1 *Peter* 5: 8.

p. 123. purged from all iniquity—1 *Sam.* 3: 14 (iniquity of Eli's house shall not be purged). *Is.* 27: 9 (shall the iniquity of Jacob be purged).

p. 129. in Zion, where the precious dew falls daily on Aaron's beard."— *Ps.* 133: 2 (It is like the precious ointment upon the head that ran down unto the beard: even unto Aaron's beard . . .).

p. 142. But the Lord who taketh away can restore tenfold.—*Job.*

p. 146. Remember Hazael, who said, 'Is thy servant a dog, that he should do this great thing?'—2 *Kings* 8: 13.

347

p. 146. wilt thou obey, even as Samuel did?—*Sam.*

p. 147. Satan, in some shape, seeking whom he might devour.—1 *Peter*
5: 8 ("may" for "might").

p. 149. pillar of the church—1 *Tim.* 3: 15 (church, the pillar and ground
of the truth).

pp. 153, 169, 184, 194. the Lord's Prayer

p. 161. It is as if the devils, whom our Lord banished into the herd of
swine, had been permitted to come again upon the earth . . .—
Mark 5, *Luke* 8.

p. 165. we are told to pray for them that spitefully use us, and to do good
to them that persecute us . . .—*Mat.* 5: 44.

p. 170. a baptized Christian who had betrayed the Lord, even as Judas
did,—*Gospels.*

p. 172. the unpardonable sin against the Holy Ghost.—*Mark* 3: 29,
Luke 12: 10 (blaspheming against the Holy Ghost shall not be forgiven unto men).

p. 174. for she had faith in Lois's power over her son, as being akin to
that which the shepherd David, Playing on his harp, had over
King Saul sitting on his throne.—1 *Sam.* 16: 23.

p. 174. Lead me not into temptation!—*Lord's Prayer.*

p. 176. Yet Scripture says that we are not to suffer witches in the land,—
Ex. 22: 18 (Thou shalt not suffer a witch to live).

p. 179. How beautiful is the land of Beulah,—*Is.* 62: 4 (Bunyan, *Pilgrim's Progress*).

p. 182. unbelieving Sadducees—*Mat.*, *Acts.*

pp. 183-4. Jesus . . . the Assembly's Catechism . . . Book of Common
Prayer . . . the Roman mass-book . . . the Prayer-book

p. 195. Then all the girls began "to tumble down like swine", to use the
words of an eyewitness.—*Mat.* 8: 32 (herd of swine ran violently
down).

p. 197. If you will confess, there may yet be balm in Gilead.—*Jer.* 8: 22
(Is there no balm in Gilead?).

p. 204. the marvellous and sorrowful story of One who died on the cross
for us and for our sakes—*Gospels.*

p. 205. holy fragments of the Psalms

p. 207. such evidence against the accused, as, . . . we justly fear was insufficient for the touching the lives of any (Deut. XVII. 6) . . .
—*Deut.* 17: 6.
to bring upon ourselves and this people of the Lord the guilt of
innocent blood; which sin, the Lord saith in Scripture, he would
not pardon (2 Kings XXIV. 4) . . .—2 *Kings* 24: 4.

p. 208. that his sin may be blotted out—*Neh.* 4: 5 (Let not their sin be
blotted out).

The Manchester Marriage:

p. 497. in a spirit not unlike that of Ruth, entreated that, come what
would, they might remain together.—*Ruth.*

p. 501. Will you have me to be thy wedded husband, and serve me, and love me, and honour me—*Form of Solemnization of Marriage.*

Mary Barton:

Preface. widow's mites—*Mark* 12: 42–44.

p. 18. as separate as Dives and Lazarus, with a great gulf betwixt us: (p. 101. the old parable of Dives and Lazarus.)—*Luke* 16 (Dives in the Vulgate version).

p. 18. earning her bread by the sweat of her brow, as the Bible tells her she should do, . . .—*Ge.* 3: 19 (in the sweat of thy face).

p. 18. If I am sick do they come and nurse me?—*Mat.* 25: 36 (I was sick, and ye visited me . . .)

p. 43. the grand supplication, "Lord, remember David".—*Ps.* 132: 1.

p. 62. and no man gave unto them—Cf. *Mat.* 25: 42 (ye gave me no meat . . .).

p. 62. Love strong as death—*Can.* 8: 6 (love is strong as d.)

p. 65. silver and gold he had none—*Acts* 3: 6 ("have I" for "I had").

p. 69. a' about God being our Father

p. 69. Han they done as they'd be done by for us?—*Mat.* 7: 12.

p. 77. neighbours, in the good-Samaritan sense of the word—*Luke* 10.

p. 80. who had led me through the wilderness—*Ps.* 106: 9 (he led me through the depths as through the wilderness).

p. 80. His will be done

(God's will be done p. 106

Thy will be done p. 145

God's will be done! p. 293

His will be done p. 309)—*Lord's Prayer.*

p. 83. the old leaven, infused years ago by her aunt Esther,—1 *Cor.* 5: 6 (a little leaven leaveneth the whole lump).

p. 94. All flesh is grass; here to day and gone to-morrow, as the Bible says.—*Is.* 40: 6 (all fl. is gr.). *Mat.* 6: 30 (the grass which today is and tomorrow is cast into the oven).

p. 99. like the Conqueror on his Pale Horse,—*Rev.* 6: 8 (a pale horse, his name . . . was death).

p. 100. Comfort ye, comfort ye, my people, saith your God.—*Is.* 40: 1.

p. 103. i' the sight o' God

p. 113. Return of the Prodigal—*Luke* 15.

p. 114. Former times had chastised them with whips, but this chastised them with scorpions—1 *Kings* 12: 11 (my father chastised you with whips but I will . . .).

p. 124. as ever Cain killed Abel

(p. 307 marks of Cain)—*Ge.* 4.

p. 129. to love you and cherish you—*Form of Solemnization of marriage.*

p. 138. he was the only son of his mother, and she was a widow—*Luke* 7: 12.

p. 138. the thought of his mother stood like an angel with a drawn sword in the way to sin—*Nu.* 22: 23 (ass saw angel, his sword drawn); *Chron.* 21: 16.

p. 146. any stumbling-block in your path

p. 146. See now the Lord has put coals of fire on my head—*Prov.* 25: 22.

p. 146. an unbelieving Thomas—*John* 20.

p. 146. Wait patiently on the Lord—*Ps.* 40: 1 (I waited patiently for the Lord). *Ps.* 27: 14 (wait on the Lord . . .).

p. 155. Sick, and in prison, and ye visited me—*Mat.* 25: 36, 43.

p. 159. Blessed are the pure in heart, for they shall see God—*Mat.* 5: 8.

p. 164. Rest that is reserved for the people of God.—*He.* 4: 9 (remaineth a rest to the people of God).

p. 169. they know not what they do.—*Luke* 23: 34.

p. 209. Stricken of God and afflicted—*Is.* 53: 4.

p. 209. nigh unto death—*Ph.* 2: 27.

p. 212. hanged as high as Haman.—*Esther* 7.

p. 213. Where the wicked cease from troubling, and the weary are at rest.—*Job* 3: 17.

p. 213. And God shall wipe away all tears from their eyes (p. 295 where the Lord God wipes away all tears)—*Is.* 25: 8 (Lord God will w. a. tears from off all faces).

p. 218. It would be like seething a kid in its mother's milk, and that th' Bible forbids—*Ex.* 23: 19.

p. 220. thou whited sepulchre!—*Mat.* 23: 27 (w. sepulchres).

p. 221. rocked the cradle of her "first-born"

p. 221. the Delilah who had lured him to his danger—*Judges* 16.

p. 230. that Eden of innocence—*Ge.* 2, 3.

p. 253. in your judgment remember mercy, as the Bible says—*Ha.* 3: 2 (Lord, in wrath remember mercy).

p. 254. I sometimes think there's two sides to the commandment; and that we may say, "Let others do unto you, as you would do unto them",—*Mat.* 7: 12.

p. 257. the old feeling which first bound Ruth to Naomi—*Ruth.*

p. 267. and she felt it was not for her to cast stones at those who, . . .—*John* 8: 7.

p. 318. his Absalom—2 *Sam.*

p. 325. she said her "Nunc Dimittis"—the sweetest canticle to the holy. —*Luke* 2. (Cf. Bacon, *Essays 2:* the sweetest c. is *N. d.*)

p. 338. to pour oil and balm into the bitter wounds.—*Luke* 10: 43.

p. 341. in her goings-out or in her comings-in—*Eze.* 43: 11 (goings out and comings in).

p. 345. Forgive us our trespasses

(pp. 354–6. Forgive us our trespasses as we forgive them that trespass against us
Let my trespasses be unforgiven, so that I have vengeance for my son's murder

Forgive us our trespasses, as we forgive them that trespass against us)—*Lord's Prayer*.

p. 347. the "stalled ox"—*Prov.* 15: 17.

p. 347. her Martha-like cares—*Luke* 10, *John* 12.

p. 350. Oh, my God! comfort me, comfort me!"—*Ps.* 119: 82 (When wilt thou comfort me?).

p. 350. He had forfeited all right to bind up his brother's wounds.—*Luke* 10: 43.

p. 351. the Avenger, the sure Avenger

p. 352. before he could comprehend the Spirit that made the Life.—*2 Cor.* 3: 6 (the spirit giveth life).

p. 353. He did not know what he was doing—*Luke* 23: 34 (they know not what they do).

(p. 353. I did not know what I was doing

p. 354. They know not what they do.)

p. 356. God be merciful to us sinners—*Ps.* 67: 1 (God be m. unto us and bless us). *Litany*.

p. 359. God does not judge as hardly as man—*1 Sam.* 16: 7 (Lord seeth not as man seeth).

p. 361. mine own ewe-lamb.—*Lev.* 14: 10.

p. 375. Psalm CIII. v. 9 "For He will not always chide, neither will He kneep his anger for ever.

Modern Greek Songs:

p. 473. they accompany him on a part of his way, as Orpah and Ruth accompanied Naomi,—*Ruth* 1.

p. 474. with something of the wild entreaty of Esau when he adjured Isaac to "Bless me, also, O my father!"—*Gen.* 27.

p. 475. at the fountain; to which all Greek maidens go to draw water, as Rebekah went, of old, to the well.—*Gen.* 24.

The Moorland Cottage:

p. 295. ministers of him, to do his pleasure—*Ezr.* 10: 11, *Ps.* 103: 21; *Is.* 61: 6 (minister of our God).

p. 336. any more than the widow saw the world-wide effect of her mite—*Mark* 12: 42–44.

p. 355. live out my appointed days

pp. 355, 374. Lord! have mercy upon us!—*Litany*.

p. 369. with something like Esau's craving for a blessing.—*Gen.* 27.

p. 372. and say "God's will be done"—*Lord's Prayer*.

p. 129. Susannah and the Elders . . . Bel and the Dragon . . . *Apocryphal Books*.

Morton Hall:

p. 364. just as courteously as if she had been the Queen of Sheba, and Charles King Solomon praying her to visit him in Jerusalem.—*Kings*.

My Lady Ludlow:

p. 51. the answer in the Catechism that Mr. Horner was most fond of calling upon a child to repeat, was that to "What is thy duty towards thy neighbour?" The answer Mr. Gray liked best to hear repeated with unction was that to the question, "What is the inward and spiritual grace"? The reply to which Lady Ludlow bent her head the lowest, as we said our Catechism to her on Sundays was to, "What is thy duty towards God"?—*Book of Common Prayer.*

p. 56. Don't you know what tree we read of in Genesis?—*Gen.* 1.

p. 130. about Martha and Mary ... I had as good a right as she had to be Mary, and save my soul—*Luke* 10.

p. 131. About Mary and Martha—*Luke* 10.

p. 150. The Lord gave and the Lord taketh away. Blessed be the Lord's name.—*Job* 1: 21.

p. 152. all flesh ... was but grass—*Is.* 40: 6; 1. *Peter* 1: 24.

North and South:

p. 48. the Lord's Prayer—*Lord's Prayer.*

p. 63. the friends of Job ... "they sat with him on the ground seven days and seven nights, and none spake a word unto him; for they saw that his grief was very great".—*Job.*

p. 83. Matthew Henry's Bible Commentaries—Matthew Henry's *Bible Commentaries.*

p. 96. and longing to get away to the land o' Beulah;—*Is.* 62: 4 (Bunyan, *Pilgrim's Progress*).

p. 97. They shall hunger no more, neither thirst any more; neither shall the sun light on them, nor any heat.—*Rev.* 7: 16.

p. 109. the Book o' Revelations—*Rev.*

p. 109. wipe away all tears from all eyes—*Rev.* 7: 17.

p. 126. there are passages in the Bible which would rather imply ... that they neglected their duty as stewards—*Luke* 16, 19.

p. 132. that he is a little ignorant of that spirit which suffereth long, and is kind, and seeketh not her own.—1 *Cor.* 13: 4.

p. 147. And the name of the star is called Wormwood; and the third part of the waters became wormwood; and men died of the waters, because they were made bitter.—*Rev.* 8: 11.

p. 147. in Revelations—*Rev.*

p. 153. I would befriend Jezebel herself—*Kings.*

p. 159. in shining raiment—*Mark* 9: 3 (his raiment became shining).

p. 160. the very dogs are not pitiful in our days, as they were in the days of Lazarus.—*Luke* 16.

p. 160. purple and fine linen—*Luke* 16: 19.

p. 161. th' great battle of Armageddon—*Rev.* 16: 16.

p. 166. Solomon—*Kings.*

p. 175. even a saint in Patmos—*Rev.* 1.

p. 187. soft raiment—*Mat.* 11: 8.

p. 202. I walk pure before God!—Cf. *Ge.* 24: 40 (The Lord, before whom I walk).

pp. 211, 310. a Judas—*Gospels.*

p. 213. the New Heavens and the New Earth—*Is.* 65: 17.

p. 221. Henry's Commentaries—Matthew Henry's *Bible Commentaries.*

p. 230. they may rest from their labours—*Rev.* 14: 13.

p. 230. The weary are at rest—*Job* 3: 17 (there the w. be . . .).

p. 230. He giveth His beloved sleep—*Ps.* 127: 2.

p. 240. the fourteenth chapter of Job—*Job* 14.

p. 245. a text, "The fathers have eaten sour grapes and th' children's teeth are set on edge'.—*Eze.* 18: 2.

p. 248. King Herod—*Gospels.*

p. 264. Let not your heart be troubled—*John* 14: 1.

p. 292. a Holy of Holies—*Vulgate* (*Ex.* 26: 34).

p. 292. as "a dog, and done this thing".—*2 Kings* 8: 13.

p. 315. Who has promised to be a father to the fatherless?—*Ps.* 146: 9 (The Lord relieveth the fatherless).

p. 403. it would not do to have a Mordecai refusing to worship and admire—*Esther.*

p. 427. From everlasting to everlasting, Thou art God! *Ps.* 90: 2.

p. 436. 'Give me children, or else I die.'—*Gen.* 30: 1 (or I die).

p. 446. "Her merchants be like princes",—*Is.* 23: 8 (whose merchants are princes).

The Old Nurse's Story:

p. 428. Flesh is grass,—*Is.* 40: 6; 1 *Peter* 1: 8.

The Poor Clare:

p. 304. all the beautiful and poetic names of the Litany. "O Rose of Sharon! O Tower of David! O Star of the Sea!—*The Song of Solomon.*

p. 339. Therefore, if thy enemy hunger, feed him; if he thirst, give him drink.—*Rom.* 12: 20.

Right at Last:

p. 295. doing as you would be done by.—*Sermon on the Mount.*

Ruth:

p. 19. God watches over orphans—*Ps.* 146: 9 (The Lord . . . relieveth the fatherless).

pp. 32–3. Why art thou so vexed, O my soul; and why art thou so disquieted within me? O put thy trust in God: for I will yet thank Him, which is the help of my countenance, and my God.— *Ps.* 42.

p. 35. the Lord lift up the light of His countenance upon thee.—*Ps.* 4: 6 (Lord, lift thou up the light of thy countenance).

p. 36.   the devil goeth about as a roaring lion, seeking whom he may devour.—1 *Peter* 5: 8.

p. 36.   God judgeth not as man judgeth—1 *Sam.* 16: 7 ("seeth" for "judgeth").

p. 51.   He called it "wrestling for her soul".—*Ge.* 32.

p. 64.   dead in trespasses and sins—*Ephes.* 2: 1.

p. 70.   What have I to do with thee?—2 *Kings* 3: 13; 2 *Chron.* 35: 21; *Mark* 5: 7; *Luke* 8: 28; *John* 2: 4.

p. 80.   'doing good, hoping for nothing again'—*Luke* 6: 35 (lend, hoping . . .)

p. 83.   the tenderness which led the Magdalen aright—*Mark* 15, *Mat.* 27.

p. 85.   the Cain-like look—*Ge.* 4.

p. 98.   and two of them prayed earnestly for "them that had gone astray" —*Is.* 53: 6 (like sheep have g. a.).

p. 99.   God be merciful to me a sinner!—*Litany.*

p. 106.   she had gone astray—*Is.* 53: 6 (like sheep have g. a.).

p. 107.   and speaking to God in the spirit, if not in the words, of the Prodigal Son: "Father! I have sinned against Heaven and before Thee, and am no more worthy to be called Thy child!"—*Luke* 15: 21.

p. 110.   'Do unto others as ye would that they should do unto you'—*Mat.* 7: 12.

p. 112.   the beauty and significance of the words, "Our Father!"

p. 113.   God was "Our Father!"

p. 114.   "Our Father in heaven"

p. 114.   he was "tormented in this flame"—*Luke* 16: 24.

p. 115.   to set him up as a Solomon.—*Kings.*

p. 123.   I wish folks would be content with locusts and wild honey.— *Mat.* 3: 4 (his meat was locusts . . .).

p. 123.   whatsoever thy hand findeth to do, that do with all thy might!— *Ecc.* 9: 10.

p. 125.   gone astray—*Is.* 53: 6.

p. 127.   when the left hand did not know what the right hand did—*Mat.* 6: 3 (let not thy left hand know what thy right h. doeth).

p. 129.   One of Job's daughters: Jemima, Kezia, and Karen-Happuch.— *Job.*

p. 136.   every good law-word you put in it, sounding like, and not to be caught up as a person runs.—Cf. *Ha.* 2: 2 (he may run that readeth it).

p. 142.   I think it is for them without sin to throw stones at a poor child, —*John* 8: 7 (He that is without sin among you, let him first cast a stone at her).

p. 142.   remember where it is said, "He that spareth the rod, spoileth the child",—*Prov.* 13: 24 (He that spareth the rod hateth his son). (Butler, *Hudibras:* then spare the rod and spoil the child.)

p. 142. King Solomon . . . King Solomon's son . . . King Rehoboam . . . what is said on him, 2 Chronicles, XII. chapter, 14th v.: 'And he'—that's King Rehoboam, the lad that tasted the rod—'did evil, because he prepared not his heart to seek the Lord".—2 *Chron.* 12: 14.

p. 143. wait patiently upon God—*Ps.* 40: 1.

p. 146. with the stars that kept watch over Rizpah shining down upon her, —2 *Sam.* 21: 8–10.

p. 146. Thy will, not mine, be done.—*Mat.* 26: 39.

p. 158. to pull out the mote from any one's eye—*Mat.* 7: 3 (the mote that is in thy brother's eye).

p. 171. The old anger that wrought in the elder brother's heart, till it ended in the murder of the gentle Abel,—*Ge.* 4.

p. 173. it is more blessed to be loved than to be beloved.—*Acts* 20: 35 (to give than to receive).

p. 178. We are not to do evil that good may come—*Rom.* 3: 8.

p. 180. little cloud no bigger than a man's hand—1 *Kings* 18: 44 (little cloud . . . like a . . .).

p. 190. Lead us not into temptation, but deliver us from evil.—*Lord's Prayer.*

p. 190. The words "stormy wind fulfilling His word"—*Ps.* 148: 8.

p. 191. a very present help in time of trouble—*Ps.* 46: 1 (a v. p. h. in tr.).

p. 192. Thy will be done!—*Lord's Prayer.*

p. 196. Hills from whence cometh our help—*Ps.* 121: 1 (my help).

p. 197. The second lesson for the morning of the 25th of September is the 26th chapter of St. Matthew's Gospel. And when they prayed again Ruth's tongue was unloosed, and she also could pray, in His name who underwent the agony in the garden.—*Mat.* 26.

p. 198. from strength to strength.—*Ps.* 84: 7.

p. 199. for His mercy endureth for ever.—*Ps.* 136: 1.

p. 218. But after this Ruth "clave unto her".—*Ruth* 1: 14.

p. 218. a rock in the dreary land, where no shadow was.—*Is.* 32: 2 (the shadow of a great rock in a weary land).

p. 225. that Hope and Faith which is the Spirit that maketh alive.—2 *Cor.* 3: 6 (the spirit giveth life).

p. 235. shake her off from you, as St. Paul shook off the viper—even into the fire.—*Acts* 28: 5.

p. 244. —that gentle, tender help which Jesus gave once to Mary Magdalen—*Mark* 15; *Mat.* 27. *Luke* 8, 24; *John* 19, 20.

p. 249. Ask, and it shall be given unto you.—*Mat.* 7: 7 (given you).

p. 256. she "accepted her penance".—Cf. *Lev.* 26: 41 (they then accept of the punishment).

p. 257. a pillar of fire—*Ex.* 13: 21.

p. 263. and he worked the more diligently while "it was yet day".—2 *Sam.* 3: 35. *John* 9: 4 (I must work . . . while it is day).

p. 267. a "law unto himself",—*Rom.* 2: 14 (a law unto themselves).

pp. 294-5. for, since the days of King Belshazzar, the solemn decrees of Doom have ever seemed most terrible when they awe into silence the merry revellers of life.—*Daniel* 5.

p. 299. She will be in the light of God's countenance . . .—*Ps.* 4: 6 (the light of thy countenance upon us).

p. 299. many arose and called her blessed—*Prov.* 31: 28 (Her children arise up, and call her blessed).

pp. 317-18. the seventh chapter of Revelations, beginning at the ninth verse . . . "And he said to me, These are they which came out of great tribulation, and have washed their robes, and made them white in the blood of the lamb.

"Therefore are they before the throne of God, and serve him day and night in his temple; and he that sitteth on the throne shall dwell among them.

"They shall hunger no more, neither thirst any more; neither shall the sun light on them, nor any heat.

"For the Lamb which is in the midst of the throne shall feed them, and shall lead them unto living fountains of waters, and God shall wipe away all tears from their eyes." *Rev.* 7: 14—17.

Six Weeks at Heppenheim:

p. 370. doing evil that possible good might come.—*Rom.* 3: 8.

The Squire's Story:

p. 540. a thorn in the popular Mr. Higgins's side—2 *Cor.* 12: 7.

p. 540. this female Mordecai—*Esther.*

p. 545. once I read in the Bible that "Charity covereth a multitude of sins".—1 *Peter* 4: 8.

Sylvia's Lovers:

p. 41. I' Donkin be Solomon, thou must be t' Queen o' Sheba; (p. 154, King Solomon.)—*Kings.*

p. 58. a sermon on the text, "In the midst of life we are in death";— *Book of Common Prayer:* Burial of the dead.)

p. 72. an' if there's a gnashing of teeth,—*Mat.* 22: 13 (There shall be weeping and gnashing of teeth).

p. 86. as dead as Noah's grandfather

p. 87. But all a could think on was, "What is your name, M or N?"— *Catechism* (N or M).

p. 111. Give me Sylvia, or else I die."—*Gen.* 30: 1 (give me children or I die.)

p. 124. to cry out in his heart *vanitas vanitatum*—*Ecc.* 1, 2; 12: 8 (*Vulgate:* vanitas vanitatum et omnia vanitas).

p. 140. Satan is desiring after yo' that he may sift yo' as wheat.—*Luke* 22: 31 (Satan desired to sift you).

p. 176. Hazael, "Is thy servant a dog that he should do this thing?"—
2 *Kings* 8: 13 (this great thing).

p. 196. the Mordecai sitting in Haman's gate;—*Esther.*

p. 210. where there's neither marrying nor giving in marriage—*Mat.*
22: 30 (For in the resurrection they neither marry, nor are given
in marriage).

p. 212. the few verses in Genesis in which Jacob's twice seven years'
service for Rachel is related,—*Ge.* 29.

p. 213. seven years and maybe seven years more—*Ge.* 29.

p. 221. seething the kid in its mother's milk—*Ex.* 23: 19 (Thou shalt not
seethe a kid in his . . .).

p. 266. But He "who knoweth our frame, and remembereth that we are
dust,—*Ps.* 103: 14.

p. 266. The text was Zechariah VII, 9, 'Execute true judgment and show
mercy'.—*Zech.* 7: 9.

p. 286. It's said in t' Bible . . . that we're to forgive. *Mat.* 18: 22.

p. 286. yo' pray to be forgiven your trespasses, as you forgive them that
trespass against you.—*Lord's Prayer.*

p. 290. From him that would ask of thee turn not thou away,—*Mat.* 5:
42 (. . . borrow of thee, turn not away).

p. 293. no out-door animals to look after; the "ox and the ass"—Response
to 10th Commandment: nor his ox nor his ass.

p. 354. like Cain—*Ge.* 4.

p. 355. The Lord make His face to shine upon thee!—*Ps.* 31: 16 (make
thy face to shine upon thy servant).

p. 358. wrestling with the Lord—*Ge.* 32: 24 (There wrestled a man with
him until the breaking of the day; . . . as he wrestled with him).

p. 361. the first chapter of Genesis.—*Ge.* 1.

p. 365. the pomp of King Solomon—*Kings.*

p. 365. some fifty, some an hundred fold.—*Mat.* 13: 8 (some an hundredfold, some sixtyfold).

p. 384. Mount Carmel, where the prophet Elijah was once, . . .—1 *Kings*
18 ff.

p. 411. For the Scripture says he's t' fayther o' lies.—*John* 8: 44 (devil
is a liar, and father of it).

p. 418. With God all things are possible.—*Mat.* 19: 26.

p. 418. but his place knew him not—*Job* 7: 10 (He shall return no more
to his house, neither shall his place know him any more).

p. 423. but it was as nothing to her.—*Lamentations* 1: 12 (Is it nothing
to you, all ye that pass by?).

p. 424. I forgot to do to thee as I would have had thee to do to me.—
Mat. 7: 12.

p. 425. I think I shall go about among them as gnash their teeth for iver,
while yo' are where all tears are wiped away—*Mat.* 8: 12 (There
shall be weeping and gnashing of t.) *Rev.* 7: 17 (God shall wipe
away all tears from their eyes).

p. 426. Thy will be done—*Lord's Prayer.*

p. 427. to be like Abraham, who was called the friend of God, or David, who was said to be the man after God's own heart, or St. John, who was called "the Beloved".—*John* 19: 26. (Cf. *Deut.* 33.)

p. 427. the "way to escape"—1 *Cor.* 10: 13.

p. 428. Lord, forgive us our trespasses as we forgive each other!—*Lord's Prayer.*

p. 428. that bringeth glad tidings of great joy . . .—Supplement to the New Version of the Psalms (1700): While Shepherds Watched.

p. 429. he is gone where there is no more sorrow, and no more pain—*Rev.* 21: 4 (there shall be no more . . . sorrow . . . neither . . . any more pain).

p. 430. there shall be no more sea—*Rev.* 21: 1 (and there was no more sea).

p. 506. some fifty, some an hundred fold;—*Mat.* 13: 8 (But other fell into good ground, and brought forth fruit, some an hundredfold, some sixtyfold, some thirtyfold).

Traits and Stories of the Huguenots:

p. 340. If I am bereaved of my children, I am bereaved,—*Ge.* 43: 14 (If I be bereaved . . .).

p. 501. an edition of the Psalms of David—*Psalms.*

The Well of Pen-Morfa:

p. 362. to take her for better, for worse—*Form of Solemnization of Marriage.*

p. 363. As surely as the Saviour brought the son of a widow from death to life, for her tears and cries—*Luke* 7.

p. 367. the awful agony in the Garden—*Mark* 14.

p. 367. he "suffered long, and was kind".—1 *Cor.* 13: 4 (Charity suffereth long and is kind).

p. 368. He giveth and he taketh away.—*Job.* 9: 12.

Wives and Daughters:

p. 94. an offering of first-fruits—Cf. *Ex.* 22: 29 (to offer first of thy ripe fruits).

p. 163. I can break through the withes of green flax with which they try to bind me.—*Judges* 16: 7 (If they bind me with seven green withs).

p. 216. being all things to all men—1 *Cor.* 9: 22.

p. 217. her place knew her no more.—*Job* 7: 10 (neither shall his place know him any more).

p. 244. Have mercy upon me, for I am very miserable.—*Litany* (Have mercy upon us miserable sinners).

p. 251. Give me the portion that falleth to me.—*Luke* 15: 12.

p. 333. to "scatter his enemies".—*Ps.* 68: 1 (let his enemies be scattered).

p. 336. a rock of strength, under whose very shadow there is rest.—*Is.* 32: 2 (as the shadow of a great rock).

p. 343.   he would have smote his breast—*Luke* 18: 13 (publican smote upon his breast).

p. 399.   Her constant prayer, "O my lord! give her the living child, and in no wise slay it", came from a heart as true as that of the real mother in King Solomon's judgment.—1 *Kings* 3: 26.

p. 427.   Grow in grace,—2 *Peter* 3: 18.

p. 478.   thinking of him as a staff and a stay—*Ps.* 18: 18 (the Lord was my stay).

p. 533.   God's will be done—*Lord's Prayer*.

p. 550.   'all the appointed days', as is said in the Bible.

IV

REFERENCES TO FAIRY TALES, etc.

the old rigmarole of childhood. In a country there was a shire, and in that shire there was a town . . .
(*Wives and Daughters*, p. 19.)

(like the heroes and heroines in fairy-tales) "marry, and live very happily ever after.
(*The Life of Charlotte Brontë*, p. 366.)

"And they lived together very happily ever after."
(*Modern Greek Songs*.)

she was like the fairy-gifted child, and dropped inestimable gifts.
(*The Well of Pen-Morfa*.)

References to the Arabian Nights and the Tales of the Genii: Like the Caliph in the Eastern story (the eastern King), a whole lifetime of possibilities passed through her mind in an instant; Sindbad the Sailor; Aminé; "old lamps for new"; Prince Caramazan; Princess Badoura; Alnashar visions; the fisherman and the genie;
(*Cranford, Mary Barton, The Moorland Cottage, North and South, Ruth, Wives and Daughters*.)

King Arthur's Knights
(*Curious If True*.)

Babes in the Wood.
(*Wives and Daughters*.)

Bluebeard.
(*Cranford, Curious If True*.)

Cinderella.
(*Curious If True, North and South, Wives and Daughters*.)

Daniel O'Rourke.
(*North and South, Wives and Daughters*.)

Dick Whittingdon.
(*Curious If True, My Lady Ludlow*.)

The Faithful John.
(*Wives and Daughters*.)

La Fée-marraine.
(*Curious If True.*)

Fortunio's servant Lightfoot.
(*Modern Greek Songs.*)

Jack the Giant-killer.
(*Curious If True.*)

Knights of the silver shield.
(*Wives and Daughters.*)

Monsieur Ogre.
(*Curious If True.*)

Little Red Riding Hood.
(*Curious If True, French Life, Sylvia's Lovers.*)

Puck or Robin Goodfellow.
(*Libbie Marsh's Three Eras.*)

Riquet-with-the-tuft.
(*Company Manners, Ruth.*)

Robin Hood.
(*Modern Greek Songs.*)

The Seven Sleepers.
(*Wives and Daughters.*)

The Sleeping Beauty.
(*Company Manners, Cousin Phillis, Curious If True, The Moorland Cottage, North and South, Wives and Daughters.*)

The White Cat.
(*Company Manners.*)

The little boy in the child's story, who asks all sorts of birds and beasts to come and play with him; and, in every case, receives the sober answer, that they are too busy to have leisure for trivial amusements.
(*Wives and Daughters.*)

The shield of the knight in the old story.
(*Wives and Daughters.*)

V

BOOK TITLES, etc.

"Housewife's Complete Manual"
(*Cousin Phillis*, p. 209.)

a Peerage
(*Cranford*, p. 87.) (Cf. *Wives and Daughters*, pp. 270, 304: One of the few
books . . . was bound in pink. . . . The "Red Book".)

Eugénie de Guérin
(*French Life*, p. 653.)

the authorised report of the trial for murder of Madame la Marquise de
Gange.
(*French Life*, p. 664.)

"The Death of Abel",
(*Half a Lifetime Ago*, p. 247.)

The British Essayists.
(*The Life of Charlotte Brontë*, p. 82, *Wives and Daughters*, p. 435.)
(The British Essayists; with prefaces, historical and biographical, by A.
Chalmers. 38 vols. London 1823.)

the Bibliotèque Choisie des Pères de l'Eglise.
(*The Life of Charlotte Brontë*, p. 152.)

Dr. Arnold's Life
(*The Life of Charlotte Brontë*, p. 323.)
(The Life and Correspondence of Thomas Arnold.)

the preface to Sir J. E. Smith's Life.
(*Mary Barton*, p. 45.)
(Scottish physician and botanist.)

Jack Sheppard romances
(*Mary Barton*, p. 214.)

The Female Jesuit.
(*Morton Hall*, p. 362.)

a volume of engravings from Mr. Hogarth's pictures
(*My Lady Ludlow*, p. 45.)

"Old and young, boy, let 'em all eat, I have it;
Let 'em have ten tire of teeth apiece, I care not."
Rollo, Duke of Normandy.
(*North and South*, p. 167.)—*The Rolliad*.

Facciolati
(*Ruth*, pp. 76, 90.)

the Complete Farrier
(*Sylvia's Lovers*, p. 211.)
(Rob. Farrier, English subject painter, 1796–1879.)

The Farmer's Complete Guide.
(*Sylvia's Lovers*, pp. 261, 276.)

Lodge's Portraits
(*Wives and Daughters*, p. 36.)
(Wm Lodge, English engraver, 1649–89.)

the 'Beauties of England and Wales'
(*Wives and Daughters*, p. 506.)

VI

NAMES OF NEWSPAPERS AND MAGAZINES

The *Athenaeum*. (*A Dark Night's Work, The Life of Charlotte Brontë.*)
Blackwood. (*Cranford, Wives and Daughters.*)
Chambers's Journal. (*Disappearances, The Life of Charlotte Brontë.*)
The *Courier*. (*Mary Barton.*)
The *Daily News*. (*The Life of Charlotte Brontë.*)
The *Edinburgh Review*. (*The Life of Charlotte Brontë, Wives and Daughters.*)
The *Examiner*. (*Christmas Storms and Sunshine, The Life of Charlotte Brontë.*)
The *Flying Post*. (*Christmas Storms and Sunshine.*)
The *Galignani*. (*Cranford, A Dark Night's Work.*)
The *Gazette*. (*Cousin Phillis, My French Master.*)
The *Gentleman's Magazine*. (*Cranford, Sylvia's Lovers.*)
(Old Urban [*The Squire's Story*]. Old Urban = the pseudonym for the
  editor of the *Gentleman's Magazine*.)
The (*Manchester*) *Guardian*. (*Mary Barton, Two Fragments of Ghost Stories.*)
The *Hamley Examiner*. (*A Dark Night's Work.*)
Household Words. (*Disappearances, Modern Greek Songs.*)
The *Illustrated News*. (*The Shah's English Gardener, The Squire's Story.*)
The *Lancet*. (*Mr. Harrison's Confessions.*)
The *Leeds Mercury*. (*The Life of Charlotte Brontë.*)
The *Literary Gazette*. (*The Life of Charlotte Brontë.*)
The *Lounger*. (*The Life of Charlotte Brontë.*)
The Milton Times. (*North and South.*)
The *Mirror*. (*The Life of Charlotte Brontë.*)
The *Morning Chronicle*. (*Wives and Daughters.*)
The *Northern Star*. (*Mary Barton.*)
The *Palladium*. (*The Life of Charlotte Brontë.*)
Philologus. (*The Squire's Story.*)
The *Post*. (*Christmas Storms and Sunshine.*)
La Presse. (*French Life.*)
The *Quarterly Review*. (*The Life of Charlotte Brontë, Wives and Daughters.*)
The *Rambler*. (*The Life of Charlotte Brontë.*)
La Revue des Deux Mondes. (French Life.)
St. James' Chronicle. (*Cranford.*)
The *Spectator*. (*The Life of Charlotte Brontë.*)
The Times. (*A Dark Night's Work, The Life of Charlotte Brontë, The Moorland Cottage, North and South, Ruth, The Shah's English Gardener, Wives and Daughters.*)
The *Woodchester Herald*. (*The Moorland Cottage.*)

VII

UNTRACED QUOTATIONS

An Accursed Race:

p. 200.   do we not read of the incense of good workers, and the fragrance
of holiness?
(Cf. *Sylvia's Lovers*, p. 139: "Neither do godly ways savour de-
licately after the pleasures of the world",)

Company Manners:

p. 511.   they are the "mere material with which wisdom (or wit) builds".

p. 509.   like Keeley in the "Camp at Chobham",

p. 493.   Lady O'Looney, of famous memory

p. 498.   "Of sweetbreads they'll get mony an ane,
Of Sablé ne'er anither."

Cousin Phillis:

p. 182.   the psalm "Come all harmonious tongues" to be sung to Mount
Ephraim tune.

Cranford:

p. 27.   "But don't you forget the white worsted at Flint's" of the old
song.

p. 97.   the old tapestry story.

A Dark Night's Work:

p. 16.   like the famous Adam and Eve in the weather-glass: when the one
came out the other went in.

French Life:

p. 643.   a more than charming hostess, whose virtues, which were the
real source of her charms, have ere this "been planted in our
Lord's garden"

p. 644.   the old epitaph—
They were so one, it never could be said
Which of them ruled, and which of them obeyed.
There was between them but one dispute,
'Twas which the other's will should execute.

p. 665.   When first she came to town
They ca'ed her Jess MacFarlane
But, now she's come and gone,

They ca' her The Wandering Darling.
(Cf. *Sylvia's Lovers*, p. 81: the lover of Jess MacFarlane—
"I sent my love a letter,
But, alas! she canna read,
And I lo'e her a' the better."
Mr. Harrison's Confessions, p. 422: She was silent now, and 'I lo'ed her a' the better'.)

Libbie Marsh's Three Eras:
p. 464. its "verdurous walls"
p. 468. one of the children's hymns—
"Here we suffer grief and pain,
Here we meet to part again;
In Heaven we part no more.
Oh! that will be joyful",
(Cf. p. 469: "In Heaven we part no more.")

The Life of Charlotte Brontë:
p. 10. From Penigent to Pendle Hill,
From Linton to Long-Addingham
And all that Craven coast did tell, etc.
p. 266. before "the desk was closed, and the pen laid aside for ever".

Lizzie Leigh:
p. 411. "Not all the scalding tears of care
Shall wash away that vision fair;
Not all the thousand thoughts that rise,
Not all the sights that dim her eyes,
Shall e'er usurp the place
Of that little angel-face."

Mr. Harrison's Confessions:
p. 397. the Little German canon . . ." 'Oh wie wohl ist mir am abend',
etc.
p. 402. Sleep, baby, sleep!
Thy rest shall angels keep;
While on the grass the lamb shall feed,
And never suffer want or need.
Sleep, baby, sleep.
p. 403. I was one of the 'Peculiar people, whom Death had made dear'.
(Cf. *The Life of Charlotte Brontë*, p. 321: "Peculiar people whom Death had made dear."
North and South, p. 269: one of those peculiar people who are bound to us by a fellow-love for them that are taken away . . .
p. 292: this one conversation made them peculiar people to each other;)
p. 407. "Hould me, or I'll fight", as the Irishman said.

p. 446. the negro song—
"'Who's dat knocking at de door?'

The Manchester Marriage:
p. 513. she's at the time of life when they say women pray for husbands—
'any, good Lord, any'

Mary Barton:
p. 20. "Polly, put the kettle on,
And let's have tea!
Polly, put the kettle on,
And we'll all have tea."

p. 34. "in the days of long ago"

p. 76. "How infinite the wealth of love and hope
Garnered in these same tiny treasure-houses!
And oh! what bankrupts in the world we feel,
When Death, like some remorseless creditor,
Seizes on all we fondly thought our own.
"The Twins."

p. 84. "Deal gently with them, they have much endured;
Scoff not at their fond hopes and earnest plans,
Though they may seem to thee wild dreams and fancies.
Perchance, in the rough school of stern Experience,
They've something learned which Theory does not teach;
Or if they greatly err, deal gently still,
And let their error but the stronger plead
'Give us the light and guidance that we need!'
Love Thoughts.

p. 98. 'What a single word can do!
Thrilling all the heart-strings through,
Calling forth fond memories,
Raining round hope's melodies,
Steeping all in one bright hue—
What a single word can do!'

'What a single word can do!
Making life seem all untrue,
Driving joy and hope away,
Leaving not the cheering ray,
Blighting every flower that grew—
What a single word can do!'

p. 103. That of no wife toke he non offering
For curtesie, he sayd, he n'old non.

p. 113. "Then guard and shield her innocence,
Let her not fall like me;

'Twere better, oh! a thousand times,
She in her grave should be."
"The Outcast."

p. 155. "Know the temptation ere you judge the crime!
Look on this tree—'twas green, and fair and graceful;
Yet now, save these few shoots, how dry and rotten!
Thou canst not tell the cause. Not long ago,
A neighbour oak, with which its roots were twined,
In falling wrenched them with such cruel force,
That though we covered them again with care,
Its beauty withered, and it pined away.
So, could we look into the human breast,
How oft the fatal blight that meets our view,
Should we trace down to the torn, bleeding fibres
Of a too trusting heart—where it were shame,
For pitying tears, to give contempt or blame."
"Street Walks."

p. 165. "What thoughtful heart can look into this gulf
That darkly yawns 'twixt rich and poor,
And not find food for saddest meditation!
Can see, without a pang of keenest grief,
Them fiercely battling (like some natural foes)
Whom God had made, with help and sympathy,
To stand as brothers, side by side, united.
Where is the wisdom that shall bridge this gulf,
And bind them once again in trust and love?"
"Love-Truths."

p. 176. "Not for a moment take the scorner's chair;
While seated there, thou know'st not how a word,
A tone, a look, may gall thy brother's heart,
And make him turn in bitterness against thee."
"Love-Truths."

p. 197. that little Spanish air you sing 'Quien quiera'.

p. 219. "I saw where stark and cold he lay,
Beneath the gallows-tree,
And every one did point and say,
'Twas there he died for thee!'

Oh, weeping heart! Oh, bleeding heart,
What boots thy pity now?
Bid from his eyes that shade depart,
That death-damp from his brow!"
"The Birtle Tragedy."

p. 245. "And must it then depend on this poor eye
And this unsteady hand, whether the bark,
That bears my all of treasured hope and love,
Shall find a passage through these frowning rocks
To some fair port where peace and safety smile,—
Or whether it shall blindly dash against them,
And miserably sink? Heaven be my help;
And clear my eye and nerve my trembling hand!"
"The Constant Woman."

p. 294. "Oh! sad is the night-time,
The night-time of sorrow,
When, through the deep gloom, we catch but the boom
Of the waves that may whelm us to-morrow."

p. 375. "Clap hands, daddy comes,
With his pocket full of plums.
And a cake for Johnnie."

The Moorland Cottage:
p. 326. "melodies of the everlasting chime"
(Cf. *Ruth*, p. 48: 'There are in this loud stunning tide
Of human care and crime,
With whom the melodies abide
Of th' everlasting chime,
Who carry music in their heart
Through dusky lane and crowded mart,
Plying their task with busier feet,
Because their secret souls a holy strain repeat.)

p. 337. a story in "Evenings at Home" called the Transmigrations of
Indra?

p. 379. poor people "in that new world which is the old".

North and South:
Preface. "Beseeking him lowly, of mercy and pité,
Of its rude makyng to have compassion."

p. 9. "Haste to the Wedding."
p. 100. "Well—I suppose we must"
Friends in Council.

p. 291. "There's nought so finely spun
But it cometh to the sun." ...
He was deeply interested in all her father said
"Of death, and of the heavy lull,
And of the brain that has grown dull."

p. 366. Je ne voudrois pas ... (long prose quotation)
p. 461. "Pack Clouds Away."

369

Ruth:
p. 43. "wi' their dear little bairnies at hame";
p. 89. "the sweep of eternity is large"
p. 94. announced their approach as effectually as the "trumpets' lordly blare" did the coming of Abdallah.
p. 100. 'Thine own sweetheart
Till death doth part',
p. 112. The earth was still "hiding her guilty front with innocent snow",
p. 121. 'Dance, thumbkin, dance—dance ye merry men every one.'
p. 133. "As I was going to Derby, sir,
Upon a market-day."

Six Weeks at Heppenheim:
p. 381. the German harvest-hymn
Wir pflügen und wir streuen
Den Saamen auf das Land;
Das Wachsen und Gedeihen
Steht in des Höchsten Hand.
Er sendet Thau und Regen,
Und Sonn und Mondenschein;
Von ihm kommt aller Segen,
Von unserm Gott allein.
Alle gute Gabe kommt her
Von Gott dem Herrn,
Drum dankt und hofft auf Ihm.

Sylvia's Lovers:
p. 27. "Out of strife cometh strife."
p. 79. a sea ditty, . . ., the burden of which was, "for I loves the tossin' say!"
p. 166. "damn the faults we have no mind to"
p. 293. if she preferred to "sit in her parlour and sew up a seam".
p. 318. "all on board perished"

Wives and Daughters:
p. 41. the *Che sarà sarà*
p. 265. that little French ballad ... The refrain is—
Tu t'en repentiras, Colin,
Tu t'en repentiras, Colin,
Car, si tu prends une femme,
Tu t'en repentiras.
p. 293. resembling "a Katherine pear on the side that's next the sun".
p. 344. It was the old fervid tenderness: "Do not wish for the moon, O, my darling, for I cannot give it thee."
p. 360. "her pretty lips with blackberries were all besmeared and dyed";
p. 411. 'M. de la Palisse est mort
En perdant sa vie;

Un quart d'heure avant sa mort
Il était en vie'

p. 427. "As tall and as straight as a poplar tree!" as the old song says.

p. 435. Cynthia had been "in the world", had "beheld the glare and glitter and dazzling display of London",

p. 468. cuishla ma chree,
pulse of my heart—

p. 470. something of the "toujours perdrix" feeling

p. 479. "shouldering the crutch, and showing how fields were won"—

p. 563. Nor did he say, 'Caesar and Pompey berry much alike, 'specially Pompey', which is the only specimen of negro language I can remember

MRS. GASKELL'S WORKS WITH DATES OF FIRST APPEARANCE

18 37. Jan. *Sketches Among the Poor, No. 1.* (Poem by Mr. and Mrs. Gaskell. *Blackwood's Magazine.*)

1840. *Clopton Hall.* (Wm Howitt's *Visits to Remarkable Places.*)

1847. *Libbie Marsh's Three Eras.* (*Howitt's Journal.*)
The Sexton's Hero. (*Howitt's Journal.*)

1848. *Christmas Storms and Sunshine.* (*Howitt's Journal.*)
Oct. *Mary Barton.* (Chapman & Hall.)

1849. July–Nov. *Hand and Heart.* (*Sunday School Penny Magazine.*)

1850. March 30. *Lizzie Leigh.* (*Household Words* from March 30.)
Nov. 16–23. *The Well of Pen-Morfa.* (*Household Words.*)
Dec. 28. *The Heart of John Middleton.* (*Household Words.*)
Dec. *The Moorland Cottage.* (*Chapman & Hall.*)

1851. Feb.–April. *Mr. Harrison's Confessions.* (*Ladies' Companion.*)
June 7. *Disappearances.* (*Household Words.*)
Dec. 13–May 21, 1853. *Cranford.* (*Household Words.*)

1852. Jan.–April. *Bessy's Troubles at Home.* (*Sunday School Penny Magazine.*)
June 19. *The Shah's English Gardener.* (*Household Words.*)
Dec. *The Old Nurse's Story.* (*Household Words.*)

1853. Jan. *Ruth.* (Chapman & Hall.)
Jan. 22. *Cumberland Sheep Shearers.* (*Household Words.*)
Oct. 22. *Bran.* (Poem. *Household Words.*)
Nov. 19–26. *Morton Hall.* (*Household Words.*)
Dec. 20. *Traits and Stories of the Huguenots.* (*Household Words.*)
Dec. 17–24. *My French Master.* (*Household Words.*)
Dec. *The Squire's Story.* (*Household Words.*)
Dec. *The Scholar's Story.* (Poem. *Household Words.*)

1854. Feb. 25. *Modern Greek Songs.* (*Household Words.*)
May 20. *Company Manners.* (*Household Words.*)
Sep. 2–'Jan. 17, 1855. *North and South.* (*Household Words.*)

1855. Aug. 25. *An Accursed Race.* (*Household Words.*)
Oct. 6–20. *Half a Lifetime Ago.* (*Household Words.*)

1856. Dec. 13–27. *The Poor Clare.* (*Household Words.*)
Dec. 27. *A Christmas Carol.* (Poem. *Household Words.*)

1857. *The Life of Charlotte Brontë.* (Smith, Elder & Co.)
Introduction to M. S. Cummins' *Mabel Vaughan.* (Sampson Low & Co.)

1858. Jan. *The Doom of the Griffiths.* (*Harper's Magazine.*)
June 19–Sep. 25. *My Lady Ludlow.* (*Household Words.*)
Nov. 27. *Right at Last.* Original title: *The Sin of a Father.* (*Household Words.*)
Nov. *The Half-Brothers.* (The *Dublin University Magazine.*)
Dec. *The Manchester Marriage.* (*Household Words.*)

1859. *Round the Sofa and Other Tales.* (Except the introductory story, a republication of old stories. Sampson Low & Co.)
Oct. 8–22. *Lois the Witch.* (*All the Year Round.*)
Dec. *The Crooked Branch.* Original title: *The Ghost in the Garden Room. All the Year Round.*)

1860. Feb. *Curious if True.* (*Cornhill Magazine.*)

1861. Jan. 5–19. *The Grey Woman.* (*All the Year Round.*)

1862. May. *Six Weeks at Heppenheim.* (*Cornhill Magazine.*)
Preface to Vecchj's *Garibaldi at Caprera.* (Macmillan & Co.)

1863. Jan. 24.–March 21. *A Dark Night's Work.* (*All the Year Round.*)
March 21. *An Italian Institution.* (*All the Year Round.*)
Nov. 28. *The Cage at Cranford.* (*All the Year Round.*)
Nov.–Feb. 1864. *Cousin Phillis.* (*Cornhill Magazine.*)
Dec. *Crowley Castle.* (*All the Year Round.*)
Sylvia's Lovers. (Smith, Elder & Co.)
Robert Gould Shaw. (Short article. *Macmillan's Magazine.*)

1864. April–June. *French Life.* (*Fraser's Magazine.*)
Aug.–Jan., 1866. *Wives and Daughters.* (*Cornhill Magazine.*)

1865. Contributions to the *Pall Mall Gazette.* (Journalism.)

1906. *Two Fragments of Ghost Stories.* (The Knutsford edn.)

1923. *My Diary. The early years of my daughter Marianne.* By Elizabeth Cleghorn Gaskell. Privately printed by Clement Shorter. London, 1923. (Begun March 10, 1835, ended Oct. 28, 1838.)

BIBLIOGRAPHY

(Works of reference, such as *The Dictionary of National Biography* and *The Oxford Dictionary of Quotations*, are not included.)

1. MANUSCRIPT MATERIAL

a. In the British Museum, London:
Notes and letters from Mrs. Gaskell to F. J. Furnivall and John Forster.
b. In the Victoria and Albert Museum, London:
Letters from Mrs. Gaskell to W. S. Landor.
c. In the John Rylands Library, Manchester:
MSS of *The Grey Woman* and *Wives and Daughters*, letters from various contemporaries addressed to Mrs. Gaskell or to the Rev. Wm Gaskell, an autograph collection (consisting chiefly of letters) made by Mrs. Gaskell. Many of the letters in this library are printed in *Bulletin of the John Rylands Library, Manchester, Vol. 19. No. 1. January 1935*.
d. In the Brotherton Library, Leeds:
The Shorter Collection, including letters addressed to Mrs. Gaskell, letters and copies of letters from Mrs. Gaskell to various friends and relatives, from Meta Gaskell to her sister Marianne, from the Rev. Wm Gaskell to his sister Eliza, from Mrs. Gaskell's two eldest daughters to Mr. Shorter, from Mrs. Gaskell's stepmother to Mrs. Lumb, from Mrs. Gaskell's cousin Marianne Lumb to her mother, an unpublished review of *Mary Barton*, the copy of a Rough Draft of *Mary Barton*, an unfinished MS, *Life and Letters of Mrs. E. C. Gaskell*, by Jane Coolidge.

2. EDITIONS OF MRS. GASKELL'S WORKS
to which page numbers refer.

(Deviations from this list are noted in the text.)

The Knutsford Edition, London, 1906:
Bessy's Troubles at Home.
Christmas Storms and Sunshine.
Clopton Hall.
Company Manners.
Crowley Castle.
Cumberland Sheep Shearers.

Curious if True.
Disappearances.
French Life.
An Italian Institution.
Loïs the Witch.
The Manchester Marriage.
Modern Greek Songs.
The Moorland Cottage.
My French Master.
The Old Nurse's Story.
Right at Last.
The Shah's English Gardener.
The Squire's Story.
Two Fragments of Ghost Stories.

Novels and Tales by Mrs. Gaskell. In seven volumes. Vol. VI. Smith, Elder, and Co. London, 1893:

Hand and Heart.
Morton Hall.
Ruth.

Pocket Edition of Mrs. Gaskell's Works. In eight volumes. Smith, Elder, and Co. London (no date):

An Accursed Race.
The Crooked Branch.
A Dark Night's Work.
The Doom of the Griffiths.
The Grey Woman.
Half a Lifetime Ago.
The Half-Brothers.
The Heart of John Middleton.
Libbie Marsh's Three Eras.
Mr. Harrison's Confessions.
My Lady Ludlow.
North and South.
The Poor Clare.
Round the Sofa.
The Sexton's Hero.
Six Weeks at Heppenheim.
Traits and Stories of the Huguenots.
The Well of Pen-Morfa.

Everyman's Library. Edited by Ernest Rhys. London and New York:

The Life of Charlotte Brontë.
Sylvia's Lovers.

The World's Classics edition. London 1906–19:
Bran.
The Cage at Cranford.
A Christmas Carol.
The Scholar's Story.
Sketches among the Poor, No. 1.

The Chiltern Library, John Lehmann. Paulton and London, 1947–8:
Cousin Phillis.
Cranford.
Mary Barton.

My Diary. The early years of my daughter Marianne. By Elizabeth Cleghorn Gaskell. Privately printed by Clement Shorter. London, 1923.

3. WORKS BY OTHER AUTHORS.

(Editions are not specified, as references are made to chapters, not to pages.)

Austen, Jane, *Works.*
Bremer, Fredrika, *Works.*
Brontë, Anne, *Agnes Grey.*
Brontë, Charlotte, *Works.*
Brontë, Emily, *Wuthering Heights.*
Browning, Elizabeth Barrett, *Aurora Leigh.*
Burney, Frances, *Evelina, or the History of a Young Lady's Entrance into the World.*
Carlyle, Thomas, *Sartor Resartus.*
Charlotte Elizabeth (Mrs. Phelan, Mrs. Tonna), *The Wrongs of Woman.*
——, *Helen Fleetwood.*
——, *Rachel, or Little Faults.*
Chorley, Henry F., *Pomfret; or, Public Opinion and Private Judgment.*
Defoe, Daniel, *Moll Flanders.*
——, *Roxana, or, The Fortunate Mistress.*
Dickens, Charles, *Works.*
Disraeli, Benjamin, *Sybil.*
Eliot, George, *Scenes of Clerical Life.*
——, *Adam Bede.*
——, *Silas Marner.*
Goldsmith, Oliver, *The Vicar of Wakefield.*
Kingsley, Charles, *Yeast.*
——, *Alton Locke.*
——, *Cheap Clothes and Nasty.*
Martineau, Harriet, *Deerbrook.*
Norton, Caroline, *The Child of the Islands. A Poem.*
Richardson, Samuel, *Pamela, or, Virtue Rewarded.*
Sedgwick, Miss, *Home.*

4. HISTORY OF LITERATURE, CRITICISM, BIOGRAPHY
(Books.)

Bentley, Phyllis, *The Brontës*. London, 1947.

Bowen, Elizabeth, *English Novelists*. London, 1946.

Bullett, Gerald, *George Eliot, her life and books*. London, 1947.

Burton, Hester, *Barbara Bodichon*. *1827–1891*. London, 1949.

Butler, Samuel, *The Life and Letters of Dr. Samuel Butler*. London, 1896.

The Cambridge History of English Literature. Cambridge, 1920–27.

Carlyle, Alexander, ed., *New Letters and Memorials of Jane Welsh Carlyle*, Annotated by Thomas Carlyle and edited by Alexander Carlyle, with an introduction by Sir James Crichton-Browne. London and New York, 1903.

Cazamian, Louis, *Le Roman social en Angleterre*. Paris, 1904.

Cecil, David, *Early Victorian Novelists. Essays in revaluation*. London, 1934.

——, *Hardy the Novelist*. London, 1943.

——, *Jane Austen*, Cambridge, 1935.

Chadwick, Mrs. Alice, *Mrs. Gaskell, Haunts, Homes, and Stories*. New and revised edn. London, 1913.

Chesterton, G. K., *The Victorian Age in Literature*. London, 1913.

——, *Charles Dickens*. Zephyr Books edn. Stockholm, 1946.

Chorley, Henry Fothergill, *Autobiography, Memoir, and Letters*. Compiled by Henry G. Hewlett. London, 1873.

Clarke, Charles and Mary Cowden, *Recollections of Writers*. London, 1878.

Gathered Leaves from the Prose of Mary E. Coleridge with a memoir by Edith Sichel. London, 1910.

Cook, Sir Edward, *The Life of Florence Nightingale*. London, 1914.

Cross, J. W., *George Eliot's Life* (3 vols.) Edinburgh and London.

The Letters of Charles Dickens. Edited by his sister-in-law and his eldest daughter. London [1880–2].

Dimnet, Ernest, *The Brontë Sisters*. Translated from the French by Louise Morgan Sill. New York (no date).

Dullemen, J. J. Van, *Mrs. Gaskell: Novelist and Biographer*. Amsterdam, 1924.

Erskine, Mrs. Steuart, *Anna Jameson, Letters and Friendships. 1812–1860*. London, 1915.

Escoube, Lucienne, *Emily Brontë et ses Démons*. Paris, 1941.

Evans, John, *Lancashire Authors and Orators*. London, 1850.

ffrench, Yvonne, *Mrs. Gaskell*. London, 1949.

Fletcher, Mrs., *Autobiography. With letters and other family memorials. Edited by the survivor of her family*. Edinburgh, 1875.

Forster, John, *The Life of Charles Dickens*. London [1872–4].

Fox, Franklin, *Memoir of Mrs. Eliza Fox, to which extracts are added from the journals and letters of her husband, the late W. J. Fox M. P. for Oldham*. London, 1869.

Gosse, Edmund, *A History of Eighteenth Century Literature*. London, 1889.

Haldane, Elizabeth C. H., *Mrs. Gaskell and her Friends*. London, 1931.

——, *George Eliot and her Times. A Victorian Study*. London, 1927.

Hanson, Lawrence and E. M., *The Four Brontës*. London, New York and Toronto, 1949.

Hare, Augustus J. C., *The Story of my Life*. London, 1896.

Hennessy, Una Pope, *Canon Charles Kingsley. A Biography*. London, 1948.

Herford, Brooke, *Travers Madge: A Memoir*. London, 1867.

Holland, Bernard, ed., *Letters of Mary Sibylla Holland. Selected and edited by her son, Bernard Holland*. 2nd edn, London, 1898.

Holland, Sir Henry, *Recollections of Past Life*. London, 1872.

House, Humphry, *The Dickens World*. 2nd edn. London, New York and Toronto, 1942.

Howitt, Margaret, ed., *Mary Howitt. An Autobiography*. London, 1889.

Ireland, Mrs. Alexander, *Selections from the Letters of Geraldine Endsor Jewsbury to Jane Welsh Carlyle*. London, 1892.

Irvine, Wm Fergusson, ed., *A History of the Family of Holland of Mobberley and Knutsford. From materials collected by the late Edgar Swinton Holland*. Privately printed. Edinburgh, 1902.

James, Henry, *William Wetmore Story and his Friends. From letters, diaries, and recollections*. Edinburgh and London, 1903.

Johnson, George W. and Lucy, A., *Josephine A Butler, an autobiographical memoir. With Introduction by James Stuart*. Bristol and London, 1909.

Johnson, R. Brimley, *The Women Novelists*. London, 1918.

Kenyon, Frederic G., ed., *The Letters of Elizabeth Barret Browning edited with biographical additions*.

Charles Kingsley, His Letters and Memories of his Life, edited by his wife. London, 1901.

Lamm, Martin, Dickens och hans romaner. Stockholm, 1947.

Leavis, F. R., *The Great Tradition*. London, 1948.

Legouis, Emile, and Louis Cazamian, *A History of English Literature*. Revised edn. London, 1945.

MacCarthy, B. G., *Women Writers. Their Contribution to the English Novel 1621–1744*. Oxford, 1946.

——, *The Later Women Novelists*. Oxford, 1947.

Martineau, Harriet, *Autobiography. With Memorials by Maria Weston Chapman*. 2nd edn. London, 1877.

Melville, Lewis, *Victorian Novelists*. London, 1906.

Letters of Charles Eliot Norton. With Biographical Comment by his daughter Sara Norton and M. A. De Wolfe Howe. London, 1913.

O'Meara, Kathleen, *Madame Mohl. Her Salon and her Friends. A Study of Social Life in Paris*. London, 1885.

Payne, George A., *Mrs. Gaskell. A Brief Biography*. Manchester, 1929.

Pearson, Hesketh, *Dickens. His Character, Comedy and Career.* New York, 1949.

Pole, William, *The Life of Sir William Fairbairn, Bart. Partly written by himself.* London, 1877.

Quennell, Peter, *John Ruskin. The Portrait of a Prophet.* London, 1949.

Quiller-Couch, Sir Arthur, *Charles Dickens and Other Victorians.* Cambridge, 1925.

Raleigh, Sir Walter, *The English Novel.* London, 1894.

Renton, Richard, *John Forster and his Friendships.* London, 1912.

Rhotert, Karl, *Die Frau bei George Eliot.* Berlin, 1915.

Ritchie, Lady, *Blackstick Papers.* London, 1908.

Sampson, George, *The Concise Cambridge History of English Literature.* Cambridge and New York, 1946.

Sanders, Gerald De Witt, *Elizabeth Gaskell. With a bibliography by Clark S. Northup.* New Haven and London, 1929.

Schück och Warburg, *Illustrerad svensk litteraturhistoria.* Tredje, fullständigt omarbetade upplagan. Utgiven av Henrik Schück. Sjätte delen. Stockholm, 1930.

Shaen, Margaret J., *Memorials of Two Sisters. Susanna and Catherine Winkworth.* London, New York, Bombay, and Calcutta, 1908.

Shorter, Clement, *The Brontës. Life and Letters.* London, 1908.

Simpson, M. C. M., *Letters and Recollections of Julius and Mary Mohl.* London, 1887.

Solly, Henry Shaen, *The Life of Henry Morley.* London, 1898.

Strachey, Lytton, *Queen Victoria.* (Phoenix Library, London 1937.)

Alfred Lord Tennyson. A Memoir. By his son. London, 1897.

Traz, Robert de, *La Famille Brontë.* Paris, 1939.

Trollope, Anthony, *An Autobiography.* With an Introduction by Charles Morgan. London, 1946.

Whitehill, Jane, *Letters of Mrs. Gaskell and Charles Eliot Norton 1855–1865.* London, 1932.

Whitfield, S. Stanton, *Mrs. Gaskell. Her Life and Work.* London, 1929.

Wollweber, Carola, *Der Soziale Roman der Mrs. Gaskell.* Dissertation. Giessen, 1928.

5. (SOCIAL) HISTORY, EDUCATION, LEGISLATION. (Books.)

Bryant, Arthur, *English Saga 1840–1940.* London, 1940.

Blease, W. Lyon, *The Emancipation of English Women.* London, 1910.

Chapone, Mrs., *Letters on the Improvement of the Mind;* Gregory, Dr., *A Father's Legacy to his Daughters;* Pennington, Lady, *A Mother's Advice to her Absent Daughters.* (In one vol.) Edinburgh, 1821.

Courtney, Janet E., *The Adventurous Thirties. A chapter in the women's movement.* London, 1933.

Gregory (See Chapone).

Jameson, Mrs., *Characteristics of Women, moral, poetical and historical.* London, 1832.

——, *Memoirs and Essays illustrative of Art, Literature, and Social Morals.* London, 1846.

Hecker, Eugene E., *A Short History of Women's Rights.* New York and London, 1910.

Holt, Raymond V., *The Unitarian Contribution to Social Progress in England.* London, 1938.

Markham, Thomas Hugh, *The Divorce and Matrimonial Causes Acts of 1857 and 1858, with all the decisions, new rules, orders, and table of fees, &c.* London, 1858.

Mayhew, Henry, *London Labour and the London Poor.* London, 1862.

Neff, Wanda Fraiken, *Victorian Working Women. An Historical and Literary Study of Women in British Industries and Professions 1832–1850.* London, 1929.

Pennington (See Chapone).

Percival, Alicia C., *The English Miss To-Day and Yesterday. Ideals, methods and personalities in the education and upbringing of girls during the last hundred years.* London, 1939.

Pinchbeck, Ivy, *Women Workers and the Industrial Revolution 1750–1850.* London, 1930.

Reid, Mrs. Hugo, *A Plea for Woman: Being a vindication of the importance and extent of her natural sphere of action.* Edinburgh, London and Dublin, 1843.

Reiss, Erna, *Rights and Duties of Englishwomen.* Manchester, 1934.

Rousseau, Jean-Jacques, *Emilius or An Essay on Education. By John James Rousseau, Citizen of Geneva. Translated from the French. The Fifth Book. Sophia; or the Woman.* London, 1763.

Ruskin, John, *Lecture II. Lilies. Of Queens' Gardens.* Delivered at Manchester in 1864.

Sandford, Mrs. John, *Woman in her Social and Domestic Character.* London, 1831.

——, *Female Improvement.* London, 1836.

Stowe, Harriet Beecher, *Sunny Memories of Foreign Lands.* London 1854.

Trevelyan, G. M., *History of England.* 2nd edn. London, New York and Toronto, 1927.

——, *English Social History. A Survey of Six Centuries. Chaucer to Queen Victoria.* 2nd edn. London, New York and Toronto, 1946.

Wollstonecraft, Mary, *A Vindication of the Rights of Woman.* With an Introduction by Elizabeth Pennell. London.

Ideas and Beliefs of the Victorians, an historic revaluation of the Victorian Age. Series of talks broadcast on the B.B.C. Third Programme. Published by Sylvan Press Limited, London, 1949.

6. ARTICLES. (Arranged chronologically.)

Athenaeum, Oct. 21, 1848. Rev. of *Mary Barton*. (Pp. 1050–1.)

New Monthly Magazine. Vol. 82, being the first part for 1848. "The Cagots" (Pp. 437–41.)

New Monthly Magazine, Nov. 4, 1848. *Rev. of Mary Barton*. (Pp. 406–8.)

Eclectic Review, Jan. 1849. Rev. of *Mary Barton*. (Pp. 51–63.)

Prospective Review, Feb. 1849. J. J. Taylor, Rev. of *Mary Barton*. (Pp. 36–57.)

British Quarterly Review, Feb. 9, 1849. Rev. of *Mary Barton*. (Pp. 117–36.)

Westminster Review, April, 1849. E. W.; Rev. of *Mary Barton*. (Pp. 48–63.)

Edinburgh Review, April, 1849. William Rathbone Greg, Rev. of *Mary Barton*. (Pp. 402–35.)

Fraser's Magazine, April, 1849. "Letter of Advice from an Experienced Matron to a Young Married Lady." ·

Fraser's Magazine, April, 1849. "Recent Novels." (Pp. 417–32.)

Eclectic Review, June, 1849. Walter Savage Landor, "To the Author of Mary Barton".

Westminster Review, Jan., 1850. "Woman's Mission." (Pp. 352–78.)

Edinburgh Review, Jan., 1850. Rev. of *Shirley*.

Westminster Review, April–July, 1850. "Prostitution." (Pp. 448–506.)

———. "Histoire Morale des Femmes." (Pp. 516–30.)

Athenaeum, Dec. 21, 1850. Notice of *The Moorland Cottage*. (Pp. 1337–8.)

Westminster Review, April–July, 1851. "Enfranchisement of Women." (Pp. 289 ff.)

British Quarterly Review, June–Sep., 1851. "Revolutionary Literature." (Pp. 491–543.)

Athenaeum, Jan. 15, 1853. Rev. of *Ruth*. (Pp. 76–8.)

Sharpe's London Magazine, Jan. 15, 1853. Rev. of *Ruth*.

Literary Gazette, Jan. 22, 1853. Rev. of *Ruth*.

Living Age, March, 1853. Rev. of *Ruth*. (Pp. 543–5.)

Eliza Cook's Journal, March, 1853. Rev. of *Ruth*. (Pp. 277–80.)

English Review, April, 1853. Rev. of *Ruth*. (Pp. 193–4.)

Tait's Edinburgh Magazine, April, 1853. "The Story of Ruth." (Pp. 217–20.)

Westminster Review, April, 1853. "Ruth and Villette." Pp. 474–91.

Prospective Review. May, 1853. Rev. of *Ruth*.

North British Review, May, 1853. Rev. of *Ruth*. (Pp. 151–74.)

Putnam's Monthly Magazine, May, 1853. George William Curtis, "Villette and Ruth". (Pp. 535–539.)

Gentleman's Magazine, July, 1853. "The Lady Novelists of Great Britain."

Athenaeum, April 7, 1855. Rev. of Mrs. Jameson's "Sisters of Charity".

———, Rev. of *North and South*.

Blackwood's Edinburgh Magazine. May, 1855. "Modern Novelists—Great and Small." (14 pp.)

Revue des Deux Mondes, Oct. 1, 1855. Emile Montégut, "Le Roman de moeurs industrielles en Angleterre". (Pp. 115–146.)

Eclectic Magazine, Feb., 1856. "The Author of *Mary Barton*." (Pp. 259–63.)

Rev. Wm Gaskell, "A Time of War and a Time of Peace". (Sermon preached May 4, 1856.) (London, 1856.)

Edinburgh Review, July, 1857. Wm Rathbone Greg, "The Licence of Modern Novelists". (Pp. 124–56.)

Athenæum, April 4. (Pp. 427–9.)
Tait's Edinburgh Review, May. (Pp. 292–6.)
Fraser's Magazine, May. (Pp. 569–582.)
Gentleman's Magazine, June. (Pp. 688–94.) | 1857, Rev. of *The Life of*
Christian Observer, July. (Pp. 487–90.) | *Charlotte Brontë*
British Quarterly Review, July.
Christian Remembrancer, July. (Pp. 87–145.)
Westminster Review, July.

Westminster Review, April, 1863. Notice of *Sylvia's Lovers*.

Westminster Review, July, 1863. Rev. of *A Dark Night's Work*. (Pp. 304–7.)

Athenaeum, Nov. 18, 1865. "Mrs. Gaskell."

James Drummond, "The Holiness of Sorrow: a Sermon Preached in Cross Street Chapel, Manchester, on Sunday, Nov. 19, 1865, on the Sudden Death of Mrs. Gaskell".

Macmillan's Magazine. Dec., 1865. David Masson, "Mrs. Gaskell". (Pp. 153–6.)

Nation. Dec. 14, 1865. (P. 750.)

Athenaeum. Jan. 13, 1866. "Fredrika Bremer."

Athenaeum. March 3, 1866. Rev. of *Wives and Daughters*.

British Quarterly Review. April 1, 1867. "The Works of Mrs. Gaskell." (Pp. 399–429.)

Cornhill Magazine. Feb., 1873. G. B. Smith, "Mrs. Gaskell and her Novels". (Pp. 191–212.)

National Home Reading Union Magazine, April, 1878. M. Ainsworth, "The Labour Movement in Fiction. Mary Barton."

Manchester City News. June 22, 1878. R. E. Bibby, "Mary Barton and Greenhey's Fields".

Fortnightly Review, Sep., 1878. William Minto, "Mrs. Gaskell's Novels". (Pp. 353–69.)

Josephine Butler, "Social Purity". London, 1879. (Address given at Cambridge, May, 1879.)

Manchester City News, Jan. 3, 1880. "Miss F. Masson. A Biographical Sketch."

Manchester Guardian, June 12, 1884. Obituary of Mr. Gaskell.

Manchester Guardian, Sep. 29, 1891. "The Anniversary of the Birth of Mrs. Gaskell."

Anne Thackeray Ritchie, Preface to *Cranford*. London, 1891.

Good Words, Sep., 1895. Margaret Howitt: "Stray Notes from Mrs. Gaskell". (Pp. 604–12.)

Atlantic Monthly, April, 1896. Alice Brown, "Latter-day Cranford".

Bookman, June, 1896. Clement K. Shorter, "Mrs. Gaskell and Charlotte Brontë". (Pp. 313–24.)

Cooperative News, Nov. 7, 1896. Rev. of C. K. Shorter, *Charlotte Brontë and her Circle*.

New Saturday, Jan. 16, 1897. Herbert Paul, "Appreciation of Mrs. Gaskell".

Woman at Home. March, 1897. Sarah A. Tooley, "Ladies of Manchester". (Pp. 488–9.)

H. D. Traill, Introduction to the Centenary edn of Carlyle's Works. (Chapman & Hall, London, 1897.)

Sketch, March 1, 1899. George A. Payne, "A Memorial to Mrs. Gaskell".

Manchester Guardian, March 4, 1899. "Sandlebridge and its Associations".

Sunday Magazine, May, 1899. A. G. Skinner, "A Cheshire May Queen."

Manchester Herald, Jan. 6, 13, 1900. George A Payne, "Mrs. Gaskell and Knutsford".

Gentlewoman, Jan. 5. (p. 30), 1901. Mrs. Wilfred Meynell, "Women in Literature".

Manchester Guardian, Jan. 8, 1901. "Knutsford as Cranford."

Literary World, Feb. 8, 1901. "Knutsford as Cranford."

Manchester Quarterly, July, 1902. (Pp. 195–228.) John Mortimer, "Lancashire Novelists; Mrs. Gaskell". (Pp. 195–228.)

Manchester City News, 1903. Henry Thomas Crofton, "Mary Barton's Farm".

Chamber's Cyclopaedia of English Literature, Jan., 1903. Sir Wm Robertson Nicoll, "Mrs. Gaskell". (Pp. 527–8.)

Manchester Guardian, Feb. 10, 1903. "Edna Lyall."

Treasury, May 1, 1903. Joshua Grant, "May-Day at Cranford". (Pp. 720–4.)

Manchester City News, Sep. 5, 1903. Rev. of Green's Hand List.

Manchester Guardian. Jan. 25, 1904. "A Cyclist on Sandlebridge and its Associations."

Notes and Queries, March 5, 1904. Joseph Rogers, "Mrs. Gaskell's Sylvia's Lovers". (Pp. 187–8.)

Manchester Guardian. Nov. 11, 1904. Wm. E. A. Axon, "Pepperhill Farm".

Manchester Guardian, Nov. 16, 1904. "Greenheys Fields and 'Mary Barton'."

Manchester Guardian, Oct. 7, 10, 11, Nov. 14, 1905. "Mrs. Gaskell and Knutsford."

Manchester Guardian, Nov. 15, 24, 1905. "Mary Barton."

Manchester Guardian, Nov. 22, 1905. "Mrs. Gaskell and Moss Side."

National Home Reading Union Magazine, Sep., 1905. "Mary Barton." (Pp. 18–21.)

A. W. Ward, Biographical Introduction and Introductions to Mrs. Gaskell's Works in the Knutsford Edn., 1906.

Manchester Guardian, Sep. 4, 1906. C. H. H., "Mrs. Gaskell".

National Home Reading Union Magazine, Sep., 1906. Rev. of *North and South*. (Pp. 22–4.)

Times Literary Supplement, Sep. 14, 1906. Rev. of the Knutsford edn. of Mrs. Gaskell's Works.

Daily Chronicle, Sep. 22, 1906. Rev. by George Sampson of *Mary Barton* and *Cranford*.

Yorkshire Weekly Post, Sep. 29, 1906. "The Knutsford edition."

Clement K. *Shorter*, Prefaces to Mrs. Gaskell's works in the World's Classics edn., 1906–19.

Manchester Evening News, Oct. 20, 1906. Rev. of *North and South*.

Academy, Nov. 24, 1906. Rev. of the Knutsford edn. (Pp. 519–20.)

Manchester Guardian, Jan. 10, 1907. M. G., "The Knutsford Edition".

Manchester City News, Feb. 16, 1907. George A. Payne, "Cranford".

——, Feb. 23, 1907. Sarah Cash, "Mrs. Gaskell and Knutsford".

Knutsford Advertiser, March 22, 1907. "The Memorial to Mrs. Gaskell."

Manchester Guardian, March 25, 1907. "Some Appreciations."

Nation, April 11, 1907. Paul Elmer Moore, Rev. of the Knutsford edn.

Manchester Evening News. May 9, 1907. "Mary Barton Banned."

Yorkshire Post, May 9, 1907. "Mary Barton as a School Book."

Manchester Guardian, June 22, 1907. "The London County Council and Mary Barton."

Academy, June 22, 1907. Leading article on the banning of *Mary Barton* by the London County Council.

Manchester Evening Chronicle, June 19, 1907. Note on the banning of *Mary Barton* by the London County Council.

T. P's Weekly, June 28, 1907. "Mrs. Gaskell and Mary Barton."

Standard, July 12, 1907. "A Whitby Correspondent on the tearing down of the old shop in Bridge Street."

Sphere, July 20, 1907. "On Knutsford as Cranford."

Manchester City News, Dec. 7, 1907. " 'Cranford' once more."

William Henry Hudson, Introduction to Carlyle's *Sartor Resartus* and *On Heroes and Hero-Worship* in the Everyman edn., 1908.

Woman's World, Oct. 29, 1908. "Memories of Plymouth Grove."

Millgate Monthly, Oct., 1908. Henry Walker, "Cranford".

A. Cobden Smith, "Miss Julia Gaskell. A Memorial Address". Nov. 1, 1908.

British Weekly, Nov. 14, 1908. "The Late Miss Julia Gaskell."

Christian Life, Nov. 14, 1908. "The Late Miss Julia Gaskell." (Pp. 611–12.)

Morning Leader, Nov. 14, 1908. Article on Miss Julia Gaskell.

May Sinclair, Introduction to the Everyman edn. of *The Life of Charlotte Brontë*. 1908.

Notes and Queries, Aug. 7, 1909. "North and South in the World's Classics."

British Weekly, March 31, 1910. A Man of Kent, "Woman's Work in English Fiction".

Unitarian Monthly, April, 1910. Sarah A. Tooley, "Mrs. Gaskell."

Daily Dispatch, Aug. 18, 1910. "On the Centenary of Mrs. Gaskell."

Sunday Chronicle, Sep. 4, 1910. "The Centenary of Mrs. Gaskell, the Novelist."

Nation, Sep. 10, 1910. "The Art of Mrs. Gaskell."

Manchester City News, Sep. 10, 1910. George A. Payne, "The Gaskell Centenary".

Great Thoughts, Sep. 10, 1910. Florence Bone, "The Story of Mrs. Gaskell". (Pp. 376–8.)

Manchester Guardian, Sep. 23, 1910. "The Centenary of Mrs. Gaskell."

Illustrated London News, Sep. 24, 1910. "The Centenary of Mrs. Gaskell's Birth."

Inquirer, Sept. 24, Oct. 1, 1910. Note of the Centenary of Mrs. Gaskell.

Manchester City News, Sep. 24, 1910. "Meeting of the Manchester Literary Club."

Manchester Evening News, Sep. 28, 1910. J. M. W., "Mrs. Gaskell: An Appreciation".

Manchester Guardian, Sep. 29, 1910. Flora Masson, "The Novelist's Career".

Manchester Courier, Sep. 29, 1910. "The Gaskell Centenary."

Glasgow Herald, Sep. 29, 1910. Clement K. Shorter, "The Centenary of Mrs. Gaskell".

Standard, Sep. 29, 1910. "The Centenary of Mrs. Gaskell."

Daily Dispatch, Sep. 29, 1910. "Mrs. Gaskell. Centenary of the Author of *Cranford*."

Manchester Evening Chronicle, Sep. 29, 1910. Notice of the Gaskell Centenary.

Daily Graphic, Sep. 29, 1910. "Mrs. Gaskell's Centenary."

Manchester Guardian, Sep. 29, 1910. C. H. Herford, "Mrs. Gaskell's Powers".

——, "About the Moss Side Collection."

Daily Chronicle, Sep. 29, 1910. J. A. Hill, "On the Centenary of Mrs. Gaskell".

Liverpool Daily Post and Mercury, Sep. 29, 1910. "Centenary of Mrs. Gaskell."

Scottish Co-operator, Sep. 30, 1910. J. C., "The Centenary of Mrs. Gaskell".

Millgate Monthly, Sep., 1910. Wm. E. Axon, "The Centenary of Mrs. Gaskell". (Pp. 778–81.)

Bookshelf, Sep., 1910. "Mrs. Gaskell."

Girl's Own Paper, Oct., 1910. Howard M. Jenkins, "The Real 'Cranford'".
Review of Reviews (London), Oct., 1910. "The Centenary of Mrs. Gaskell."
Chambers's Journal, Oct. 1, 1910. Helen Melville, "Mrs. Gaskell and Cranford".
Inquirer, Oct. 8, 1910. Miss Mat. Hompes, "Mrs. Gaskell and her Social Work among the Poor".
Manchester Courier, Oct. 14, 1910. Note on Silverdale.
Manchester City News, Oct. 29, 1910. "The Gaskell Centenary."
Christian Freeman, Nov., 1910. A. W. Blundell, "Mrs. Gaskell, 1810–1910".
Christian Life, Dec. 17, 1910. "Notes of an Octogenarian Minister."
Athenaeum, Dec. 24, 1910. Notice of *Sylvia's Lovers*.
Manchester City News, Dec. 24, 1910. "Mrs. Gaskell and Christmas."
——, John Mortimer, "A Budget of Good Stories—Grave and Gay".

Reviews in 1910 of Mrs. Ellis H. Chadwick, *Mrs. Gaskell, Haunts, Homes and Stories*, in:

Nation, Jan. 18.
British Weekly, Sep. 15.
Christian Life, Oct. 15.
Daily Chronicle, Sep. 15. (Clement K. Shorter.)
Daily News, Sep. 15.
Daily Telegraph, Sep. 16.
Spectator, Sep. 17.
Sphere, Sep. 17. (Clement K. Shorter.)
Publishers' Circular, Sep. 24.
Manchester Guardian, Sep. 26.
Yorkshire Post, Sep. 28.
Times Literary Supplement, Sept. 29.
Morning Post, Sep. 29.
Treasury, Oct.
Athenaeum, Oct. 1.
Bookman. (London), Oct. (Wm. E. A. Axon.)

Inquirer, Jan. 7, 1911.
Manchester Quarterly, Jan., 1911. John Mortimer, "Concerning the Mary Barton Fields".
Sunday School Quarterly Magazine, Jan., 1911. Cobden A. Smith, "A Centenary Address: Mrs. Gaskell and Lower Mosley Street Sunday School".
Esther Alice Chadwick, Introduction to the Everyman edn. of *Sylvia's Lovers*, Jan., 1911.
Christian Life, March 4, 1911. A. Cobden Smith, "Memories of Lower Mosley Street".
Nation, June 15, 1911. "News for Bibliophiles."
Bookman, Oct. 1911. Esther Alice Chadwick, "The Gaskell Collection at Manchester."

National Home Reading Union; Young People's Magazine, Dec., 1911. Una M. Goodwin, "Cranford".

Nation (New York), Jan. 8, 1912. "The Author of *Cranford.*"

National Home Reading Union Magazine, May, 1912. C. E. Larton, "Wives and Daughters".

——, "About some of Mrs. Gaskell's other novels".

Bookman (London), Mrs. Alice H. Chadwick, "Mrs. Gaskell's Birthplace". (Pp. 160–3 XLIII.)

Everyman, Nov. 22, 1912. Margaret Hamilton, "The Women of Mrs. Gaskell."

Daily Chronicle, Nov. 25, 1912. "Doom of Clogs and Shawl."

Everyman, March 14, 1913. John K. Prothero, "*Sylvia's Lovers* by Mrs. Gaskell",

Sphere, Nov. 8, 1913. C. K. S., "A Literary Letter: The late Miss 'Meta' Gaskell".

Everyman, Jan. 9, 1914. R. E. Levey, "Mrs. Gaskell's *Mary Barton*".

Royal Exchange Assurance Magazine, July, 1914. "Manchester Memoirs."

Christian Science Monitor (Boston, Mass.), Nov. 4, 1915. "Mrs. Gaskell visits Charlotte Brontë."

British Weekly, Nov. 11, 1915. A Man of Kent, "Mr. Shorter's Edition of Mrs. Gaskell".

British Weekly, Jan. 31, 1918. Claudius Clear /Sir W. R. Nicoll/, "Mary Barton: A Tale for the Times".

Manchester City News, 19 July, 1919.

Reporters' Journal, March, 1920. C. J. Courteney, "The Charms of Mrs. Gaskell".

John O'London's Weekly, Dec. 19, 1925. E. B. Osborn, "The Tragical Comedies of Gentle Lives".

Spectator, July 6, 1929. Gilbert Thomas, "Mrs. Gaskell".

Manchester City News, 21 Feb. 1931. "Kingsley and the Gaskells. An Interesting Link."

Manchester Quarterly, 1932. W. Henry Brown, "Mrs. Gaskell: A Manchester Influence". (14 pp.)

PMLA, June, 1938. Annette B. Hopkins, "Mrs. Gaskell in France, 1849–1890". (Pp. 545–74.)

Huntington Library Quarterly, Aug., 1946. Annette B. Hopkins, "Dickens and Mrs. Gaskell". (Pp. 357–85.)

Lettice Cooper, Introduction to *Mary Barton* in the Chiltern Library edn., 1947.

Elizabeth Jenkins, Introduction to *Cranford* and *Cousin Phillis* in the Chiltern Library edn., 1947.

Margarete Lane, Introduction to *The Life of Charlotte Brontë* in the Chiltern Library edn., 1947.

Rosamond Lehmann, Introduction to *Wives and Daughters* in the Chiltern Library edn., 1948.

INDEX

(Titles of books, etc., are given under the names of the authors, except the works of Mrs. Gaskell, the titles of which are given in alphabetical order.)

ADDITIONS AND CORRECTIONS

p. 1, l. 3: NINETEENH *read* NINETEENTH

    l. 23: to men *read* to new groups of men

p. 2, n 1 l. 2: opinion *read* Opinion

p. 4, n 4 l. 5: Elisabeth *read* Elizabeth

p. 7, l. 1: redicalness *read* radicalness

    l. 5: ther *read* her

p. 9, l. 12: Falls *read* Falls,

p. 15, n 1 l. 9: taken suddenly *read* suddenly taken

p. 35, l. 14: story, *read* story.

    n 2, l. 3: full length *read* full-length

p. 39, l. 1, n 1 l. 5: women *read* women's

p. 40, n 1, l. 3: proves *read* would seem to prove

p. 49, ll. 14–15: home.³ In a letter to G. H. Lewes, Charlotte Brontë *read* home,³ and in a letter to G. H. Lewes, she

p. 55, n 5 l. 2: tick *read* rick

p. 57 n 1: Letter *read* letter

p. 73 n 1 l. 2: engagement *read* engagement,

p. 81, l. 20: him."³ *read* him."⁴

    last note: 3 *read* 4

p. 84 n 2: 689 *read* P. 689

p. 90, l. 27: stairs, 'Effie *read* stairs', Effie

p. 91 n 2: "Of "Queens' *read* "Of Queens'

p. 97, l. 4: the letter *read* the first letter

p. 103, l. 7: Stevensen *read* Stevenson

p. 132, l. 30: war *read* war,

p. 156, l. 9: conditions and the *read* conditions and her emphasis on the

    l. 16: was *read* were

p. 157 n 1: *add The Life of Charlotte Brontë*

    n 2: Pp. *read* P.

p. 160, l. 22: not go *read* not to go

p. 161, l. 10: *delete* in

p. 171, l. 29: OhI *read* Oh!

p. 180 n 1: p. 61 *read* p. 66

    l. 37: 4 *read* 5

p. 182, n 1, last line: Bulletin *read Bulletin*

p. 188, l. 6: full length *read* full-length

p. 193, l. 21: carefully, *read* carefully."

p. 196, l. 24: mind, was *read* mind was
p. 206, l. 4: an *read* on
p. 212, l. 15: realzied *read* realized
p. 238, n 3: Pinchbeck *read* Pinchbeck,
p. 248, l. 27 and *read* And
p. 249, l. 6: Dunwood *read* Dimwood
p. 252, last note: 3 *read* 4
p. 271, l. 23: step daughter *read* stepdaughter
p. 276, l. 34: In discussion *read* In a discussion
p. 277, l. 28: Charles *read* C. E.
p. 282, l. 23: *to read of*
p. 286, l. 19: Bezè *read* Bèze
         l. 21: *Charlotta read Charlotte*
p. 289, l. 12: an *read* and
p. 293, l. 10: Patient Grissil *read Patient Grissil*
p. 313, l. 40: *Song's read Songs*
p. 315, l. 5: *delete* or
p. 326, l. 10: in *read* In
p. 330, l. 36: Trackeray *read* Thackeray
p. 339, l. 40: *In the Oxford of read* In *The Oxford Book of*
p. 342, l. 19: mist *read* midst
p. 347, l. 18: Playing *read* playing
p. 350, l. 22: kneep *read* keep

04